This original and far-reaching study recounts the powerful involvement of the Catholic Church in the cultural life of France in the seventeenth century.

Professor Phillips brings together the social, religious and intellectual history of the *Grand Siècle* and focuses on the involvement of the Church in a variety of cultural domains, including literature, art, censorship and ideas, exploring the limits as well as the extent of the Church's influence, especially in its attempt to impose orthodoxy in all areas and on all sections of society. Given that orthodoxy determines the believer's inclusion or exclusion from the Church, thus implying the notion of boundaries in a context of constraint, the study is conceived according to a number of spaces. The notion of space is sometimes interpreted literally, as in the case of Port-Royal, the school and the church building, and sometimes metaphorically, as in orthodoxy itself, science and theology. The book also deals with religious attitudes to *libertinage*, atheism and deism, and with aspects of French Protestantism.

The strength of Professor Phillips's synthesis, the first of its kind to address the subject in English, lies in the breadth of its concerns and in its combination of social, religious and intellectual history.

Church and culture
in seventeenth-century France

Church and culture
in seventeenth-century France

Henry Phillips

University of Manchester

CAMBRIDGE
UNIVERSITY PRESS

Published by the Press Syndicate of the University of Cambridge
The Pitt Building, Trumpington Street, Cambridge CB2 1RP
40 West 20th Street, New York, NY 10011-4211, USA
10 Stamford Road, Oakleigh, Melbourne 3166, Australia

First published 1997

Printed in Great Britain at the University Press, Cambridge

A catalogue record for this book is available from the British Library

Library of Congress cataloguing in publication data

Phillips, Henry.
  Church and culture in seventeenth-century France / Henry Phillips.
    p.   cm.
  Includes bibliographical references and index.
  ISBN 0 521 57023 9
  1. Christianity and culture – France – History – 17th century.
  2. France – Civilization – 17th century.   3. France – Church history –
  17th century. 4. Catholic Church – France – History – 17th century.
  I. Title.
  BR845.P48   1996
  261'.1—dc20 96–20316 CIP

ISBN 0 521 57023 9 hardback

VN

Contents

Preface

This project has been a long time coming to fruition, having passed through at least two different phases. It was almost on the point of being abandoned until the timely intervention of Professor Peter Bayley of the University of Cambridge who flatteringly persuaded me to continue, and to him I owe my first debt of gratitude. The project in fact originated in a paper I was invited to give in 1982 to the Society for Seventeenth-Century French Studies, and I am therefore grateful to them for the opportunity of furthering an interest in French social and cultural history acquired in my teaching as a lecturer in the French Department of the University of Aberdeen. I must however record a particular expression of thanks to my former colleague at Emmanuel College, Cambridge, Peter Burke, who has guided me through the pitfalls of a discipline which is not my first home. Michael Moriarty, now of Queen Mary and Westfield, in the University of London, offered important encouragement at a crucial stage of writing. Joe Bergin of the University of Manchester and Lawrence Brockliss of Magdalen College, Oxford have also offered invaluable advice. Dr Anthony Wright of the University of Leeds was also kind enough to look over parts of the text. An early stage of this project benefited greatly from a substantial grant from the British Academy. I am grateful both to the Master and Governing Body of Emmanuel, and to the University of Cambridge, who were generous enough in granting me a year's study leave during which much of the work which finds its present form here was completed. The facilities of the University of Manchester have been vital to the final stages of the project. Lastly, Richard Fisher of Cambridge University Press and Monica Kendall, my copy-editor, have been of invaluable assistance in seeing the book safely through to publication.

Introduction

'Hors de l'Eglise, point de salut'. The Church is an institution with powers of exclusion and inclusion through baptism and excommunication. Excommunication can take two forms: the first excludes the individual from the sacraments, the second from the church building itself. This concept of exclusion and inclusion thus gives rise to a notion of boundaries, and boundaries suggest a space. The believer stays within those boundaries: or places himself or herself outside them, or is expelled beyond them. The threshold of the church building thus brings together what one might call the abstract space of belief and the physical consequences of believing, or going against belief in terms of a 'real' space. This book is very much about a number of such spaces.

If the Church is a space in the way I have suggested, its control over that space is in large part determined by its power to define the criteria for belonging to it. The power and authority of the Church thus rest on the enforcement of these criteria which in themselves form a space of orthodoxy where adherence to orthodoxy allows one's continuing inclusion and where challenging it leads to expulsion. Orthodoxy itself has limits to the extent that the space of belief cannot be limitless. Nor does orthodoxy brook any rivalry. Jurisdiction is indispensable in the space of the Church.

The relation of the abstract to the real is an important component of space. While Port-Royal can be construed as an abstract space in the sense that it represents a position both within the space of orthodoxy and in relation to it, it is also a real space in both its construction and destruction as buildings. The school represents at the same time the space of education as we can understand it through the content of the curriculum but also a physical confine dictating aspects of behaviour and surveillance. Similarly the church building is a symbol of the sacred and of the faith, but the symbolism is, in Catholicism at least, represented in tangible form in terms of its architectural disposition and the representations of the sacred found there. The wider space of the Church was of course a real space in the sense that it was divided into provinces, dioceses and parishes. This

1

concept of the Church as a space is reinforced by Tridentine considerations concerning residence of priests and bishops alike, those in other words who could enforce the Church's jurisdiction of its territory over the faithful who inhabited it.

What unites these spaces is that they are all related to issues of power and control. Foucault was among the first to conceive the degree to which spaces are a function of power. In his *Histoire de la folie* he remarks: 'L'Hôpital général n'est pas un établissement médical. Il est plutôt une structure semi-juridique, une sorte d'entité administrative qui, à côté des pouvoirs déjà constitués, et en dehors des tribunaux, décide, juge et exécute . . . Il est une instance de l'ordre, de l'ordre monarchique et bourgeois qui s'organise en France à cette même époque.'[1] This sort of power, the power to confine the mad or the sick, is directly connected with the power to impose definitions which are then used to legitimate the authority of certain actions. In *The Birth of the Clinic* Foucault refers to what he calls a 'political consciousness' in the discourse of disease:

Medicine must no longer be confined to a body of techniques for curing the ills and of the knowledge that they require; it will also embrace a knowledge of *healthy man*, that is, a study of *non-sick* man and a definition of the *model man*. In the ordering of human existence it assumes a normative posture, which authorizes it not only to distribute advice as to healthy life, but also to dictate the standards for physical and moral relations of the individual and of the society in which he lives.[2]

This is not dissimilar to the functioning of religious orthodoxy. The norm established by orthodoxy, an exposition of which is the eternal function of the Church, permits the identification of the heterodox and hence the definition of spiritual 'illnesses' which must be eradicated, although it turns out that the heterodox has a function too, this time in helping to define more clearly what is orthodox. All aspects of life in society have in some way a relation to the space of orthodoxy to the extent that they are judged according to its criteria. Personal adherence to that orthodoxy is required if one is to remain within the territory of the Church. But it is not a space whose boundaries are movable according to personal interpretation. Indeed the room for manoeuvre in such a space is very limited if the notion of orthodoxy is to have any sense at all. Orthodoxy militates in favour of a homogeneous space and the identity of the Church as a space rests on the universality of its beliefs, hence the very great importance placed by the Catholic Church on an unbroken tradition of biblical interpretation and religious practice from the time of Christ through the Apostles and the early Church to the present day.

---

[1] M. Foucault, *Histoire de la folie à l'âge classique* (Paris, 1989), pp. 60–1.
[2] M. Foucault (trans. A. M. Sheridan), *The Birth of the Clinic: an Archaeology of Medical Perception* (London, 1989), p. 34 (Foucault's emphasis).

The concept of power in relation to a spiritual territory is further illustrated both at the level of the kingdom and in the links between France and international Catholicism. In the first place it was the (frustrated) wish of the Council of Trent to restore the authority of the Roman Catholic Church in the territories lost to Protestantism, perhaps symbolised in François de Sales's title as bishop of Geneva. The Church in France certainly regarded some of its own territory as lost to the Huguenots, especially in cities like Nîmes and La Rochelle whose populations in the early part of the century were overwhelmingly Protestant. The Catholic hierarchy, many of whom never accepted the act of toleration constituted by the Edict of Nantes in 1598, were quite simply not prepared to share the territory of France, their own 'space', with a religious competitor. The ambition of the Church was naturally to bring Protestants back into the space of the mother Church, 'le giron de l'Eglise', which they had so heedlessly abandoned.

The desire of the Council to reassert papal over temporal authority was not generally welcome in France, and, beyond jurisdiction in matters of faith, the extension of papal authority over Churches outside Rome was not wholly acceptable to the French Church. The assertion that the pope's authority was absolute in all matters relating to the Church and superior in that regard to the temporal authority could not possibly command assent from those sovereigns who had acquired privileges in the jurisdiction of their own Churches in agreements drawn up prior to the Council. For example, the Concordat of Bologna of 1516 gave the French sovereign certain rights in ecclesiastical administration, including nomination of bishops to certain sees. The situation of the Church in France was complicated by the refusal of the temporal authorities to integrate the decrees of the Council of Trent within the system of French law. The Council was never even officially 'received', despite the unilateral declaration of reception in 1615 by the Assembly of the Clergy of France, never ratified by royal authority. Gallican liberties as, for example, inscribed in the Concordat set limits to the jurisdiction of papal authority in the kingdom which assumed great political importance, particularly in the 'affaire de la régale' and the Jansenist controversy. At one stage in the century Richelieu envisaged the possibility of a national Church separate from that of Rome with himself as its patriarch.[3]

The space of the Church, both politically and morally, was a *totalising* force as represented in the Council of Trent's intention to establish what Anthony Wright calls 'the identity of the true Catholic

[3] See J. Orcibal, 'Le Patriarcat de Richelieu devant l'opinion', in *Les Origines du Jansénisme*, vol. III (Paris, 1948), 108–46.

teaching'.[4] Such a concept was wide-ranging in its implications, and indeed the delegates who attended the Council which lasted from 1548 to 1563 saw no reason to exclude from their deliberations any issue relative to the Christian religion in action at the level of the collectivity or the individual. This involved no less than the regeneration of spirituality in all sections of the community and in all forms of activity which could be devoted to God. It also entailed the elimination of those actions and agencies contrary to the letter and spirit of the Christian religion as it came to be defined by the Council. Its ambition was that no realm of social or political life could exclude a moral or religious dimension, both of which were to be exclusively interpreted within the framework of a Christian orthodoxy.

It is clear that the cultural domain in its broadest sense was meant to come under the surveillance of the Church. In addition to the strictures imposed explicitly in the domain of art at the last session of the Council, the French Catholic Church in the seventeenth century saw it as its task to root out what it thought were the nefarious consequences of a wide range of cultural activities, especially those associated with books and the theatre. The development of ideas in the realm of the new science – which challenged a number of traditional assumptions about explanations of the physical universe – and, more generally, all formulations of belief came under the closest scrutiny. No institution or group of any sort could hope to escape the eagle eye of those determined to expel any form of deviance from what was regarded as orthodox doctrine and from what were thought of as proper standards of behaviour in a Christian society. In this light the post-Tridentine Church promoted a respect for things sacred to which a more severe definition was given than in any previous period.

At the same time as providing coherence for a subject of such wide-ranging dimensions, the idea of space or spaces offers the possibility of problematising certain crucial social, cultural and ideological relationships. The ideal of the Church imposing itself as a totalising force in the kingdom of France was not without its problems, especially in view of competing claims, or at least resistance to the claims of the Church emanating from other spaces. One of these is what we might call the space of the 'world'. Indifference to its space was not something easily tolerated by a Church eager to occupy the whole space of social and cultural activity, and it was consequently difficult to envisage a space of the world with its own logic and laws co-existing with the space of the Church in the wider sense. It might be held that some aspects of behaviour were no business of the Church, a position articulated in Molière's play, Le Tartuffe

[4] A. D. Wright, The Counter-Reformation: Catholic Europe and the Non-Christian World (London, 1982), p. 15.

(1669). The business of the Church was on the other hand deepening the faith of those who already possessed it and converting those who did not. The Church could not envisage itself being excluded from any imaginable space and its aspiration could be nothing less than 'filling the space'. The Church therefore had to persuade its constituency that leading a religious life and living a life in the world were compatible, despite the assertions of some within the space of the Church that they were not.

The modalities of persuasion were to give rise to considerable tension. The space of orthodoxy and its relation to other spaces did not always comprise a simple imposition of authority but required a certain negotiation. Two terms are important to an understanding of what follows: accommodation and assimilation. Accommodation points to two things. First, it indicates the degree to which, let us say, an idea is taken account of in order to produce a reformulation within the space of orthodoxy and which does not affect any article of faith. It may be perceived as involving not a shift in the definition of faith but a deeper understanding of it. In this case the idea is assimilated into a more general religious concept. Second, a negative sense of accommodation is one which leads to a compromise unacceptable to the unconditional guardians of orthodoxy. Some saw the accommodation of certain ideas as precisely an attack on and deformation of the original understanding of the faith. A similar definition of accommodation was ascribed to the agencies of the Church who operated in 'the world', that is to say outside the space of ordination. The Society of Jesus in particular was constantly accused, not exclusively by supporters of Port-Royal, of accommodating itself with worldly or even pagan ways in order to bring converts into the space of the Church.

A further problem was, however, that the definition of the space of orthodoxy, on which the occupation of other spaces rested, was in no way 'given'. The Church turned out not to be the homogeneous space of its aspirations. It can be reasonably argued that the limits of orthodoxy are difficult to set in advance and emerge only when they are challenged. The seventeenth-century French Church had many occasions on which to reflect on the boundaries of the space of orthodoxy, from arguments over the exact nature of Tradition, through bitter disputes over penitential theory and practice, to the limits to be set on biblical exegesis. Many also dissented from the association of Catholic orthodoxy with specific philosophical positions underpinned by the authority of St Thomas Aquinas's synthesis of Aristotelian and Christian thought. At the same time, all who participated in these disputes did not perceive themselves to be outside the space of orthodoxy and hence the space of the Church.

Finally, the Church had to contend with another agency which had its own totalising ambitions, royal power. This was evident in the unfolding of gallicanism from the time of Richelieu to the end of Louis XIV's reign, and in the desire of the monarchy to control sectors previously the domain of the Church, like charity and the book trade. Battle was joined at various stages of the century on the ethical content of foreign and domestic policy, and the degree to which the Church should influence it. Equally, royal and ecclesiastical power had a combined interest in the control of culture and control through culture. The power of the Church in these areas, especially in the face of conflicting interests between the Church and the king, proved to have its own limits.

Orthodoxy is not only a problem for the Church but also for those writing about it. If orthodoxy is not a 'given', defining the Church as the space of orthodoxy seems to be putting the cart before the horse. On the other hand, a book has to start somewhere, and it seemed appropriate to look first at the general direction in which the Church's renewal in seventeenth-century France was moving. The approach I have adopted attempts first to lay out that programme and the many levels of institutional response before introducing the heavy battalions of dissent and dissension. This is not to say that, even within broad agreement on a pastoral programme, differences did not emerge over the manner of its implementation. Indeed, the unifying theme of this study is the degree to which, even in the areas of what were in its own terms the strengths of the Church, the seeds were sown of its vulnerability to all sorts of resistances and challenges, from the response of the faithful to attempts to root out all forms of 'deviant' beliefs or representations, to the response of the Church to new ideas and individuals or groupings, within and outside the Church, considered, rightly or wrongly, as hostile.

Chapter 1, then, will set out many aspects of the Church's pastoral action in respect of what is now known as the Catholic Reform. Whatever the intentions of the Council of Trent, the Church could not effectively influence the spaces outside its immediate space unless the Church itself was reformed in a variety of ways. Promoting respect for the sacred among the faithful could be successful only if those responsible for instruction understood fully themselves the nature of the faith. If the space of the Church is ultimately defined as the space of orthodoxy as established by and subsequent to the Council of Trent, then forms of participation must conform to that orthodoxy. This applied as much to the clergy as to the laity, and the Catholic Reform in seventeenth-century France addressed both these constituencies. Indeed, the link between them was organic in the sense that one of the clergy's obligations was to produce the sound believers from among whom future members of the clergy would be recruited: hence the constant emphasis at Trent on the duties and responsibilities of the clergy, from the bottom to the top of the hierarchy.

An important aspect of this reform emphasised the specially sanctified status of the priest. While certainly the laity was made increasingly aware of its place in respect of the limits of its participation in the Church's ceremonies and organisation, the regeneration of the faithful took a variety of forms, from the promotion of a spiritual life in the 'world' by St François de Sales to the creation of lay religious societies.

A widespread religious renewal could be achieved only by a greater penetration of the mass of the faithful by the Church. Chapter 2 looks at issues raised by the promotion of religion using secular artistic forms, and also at the promotion of the Church's presence and visibility in its spiritual territory, for example through the construction of new churches and religious houses, and the reconstruction of the old, all of which was designed to 'fill the space'. The establishment of schools of all types and at all levels of society became an important medium for the communication and dissemination of orthodoxy. The school as the disseminator of a particular type of culture and comportment is the subject of chapter 3.

It is in chapter 4 that we meet dissension as a major player in this study, in the different attitudes towards the Church in France as an institution reflecting French traditions, in the various interpretations of the tradition of the Church's teaching and attitudes towards biblical exegesis. Chapters 5 and 6 take the discussion of dissension a stage further with a detailed consideration of changes in the world of ideas, particularly in the confrontation of the two great intellectual traditions of the period: Thomism/Aristotelianism and Augustinianism. The advance of Cartesianism in particular and the new science in general encouraged people to understand orthodoxy and its relation to ideas in different ways without damaging teaching concerning articles of faith. Opposition within the space of the Church to the new thinking not only detracted from the homogeneity sought by those attempting to establish post-Tridentine formulations of orthodox positions, but led to the creation of new spaces within which new ideas could be discussed and disseminated.

While Descartes and others firmly situated themselves within the Church, despite their opposition to some of its philosophical positions, others either situated themselves outside the space of orthodoxy or were constructed by the Church as existing beyond its boundaries. The Catholic Church was not without its enemies or its critics in France in the seventeenth century. Hostility towards the Church might be held to take a number of forms. Intellectual *libertin* circles adopted what I have called a critical form of belief in that, while they did not reject the place of the Church in society, they did not necessarily feel that they could or should accept as a matter of course what they were expected unconditionally to accept. On the other hand, the Church constructed others as hostile, and many clerics adopted the convenient labels of 'libertin' and 'athée' with which to categorise them. Protestants too were identified as hostile in their attack on many Catholic practices and beliefs. In the course of the century, however, it became rapidly apparent that some groups or individuals within the immediate space of the Church did not feel comfortable with ways in which, for example, debate was conducted or authority exercised. The confrontational nature of Port-Royal's increasingly hardening stance, certainly on the issue of papal, and eventually royal, authority threatened to lead to its exclusion from the space of the Church. Dissension became hostility for both sides. All these groups are discussed in chapters 7 and 8. Finally, given the extent and importance of the spaces of dissension and hostility, the Church was anxious to attempt some control of the dissemination of what it considered to be heterodox opinion both in society at large and in its own domain. Chapter 9 looks at the problems involved in such an attempt and the ways in which the Church had, from time to time, to combine with civil authority to stem the tide of 'dangerous' opinions.

All through my study, the relation of the space of orthodoxy to other spaces inevitably raises issues of the sacred and the profane, particularly the limits that can be ascribed to each. The reason for the Church's programme of elimination and reclamation derived precisely from the confusion in certain minds of the precise nature of the boundaries between them. To what degree was this situation clarified? Was the Church successful in its ambition to occupy the whole of the social and political space? To what extent did the space of ideas function independently of theological concerns? What was the significance of the creation of the Académie royale des sciences which deliberately excluded those in orders and any form of theological debate? What consequences ensued from the removal of censorship powers from the Church? An answer to these questions is attempted in my conclusion.

The breadth of this study has its own problems. Clearly the number of spaces that can be identified in the cultural domain will vary according to the vantage-point adopted or even according to one's preferences. Boundaries are notoriously mobile and I am not unaware of the infinite nature of space. The spaces I have picked out in this study are meant to represent as best as possible the range of activity in cultural life which the Church felt it necessary to scrutinise. I do not pretend for a moment that the list is either exhaustive or complete. I have wished simply to focus attention on what one might call cultural products such as art, literature, ideas and beliefs, all of which, for the faithful or others, sustained a relationship, a way of living and coping, an interface with life in this world and, where relevant, the next.

1   The spaces of belief

Introduction

After the period of religious wars which, in part at least, prevented France from initiating the reforms promoted by the Council of Trent, the seventeenth century witnessed the growth of a movement within the Church which sought to transform all aspects of social, religious and even political life. The Church's programme was inclusive in the sense that it desired no less than to make its presence felt in all areas of human activity and to ensure that the behaviour and beliefs of all those engaged in human activity acted according to the lights of orthodoxy as it had been defined by Trent and as that definition came to be refined when confronted by issues deriving from the need to control the numerous areas of public and private life which had perhaps not previously ever come under such close scrutiny.

The Catholic Reform had to perform two principal tasks, and it could not afford to put one before the other. Both had to be carried out simultaneously. The faithful at every level of society had to be brought within the space of Tridentine orthodoxy of belief and practice, and the cadres of the Church, from top to bottom, had themselves to be taught and to be trained in this orthodoxy if reform was to be successful. At this stage my principal concern is the degree to which Trent had an effect on the organisation of the Church and the faithful. At this level there could be no dispute about the need for orthodoxy and change. Here I shall address the degree to which the French Church was successful in implementing change, leaving to a later chapter the emergence of arguments concerning definitions of orthodoxy.

The Church and the clergy

The Church, throughout the seventeenth century, faced enormous difficulties in the control of its own space, perhaps the most urgent being the case of its personnel and their conception of fulfilling their duties to the diocese and to the faithful. In the first place, vocations were not all they could be. The hierarchy of the Church included a fair number of prelates who owed their positions to preferment of one sort or another, and who, in any case, found themselves in the Church for family reasons (Richelieu is a good example). It was not uncommon for positions to run in the family. For almost a century the Gondi family had the monopoly of episcopal and archiepiscopal positions in Paris. The Rohans, another noble family, were bishops of Strasbourg from 1704 to 1803. Two other important families, the La Rochefoucaulds and the Colberts, occupied a number of sees between them.[1]

Nor was the space of the seventeenth-century Church occupied in the way that the post-Tridentine Church required. Quite simply, many of its officials did not reside in the place appointed to them. This was the case both with the hierarchy and with the lower clergy. Even when the situation had improved later in the century Louis XIV could still find fifty bishops present at court to sign an anti-papal document during the affair of the *régale*, an issue concerning the crown's right to episcopal appointments which set the authority of Louis XIV against that of the pope. The lower clergy were no better. They often preferred to leave their parishes in the charge of poor-quality vicars while themselves pursuing study and other activities in the towns, especially Paris. Two famous and interesting examples spring to mind: Bossuet, perhaps the most prominent bishop of Louis XIV's reign, never resided at Meaux, and Duvergier de Hauranne, one of the fathers of Jansenism, never resided at Saint-Cyran of which he was abbé.

Indeed, one of the major reforms of Trent was the insistence on residence for all members of the hierarchy. Another of their duties was to preach. Session XXIV of the Council stipulated that the bishop or his designate must preach on Sundays and solemn feast days, and during periods of fasting (Advent and Lent) he must preach every day or at least three days a week if judged appropriate. In addition the bishop had to undertake each year a pastoral visit of his diocese. Some bishops clearly rose to the challenge. Jean-Baptiste Gault, bishop of Marseille, resided in the Hôtel-Dieu and was exemplary in the austerity of his way of life, as was the legendary Pavillon, bishop of Alet. François de La Fayette, a nobleman of high rank, had been tonsured at thirteen years of age but turned out to be a strong reformer and resided permanently in his diocese of Limoges. Many, like Etienne Le Camus, bishop of Grenoble from 1671 to 1707, took their pastoral visits seriously. But not all bishops demonstrated this level of conscientiousness and application. Gabriel de Ro-

---

[1] J. Delumeau, *Le Catholicisme entre Luther et Voltaire* (Paris, 1971), p. 66.

quette, bishop of Autun, arrived in 1668 to find his see in a deplorable
state, came up against the chapter of the cathedral of Saint-Lazare, left
and returned only for the yearly synod.[2] Whatever their quality, bishops
faced a further difficulty in that they did not always have control of the
clergy in their own space. The archbishop of Reims could himself
nominate only 32 out of 517 priests in his diocese, the bishop of Avranches
21 out of 180 and the bishop of Clermont one quarter of 840. In this
diocese alone there were some 200 patrons.[3]

This lack of control may have hampered the pace of the reform of the
mores of the parish clergy, of those therefore who were supposedly in daily
contact with their flock, and Session XXII of the Council of Trent dealt
with aspects of their behaviour. While this presented the Church with one
of its major problems, it would be wise to avoid generalisations and
oversimplified judgements. A number of historians have warned us
against the tendency to think of the clergy as uniformly bad before the
Council and uniformly good afterwards.[4] No reform could have got off the
ground at all without a fair number of bishops and priests already fitted for
the task. Hence Dominique Julia has called for a more subtle periodisation
of the Counter-Reformation in France and questions whether the inspiration of Carlo Borromeo, the militant archbishop of Milan, and his model
of reform imported into France constituted the new beginning so often
advanced for the French movement. A study of the diocese of Chartres
during the first half of the seventeenth century shows that the questions
asked of parishioners in respect of the conduct of the clergy belonged to a
gallican tradition dating from as far back as the fifteenth century.[5]

It remains true that in very many cases the behaviour of the parish clergy
was a source of some anxiety. Indeed, information on the way they
behaved often came from complaints of the parishioners themselves, or
from the results of diocesan visits. The problems were numerous and
related to sexual licence, drunkenness – visits to the tavern were not rare –
swearing and even blasphemy. Priests were known to play bowls on
religious feast days with their parishioners and, in some cases, even had to
undertake manual work in order to survive financially. In Tournai the
replacement for the parish priest doubled as a barber or tailor.[6]

[2] Details concerning these and other bishops may be found in P. Broutin, *La Réforme
pastorale en France: recherches sur la tradition pastorale après le Concile de Trente*, 2 vols.
(Tournai, 1956).
[3] D. Julia, 'La Réforme post-tridentine en France d'après les procès-verbaux de visites
pastorales: ordre et résistances', in *La Società religiosa*, 311–415 (p. 291).
[4] J. Ferté, *La Vie religieuse dans les campagnes parisiennes, 1622–1695* (Paris, 1962), p. 170,
and F. Lebrun (ed.), *Histoire de la France religieuse*, vol. II, *Du Christianisme flamboyant à
l'aube des Lumières* (Paris, 1988), p. 370.
[5] Julia, 'La Réforme', 322.
[6] Delumeau, *Le Catholicisme*, p. 233.

One of the most important effects of the Catholic Reform in France was the separation of the priest from his flock, in other words the creation of a frontier between the sacred space of the priesthood and the profane activities of the flock. Everything that was unconnected with the duties of a priest as they were narrowly defined was excluded. One important consequence of this separation was that the parish priest should henceforward be sufficiently differentiated from his parishioners in terms of physical recognition. The wearing of the cassock as a mark of his special status was in the early part of the century uncommon, in Autun even as late as 1696. The separation of the priest from his flock brought with it the obligation to observe superior standards of personal behaviour and to abandon any form of work and any form of activity, such as hunting, which placed him in the profane world of his parishioners. If, in order to control it, social space was to be effectively occupied by the Church, that occupation had to be visible. The Church needed to manifest itself as present. The priest was in the social space but not of it. Although progress in the seventeenth century was uneven, the signs are that improvements in the behaviour of the lower clergy were secured. The *procès-verbaux* of diocesan visits seem to record that parishioners' complaints greatly diminished, especially in the last quarter of the century.

The progressive separation of priest and flock was accompanied by moves to improve the intellectual quality of the clergy. Many rural priests were, at the beginning of the century, unable to understand the words of the mass, and the liturgy could be said quite differently from one parish to another. How could the level of orthodoxy of the faithful be adequately controlled if the priest was unfamiliar with the full meaning of the key ceremonies of the Church? The priest had therefore to be educated to a reasonable level and needed to be equipped with a special sort of knowledge. This knowledge would have been inaccessible to the vast majority of the faithful since its source was the printed word, not only in the form of the Bible, but also in the form of a number of texts which embodied the reforming spirit of the Church. Thus the priest was to differentiate himself, at least in the rural areas where the Reform was more difficult to implant, by the possession of a library.

Few priests possessed many books in the early period of the Reform. In 1630 the curé of Dampierre had four. It was felt therefore necessary to prescribe a minimum holding of works containing guidance on priestly functions. In the diocese of La Rochelle, the number of books that a priest was required to possess progressed in stages. In 1623 they included a manual of casuistry, the decrees of the provincial council and a Tridentine catechism. In 1658 certain additions to the list included the New Testament, lives of the saints and a diocesan catechism. In 1669 the whole

Bible was prescribed along with the works of St Gregory and St Bernard, and the moral sections of St Thomas's *Secunda secundae* in the *Summa theologiae*.[7] In 1658 the archbishop of Sens prescribed some forty-seven texts among which were classic reforming texts such as Carlo Borromeo's *Instructions to confessors*, which had been officially adopted by the French Church in 1657, and St François de Sales's *Introduction à la vie dévote*.[8] That the bishops' instructions were heeded is indicated by the *procès-verbal* of a pastoral visit in the diocese of Châlons-sur-Marne which recorded that 97 out of 125 curés possessed the twelve texts which had been prescribed.[9] On the other hand no measures were ever formally taken in Paris to prescribe texts. Thus the priests of the Paris region generally possessed poor libraries.[10] But in 1695 it seems that a considerable improvement had occurred. Because of a special effort made by the diocese and because of the proximity of a stimulating intellectual environment in Paris, the clergy of the Paris region were more advanced than their counterparts in less well-policed areas of France such as the south-west or even neighbouring dioceses.[11] The universal desire to improve the space of the Church very much depended on local initiative, on the quality of the prelate in charge and even on the nature of the terrain.

Not all progress turned out to be good progress. In the diocese of La Rochelle some priests possessed important collections not only of the standard works but also of more modern authors such as Yves de Paris, a Capuchin religious moralist, Bourdoise the missionary, and Antoine Arnauld and Saint-Cyran, two Jansenist theologians. Even secular authors were represented: Charron, Pascal, Balzac, Montaigne and Corneille.[12] Some of these names obviously set alarm-bells ringing. After all, priests could not be protected from the effects of the doctrinal battles which raged in the Church in the course of our period, although possessing a particular book did not necessarily entail agreement with its contents. None the less prescription rapidly moved to proscription. The bishop of La Rochelle, Etienne de Champflour, was keen to extirpate any Jansenist influence. Certain books were therefore proscribed, especially after the condemnation of Quesnel's *Réflexions morales*, which largely gave rise to the papal bull of 1713, entitled *Unigenitus*, which was meant to resolve the Jansenist controversy once and for all. The bishop even personally inspected the libraries of some religious houses.[13] One can also imagine that a close eye was kept on the collections of parish priests. One

[7] L. Perouas, *Le Diocèse de La Rochelle de 1648 à 1724: sociologie et pastorale* (Paris, 1964), p. 253.
[8] Delumeau, *Le Catholicisme*, p. 271.   [9] Julia, 'La Réforme', 349.
[10] Ferté, *La Vie religieuse*, p. 191.   [11] Ibid., p. 195.
[12] Perouas, *Le Diocèse de La Rochelle*, p. 263.   [13] Ibid., p. 375.

of the problems of a more educated clergy was that new or alternative ideas suddenly became accessible and orthodoxy was threatened. The agent of control needed even closer surveillance. Libraries suddenly became potential spaces of subversion.

Other means adopted to improve the intellectual quality of the clergy comprised the establishment of conferences where the priest's knowledge of doctrinal matters would be further refined, along with the establishment of seminaries where priests could be isolated from the contamination of their flock and learn all the rudiments of their profession in a controlled environment. The success of the seminary was late in coming, and its progress was uneven. Thirty-six were created between 1642 and 1660, and a further fifty-three from 1660 to 1680. By the end of the eighteenth century there were seminaries in 122 out of 134 dioceses. Even at the end of the Ancien Régime a geographical uniformity had not been achieved, thus testifying to the enormity of the problems faced by the seventeenth-century hierarchy who very often lacked the necessary funds to found these institutions.

It is not generally until the end of the century that we see the success of the seminary from which the new type of priest emerged into the world. La Rochelle is a good example. A significant difference could be discerned in the intellectual quality of priests ordained before the establishment of the seminary in 1657 and those ordained after, and this is illustrated in part by the greater number of books possessed by the 'new' priests. The early establishment of the seminary can in this case be explained by pressures arising from the existence of the frontier between the Protestant and Catholic worlds, where the difference in quality between the pastor and the priest was considered disadvantageous to the evangelising efforts of the Catholic Church. After 1657 Catholic priests were scarcely inferior to their Protestant counterparts.[14] The culture of the pastor could only be answered by the culture of the priest. The elimination of the frontier between the two faiths, that is to say the conversion and assimilation of Protestants, depended on the education of the Catholic clergy.

Despite the immense difficulties that a kingdom as large and as diverse as that of France posed, the Church was vigorously implanting itself and enhancing its visibility in the social space, as is testified by the geographical penetration of religious houses in France. For our period, historians have calculated that there were some 15,000 convents in France, nearly half of which were new foundations.[15] In just three archdeaconries of the diocese of Paris, nine abbeys and three male priories were established in

[14] Ibid., pp. 263–4.
[15] A. Latreille, E. Delaruelle and J.-R. Palanque (eds.), *Histoire du catholicisme en France*, 3 vols. (Paris, 1957–62), II, 282.

1622.[16] In the diocese of La Rochelle sixty-three new religious houses were established between 1648 and 1724. The increase in the number of regulars in the century was of the order of 60–80 per cent, while correspondingly the secular clergy declined by 10 per cent over seventy-five years.[17] The participation of the regular clergy in the regeneration of faith in the faithful, in their role as preachers and directors of conscience, was not without controversy. Such was the extent of their growth that Colbert attempted in 1666 to reduce the number of religious by forbidding the establishment of new communities without the express permission of the king.[18] The success of the Catholic Reform was seen to come into conflict with the state whose mercantilist economic policy was dependent on manpower. Celibates deprived the economy of their own labour and that of possible future generations. The kingdom would be unable to fill its own space.

Church and society

The Catholic Reform at the level of the faithful was, in the eyes of the Church, a totalising phenomenon and did not recognise autonomous secular spaces. That is to say that there was no corner of social life which it regarded as beyond its control. But the Church's control of the faithful could not proceed in quite the same way as the control of its own personnel. Quite simply, there was no law against sin. No collective judicial constraint could be brought to bear on those, say, who wished to spend their whole day in pleasurable pursuits without there being any obvious detriment to the welfare of others. In this perspective, the control of the faithful had to be of a different order. The Church, if it was to succeed in its mission of evangelising society, had still to occupy the social space but it had to be careful in its strategy. One of the real innovations of the Counter-Reformation was the invention of different approaches to the manifold problems the social space posed.

The Jesuits were quick to realise the advantages that could accrue from their physical location in Paris. One aspect of their own strategy was very much geographical. The professed house was established in an area which by tradition, a tradition enhanced by Henri IV's urban vision, contained the fashionable town residences of the court aristocracy. The Eglise Saint-Louis, close to the Louvre, frequented by Louis XIII and his Court, was therefore a focus of worldly society. There the Society of Jesus, not without design, concentrated those of its forces which specialised in

[16] Ferté, *La Vie religieuse*, p. 109.
[17] Perouas, *Le Diocèse de La Rochelle*, pp. 437 passim.
[18] Latreille (ed.), *Histoire du catholicisme*, II, 375.

preaching, spiritual direction, the foundation of lay congregations and the publication of books in the vernacular for the use of the laity. The provincial and the king's confessor also resided there.[19]

Not all sections of the Church agreed on the strategies chosen by its constituent parts. The conversion of an educated and sophisticated social élite would seem to require different methods than those required to convert rural communities, although the essence and the strength of the message was ultimately the same. The calibre of the priest would also differ, therefore, according to circumstances. The problem is the extent to which the space of the Church accommodated itself with the space of society. A frontier existed between the two built on divergences in the priorities of those who occupied those spaces. It was of course the aim of the Church to assimilate the social world, to 'christianise' it. In so doing, however, it ran the risk of being assimilated by society, of being compromised by secularism, of conceding too much of its own space. Did the Church control the social world, or did the social world ultimately control the Church?

The Church faced a crucial choice: what sort of Christianity was it to offer the faithful? Some, notably the Jansenists and their followers, assessed the situation in historical terms and emphasised the degree to which religion had, according to them, been corrupted by a whole variety of trends, including scholasticism, the influence of stoicism from the time of St Ambrose and what might be seen as the abasement of the spiritual life following the influence of the paganising elements of the Renaissance. They found their answer in the purity of belief associated with the period of the primitive Church, more particularly of the Church of St Augustine, which they wished to instil in the faithful of their own time. Others proposed an alternative solution, in a sense no less historical. Was it not better to appropriate the positive aspects in the heritage of the Renaissance and remove its poisonous elements, thus offering the Christian of middling virtue a religion adapted to his or her moral stature? What use would a too demanding form of religion be when its sole consequence would be to empty the churches? In these responses lies the confrontation between the uncompromising and purist perspective of radical Augustinianism and a more flexible Christian humanism which positively assimilated certain values deriving from the world and to which the world was attached, in order better to convert it.[20] The tension between these two perspectives is the history of the Church in its social role in seventeenth-century France.

---

[19] M. Fumaroli, *L'Age de l'éloquence: rhétorique et 'res literaria' de la Renaissance au seuil de l'époque classique* (Geneva, 1980), p. 248.

[20] H. Busson, *La Religion des Classiques, 1660–1685* (Paris, 1948), pp. 64–5.

St François de Sales (1567–1622) was one of the major reforming figures who, in France, formulated a possible strategy for directing the conscience of those in the social space. A singularly important innovation in the century was the development of a more personal approach to salvation and one which used a language more adapted to the individual Christian. This is crystallised in one of the most successful books of the whole century, the *Introduction à la vie dévote*, which was published in 1609 and which ran to forty editions in ten years. The approach of St François was so innovative that he was forced to defend himself from the accusation that the responsibilities of a bishop were too important for time to be spent on a 'distraction'.[21] He was in any case a remarkable episcopal figure who gave a personal lead on a number of levels. He urged an unadorned language in preaching, he personally catechised children – something unusual for a prelate at the beginning of the seventeenth century – and he worked in close association with the priests of his diocese.[22]

There are two striking aspects to his innovations. The first was stylistic. The *Introduction* is entirely free of the cumbersome quotation from theological writings which was customary in such works: the learned don't need them and the rest aren't interested.[23] Moreover, St François aimed to unite the useful with the agreeable in his work, thus reflecting a theme derived from Horace's *Ars poetica* which was to become an important literary principle during our period and beyond. A remarkable feature of his style is its personal tone in which the reader is addressed as 'Mon cher lecteur', and where the addressee is Philothée, a devout society woman. This particular approach raised an important point concerning the degree to which the director of conscience could be close to the individual Christian. What degree of familiarity was possible if the priest was at the same time to remain separate from the mass of the faithful? Certainly, the priest did not 'share the world' of the penitent. So what was the precise frontier between the religious and the secular in these circumstances?

The *Introduction* addresses principally the compatibility of Christian life with social demands. In a sense such an approach already suggests two spaces, and not a unified space. The question remains: is it possible to live in both the space of the Church and the space of society? St François argues according to the difference between conceptions of the world for the priest and for the individual lay Christian. It would clearly be a

---

[21] St François de Sales (ed. Ch. Florisoone), *Introduction à la vie dévote*, 2 vols. (Paris, 1961), I, 10.
[22] Broutin, *La Réforme pastorale*, I, 79–80 and 80–3.
[23] François de Sales, *Introduction*, I, 4.

nonsense for the artisan to be at church all day like the priest, for such a form of worship would be ridiculous, exaggerated and unbearable. But it would be equally ridiculous to expect a religious to be available for all sorts of meetings in the same way as a bishop. Different estates require different sorts of devotion. The weakness of works of piety in the past, he argues, is that they have mostly been written for those already in retreat from the world. My intention, he writes, is to instruct those in the towns, in households, at Court and those who, on the pretext that their condition obliges them to live 'une vie commune quant à l'exterieur', do not think that anyone can aspire to a high level of Christian piety while pressed by temporal affairs.[24] So, there is a form of devotion corresponding to each station in life, whether it be in the kitchen or in service of any sort, however humble.[25]

What of those times when obligations in the world prevent the Christian from concentrating on devotion? Do these escape the space of the Church? Certainly St François envisages that the Christian in the world must pass from one state to another, that is to say from a state of prayer to the occupations that are his or her legitimate concern. The lawyer must leave prayer to plead a case; the wife must attend to her domestic duties.[26] But even within the occupations of the world a space must be kept for meditation. Thus the outer space of the world is kept at bay by the inner space of solitude, even amidst business and conversation.[27] At the same time, St François envisages that the Christian is engaged in social duties which are as much the will of God as devotion itself.[28] Thus, in any case, the space of the world is assimilated within the space of devotion. Legitimate occupations are in themselves sanctified. Devotion even enhances the occupations of the world.[29]

Although he was mostly associated with the social élite of France, St François was concerned in fact with the whole of the laity. This 'volonté d'universel' was quite new at the time,[30] and even a subject of scandal.[31] He showed that the space of the world could be a part of the space of the Church. Equally, his witness is an example of how the Church could come to occupy a part of domestic space. Those who inhabit it must recognise the form of devotion most appropriate to them. Perhaps the most crucial aspect of Salesian spirituality was that his laicisation of piety inscribed the notion of the priesthood of all believers within Roman orthodoxy.[32] Louis Cognet understands the essence of Salesian spirituality as 'une véritable

---

[24] Ibid., p. 8.   [25] Ibid., pp. 129–30.   [26] Ibid., p. 85.   [27] Ibid., p. 91.
[28] Ibid., p. 93.   [29] Ibid., pp. 21–2.
[30] Lebrun (ed.), *Histoire de la France religieuse*, II, 352.
[31] F. Lebrun (ed.), *Histoire des Catholiques en France* (Paris, 1980), p. 86.
[32] Lebrun (ed.), *Histoire de la France religieuse*, II, 354.

réaction personnaliste' which, in turn, seeks to emphasise the obligation of individual Christians.[33]

St François's approach is not without its difficulties, and his views on certain matters could be interpreted in a way they were perhaps not intended to be. The problem remains the degree to which the world can be accommodated. One cannot say that St François's view of devotion placed great demands on the Christian. He advises Philothée that she must, on feast days and Sundays, attend matins and vespers 'tant que votre commodité le permettra'.[34] While it was never expected that individuals attend all possible services, the way in which the exemption is expressed is interesting. The greatest difficulty with some aspects of St François's advice is what it can be held to legitimate, especially since it clashes with an alternative tradition on the nature of life which adopts a much more rigorist position.

The subject of *divertissement* attracted much discussion in pious works and in sermons where the central problem was identified as the status of pleasure in the life of the Christian. The orthodox position held that the world is full of the concupiscence of the flesh, with the result that any occasion on which we encourage our concupiscence to act is sinful, even if we expose ourselves only to the possibility of sin rather than to direct participation in it. All theologians agree that some diversion is necessary from the pressures of daily life and work. But two things are important to recognise: the first is that *divertissement* is legitimate only in so far as it allows us to rest, to 're-create' ourselves; the second is that we must not undertake as part of our *divertissement* activities which would be detrimental to a state of renewal. Most religious moralists argue that, given man's nature, he will seek pleasure for its own sake in activities which are clearly not designed to send him back to his duties refreshed.

On a number of occasions in the course of the century, the name of St François was invoked as an authority in the legitimation of dancing and theatre, both of which, even in non-Augustinian traditions, were highly suspect forms of recreation. The difficulty arose from St François's notion that dancing and theatre (two items, it must be said, in a list of five including games, banquets and 'les pompes') are not in themselves evil but indifferent, since they can be well- or ill-used. Religious moralists generally reject the favourable interpretation that can be put on these words, pointing out that St François laid down so many conditions to be observed (actually in the specific case of dancing) that such activities could never be considered legitimate. It is true that the reference to drama occurs in a chapter which deals with purging oneself of becoming addicted

[33] Broutin, *La Réforme pastorale*, I, 94.   [34] François de Sales, *Introduction*, I, 33.

to dangerous and superfluous things, but there is sufficient ambiguity for the implication to be drawn that a liberal approach compromises with the values of the world, in themselves based on dubious forms of pleasure.

Indeed St François's attitude sets out to maintain a balance between necessary contact with others in society and avoiding unnecessary occasions of intercourse. Deliberately to seek conversation and deliberately to avoid it are two extremes which are reprehensible in 'la dévotion civile': one leads to idleness while the other shows disdain for our fellow-creatures.[35] The failure to proscribe dancing absolutely thus leaves the responsibility with the individual who must exercise a sort of self-control. As one historian defines it, devout humanism designates the tendency of many seventeenth-century writers to see the glory of God in the whole of human life and to admire at the same time God the creator and man as the image of God's work. That, he adds, is a balance which is difficult to achieve.[36] For others, however, it is a balance impossible to achieve in the space of the world, and certainly not one that the individual Christian can be trusted with.

Church and societies

With the example of St François de Sales I have been concerned to illustrate one way in which the Church acts in the space of the world in a visible way. His lead in that personal and individual approach was followed by many others to the extent that the personal form of the pastoral letter became a genre of religious writing. Alongside this personal intervention in the space of society, there existed an associative form of intervention. During the century a number of societies were formed by both clerics and lay persons which sought to bring about changes in behaviour towards the sacred at all levels of social life. These societies, often secret, promoted Christian action through individual members of the societies, or through those outside them who were unaware of the existence of these societies. They were further manifestations of the desire of many within the Church to exercise a tighter control over the lives of the faithful.

The most famous of these societies is the Compagnie du Saint-Sacrement. The Compagnie was in essence a secret society, composed of laymen and clerics, which kept no written record of its proceedings and launched its initiatives without the participants being aware of the existence of the Compagnie. Alain Tallon, its most recent historian, confirms the geographical spread of the Compagnie which, thirty years

[35] Ibid., p. 65.
[36] Lebrun (ed.), *Histoire de la France religieuse*, II, 351.

after its foundation between 1627 and 1630, had 4,000 members in sixty towns.[37] Its mainly urban nature was complemented by 'petites compagnies' which operated in rural areas.[38] Of its known members, 501 out of 990 were laymen, including Lamoignon, the *lieutenant civil* of Paris at the beginning of Louis XIV's reign and, indeed, the lay members came most often from the *robe* or the milieu of the *parlement*. The clerical members, Bossuet and St Vincent de Paul among them, included thirty-nine bishops. Regulars were strictly excluded. Although there was a distrust of Jansenism, all the spiritual families of Catholicism were represented.[39]

The Compagnie's aim was in many ways to police the sacred in the social space. Its members orchestrated attacks on Molière's *L'Ecole des femmes*, *Le Tartuffe* and *Dom Juan*. They enforced greater respect for the sacraments, such as kneeling as the sacraments were carried through the streets to the dying. They attempted to curb what they regarded as the excesses of the Carnaval, and had a network of spies who informed, for example, on butchers who sold meat on Fridays. They also sought to have sacred images removed from the signs outside private dwellings, and mounted crusades against the Protestant Church, being responsible for the removal of rights from Huguenot doctors in Lyon.

This negative side should not, however, be allowed to dominate the picture of the Compagnie. Even their punitive actions were undertaken on the basis of a certain attitude to the sacred and its role in the social space. Their spying and delation became necessary only when they felt that the civil authorities had let them down.[40] On the positive side they initiated much charitable work. St Vincent de Paul was, before he became a member, unaware that he himself was working on behalf of the Compagnie. In a sense, the charitable work of the Compagnie was partly inspired by their concern that the care for the poor had become too much of a lay programme without the necessary religious input,[41] something which became increasingly true in the second half of the century when the Compagnie had ceased to be.

The dynamics of the Compagnie stemmed equally from the promotion of a personal reflection on spiritual edification.[42] The Compagnie in fact highlights many of the issues I have been dealing with hitherto in terms of the relation of the social to the religious space. It fulfilled two roles, both of which are directly related to the separation of the priest from his flock. The first enabled the secular clergy to move out from its isolation and to meet with pious members of the laity in a new sort of community where it could confront the sort of problems common to all those who wished to promote

[37] A. Tallon, *La Compagnie du Saint-Sacrement, 1629–1667: spiritualité et société* (Paris, 1990), pp. 22–5.   [38] Ibid., p. 35.   [39] Ibid., pp. 26–7.
[40] Ibid., p. 61.   [41] Ibid., p. 58.   [42] Ibid., p. 37.

a certain idea of the sacred.[43] The second provided the laity with a means of playing a role in the Church militant of the seventeenth century. More than this, the laity could almost aspire to the sanctity attaching to the priesthood.[44] The fervour of the laity was such that private houses used as meeting places could sometimes be treated as if they were chapels. In Grenoble, holy water could be found at the entrance of one such place.[45] Moreover, the Compagnie was also an organisation determined by its nature as a religious fraternity where the spirit of the primitive Church overrode any social divisions.[46]

Serious weaknesses, however, made themselves felt at the heart of the conception lay members of the Compagnie had of themselves, and they illustrate tensions created by the aspiration of lay persons to a special status within the space of the Church. The appropriation by the laity of a clerical voice worked in some ways to undermine the dynamics of the Compagnie in moving its members away from the lay world which they were in a good position to christianise through their action and example.[47] This weakness was compounded by the inculcation in some of the mystical notion of 'anéantissement', a concept elaborated by Cardinal Bérulle, the founder of the French Oratory, which involved the efface-ment of the self in the person of Christ, thus running counter to the notion of action in the world.[48] Another tension existed between the Compag-nie's purely spiritual aspirations and the restrictions on their actions imposed by their lay status. There emerged in the Compagnie a pessimis-tic attitude to the less than exciting nature of the sort of existence membership of the Compagnie demanded:

le rôle du chrétien dans le monde semble se limiter à être bon père, bon seigneur ou bon voisin. Certes, cela pourrait satisfaire les dévots, s'ils n'avaient pas le sentiment de l'urgence de sauver un monde qui se perd, en le sanctifiant. Le décalage entre le modèle proposé par la Compagnie et sa vision du monde est peut-être une des causes de l'échec des dévots, dans leur volonté de réformer les chrétiens du XVIIe siècle.[49]

The Compagnie simply lacked the heroic impulse of the early Church which was difficult to transpose into a time and a place already won over to Christianity. Equally, it turned out that the Compagnie's lay members could not control their own status in the space of the Church.

What was the relation of the Compagnie to the hierarchy and institution of the Church? Its members had no official sanction for their works, although, as we have seen, bishops were included in their ranks. Their relationship with bishops was not in any case founded on respect for their local authority but rather on respect for the dignity of their office. It did

[43] Ibid., p. 25.   [44] Ibid., p. 40.   [45] Ibid., p. 74.   [46] Ibid., pp. 94–5.
[47] See ibid., p. 77.   [48] Ibid., p. 97.   [49] Ibid., p. 103.

not matter that the Compagnie was not authorised by the bishop of the diocese in which it existed as long as it was authorised by another. In fact bishops were asked not to intervene in the Compagnie's actions but to use their power in its service, 'étant bien entendu qu'on révère leur dignité'.[50] In this way the Compagnie preserved its independence. In some cases the ecclesiastical hierarchy reacted unfavourably. The archbishop of Lyon was hostile to meetings of dévots in his diocese and they were discontinued for a time. The fact remains that the Compagnie was a space within a space with its own means of regulation. The Compagnie eventually attracted the attention of Louis XIV who disapproved of any organism which escaped his control, especially if it was clandestine in the way of this particular group. The Compagnie was suppressed in 1666.

But the Compagnie du Saint-Sacrement was not the only sort of religious society in the seventeenth century which included the laity within its bounds and which sought to transform the behaviour of the faithful. Under the auspices of the Jesuits, Marian congregations (or sodalities), which were predominantly male, flourished across the whole of Europe. Initially they were meant to form a link between the colleges and their former pupils. But the aim of the congregations was no less than to root Christianity in the faithful across a wide section of the population. The congregation thus formed would be 'a brotherhood constituting a model of Christian society which would serve as an example to the whole town'.[51] A sign of this in some places was that the chapel in the college was much larger than a chapel designed simply to serve the needs of the pupils, and in Grenoble and Chambéry the members built their own. In Champagne all the sodalities together added up to more than the college population and demonstrate the degree to which this form of apostleship was as important as the educational programme offered in the schools.[52]

The geographical penetration of the congregations was uneven. The sodalities were particularly strong in the east, the south and the south-east of France. As one might expect, Toulouse, renowned for the very strong Catholic inspiration of its administration, was a centre for the Marian congregations which reached even into very small villages.[53] Lille gives us some idea of the numerical implantation of the congregations: out of a total population of 45,000, 2,000 belonged to the sodalities. In Nancy, the proportion was even more impressive, 1,000 out of a population of 7,000.[54] The congregations were another aspect of the occupation of social space by the space of the Church.

---

[50] Ibid., p. 120.
[51] L. Châtellier, *The Europe of the Devout: the Catholic Reformation and the Formation of a New Society* (Cambridge, 1989), p. 5.   [52] Ibid., pp. 50–1.   [53] Ibid., p. 84.
[54] Ibid., p. 51.

Some idea of the social make-up of the sodalities can be gleaned from the example of Nancy, which, however, had its local peculiarities. In 1639 its members included merchants, artists (among whom we find Jacques Callot, the engraver), lawyers, judges, and especially ducal officials and high-ranking elements of the ducal court. Membership subsequently changed and by 1675 the sodality had become a congregation of artisans, dominated by workers in the cloth, wood and leather trades. By the end of the century, tailors and shoemakers had replaced the ducal officers, all of which reflects the decline of Nancy as a political and cultural capital, a decline due to the loss of its duke. It none the less remains that the sodalities in themselves reflected changes in the urban population over time. Such changes, Châtellier argues, reflect the specific intention of establishing a truly proportional relationship between the socio-professional categories in the locality and the groups composing the congregation which thus became a microcosm of the town: 'Rather than a consequence, the social structure of a congregation was a construct; a willed and carefully considered construct, whose purpose was the conversion of the whole town by the means clearly outlined by the founding fathers, that of the apostleship of like by like.'[55]

In the early days, despite the fact that the congregations were inspired by the Jesuits, the composition of the membership was far from partisan. There were former Protestants and men of Jansenist sympathies. As with the Compagnie du Saint-Sacrement, different currents of spirituality could come together in a united space with a common purpose. It would seem that the idea which drove in part the Parisian association was precisely 'to unite what was formerly divided, and to bring together those who seemed destined not only not to respect each other, but never even to meet'.[56]

Enrolling the laity in sodalities was directed to the control of behaviour in the community at large. The conversion of the whole social space could be founded only on the exemplary behaviour of their members. This differentiation in behaviour between members and non-members, a reflection in fact of the model of separation of priest from laity, was much encouraged, if only eventually to be effaced by the recruitment and conversion of others. This process of differentiation was further enhanced by a conventual discipline within the laity, which included, in the sixteenth century, a strong personal régime of hairshirt and scourge:

A rhythm was imposed on the year, as it was on the day. The purpose was not simply to subject piety to discipline, or to observe a liturgical year, but to live differently. The time controlled by the Church should be the whole time. Thus

[55] Ibid., p. 64.   [56] Ibid., pp. 101–2.

there would be no longer the tiniest place, or so it was hoped, from morning to night, from one year to the next, for evil.[57]

Taverns in particular were obvious no-go areas and one duty of officers of the congregation was to report those whose behaviour was scandalous.[58] The emphasis in the beginning and for a large part of the century was on the transformation of individual behaviour and on the control of individual and corporate lives according to the liturgical calendar. In due course, however, women could not be excluded from the attempt to bring about change in the laity. A shift of interest occurred from the individual in isolation to the family, which came to be regarded as an essential element of the foundation of a Christian society.[59]

But alongside the Marian congregations, secret societies were introduced, the Aa or Associations d'amis, and there were several in France from 1645. The associations were originally composed of secular priests and constituted a network of communication, a brotherhood, which covered the whole kingdom. At the beginning of Louis XIV's personal rule the consciousness of a need for secrecy would have been compounded by the realisation that the societies existed on the margins of official bodies and consisted of seculars who behaved like regulars. A higher profile could hardly have been tolerated by the king. Even the Roman authorities were unsure as to what attitude to adopt.[60] The Aas did not however remain uniquely clerical, but, in Toulouse, when the question arose of admitting adult men to the secret associations, a second association was opted for, all the better to continue that isolation of the cleric from the laity which was to be a mark of the priest's existence in rural communities in particular.[61] The essence of the secret societies was, then, to create a space within a space where certain clerics, possessing a common purpose, were distinguished from others, a sense of differentiation within the Church itself.

The most interesting aspect of the Marian congregations was perhaps the links established between civil authority and their membership. It is evident that the Jesuits were adept at modelling their strategy on differing circumstances. Châtellier describes how in some instances the Jesuits seem to have preferred to establish their societies in spaces where power was absent or remote, that is to say, Dijon, Toulouse and Lyon rather than Paris. In this sense, they implanted themselves in what Châtellier calls the interstices of power where they would find the most fertile ground. The reasons are obvious:

Would a civil authority attached to its prerogatives have found it easy to tolerate these groups of zealous Christians who arrogated to themselves, in both taverns

[57] Ibid., p. 35.   [58] Ibid., p. 57.   [59] Ibid., pp. 141–2.   [60] Ibid., pp. 70–1.
[61] Ibid., p. 83.

and streets, police powers? Would a proud bishop have viewed without concern a group of religious who attracted to their own church a large part of the male faithful of the town, at the risk of emptying the parish churches and negating all the pastoral labours of their priests?[62]

Presumably, the priests who were members of the secret societies experienced some clash of loyalties here. In any case, it provides another manifestation of the creation of independent spaces within the general space of the Church.

The *Grands* were specifically targeted and Châtellier argues that in the first half of the seventeenth century the Jesuits aimed to exert control over those in positions of power,[63] whereas the orientation of the Compagnie du Saint-Sacrement was social rather than political.[64] The world of the *parlements* too provided a fertile source of members, and interestingly so, since this world was traditionally hostile to the Society. Magistrates were members of the congregation in Toulouse, and similarly in Grenoble and Rouen.[65] The congregation of the professed house in Paris enrolled drapers, apothecaries, booksellers, minor abbés, but also figures from such diverse fields as letters, finance and the Church itself, in Vaugelas the arbiter of correct linguistic usage, Fouquet, Sublet de Noyers and the Cardinal François de la Rochefoucauld.[66] However, contact with power seems to have been discreet. Few very major figures were recruited, but when this was the case, they were those who were in daily contact with the king, influential members of the Court and the king's ministers whose presence could demonstrate 'in all circumstances, by example and, if need be, by advice, the way to behave'.[67]

Recruitment to the sodalities was not simply a local phenomenon. The aim, as illustrated by the attempt to recruit members from the regions of high administration, was to realise the Christian state, to realise a situation where the space of the Church completely overlay that of the space of the world, where no margin existed whatsoever. And this is reflected in patterns of recruitment in the sodalities nationwide where, through the presence of nobles, merchants and craftsmen, they engendered a spirit of union. The congregations were a cohesive factor which allowed the foundation of a new society: 'Every congregation member was invited to serve as a model for others, those who remained outside the association and whom it was the intention to influence in their profession, family and worldly lives.' Thus, little by little, what Châtellier calls the global change

---

[62] Ibid., p. 30.   [63] Ibid., p. 88.
[64] Tallon, *La Compagnie du Saint-Sacrement*, p. 21.
[65] Châtellier, *The Europe of the Devout*, pp. 90–1.
[66] Ibid., pp. 93–4.
[67] Ibid., p. 107.

could be realised.[68] The societies' desire was no less than to efface the frontiers which might exist between the Church and the social world. Where St François de Sales and the model he created acted on the basis of a directly personal contact with the individual Christian, the sodality, while it too desired a transformation of personal behaviour, operated more on the level of fellowship and the allegiance of the group. But the global change still rested on the personal assumption of pious behaviour in all areas of life, especially through the concept of exemplarity which, it is therefore to be noted, is not a virtue limited to the priesthood. As in the case of the Compagnie the sodalities offered ways of effacing to a degree the distance that separated the priest from the laity.

That the Compagnie du Saint-Sacrement and the sodalities were wholly dominated by men with some concessions to action on the part of women should not suggest that women were deprived of influence in the space of the Church or that their place was entirely forgotten. Jansenism as a doctrine and Port-Royal as an institution were attractions for society women who were particularly visible in their religious affiliations. Henriette d'Angleterre and Anne of Austria were especially noted for their religious fervour, and one can also point to conversions of highly placed women of the Court such as Anne de Gonzague. The example of La Fontaine's patroness, Madame de la Sablière, who exchanged a life of little virtue for work with those afflicted with incurable diseases, and the novelist Madame de Lafayette's pious last years did not go unnoticed in the space of society. Jeanne de Chantal and Madame Acarie, the latter gathering together in her hôtel her cousin Bérulle and other clerics or lay persons of great piety, were spectacular examples of the great and the holy. But while the contribution of women to the Counter-Reformation and the Catholic Reform in France was much deeper and much wider than this, the promotion of women within the Church was not uncomplicated.

The success of women in the Church can be gauged by the growth of female religious houses. From the arrival in 1601 in France of the Spanish Carmelite nuns, in Paris alone fifty-five convents were established over the next forty years. There was an increase of nuns generally in a large number of French cities such as Troyes, Blois and Reims. In 1700 there were 10–12,000 Ursulines in some 320 communities.[69] Along with the increase in the number of religious houses, the social stratum attracted by the female religious orders inevitably widened considerably in the course of the century.

One problem of women in orders derived from the space they were

[68] Ibid., p. 109.
[69] E. Rapley, *The Dévotes: Women and the Church in Seventeenth-Century France* (Montreal, 1990), pp. 20 and 48.

meant to inhabit. The question whether such women should be enclosed arose largely because of changes in the type of ministry many of them were to undertake, namely teaching and the care of the sick. Thus a new element entered the culture of the Church, the concept of a female order that was mobile, that could move from the space of the convent into the space of the world, and back again. The crossing of this frontier was a matter not to be taken lightly. The Visitation, founded by Jeanne de Chantal under the direction of St François de Sales, is a good illustration of the choice between closure and greater mobility. Their task was to visit the sick and the poor, a task which would obviously have been obstructed, not to say negated, by *clausura*, and indeed the initial experiment proved unsuccessful, since the nuns were ordered to remain in their convent.[70] But an initiative was launched which proved in the end unstoppable. The question of *clausura* simply fell by *force majeure* when it was realised that the ministry of women was necessary on quite a scale if there was to be an adequate catechisation of girls.

The matter of vows which in themselves ensured that an order should remain closed posed a further problem. Eventually, a way round this was discovered, particularly in the case of the Filles de la Charité, who took private vows but without witnesses. In this way congregations of 'filles séculières' were created.[71] But the mobility of women in these innovative orders in seventeenth-century France did pose a real legal difficulty for families. If a woman was not a member of a closed order and was unbound by vows, she would presumably be able to move back into the space of the family, with all the financial problems that that involved.[72]

It so happens that not all within the Church considered vows as conferring any special status or as having the degree of importance ascribed to them by others. St François de Sales was among those who placed less emphasis on vows and who argued that perfection came from the individual and not from his or her state, that 'the state of religion, even though called a "state of perfection", did not infallibly insure spiritual perfection'. St François therefore took the side of the secular against the regular clergy.[73] This was an attitude which could not fail, if only implicitly, to promote the image of the laity and to lessen that distance between the priest and his flock, paradoxically so much a central plank of the Catholic Reform.

One element noted as important in the diocese of La Rochelle was the quality of the Catholic clergy as opposed to that of the Protestant pastor. Similarly, one aspect of the promotion and education of women in the

---

[70] Ibid., pp. 40–1.   [71] Ibid., pp. 74 and 85.   [72] Ibid., p. 115.
[73] C. Williams, *The French Oratorians and Absolutism, 1611–1641* (New York, 1989), pp. 174–5.

seventeenth century was, according to Rapley, the unfair comparison that could be made between Catholic and Protestant women. We know that the Reformation had been particularly successful with women, for example in their access to Scripture, their ability to dispute and even to teach, although it is fair not to overestimate the liberation of Protestant women. There could on the other hand (apart from the issue of celibacy) be no equivalent in France of Rembrandt's portrait of a pastor discussing the Scriptures with his wife. As Rapley comments:

Heretic women were dabbling in theology when they would have been better employed at their distaffs: that was reason enough why Catholic women should not do the same. In any case all catechizing by the laity was contrary to the spirit of the Catholic pastoral reform. According to the Council of Trent and succeeding councils in France, the instruction of the people in the faith was the prerogative of the parish clergy.[74]

Two frontiers were then crossed, that between the faiths and that within the faith.

While the promotion of women was unquestionably an important development in the seventeenth-century French Church, and reflected the growing importance of the role of the laity in a fairly spectacular form, the general view of women was still fundamentally negative and exclusionist. In 1607 the Dominican Coëffeteau was ordered to desist from translating St Thomas's *Summa theologiae* for fear that women would be able to read it. Women were regarded as intellectually weak as a gender and creatures of excessive imagination, whose role it was to submit to the Church. Claude Fleury regarded women educated in religion as a necessity but also a danger: 'si elles sont savantes, il est à craindre qu'elles ne veuillent dogmatiser, et qu'elles ne donnent dans les nouvelles opinions'.[75] The fact remains that the Catholic and Protestant Reforms, in comparison with previous periods of the history of Christianity in the West, offered women a degree of initiative and the possibility of participating in the work of the Church to an unprecedented degree.

Church and people

Consideration of the space of the Church in relation to the space of society can be widened by shifting the emphasis substantially although not entirely from the urban to the rural. The cities and the countryside posed different problems for the Church, if only because in some respects the countryside proved more difficult to penetrate both physically and

---

[74] Rapley, *The Dévotes*, p. 117.
[75] C. Fleury, *Traité du choix et de la méthode des études* (Paris, 1686), p. 267.

mentally. It is always difficult to try and reconstruct the degree of irreligion in the past. What seems easier to reconstruct are the different ways in which belief was constructed. The rural areas of France (in the middle of the century 19 out of 20 million people lived there) have certainly attracted the overwhelming attention of historians, although it must surely be assumed that certain types of belief not wholly consistent with orthodoxy as defined by Trent, and which I shall call deviant belief, existed in the towns. Rituals not originating in Christianity itself, such as fireworks on the eve of St John, and occasions for burlesque ceremonies such as the Carnaval, survived throughout our period, and many did not consider such things as inconsistent with Catholic (or Protestant) belief. Peter Burke describes a ceremony of the journeymen hatters, saddlers and other craftsmen of Paris which involved the pouring of water over the head of a new recruit in the form of a mock baptism. This was condemned in 1655.[76] Rural culture differs from urban culture in its contact with the environment, since life in rural areas is more closely associated with the forces of nature. Belief in this sense is a function of space. Fears, real or imagined, are different and are increased by the often isolated nature of the rural community. The nature of individual and collective belief, subject to all these pressures, placed orthodoxy itself under pressure, if it was ever at any time clearly understood.

It is some years now since Jean Delumeau obliged historians to discard the idea of a golden age of belief existing some time in the Middle Ages which fell into decline thereafter. We have to take account in rural areas not of a reawakening of Christianity as defined by the reforming clergy but rather of an awakening.[77] In an unlettered and unenlightened population, for a long time steeped in an animist conception of the world, Christian ceremonies had a tendency to 'se "folkloriser"'. A backward mentality and the influence of an archaic civilisation meant that this tendency extended to beliefs themselves, thus producing a sort of paganism.[78] The deviant belief or beliefs resulting from all these things was prevalent throughout France, although the population as a whole considered itself to be Christian and had no idea it practised a form of religion condemned by the Church.[79]

It is important not to confuse deviant belief with witchcraft. Certainly the conditions of life of the rural communities were responsible for both phenomena. But the sort of religion that Delumeau is describing had no

---

[76] P. Burke, *Popular Culture in Early Modern Europe* (Aldershot, 1978), p. 210.
[77] Delumeau, *Le Catholicisme*, p. 234.
[78] Ibid., p. 244.
[79] J. Delumeau, *La Peur en Occident, XIVe–XVIIIe siècles: une cité assiégée* (Paris, 1978), p. 369.

organised pantheon of gods, no priests or priestesses, and no doctrine: 'Il était peut-être vécu, mais il n'était ni pensé ni voulu.'[80] Because of particular conditions of life, Christianity was, in other words, assimilated by a world it did not itself control. In these circumstances a clear frontier between the sacred and the profane needed to be marked out. Both Reforms, Protestant and Catholic, saw that as one of their principal tasks not only among the faithful but also among the clergy who might share aspects of the culture of their flock. The Church, at least at the beginning of the Catholic Reform in France, did not constitute one block and the masses another.

The situation as perceived by those who attempted to rectify what they regarded as the deplorable spiritual condition of the faithful can, allowing for some polemical exaggeration, be summarised by the view of le Père Boschet that faith entered Brittany 'comme au commencement de l'Eglise'. Other parts of France were no exception. In Brittany women were described as sweeping the dust from the nearest church to their village and throwing it in the air to bring a favourable wind for their sailor husbands and sons. Some practices of the sixteenth and seventeenth centuries in Lorraine, while associated with saints, were otherwise not Christian at all.[81] The tenacity of these beliefs, given the onslaught that the rural communities faced in the course of our period, was truly remarkable. In Autun, a bull was sacrificed to the Virgin in 1686 in order to protect cattle from the plague.[82]

The ways in which the boundary between the sacred and the profane became blurred and the opportunities for sections of the rural population to assimilate elements of religion to construct their way of life on their own terms were numerous. The festivities focusing on 'ducasses' and 'kermesses', and feast days of patron saints, could often be prolonged by up to a week.[83] The liturgical calendar gave rise to ceremonies which were appropriated by the people as occasions for enjoyment through dancing, games but also drunkenness and sexual licence.[84] The Church calendar also coincided with the cycle of life determined by nature, the winter cycle culminating in the Carnaval, and the spring–summer cycle centring on the Saint-Jean.[85] These festivals were therefore much more than religious festivals, if, of course, they were ever really that, perhaps a bit like the

[80] Ibid.
[81] Delumeau, Le Catholicisme, pp. 238–9.
[82] Ibid., p. 256.
[83] R. Muchembled, Culture populaire et culture des élites dans la France moderne, XVe–XVIIIe siècles: essai (Paris, 1978), pp. 124 and 170.
[84] R. Muchembled, La Violence au village, XVe–XVIIe siècles: sociabilité et comportements populaires en Artois du XVe au XVIIIe siècle (Paris, 1989), pp. 339–40.
[85] Ibid., p. 353.

modern Christmas. The mingling of the sexes at times of pilgrimage certainly didn't shock the peasants but gradually gave rise to prohibitions. In addition, cemeteries were not places of solemnity in the early modern period but places of games and meals. Once again the space of the church was the scene of activities which ran counter to the new form of respect demanded for the sacred. Muchembled argues that all these occasions marked the solidarity of the community and its own mastery over space, time, social relations and happiness such as their life could offer.[86] Why should the clergy not also be part of that sense of community?

The reforming Church simply could not permit recourse to its own space on the terms and initiative of the ignorant faithful. Either these practices had to be eliminated or they had to be brought within the bounds of orthodoxy. This could not take place while priests, creating a sort of counter-visibility, participated in, and seemed to legitimate by their presence, survivals of 'pagan' ceremonies. These sometimes took place under the auspices of bishops, as in the ceremony of the *noircis* in Vienne.[87] In the course of the century, however, such accommodation disappeared and a much harsher view was taken of clerical participation, as in Chalon-sur-Saône in 1648. The representatives of the reforming Church had themselves to be seen to understand the distinction of the sacred from the profane, if they were to inculcate a sense of this frontier in the faithful: one more reason behind the reinforcement of the concept of the priesthood in post-Tridentine Europe, and the separation, even isolation, of the priest from his flock. The priest could not afford to be associated with magic.[88] Hence too the effort on the part of the Church to root out any matter which could not be properly accredited from its own space. Jean de Launoi was a great crusader against false relics and apocryphal saints. Jean-Baptiste Thiers discredited the holy tear of Christ in Vendôme, and in Vienne, Paris and Soissons provincial synods in 1676 and 1686 rid their breviaries and missals of legends which could no longer be sustained, forty of them in Paris alone.[89]

The harsher view of pleasure which took root in the course of the seventeenth century underpinned the campaign by the Church authorities during which they set out to separate, even to ban, enjoyment in religious festivities. Pilgrimages were no longer to include members of both sexes. Under the influence of the Church the secular authorities sometimes set a limit on the number of guests at weddings for fear of public disorder. More particularly, the occasions of baptisms and marriage were solemnified. Whereas, in a rural community, dancing, especial-

---

[86] Muchembled, *Culture populaire*, p. 126.
[87] Delumeau, *Le Catholicisme*, p. 258.   [88] See ibid., p. 262.
[89] Latreille (ed.), *Histoire du catholicisme*, II, 443.

ly on the occasion of a marriage, constituted a demonstration of virility and sexual prowess for those directly concerned, in the eyes of the Church it was a profanation of what was, after all, a sacrament.[90] Indeed, the Church sought to eliminate dancing from all ceremonies related to the Church, so that the sacred was prevented from becoming an occasion for the profane. But Muchembled's assertion of a discriminatory attitude between popular and élite forms of dancing is inaccurate.[91] The rigorist clergy attacked dancing, even or especially at Court, as highly dangerous since it offered an opportunity for the two sexes to come into public physical contact.

One means of countering the assimilation of the sacred by the profane was to reverse the process. Thus some types of ceremony were taken over by the Church. The May celebrations, in their origin rites of fertility, were eventually transformed into a celebration of the Virgin no less. Such a move had one important consequence: the greater control exercised over its own ceremonies in particular, was that the faithful, from being active participants, became spectators.[92] The Church multiplied the number of processions and ceremonies in the towns and in the villages as a way of turning the faithful away from more dubious practices,[93] a case perhaps of 'épater la populace'. Religion became a sort of diversion. Crucially, however, the faithful were now deprived of ownership of festivity. Their inclusion in the Church was subject to the severest controls, to the extent that they became a part of it on strictly limited terms, and certainly no longer their own. The Church began to impose its own concept of the space and the place of the faithful within it.

The organisation of that space began with the church building itself. In terms of behaviour the authorities were engaged in a constant fight against profane attitudes inside the space of the sacred. Dominique Julia asserts that the *procès-verbaux* of episcopal visits allow us to glimpse two opposing perceptions of what the church represented as a place. For the reforming bishop or his deputy, it was a sacred place which contained the body of Christ. For the faithful the church acted as a 'maison commune', as a meeting point and as somewhere to hold village assemblies. In time of peace the church functioned as a repository for valuable objects and money boxes; in time of war, as a granary. People behaved within that space as they did outside: they talked and wandered about.[94] They brought the 'outside' into the church. Muchembled records complaints

---

[90] See R. Muchembled, *L'Invention de l'homme moderne: sensibilité, moeurs et comportements collectifs sous l'Ancien Régime* (Paris, 1988), pp. 272–3.
[91] See ibid., p. 272.
[92] Muchembled, *Culture populaire*, p. 159.
[93] Ibid., p. 261.   [94] Julia, 'La Réforme', 353.

made in 1619 and 1633 about people turning their backs on the priest during the office of the mass and even cases of transvestism.[95] From a collective solidarity where the sacred and the profane, or at least the secular, combined, it was demanded that the faithful be taught to understand the space of the sacred as a place of personal introspection where the exterior signs of the faith reflected the relationship established from within between man and God. Different places required different ways of behaviour, and a comportment associated with the space of the world was out of place in church. Not even the clergy could be relied upon to maintain the frontier between the sacred and the profane within the space of the sacred. Priests were forbidden to make any announcements of a purely secular nature from the pulpit, although it appears that the hierarchy made little headway on this point.[96]

Of particular note is the attitude towards women in church who were often obliged to stand apart from the men for fear of the temptations of the flesh, certain parts of which were exposed, thus potentially interfering with the sacred character of the ceremony.[97] The idea of exemplary behaviour in church was intended to be extended beyond it. In this the importation of the outside into church was reversed so that the mode of behaviour in a sacred place was also meant to become the norm outside it. A key space in the villages and the towns was the tavern, a place of swearing, blasphemy and other forms of deviance, to the extent that it came to be seen as the negative image of the church as a collectivity,[98] another sort of counter-space. Indeed the taverner, to use Gabriel Le Bras's expression, was the 'anti-curé'.[99] Muchembled argues that, with the promotion of female forms of devotion and the general culpabilisation associated with their gender, the model of the separation of the sexes that the church provided was to be adopted in other sorts of public place. The tavern in particular became a no-go area.[100]

The inevitable concentration on separation and the frontier between the sacred and the profane was, however, complemented by attempts on the part of sections of the Church to bring the laity more into the space of the Church by altering forms of participation during the liturgy. The initiative was delayed because quite simply no translation into French of the liturgical prayers existed until 1679. The Jansenists found themselves in the vanguard of the reform of liturgical practices. Joseph de Voisin, a sympathiser of Port-Royal, had in fact provided one in 1660 but it had been condemned by the Assembly of the Clergy of France. In the diocese

---

[95] Muchembled, *L'Invention*, pp. 260–1.   [96] Julia, 'La Réforme', 352–3.
[97] Muchembled, *L'Invention*, pp. 261 and 266–7.
[98] Ibid., p. 262.   [99] Julia, 'La Réforme', 355.
[100] Muchembled, *L'Invention*, p. 267.

of Paris a translation was produced by the archbishop, Harlay de Champvallon, and from 1680 translations were in current use, but to what extent is unclear. These innovations, in encouraging the priest to speak out loud and in providing the faithful with the means to follow what was being said, aimed to make the mass more of a common celebration. On the other hand, certain limits were quite clearly set. The congregation was not encouraged to say the prayers along with the priest, since it was inconceivable that the lay Christian should be able to 'imitate' the officiant priest in part of his functions. Practices seem also to have differed widely. In some places the canon was recited at a murmur, in others loud enough for the congregation to hear and follow it. The mass continued to be said always in Latin. Indeed at the end of the century many diocesan orders stipulated that the canon had to be recited in a soft voice.[101]

On this point the Church at the very least offered an ambiguous message on where the frontier between the priest and the individual Christian stopped in their relation to the God they shared. Once again the Church seemed to hesitate between the concept of the faithful as simple recipients of the culture of the Church, where strict controls prevented them from 'going too far', and the concept of the faithful as participants in that culture. The view of the Church was clearly determined by its fear that the control of the clergy over the laity would be weakened by any suggestion, as in Protestantism, that the cleric was anything less than a very special person.

A similar problem arose with the reading of the Bible in the vernacular. The Church was not opposed in principle to the translation of the Scriptures but considered Protestant practices as leading to all sorts of dangerous possibilities, none of them advantageous to orthodoxy. Access to the Scriptures was thus very strictly controlled. Jansenist interest in translations of the liturgy was complemented by the belief that the laity had a right to instruct itself in the truths of the Christian religion and to this end supported translations of the Bible. One of the most successful was the so-called *Nouveau Testament de Mons* (1657) which was eventually placed on the Index.[102] Jansenists were not, however, unanimous on this matter, with de Barcos defending the notion of scriptural obscurity as protecting the interests of religion while Arnauld espoused the cause of translation promoting piety through accessibility to the truths of the faith: 'this opinion [that one must possess a knowledge of Latin and a profound intellect] rests on an equally false premise, that sacred writings are so obscure throughout and so difficult to understand even in matters

[101] Julia, 'La Réforme', 379.
[102] A. Sedgwick, *Jansenism in Seventeenth-Century France: Voices from the Wilderness* (Charlottesville, 1977), p. 162.

pertaining to morals that these sorts of people have no right to believe that they will understand them upon reading them'.[103]

Richard Simon, one of the originators of biblical exegesis in France, recognised the difficulties presented by easy access of the faithful to the Bible: the arrival of new sects meant that individuals had strayed from the path of Tradition and had interpreted the texts in their own way without consulting those whose legitimate task it was to protect the truth of its meaning.[104] The priest, as the guardian of the space of the Church, was thus a necessary screen between the text and its reader. The text itself was a space which it was not given to just anyone to enter and from which certain categories of people must in any case be excluded. According to Ménestrier, a Jesuit best known for his contributions to Louis XIV's entertainment, the lower classes and women, two sections of society he regards as leading elements of the Reformation, should be forbidden to indulge in such reading.[105]

What exactly does 'reading the Scriptures' mean for the Church? For a start it is not a solitary act since that would take the activity of reading outside the control of the Church. Conditions must therefore be established which pre-empt the dangers I have described, conditions which, according to Arnauld, include the complete acceptance of the tradition of the Church and of the authorised judgements of those who have charge of that tradition. Only then can one read faithfully and with humility, and in the conviction that nothing one reads can contradict the teaching of the Church. Suspension of judgement had to be exercised at the first sight of difficulty.[106]

Others too stress the reliance on authority. Fénelon, a prelate who became involved in doctrinal disputes with Bossuet, asserts that listening to priests explaining the Scriptures, and thereby giving access to those sections of the Bible which are proportionate to the needs of the faithful, is the equivalent of reading them. In other words priests are the living Scripture. The fact is that Scripture can only be made available to those prepared for it and the reason Fénelon adduces is the same as that adduced by others for the more strictly controlled form of liturgy. The modern Church is no longer in the same situation as at the time of the primitive Church when the Christian community was united and uniformly holy. The Christians of today are now less obedient, many adhering to the faith in name only.[107] Reading the Bible is not interpreta-

[103] Quoted in Sedgwick, *Jansenism*, p. 163.
[104] R. Simon, *Histoire critique du Vieux Testament* (Amsterdam, 1685), p. 330.
[105] Le Père C.-F. Ménestrier, *Bibliothèque curieuse et instructive* (Trévoux, 1704), p. 6.
[106] G. Tavard, *La Tradition au XVIIe siècle en France et en Angleterre* (Paris, 1969), pp. 117–19.
[107] Ibid., pp. 209–11.

tion as a free exercise but rather like following the prayers of the liturgy: the reader is a recipient of the text and not a participant in it. Reading thus constitutes a reaffirmation of faith rather than an exploration of faith and is in this sense a collective rather than an individual act, even if the text is read in private. Reading must always be undertaken within the space of the Church.

If many sections of the Church were uneasy about the inclusion of the faithful in the recitation of the liturgy and the reading of the Bible, other texts existed which, in the realm of popular culture, the Church itself showed an interest in, although the extent or manner of its interest or the modalities of its intervention are somewhat unclear. In the course of the century the less literate or unlettered masses began to have access to written culture in the form of the *Bibliothèque bleue*, whose main publishing centre was in Troyes. It was an enormous success in the seventeenth and eighteenth centuries, and the little books, of few pages and printed on blue paper, sold in huge numbers. But the phenomenon itself has given rise to some controversy and to differing interpretations of its social significance focusing on the relationship of the writers and publishers to the public, and on the nature of that public. Who read these books, and whom did they target? Were they, in the seventeenth century, mainly pitched at an urban public, or did they also reach peasant communities? In this case how were they made accessible to an illiterate population? Did an oral culture still overlay the written one? Or were they more successful with the *laboureurs* of the relatively more literate north and with other sections of the population, including noblewomen?

According to Roger Chartier there is no doubt that the *Bibliothèque bleue*, a form of culture originally reserved for a social and cultural élite, became more widely available and, in the process, disseminated an alternative cultural model which offered 'un savoir-vivre et un savoir-être en société'.[108] Chartier maintains that the Church seized on these developments, in part a natural consequence of the growth of the book trade as a whole, in order to undertake the conquest of the masses. They used the blue books in other words as the scaffolding to support the reconstruction of the faithful's conduct and beliefs.[109] The Troyes publishers, among others, thus disseminated for mass circulation material directly relevant to the new forms of devotion which were being encouraged.[110] A formal alliance between the publishers and the Church is on the other hand difficult to imagine. The space of commerce would surely have

[108] R. Chartier, M.-M. Compère and D. Julia (eds.), *L'Education en France du XVIe au XVIIIe siècle* (Paris, 1976), p. 142.
[109] R. Chartier, *Lectures et lecteurs dans la France d'Ancien Régime* (Paris, 1987), p. 214.
[110] Chartier, *Lectures et lecteurs*, p. 250.

operated according to its own laws. What may be clear is that the publishers themselves would have been aware of aspects of the Reform and knew that a ready market awaited them.

The blue books certainly contained a variety of material related to religion in one way or another, not all of it perhaps in the form which the Church would have wished. One could find a corpus of *sententiae* geared to simple belief and which reflected a form of popular Catholicism, collections of prayers addressed to saints and accounts of certain devotional exercises. Some collections specified prayers related to indulgences.[111] One could read the lives of the saints, hymns – with no musical notation but with references to well-known songs – the story of Christmas, and accounts of the Immaculate Conception not always told in a spirit of reverence.[112] The almanacs even contained expressions of anti-religious feeling.[113] Many of the lives of the saints point up what we have come to think of as the specific themes of the Catholic Reform and the Counter-Reformation such as conversion, but they also have a regional orientation, as one might expect. They propagate the notion of contempt for the world, for women and for the temptations of the flesh.[114] While the retelling of these stories is not concerned with historical accuracy, Mandrou does refer to a life of St Augustine written by 'theologians' who had obtained prior permission for publication.[115] How seriously one can take this is another matter. It is, however, interesting to note with Mandrou that, at the very time the Church was attempting to root out – both in popular belief and in the paintings of artists – the legends of dubious saintly acts which the Christians of the Middle Ages and beyond had no difficulty in accepting, these very things should be disseminated by the blue books.[116]

As in the case of attendance at church, the theme of conduct was of particular concern. As early as 1600, the *Bibliothèque bleue* was one means of disseminating newly defined standards of behaviour.[117] But there were two beneficiaries in the area of conduct, the civil and religious authorities. In this case the space of the Church and the space of society exactly coincided. Chartier argues that the same will presided over the control of secular space in the promotion of certain standards of comportment and

---

[111] R. Mandrou, *De la Culture populaire aux XVIIe et XVIIIe siècles: la Bibliothèque bleue de Troyes* (Paris, 1964), pp. 86–8.

[112] Ibid., pp. 77–80.

[113] G. Bollème, *Les Almanachs populaires aux XVIIe et XVIIIe siècles: essai d'histoire sociale* (Paris, 1969), p. 57.

[114] Mandrou, *De la Culture populaire*, p. 94.

[115] Ibid., pp. 91–3.

[116] Ibid., p. 97.

[117] R. Chartier (ed.), *A History of Private Life*, vol. III, *Passions of the Renaissance*, trans. A. Goldhammer (Cambridge, Mass. and London, 1989), 181.

the control of religious space in the ejection from it of irreverent behaviour and types of excess: 'Books of manners were intended to create conditions under which social intercourse would be easier and more in conformity with the heightened requirements of religion. Readers were exhorted to abide by ever more imperative and intensive rules.'[118]

If the Church's connection with the blue books may not have been determined by a conscious programme, the very opposite is true of its intervention through missions in the rural territory of France. The missions constituted a form of evangelisation from outside the rural space, simply because intervention from within it was impossible until the rural clergy was of an adequate quality to undertake that task on its own. Progress as always was slow and uneven. It was clear, however, that something dramatic was required if any progress at all was to be made. For the seventeenth century as a whole, at least once the Tridentine reform got under way, a 'pastorale de choc' was the only way to convert the mass of so-called Christians.[119] Not that, in essence, the message was any different for Christians of differing social statuses. The image of a God, who was infinitely good but who meted out at the same time terrible punishment, was an image ceaselessly propagated by the Catholic clergy and an image which was ingrained in the system of belief of the social élite.[120] In addition the clergy spared nobody's feelings, especially in its concept of theft: professions which jeopardised individual salvation included those of the merchant and the lawyer, as well as trades like the butcher and the baker.[121]

But if the Church's message was universal and without distinction of culture, the methods adopted to convert the mass of the faithful could not always be the same as those adopted in the context of high society. While all sections of the population came into contact with missionaries in the course of the century – the kingdom of France itself was regarded as a 'pays de mission' – the missions were mostly directed at the rural communities. And missions constituted a real invasion of rural space. Religious orders, such as St Vincent's Lazaristes, were created especially for this purpose, and a number of individual priests devoted a high proportion of their career to christianising the masses. St Jean Eudes spent more than 65 per cent of his ministry in rural parishes. From 1640 to 1683 le Père Manoir undertook 375 missions in Brittany alone.[122]

The method of the missionaries was to arrive in a village in groups of

---

[118] Chartier, *Lectures et lecteurs*, p. 384.
[119] J. Delumeau, *Le Péché et la peur: la culpabilisation en occident, XIIIe–XVIIIe siècles* (Paris, 1983), p. 384.
[120] Ibid., p. 447.
[121] Ibid., p. 479.
[122] Delumeau, *Le Catholicisme*, pp. 276–9.

four to eight with the aim of catechising the whole population, and administering to all their other spiritual needs. They taught the four main prayers, the *Pater*, *Ave*, *Credo* and *Confiteor*, all the time with the underlying aim of rooting out what they regarded as superstition, indeed of arriving at a situation where the faithful no longer felt the need to have recourse to beliefs outside the space of the sacred as now defined by the reforming clergy. In this way cultural particularisms could be replaced by the universal and univocal message of Christian orthodoxy and by a religious conformism which transcended individual difference.

Once an area had been visited, it would be returned to after eight years or so, or such was the ideal. The missions were often spectacular, even theatrical in nature: processions were held, crosses were planted and suspicious books were burned with the whole community in attendance, so great was the missionaries' desire that individuals should see themselves as part of a Christian collectivity meeting under the visible signs of the faith. In this way, the absence of the missionaries would be compensated for by the presence of the images, crosses and other symbols of belief left behind. The Church was anxious in this way to fill the space with representations of itself, just as the cassock-wearing priest was himself a visible sign of the Church and distinct from other men.

The spectacular nature of the mission responded to the need to adopt a simple but forceful form of teaching for a population whose mental categories were fairly crude.[123] Moreover, that teaching was often communicated in the language of the community itself (very rarely French as we know it). In Brittany non-native speakers were obliged to learn Breton, and Godeau, bishop of Vence and then of Grasse, himself a northerner, preached in Occitan. Language was then one aspect of culture which the priest had to share with his flock, one case at least of the Church moving out into the world, but with the express aim of bringing that world into the space of the Church.

Indeed the missions appropriated in their turn the social space of the community. Just as the people had seized on religious occasions for their own secular manifestations of joy, so the missionaries adapted their proselytising to the rhythm of the peasant's daily life, as in the order of the day issued by St Vincent de Paul.[124] Le Père Bourdoise deliberately chose the day of the patron saint of the village on which to preach,[125] the day which was so often the excuse for a party. In the end, given the multiplication of ceremonies, of processions, of parading of miracles, it was almost impossible not to 'faire preuve de catholicisme'.[126] No-one

---

[123] Ibid., p. 276.
[124] Ibid.   [125] Ferté, *La Vie religieuse*, p. 199.
[126] Muchembled, *Culture populaire*, p. 263.

could avoid being a part of the space of the Church, at least in appearance.

One aspect of popular culture which the Church wished especially to eliminate was witchcraft, although Muchembled maintains that one of the reasons for the phenomenon was that neither the state nor the Church succeeded in providing a reassuring environment, either spiritually or physically.[127] The Church, another historian argues, almost legitimated witchcraft in its insistence on the existence of the devil and his powers of intervention in daily life, thus contributing to the confusion of the faithful and to belief in magic,[128] and offering one more instance when the militant action of the Church could be turned against itself. The Church was responsible for creating in some part its own counter-space.

Conclusion

If the Church was the main agency which offered the rural and urban masses an alternative culture, what conclusions can we draw in respect of its effect on the mass of the population, and especially on the rural population which was, in the eyes of the Church, so riddled with superstitious and deviant belief? Peter Burke argues that the reform of popular culture had a positive and negative side. On the one hand the Protestant and Catholic Reformations tried to reach the craftsmen and peasants.[129] Indeed these sections of the population had been relatively untouched by new forms of devotion with little or no access to certain of the forms in which it was available, notably the printed word. But Burke also points to the negative side, the inevitable element of suppression and repression that affected many items of traditional popular culture: 'The ethic of the reformers was in conflict with a traditional ethic which is harder to define because it was less articulate, but which involved more stress on the values of generosity and spontaneity and a greater tolerance of disorder.'[130]

To what extent then was the Catholic Reform successful? Is Delumeau right to suggest that the new form of devotion promoted among the masses was working? If the measure of the degree of a greater sense of religious feeling is determined by the number of those performing their Easter devotion – the most important occasion of the religious year with its emphasis on general confession – then the Reform had done a good job. In many areas the proportion of 'non-pascalisants' was by the end of the seventeenth century very small. It also seems that illegitimate births decreased in the course of the century, at least those that could be

[127] Ibid., p. 133.
[128] Lebrun (ed.), *Histoire de la France religieuse*, II, 549.
[129] Burke, *Popular Culture*, p. 208.   [130] Ibid., p. 213.

counted. A much wider knowledge of the text of prayers and a greater understanding of the elements of faith took root with a large proportion of the population.[131]

But it could be argued that Counter-Reformation religion had its price, particularly in the relationship of the new priest with his flock, and that the wholesale rejection of popular culture and religion by the ecclesiastical élite eventually presented difficulties for the Church, which came to be identified uniquely with the clergy.[132] The faithful were simply seen as subordinates.[133] The separation of the priest and his flock produced nothing less than an 'étrangéité culturelle'.[134] Rather than the space of the Church overlaying the space of society, it had simply succeeded in perpetuating their continued separation. The separation of the priest and his flock led therefore in many cases to a distance that could not ultimately be breached. Paradoxically, post-Tridentine religion had the effect of turning large sections of society away from religion. The Church contributed to emptying its own space, although one must surely not exaggerate too greatly the decline of Christianity in France even towards the end of our period. The way in which the Church protected its own space did not ensure, and even worked against, the total occupation of social space it desired. The frontier so carefully established between the sacred and the profane maintained another frontier between the Church and the people.

Dominique Julia too believes that the strict code of behaviour in church which had been imposed by the end of the eighteenth century concealed a situation which was not advantageous to the Church.[135] The entrenchment of the Reform in the population could only come about by a 'déracinement', since all conquest presupposes destruction. Did all the prohibitions have the opposite effect after all? Was the silence of the faithful respectful or empty?[136] An example in practical terms would be the low level of clerical vocations from the rural areas of the diocese of Paris where priests from outside the region had to be imported into the parishes. Indeed it has even been suggested that the influence of Jansenism in the Paris basin contributed to the eventual dechristianisation of the area.[137] On the other hand a counter-example existed in Pavillon, one of the Jansenist saints, who scored an enormous success in his severe reform of the diocese of Alet.

At the level of control, success was – as one might expect in a kingdom as large as that of France – at the very least uneven. Traditional practices

---

[131] Delumeau, *Le Catholicisme*, p. 283.
[132] Lebrun (ed.), *Histoire de la France religieuse*, II, 436.
[133] Ibid., p. 86.
[134] Julia, 'La Réforme', 378.   [135] Ibid., 353.   [136] Ibid., 397.
[137] P. Chaunu, 'Jansénisme et frontière de catholicité, XVIIe et XVIIIe siècles: à propos du Jansénisme lorrain', *Revue historique*, 227 (1962), 115–38 (p. 134).

seem to have survived clandestinely in the seventeenth century only to
reappear in the eighteenth.[138] Indeed the continuing need on the part of
bishops, right up to the end of the century and beyond, to repeat
prohibitions of certain types of behaviour and practices testifies to the
tenacity of some traditions and to the resistance offered by the population
to the efforts of the Church to bring radical change to its communities.[139]
There was much resistance, for example, to the Christian adaptation of
pre-Christian ceremonies or celebrations, or to forms of devotion to which
the faithful had become attached. After Louis XIV's annexation of
Hainaut, bishops favourable to Port-Royal found it difficult to impose
their will. In 1674 Gilbert de Choiseul's attempts to purify Marian
devotion incurred the wrath not only of the faithful but also of the parish
clergy.[140] The traditional stories of the linen workers which flourished in
the Trégorrois region of Brittany all through the Ancien Régime reveal a
community which was not only anti-clerical but also anti-Christian in its
belief in the superiority of the forces of nature over those of orthodox
religion.[141] And the Church did not wholly succeed in preventing the
faithful from integrating Church ceremonies into their own world rather
than the reverse.[142] Nor did the Church manage, despite continual efforts,
to curb the societies of penitents, and they increased in number in some
dioceses. The societies went their own way in organising public ceremonies or private ones in their own chapels, thus demonstrating a lay fervour
beyond the control of the clergy.[143] Essentially, the conflict of two cultures
represented on the one hand by an ebullience and a sense of joy, and on
the other by a form of ordered ceremonial whose logic was external to the
participants, was never satisfactorily resolved by the Church. Quite
simply, as far as processions were concerned, for example, the demand for
orderly conduct was 'NEVER' observed.[144] The people proved resilient in
the defence of their own space.

[138] Muchembled, *L'Invention*, p. 183.
[139] Muchembled, *La Violence au village*, pp. 363 and 371.
[140] Lebrun (ed.), *Histoire de la France religieuse*, II, 437.
[141] Ibid., p. 434.
[142] Julia, 'La Réforme', 387.
[143] Ibid., 383.
[144] Ibid., 385 (Julia's emphasis).

2 The spaces of representation

Introduction

If it was important for the Church to improve the understanding of the faith at every level of society, it then became especially important to reinforce it through certain means of representation and, as a consequence, to police the form and content of those representations. Of necessity the Church became involved as much in the processes of the production of images and books in particular as in the provision of guidance for the space of representation itself. The Church maintained an important presence in the world of literature in seventeenth-century France, not least because the Church provided important writers from its own ranks. The participation by certain members of the clergy in the domain of worldly literature produced what some believed to be an all too apparent compromise with the social space. On the other hand there were lay writers who in many ways espoused the cause of Christianity in their promotion of values intended to counter those emanating from pagan traditions. Throughout the century, the Church attempted to control all aspects of the written word often as part of a repressive agenda. The theatre in particular attracted the attention of its most rigorist representatives.

Of the utmost importance was the presence of the Church in the world of art and architecture. If one of the aims of the post-Tridentine Church was to 'fill the space', how better to do it than to fill it with its own buildings and to fill those buildings with images representing the sacred through its doctrine and teaching? The Church's task in evangelising the whole of society and in sanctifying daily life could not but embrace the artistic world. Indeed the role of art in service to the Church entailed a particular type of relationship with architects but especially with sculptors and artists, for there could be no point in establishing what was orthodox if artists were then to subvert that orthodoxy in the images they produced. The Church therefore had an interest in controlling that relationship. The Council of Trent paid some attention to these matters at its last session on 4 December 1563. Clearly the Church could count on a fair degree of religious culture from its artists, many of whom exhibited an obvious and public degree of personal religious commitment. But placing one's art in the service of the Church demanded a willingness to accept submission to its authority, thus reducing the possibility of an autonomous artistic space in matters of religious painting.

The Church's interest in art and architecture as an institution was accompanied by a wide interest on the part of the laity in the promotion of church building and decoration. Individuals also commissioned pious works of art as well as private chapels or tombs. Only in its public manifestations could such private enterprises be controlled. The Church well knew that art could purvey a different sort of culture, one, moreover, which found easy access among certain sections of the educated population. How could it ensure surveillance of that culture? Could it ensure it at all?

Churches and the church

If the Church was visible in the seventeenth century through one thing alone, it would be through its buildings. It is absurd to suggest that such visibility was original to our period. The seventeenth century in France did, however, witness a considerable expansion in the construction of ecclesiastical buildings, if only as a result of the expansion of religious orders and the spread of schooling under the aegis of various agencies within the Church. An additional feature of the situation in seventeenth-century France was that some regions more than others were in need of a programme of restoration because of the ravages of the wars of religion. In the Beauce alone, three hundred churches were destroyed. But the restoration of churches and decrepit monastic buildings was undertaken with the encouragement of royal authority and, symbolically in this regard, Henri IV himself was a great builder of churches. Initiatives came not only from the ecclesiastical authorities but also from the local laity, often the seigneurs, who were often involved in the 'conseils de fabrique' which determined the nature of the works and what sort of decoration there should be. The all-pervasive architectural presence of the Church and of churches, along with other symbolic monuments, meant that the countryside was full of the signs of religion. The sacred had invested the social space in a permanent and immovable way.

The towns in particular benefited from this aspect of the programme of religious reconstruction. Quite naturally Paris is a spectacular example where, it was said, no street was complete without its church or religious house. Striking examples include such landmarks as the chapel of the Sorbonne, the Val de Grâce and the chapel of Saint-Sulpice (not however completed in the seventeenth century). An essential part of the urban landscape were the houses of the Faubourg Saint-Honoré where the Dominicans, the reformed Cistercians, and the Capuchins resided. Then there were the Capucines, the Dames de l'Assomption, the Daughters of St Thomas and the convent of the Conception. Architecture was even one means of maintaining a visible link with Rome through the chapel of the Feuillants, based on Vignola's Il Gesù, the Jesuit chapel of the rue Saint-Antoine and the church of Saint-Gervais.[1] The Paris monasteries with their cloistered gardens fostered a relationship with society that may not have been entirely devotional in nature. Their rural atmosphere and exclusiveness, peopled no doubt by the well-born, radiated an aristocratic air, and they became fashionable places of worship.[2] The area of Port-Royal, moreover, with its mixture of hôtels and monasteries – the latter too headed by individuals of high social rank – resembled the social composition of the Paris of the fourteenth and fifteenth centuries where the lord's residence was close to the abbey. The architecture may have been different but 'the agglomeration of secular and religious constructions in one quarter represented a type of urban construction, often repeated, of feudal Christian society'.[3] Society assimilated the Church.

But the religious space itself had to be of the right quality if it was to induce the correct attitude in the faithful. One area in which one might imagine ecclesiastical control to be absolute would be its own space, that is to say the church as a building along with what it contained. The church was after all a function of control of the faithful in that it brought them in direct contact with a form of the sacred which had been officially sanctioned. It was also the place from which, through preaching, the majority of the population would receive the teaching of orthodoxy, and the influence of the church as a place could – as we have seen through the sort of behaviour encouraged within its precincts – act as a model beyond them.

Creating the right sort of space involved some architectural changes within existing edifices or a different sort of architecture for new ones. The number of pews was either reduced or regularised (they could give rise to social conflict), tombs were levelled, naves paved, side-chapels repaired. Indeed these were organised in some order of priority along the nave. At the top end of the sanctuary, at the level of the main altar, one would find altars consecrated to those aspects of devotion promoted by the Counter-Reformation itself, such as the Holy Family and St Joseph, whereas those representing the more traditional devotions were relegated to the other

[1] O. Ranum, *Paris in the Age of Absolutism: an Essay* (New York, 1968), pp. 127–8.
[2] Ibid., p. 121.   [3] Ibid, pp. 96–7.

end. Moreover, the ornamentation of these altars was also strictly regulated, the iconography of the latter being more sumptuous than that of the former.[4] In general terms the number of altars was sometimes reduced, especially those not well maintained, and disfigured images were removed, all this on the orders of the bishops as they inspected the parishes.

Most attention was paid to the main altar, the focus of the mass, where much effort was put into making it an object worthy of respect by, for example, the purchase of silver vases.[5] Ornaments of this sort were intended to induce greater respect and to encourage a greater level of dignity in the behaviour of the faithful. One of the most important aspects of the altar, however, was its visibility. Often on the initiative of the priest the altar was raised and the rood screen replaced by a simple balustrade, thus providing a means by which the faithful could be brought closer, this time physically, to the eucharistic liturgy,[6] a practice adopted across Europe. In addition the so-called 'Jesuit' architecture was developed whereby a single nave contributed to the visibility of the altar and the sacraments,[7] although it must be said that some scholars dispute the existence of a 'Jesuit style' which was in any case not adopted in non-Jesuit churches of the Counter-Reformation or Baroque periods.[8] Pierre Moisy argues that no convincing case could be made for the existence of a Jesuit architectural doctrine and at the very most the order followed a 'tendance d'esprit'.[9] While a certain sobriety of style, based on the single nave, may have emerged, Rome did not pronounce in favour of any particular style.[10]

Images

There is a particular reason for the explosion of images in Counter-Reformation culture. Quite simply, their place had to be re-established in the light of the rejection of images as idolatrous by the Protestant Reformation. At the same time Catholic theologians were aware of the need to establish precisely what images were meant to represent, especially when, in popular belief, images became invested with magic properties outwith the domain of the orthodox. The image is a stimulus to a reverent attitude, having no other virtue than, in Bossuet's words, to produce by its

[4] R. Taveneaux, *Le Catholicisme dans la France classique, 1610–1715*, 2 vols. (Paris, 1980), II, 454.

[5] Perouas, *Le Diocèse de La Rochelle*, p. 283.

[6] Delumeau, *Le Catholicisme*, p. 287.

[7] Latreille (ed.), *Histoire du catholicisme*, II, 397.

[8] Wright, *The Counter-Reformation*, p. 224.

[9] P. Moisy, *Les Eglises des Jésuites de l'ancienne assistance de France* (Rome, 1958), p. 69.

[10] Ibid., p. 61.

resemblance the memory of the original.[11] Questions naturally arose concerning the precise measure of that 'resemblance'. What is certain is that they must contain nothing which is either distracting or unorthodox.

Perhaps the content of images might be measured according to their aim. Here a distinction might be drawn between the teaching of the word and the significance of the images surrounding the faithful. According to Dupront, the image of things sacred is 'manifestante' rather than 'enseignante'. That is to say that the image does not in itself produce belief but reinforces it.[12] Is this what Bossuet means by images as a sort of 'pieuse lecture'?[13] If so, it is a controlled reading, like the reading of the Bible by the faithful. The image should not generate new meaning and give rise to interpretation. That is the domain of the preacher. The image-maker must take the source of the religious image as his absolute and authoritative measure of the correctness of any representation. Any deviation from this encourages a search for the reasons for difference: 'plus l'image choque les critères habituels, plus elle contraint à la recherche du sens'.[14] Close scrutiny of images was, in principle at least, paramount.

The Council of Trent itself addressed the question of images and sought to remove any abuse which had crept into the representation of the sacred, stipulating that: 'no images [suggestive] of false doctrine, and furnishing occasion of dangerous error to the uneducated be set up'. All elements of superstition should therefore be removed and all lasciviousness avoided: 'Let so great care and diligence be used herein by bishops, as that there be nothing seen that is disorderly, or that is unbecomingly or confusedly arranged, nothing that is profane, nothing indecorous, seeing that holiness becometh the house of God.'[15] The Tridentine delegates themselves did not prescribe the form that religious art should take but simply determined its moral and spiritual ends.[16] On the other hand, they had some idea of what it should not be.

In fact interpretation of the restrictions of Trent had enormous influence on the attitudes bishops adopted in their dioceses. Bossuet asserted that bishops have the controlling role in the representation of God in human form.[17] Bishops were accordingly attentive to images on their visits to parishes, and they or their deputies were anxious to induce the 'proper' form of respect especially for the representation of saints. So,

[11] J.-B. Bossuet, Œuvres, 48 vols. (Paris, 1828), XXXI, 242–3.
[12] A. Dupront, Du Sacré: croisade et pèlerinages; images et langages (Paris, 1987), p. 120.
[13] Bossuet, Œuvres, XXXI, 244.
[14] Dupront, Du Sacré, p. 127.
[15] J. W. Waterworth (trans.), The Canons and Decrees of the Council of Trent (London, 1888), pp. 235–6.
[16] Taveneaux, Le Catholicisme, II, 448.
[17] Bossuet, Œuvres, XXXI, 242.

St Anthony goes, as does the hunt in the case of St Hubert. Nor are there any more saints on horseback. A parish church of the diocese of Chartres was ordered in 1668 to remove an image of St Martin on horseback that was turned towards the sacraments. This meant that the officiating priest raised the host at the feet of the horse, something the visitor found shocking. Patron saints of corporations were also proscribed. Images of St Crispin and St Crispinian had to be removed from the church at Clamecy because their depiction as cobblers was considered grotesque.[18]

The prohibition of nudity produced one particular victim, St Sebastian. Seventeen cases were condemned in the diocese of Auxerre alone. Concern was expressed for historical accuracy to the extent that a banner of the Virgin giving the scapular to St Peter and St Paul was condemned. At Courchon it was ordered that the image of Christ on the shoulders of St Christopher should be wiped from the portrait since it was an absurd fantasy of artists. The space of the painting was no longer considered a neutral space and certainly not one over which the artist had ownership. For example, the importance of some figures could be diminished in the eyes of the authorities because of overcrowding. One painting was found to be too full of figures with the result that the saints appeared to have equal status with God. Everything had to be removed except the figures representing the Trinity.[19]

This suppression of images, another alienating factor generated by the Church, did not go unopposed. A study of altar screens in Brittany has revealed that traditional representations of saints, particularly those with the power to protect from and cure the plague, are much more numerous than the representation of the saints imposed by the Counter-Reformation. And the high point of construction of these screens was between 1660 and 1720.[20] In general, however, all animals except lambs, doves and serpents were banned from altar screens.[21] The ability of the ecclesiastical authorities to generate resistance is illustrated by an occurrence in the diocese of Sens in 1648 when the archbishop ordered that a statue of St Eloi – depicted as a blacksmith complete with hat and anvil, and which he considered ridiculous – should be removed and buried. The parishioners revolted but were eventually defeated.[22] The problem for the authorities was that, in this sort of representation, the images of the saints were too closely tied to popular belief and to the way of life of the parishioners. The sacred was insufficiently distinguished from the profane. In Peter Burke's happy phrase, familiarity breeds irreverence.[23]

---

[18] Julia, 'La Réforme', 335–6.   [19] Ibid., 334–7.   [20] Ibid., 339–40.
[21] Lebrun (ed.), *Histoire de la France religieuse*, II, 441.
[22] Julia, 'La Réforme', 337–8.
[23] Burke, *Popular Culture*, p. 212.

Restrictions on the representation of the sacred were not limited to the domain of popular culture. The Church attempted to change the traditions of centuries in the case of all artists. Much religious art in seventeenth-century France became more severe, with no superfluous episodes and no elements which would diminish respect for the Scriptures. This was particularly true of representations of the crucifixion where the number of figures concentrates attention more fully on Christ himself (Poussin is exceptional in one of his own portrayals of this scene). The beauties of landscape, still life, scenes which gave a sense of familiarity to a particular biblical event, were sacrificed to the new austerity.[24] Limits were imposed on the artist in the invention of his own details, certainly as far as the central episode was concerned, and his painting had to reflect exactly the text of Scripture. Examples of these new attitudes are legion. The Virgin could no longer be depicted as swooning before the cross and was to be depicted as standing since no reference in the Gospels indicates any other position. Philippe de Champaigne respects this injunction but Simon Vouet does not.[25] The Church considered it an error to depict Christ as leaving an empty tomb. Again Philippe de Champaigne conforms, as against Le Brun who continues the tradition. The latter, however, banished animals from the scene of the nativity on the grounds that no mention is made of them in the Gospels of Matthew and Luke. Vouet and Le Nain, but by no means all artists, follow this example.[26] Artists hesitated therefore between staying with the tradition and opting for the more rigorous position. Private commissions of course posed a certain number of problems, at least in theory. Artists often had to accede to the requests of patrons who preferred the previous forms to the new ones. [27]

Other traditional elements were held to be less than respectful, such as the representation of St Peter as balding (Le Sueur depicts him with flowing locks).[28] The child Christ is no longer supposed to be portrayed as lying naked on the ground, and the nativity reflects consequently, not the abandonment of the Holy Family, but the moment at which Christ is for the first time recognised as the Son of God.[29] Some details are however left open, such as whether Christ was nailed to the cross on the ground (theologians hesitate whereas artists all follow the tradition of the cross on the ground), the side on which the Roman soldier pierced Christ with the lance and the number of nails for the feet. Vouet depicts sometimes three,

[24] E. Mâle, L'Art religieux après le Concile de Trente: étude iconographique de la fin du XVIe siècle, du XVIIe, du XVIIIe; Italie, France, Espagne, Flandres (Paris, 1932), pp. 4–5.
[25] Ibid., p. 8.   [26] Ibid., pp. 248–9.   [27] Ibid., p. 232.
[28] Ibid., p. 233.
[29] Ibid., p. 243.

sometimes four.[30] One of the interesting changes is in the depiction of the
Holy Family where the tradition, dating from the Middle Ages, often
emphasised a domestic scene. One detail in Claude Vignon's nativity
shows angels helping Mary to prepare the baby's food. This is no longer
consonant with the gravity of the new forms of devotion.[31] Again,
therefore, the space of the Church as it is represented in the portrayal of
biblical events ejects from that space any resemblance with the space of
the world. From 'manifestation', art becomes simply 'représentation'.[32]

Thus a growing tendency towards a literal truth led to the wholesale
rejection of legends which had delighted for centuries. No compromise
was permitted and the space of the Church had to be purified of its profane
elements. Mâle comments that for some, however, it must have been
painful to be cut off from the past in this way, and indeed absolute
obedience was never ensured, not least because elements within the
Church itself remained attached to traditional representations, especially
in the religious orders. The Church hesitated and, as an institution,
showed itself to be more lenient than some of those who spoke for it,
continuing to allow the representation of apocryphal legends and episodes
from *The Golden Legend* into the period of Louis XIV.[33]

The views of some artists and art theorists came close to agreement
with the attempts by the Church to exclude from representations of the
sacred in painting anything which conflicted with the truth or reverence
for Scripture. Their response embraced not only questions of tradition as
against the new stipulations but also the legitimacy of using ornamentation imported from the world of antiquity, from the world of real pagans.
Florent le Comte argued that the painter should depict nothing that is
incompatible with Christianity and for him that includes anything from
ancient myth,[34] although Testelin would yield to *force majeure* and accede
to the request of patrons.[35] Michelangelo, a favourite target for French
critics of the seventeenth century, is according to these principles taken to
task for having included Charon in his depiction of the *Last Judgement* in
the Sistine Chapel. Catherinot criticises Rubens's mixture of the sacred
and the profane in his *Marie de Médicis* cycle,[36] while Félibien, Poussin's
biographer, remarks that Tempesta's inclusion of figures such as Venus

[30] Ibid., pp. 267–75.
[31] Ibid., p. 310.
[32] Julia, 'La Réforme', 340.
[33] Mâle, *L'Art religieux*, p. 511.
[34] F. Le Comte, *Cabinet des singularitez d'architecture, peinture, sculpture et graveure*, 3 vols.
(Brussels, 1702), III, 51.
[35] H. Testelin, *Sentimens des plus habiles peintres sur la pratique de la peinture et sculpture* (Paris,
1696), p. 21.
[36] N. Catherinot, *Traité de peinture (18 octobre, 1687)* (no place, no date), p. 20.

and Hymen in religious subjects is offensive to Christians.[37] Domenichino also comes in for this sort of criticism.[38] It is no coincidence that many of these examples are Italian.

It was of course impossible to object to the exclusion of irreverence from religious painting; in the course of the century objection was made to the portrayal of the Virgin praying in close proximity to a monkey. It was also difficult to disagree with the exclusion of the incongruous, like St Joseph praying with a rosary or the inclusion of buildings in paintings of Adam and Eve. The problem was how to come to an overall consensus on what constituted the irreverent or the incongruous. That artists were aware of the strictures which some sought to impose is clear from the strength of purpose with which they resisted attempts to control their artistic output. Catherinot, the censor of Rubens, and Du Fresnoy both stipulate that artists should be free to add ornaments when they do not corrupt the subject they embellish.[39] Félibien follows his criticism of Tempesta with the observation that other sorts of figures, like those representing the passions or the virtues, are quite legitimate.[40]

Roger de Piles, theorist, painter and spy, was among the most eloquent of those pleading for some compromise in allowing for the continuance of what artists had been doing for years without any obvious diminution in belief. He concedes that licence must be appropriate but this very appropriateness is a condition of producing a good effect, for this is the only way the artist can effectively achieve his aim.[41] While the Christian painter must never alter the truth of history, he can, through the use of licence, bring us to a greater understanding of the subject. Licence is an adjunct rather than an obstacle to meaning. Indeed, in many cases, examples of licence where the gods are not clearly identified, is the only way the artist can underline the meaning of the painting.[42] Dupuy du Grez seems to suggest that in sculpture in particular the artist has no 'long hand' in which to convey meaning, and that the use of allegorical figures takes us straight to the point.[43] Moreover, Roger de Piles regards these figures as 'invisible', by which he presumably means transparent, since they contribute to the sense. Some might, however, argue that any addition to the source would constitute a new interpretation. Roger de Piles has in that

---

[37] A. Félibien des Avaux, *Entretiens sur les vies et sur les ouvrages des plus excellens peintres anciens et modernes*, 4 vols. (London, 1705), II, 278.

[38] F. Charpentier, *Carpentariana, ou Remarques d'histoire, de morale, de critique, d'érudition et de bons mots de M. Charpentier de l'Académie françoise* (Paris, 1724), pp. 396–7.

[39] Catherinot, *Traité*, p. 9, and C. A. Du Fresnoy, *L'Art de peinture* (Paris, 1673), pp. 135–6.

[40] Félibien, *Entretiens*, II, 278.

[41] R. de Piles, *L'Idée du peintre parfait* (Paris, 1707), p. 42.

[42] Ibid., pp. 44–5.

[43] B. Dupuy du Grez, *Traité sur la peinture pour en apprendre la teorie & se perfectionner dans la pratique* (Toulouse, 1699), p. 308.

case another argument up his sleeve. Christian art is aimed not at unbelievers but at believers who have already rejected the pagan world and who will interpret the painting in a Christian way.[44] Thus the Christian is able to distinguish between the literal and the figurative. For the Christian these figures can only be figurative.

Generally, artists and theorists cried injustice at the thought of being deprived of the use of allegorical figures, especially when councils of the Church had permitted the use of allegorical representation. Roger de Piles refers to the Council of Nicaea as permitting the representation of God and the angels in human form. The search for authorities goes even further, and Daniel 9:21 and Psalm 98:8 are quoted as texts legitimating the depiction of angels and the depiction of the inanimate as animate. Scripture allows therefore a language of accommodation whereby the means of understanding is proportionate to the intelligence of humanity. Allegory brings out that meaning in palpable form.[45] A sacred text thus legitimates an element of initiative and freedom for the artist in the domain of the sacred.

The essential theme of this discussion has been the acceptability of elements belonging to one domain in another domain. If a frontier exists between profane and religious art, and it is forbidden to import elements of one into the other, the exact position of that frontier is far from obvious, since the theorists argue that allegorical figures are not in fact pagan in intention. If the intention behind the painting is sincerely Christian, then the means employed are appropriate to that context. That there was, however, a frontier between religious and profane painting is made clear by Emile Mâle, who makes the point that even the Church could not give up traditions in art it had inherited from antiquity. The Church's idea of the pictural space was thus far from clear, or at least no consensus existed as to exactly what it was. A line was drawn at nudity which was relegated to the domain of the profane although objected to even there. According to Mâle, the depiction of the gods of antiquity is where the artist could work with 'toute sa liberté'.[46] In this sense the spaces of both the artist and the Church were by no means homogeneous. As Anthony Wright says of Trent: 'As an assembly of bishops, not specialists, the Council naturally produced statements which were general rather than specific, negative rather than positive, and confined to the religious as opposed to the secular arts.'[47]

However much artists hesitated in their adherence to the new strictures, we should not think that they were reluctant in their adherence to the faith. Many of them led exemplary Christian lives and even practised their

[44] Piles, *L'Idée*, pp. 44–6.   [45] Ibid., pp. 46 and 43.   [46] Mâle, *L'Art religieux*, pp. 1–3.
[47] Wright, *The Counter-Reformation*, p. 230.

art within the space of the Church itself. Jean Boucher had his studio in one of the towers of Bourges cathedral, and he worked only for convents and churches. Callot and Michel Serre always started their day with mass. Claude Deruet had a chapel built for his tomb in the house of the Carmelites in Nancy; the sculptor Puget had a chapel in Sainte-Madeleine near Toulouse, and Le Brun had his own chapel at Saint-Nicolas-du-Chardonnet.[48] The Church had painters in its ranks, among the Dominicans, the Carthusians and other religious orders.[49]

Many of the issues relating to Counter-Reformation art as I have described it come together in two of the greatest French artists of the seventeenth century, Philippe de Champaigne (1602–74) and Nicolas Poussin (1594–1665). They are useful to us here in that each in his own way had an important place at the centre of French art in our period. They were also at the centre of certain controversies surrounding religious representation and therefore provide a focus for the problems artists faced in this particular domain.

The degree to which artists internalised the external constraints of the Church, becoming in this way a part of the space of the Church, is illustrated by the example of Philippe de Champaigne. He was at one stage a very successful court painter and achieved the rank of 'premier peintre du Roi'. He later became associated with Port-Royal, devoting himself from this time to religious art. Some indication of the painter's attitude towards his art can be found in the contents of his library where Plutarch and Seneca, representatives of stoicism, are the only pagan authors to figure. By far the largest section consisted of religious works including the patristic authorities and Arnauld's *Fréquente communion* (but no copy of Jansenius's *Augustinus*). There were no texts of the profane writers of the time. One surprise: the *Hieroglyphica seu de sacris Aegyptiorum aliarumque gentium literis commentarii*, written by Valeriano, a humanist at the papal court, who borrowed much more from ancient sources than he did from Scripture. It appears that this work was the source of Philippe de Champaigne's moral symbols or signs which were able to convey a mystical or spiritual quality.[50] As a rule he normally eschewed straightforward mythological subjects, except where obliged by patrons as at the château of Vincennes and the Tuileries.[51] According to Félibien, he also avoided as much as he could the depiction of nudity.[52]

To what extent did Philippe de Champaigne, in more than one hundred biblical paintings, obey the strictures of the Tridentine decrees on art as they were interpreted by sections of the French Church? Some examples

---

[48] Mâle, *L'Art religieux*, pp. 12–13.   [49] Ibid., p. 15.
[50] B. Dorival, *Philippe de Champaigne, 1602–1674* (Paris, 1976), pp. 80–1.
[51] Ibid., pp. 61–4.   [52] Ibid., p. 69.

we have already referred to. But on the whole there are few apocryphal subjects (a particular target of the censors), and those there are come from the early part of his career. All the other sacred pictures are either mentioned in Scripture or, like the *Assumption*, sanctioned by recognised authorities. He adheres strictly to scenes as described in the original source with the exception of *Woman of Canaan*, where he drew on a number of sources. In this he distinguished himself from other artists on a number of points, such as the depiction of Christ on the cross with his head lowered and the omission of angels at the Ascension, since in the Acts of the Apostles it is made clear that the angels appeared only after the event.[53]

Philippe de Champaigne accepted many commissions from religious orders, such as the Carthusians, but his main association from about 1645–7 was with Port-Royal where one of his daughters was a nun. As one might therefore expect, his star began to wane with the Court but the real decline of his importance as a royal painter dates from 1654–61.[54] The concept of art was not unconditionally welcome at Port-Royal which emphasised the renunciation of the vanities of the world. Hence there are few portraits, but those painted by Philippe de Champaigne certainly bear out the austerity of the spiritual atmosphere reigning at the focal point of Jansenism where the world remains firmly outside the space of the picture. Other sorts of paintings reflect, however, the historicism of Port-Royal with respect to the primitive Church in particular. In his use of symbolism, he follows the Christocentrism of the Jansenists and their emphasis on the Passion, as in the *Good Shepherd* when he places at the feet of Christ a branch of thorns in order to represent the relationship between the shepherd and the sacrifices he makes for his flock.[55]

We have therefore the picture of an artist whose overriding culture was Christian, desirous of the strictest orthodoxy, although not of complete literalness, since he includes a symbolism which was not always derived from purely Christian sources. It is also interesting that, at a time when it was increasingly felt to be legitimate (and correct) to portray Christ and the disciples at the Last Supper reclining on triclinia, Philippe de Champaigne should present Port-Royal with the traditional representation of the figures seated round a table on chairs.

By contrast, Poussin, for many – and certainly for the generations who composed the seventeenth-century Académie royale de peinture et de sculpture – the model of the classical artist, presents a number of problems, not least the exact degree of his adherence to the religion whose events he portrayed so often. To begin with, Poussin was attached to no

[53] Ibid., pp. 73–4.   [54] Ibid., p. 57.   [55] Ibid., p. 77.

party, especially since his almost unbroken residence in Rome from 1624 to his death in 1665 sheltered him from the pressures of the intense religious debates which often raged in France. Certainly he accepted commissions for particular sections of the French Church, like the portrait of St Francis Xavier for the altar of the Jesuit church in Paris, but he essentially found himself free from the conditions imposed on other French artists who either could not escape them or accepted them without question.

Poussin's work was known and admired (if also criticised), and much of it was produced for French patrons such as Richelieu and Chantelou. Like all artists of the period a significant proportion of his output was composed of religious painting, but here again Poussin showed himself to be of an independent mind, since even at Rome he eschewed the vogue for martyrdoms (his *Martyrdom of St Erasmus* did not much attract the favour of his contemporaries) and portraits of newly canonised saints which interested the artists of the Eternal City. Poussin's interest in religious painting returns to medieval traditions in his emphasis on categories of subject concerned with salvation, especially in the *Moses* cycle which, in the context of the seventeenth century, was unusual.[56] But Poussin did not neglect the major episodes of the New Testament, including the life and passion of Christ. Perhaps the most remarkable paintings of Poussin are the two sets of *Sacraments*, one painted for Cassiano dal Pozzo, secretary to the influential Cardinal Barberini and his friend and mentor in Rome, the other for Chantelou in France.

How does Poussin stand in relation to Philippe de Champaigne in terms of the respect accorded to the Tridentine decrees on art, particularly with regard to orthodoxy? There is no doubt that Poussin too was anxious to conform to the text of the Gospels in an often literal sense, as two examples in particular demonstrate. The first contains the unusual feature of the cave tomb with a mourning figure in *Christ and the Woman of Samaria*. Poussin refers here to two sources, one identifying the location of the incident (John 4:5) near to the parcel of land that Jacob gave to his son Joseph, the second to Genesis and Joshua which make clear that the land was to contain the tomb of Joseph. The second example is Poussin's *Crucifixion* which shows an open grave with a man arising from within it, a literal interpretation of Matthew 27:52.

Poussin is also attached to another form of historical accuracy which is on occasion implied by the text of the Gospels but which on others is simply a reconstruction of what must have been the case. In certain instances the text of the Gospel can make sense only if Christ and the

[56] A. Blunt, *The Paintings of Nicolas Poussin* (London, 1958), p. 179.

disciples are reclining on triclinia, thus explaining the otherwise disrespectful posture of St John the Apostle at the Last Supper. This is also true of the positioning of the woman described in the washing of the feet in the house of Simon the Pharisee in Luke 7:38 depicted in the two series of the *Sacraments* (*Penance* and *Confession* respectively). However, nothing in the text of the Scriptures would allow Poussin to portray the Virgin sitting cross-legged on a cushion in the second version of the *Annunciation*, although historically it is probably accurate as a means of sitting in the Near East. Poussin's sense of historical accuracy is even more acute in his representation of scenes from the early Church, such as the *Sacrament* of *Confirmation* where details of architecture and costume in the depiction of Christian practice in the catacombs are of remarkable fidelity to the originals.

The religious painting of Poussin was not without its critics during his own time. Some complained that the figure of St Francis Xavier in his portrayal of the miracle resembled a thundering Jupiter rather than a saint. Among Poussin's critics we would not be surprised to find Philippe de Champaigne who, in a lecture at the Académie royale de peinture et de sculpture, objected to the fact that Poussin had, in his *Eleazer and Rebecca at the Well* (Louvre), omitted the camels mentioned in the text of the Bible (they are included in the two other versions of the same subject attributed to Poussin). Charles Le Brun, the artist-head of the Académie, replied that Poussin had obviously wished to avoid the beholder being distracted by the minutiae of the incident in order to concentrate better on the principal idea of the subject,[57] in fact a perfectly Counter-Reformation response in itself. The major controversy surrounding Poussin's depiction of biblical subjects among contemporaries concerned the celebrated painting of the *Israelites gathering Manna* where there are serious discrepancies with the biblical text, including the fact that the manna had lain on the ground like dew rather than falling from heaven, as in the painting.[58]

Modern critics have always demonstrated a good deal of unease on the matter of Poussin's religious sincerity, and here we are to a certain extent confronted with the problem of the frontier between the sacred and the profane, never an issue with Philippe de Champaigne. First, Poussin includes the Nile river god in some of the paintings of the *Moses* cycle. Second, he includes Roman imagery, such as the suckling of the old woman to the detriment of the child in the *Israelites gathering Manna*. Third, he borrows figures from some of his profane paintings for his religious paintings, as in the close modelling of the Virgin in the Washington *Assumption* on the face of the poet in the *Inspiration of the Poet*.

[57] H. Jouin, *Conférences de l'Académie royale de peinture et de sculpture* (Paris, 1883), pp. 93–4.
[58] Ibid., pp. 62 ff.

Most of all Poussin can be held to have adhered to the views of the circle around Cassiano dal Pozzo which, for example, established an analogy between the sacraments and the mysteries of Greek religion where the sacraments 'would have represented . . . the basic truth which runs through all forms of religion, whether Christian or pagan, and as such would have expressed the belief in religion as above sect or creed'.[59]

Other critics emphasise the human rather than the religious strain which runs through the paintings. The *Roccatagliata Madonna*, with its domestic playfulness, does not seem to comply with Tridentine strictures as they were subsequently interpreted, whereas, on the other hand, the *Madonna of the Steps* is a classic – and beautiful – example of respectful distance. For Châtelet the first series of the *Sacraments* is not so much a meditation on the divine mysteries as on human truth: their sacred character derives not from the intervention of the supernatural but from a humanity 'apurée jusqu'à son point de perfection'.[60] And Mikaël Alpatov regards the *Rest on the Flight into Egypt* as the depiction of the Holy Family placed in unusual circumstances where the conflict is between man and the external world rather than as an episode from the 'légende évangélique'.[61] One wonders here whether Poussin does not retain some aspects, or at least the spirit, of that tradition where the sacred is more effectively represented in familiar surroundings. On the other hand in the later paintings, and this is true of the second series of the *Sacraments* and of the later version of the *Annunciation* (National Gallery), Poussin moved towards a greater austerity in his depiction of religious subjects.

The major problem with Poussin's religious painting is the difficulty in distinguishing it in intention from the profane paintings. The question arises whether Poussin's attachment to historical accuracy was the result of his adherence primarily to religious or to intellectual principles. In other words, the desire for historical accuracy was the same whether he was dealing with a biblical subject or with a bacchanal. The intellectual approach therefore predominates over any obvious sincerity of belief. In the particular case of Poussin's own religious belief this argument has no obvious solution. Perhaps Poussin was even responsible for the secularisation of religious art. What is true is that, beyond the similarities, a good deal of diversity could exist among French painters of the seventeenth century with regard to their adherence to the rigour of the Tridentine decrees on imagery.

---

[59] Blunt, *The Paintings of Nicolas Poussin*, p. 187.
[60] A. Châtelet and J. Thuillier (eds.), *La Peinture française de Fouquet à Poussin* (Paris, 1964), II, 220.
[61] M. Alpatov, 'Poussin peintre d'histoire', in A. Chastel (ed.), *Nicolas Poussin*, 2 vols. (Paris, 1960), I, 189–99 (p. 195).

Theatre

The theatre was certainly one domain where writers made a major contribution to the cause of the Church. In the first half of the century many religious tragedies were written and performed, the favourite subject for such plays being the lives of the saints. The most famous of the religious plays of this period is unquestionably Pierre Corneille's *Polyeucte* (1641–2). But the genre of Christian tragedy did not meet with universal approval from within the world of even dramatic theorists who saw in it too much of a temptation to mix the sacred with the profane to the extent of using pagan gods in a religious context. Moreover and not unsurprisingly, Port-Royal saw in religious tragedy precisely the sorts of Roman virtues which they considered the complete opposite of Christian humility.

Pierre Corneille (1606–84) constitutes an interesting example of the attachment of the writer to the Church. After all, he retired from the stage for some seven years in order to concentrate on, among other things, translating Thomas à Kempis's *Imitation of Christ*. But his most lasting association is with the Jesuits and the essence of their spirituality, although the association is not always a straightforward one. Many aspects of Corneille's work, as is well known, reflect aspects of the spirituality of his former educators, and Corneille has always been regarded as the representative in the literature of the first half of the seventeenth century of Christian or devout humanism, where humanity in the form of the hero benefits from the more optimistic assumptions on human nature which are part of the Jesuit view of man in relation to the possibility of salvation. Corneille thus embodies the idea of Aristotelian 'grandeur' and 'magnanimité' which in Jesuit spirituality is the prelude to Christian heroic virtue.[62] The choice of pagan subjects to arouse the 'admiration' of the audience does not constitute an obstacle since, within the logic of Jesuit teaching using exempla from antiquity, the Christian soul is initiated into a form of moral sublime which is 'une première touche de la grâce'.[63]

Certain of Corneille's deviations from pure Aristotelian dramatic theory, a controversial area of discussion in the period, can also be explained by his Jesuit training or at least by the influence of a Society with which he never lost contact. Many Jesuit works of theatre in the schools reject the notion of *fatum*, of *vraisemblance* (the foundation of plausibility in orthodox dramatic theorists) and the idea of the tragic hero who is neither good nor bad. What purpose could be served by this type of hero

---

[62] M. Fumaroli, *Héros et orateurs: rhétorique et dramaturgie cornéliennes* (Geneva, 1990), p. 331.
[63] Ibid., p. 137.

for a Society which advances a Christian heroism based on a concept of redemption and revelation unknown to the pagan world? This view of the hero, contained in Corneille's three *Discours du poème dramatique*, reflects the freedom from attachment to the world which makes possible the dynamic progress of the Christian soul.[64] One essential component of the Cornelian hero is his acceptance of renunciation.

Corneille, however, also illustrates the degree to which resistance to this appropriation of literature by elements of the Church emerged in the middle of the century. Corneille's other religious tragedy, *Théodore* (1645–6), alienated those who did not wish to see the French Court transformed into a 'cour sainte'. According to Marc Fumaroli, at the time that Mazarin was attempting to bring to France the brilliant and sensual art of Rome which would make Paris, after Rome, Vienna and Madrid, the fourth capital of Catholic art, Corneille mistakenly opted for the severest form of edifying theatre as elaborated by the Jesuits.[65]

But Fumaroli himself seems to opt for a paradoxical (or inconsistent?) association of Corneille with the Jesuits. On the one hand he holds that the Jesuits had to contend with a far greater diversity of religious life in France, far more so than in the territory of the Habsburgs or the territories that owed allegiance to the pope. They could not count on the acceptance of their influence when their pupils were dispersed in a land of religious diversity. In this sense, Corneille was not and could not be a Jesuit playwright. He had himself to take account of that diversity. On the other hand, Corneille owed the most explicit allegiance to the Jesuit order and is regarded in the last quarter of the seventeenth century as the most faithful example of Jesuit dramaturgy.[66] Moreover, Fumaroli also holds that, right up to *Suréna* (1674), Corneille remained a devout humanist and the French representative of an international culture through a catholicity of style which aims at the universal not from a position of paring down and simplicity as in classicism, but from a position of eclecticism and of synthesis.[67] Corneille is thus a perfect example of the exchange between the space of the Church, albeit a section of the Church whose activities were hotly contested, and the space of the world in the form of the public theatre of predominantly secular inspiration.

It was indeed the purely secular space of much of the literature of the period which concerned religious moralists who regarded the values it represented as a sort of counter-culture which threatened their teaching at its core. Where the Church taught that the world was full of concupiscence and corruption, poetry, plays and especially novels encouraged – through their portrayal of the pleasures of carnal love and their exaltation

---

[64] Ibid., pp. 72–3.   [65] Ibid., pp. 249–50 and 254–5.
[66] Ibid., pp. 64–5.   [67] Ibid., p. 259.

of worldly pomp and ceremony – an attachment to the world which turned people away from God. Writers instilled a love of the creature rather than a love of the Creator.

The crucial arena of this discussion on the relative merits of secular literature as a moral or corrupting force was the theatre, not only through the texts performed in it, but because of the whole nature of the experience. The theatre, as a building, resembled in that sense the tavern in the world of popular culture. It acted as a rival attraction to the church, the actor mirroring the priest in his pulpit, especially as performances took place on Sundays. In the same way that the Church was visible through its churches, the culture which ran counter to it, or so the Church believed, was also visible to the extent of attracting rival publics, another way in which the theatre was considerably more dangerous than simply the printed word. The stage as a visible entity was a space where actresses in their immodest costumes proffered the temptations of the flesh, and where therefore the performances of the passions were so much more compelling than their description when read silently.

The rivalry between Church and theatre – and the parallel of the actor and the priest – is compounded by the great emphasis on moral instruction. Dramatic theorists like Jean Chapelain, also a poet and literary bureaucrat, evinced a keen awareness of what they regarded as the dangers of generating the wrong form of pleasure in the theatre. The importance of the emphasis on moral instruction emanating from the stage was that actors seemed to offer a secularised form of teaching on the passions, and reinforced the teaching of the Church on the distinction of right from wrong. Religious moralists replied that actors, whose purpose it was to arouse harmful passions in the audience, had no right or claim to usurp a teaching which could only be offered by those properly qualified, that is to say, priests. The actors' claim to teach was therefore invalid since it was absurd that the poison of passion had to be swallowed first so that it could then be countered. The Church could not be expected to look with indifference upon a secular space which seemed to arrogate to itself a task which was properly and traditionally theirs.[68]

Not that all sections of the Church reacted in exactly the same way to the theatre. After all, Richelieu was responsible for the Edict of 1641 absolving actors from the charge of infamy which, among other things, prevented them from entering holy orders. Bishops served as ushers to the public when Richelieu opened his Grand Théâtre in the Palais-Royal and prelates regularly attended theatrical performances at Court. Fumaroli points also to the trend within Jesuit attitudes to the theatre in the

[68] See H. Phillips, *The Theatre and its Critics in Seventeenth-Century France* (Oxford, 1980).

seventeenth century which aimed at bringing about a 'modération chrétienne' as proposed by Ottonelli in his *Della Moderazione cristiana del teatro* of 1646. This moderation would be the result of the educative process of the Jesuits through which many writers, actors and spectators passed.[69]

But France and the gallican Church were not in a mood to welcome a strategy of accommodation and, alone among the Catholic nations of Europe of this time, exercised the full rigour of the religious law at its disposal to deal with actors. The Edict of 1641, designed probably by Richelieu and meant to remove the scandal attached to the actor's profession, turned out to have less weight than might have been hoped by those in the acting profession, since it reflected a theological position deriving from St Thomas's lenient attitude to the concept of play which had no legal foundation in canon law. Many bishops, as was their right by virtue of the independence granted to them in such matters, included in their diocesan ritual actors, along with prostitutes and witches, in the list of those to be denied the sacraments (with all the consequences that that entailed) unless they renounced their profession. They took this action despite the new model ritual which had been published by Paul V in 1614 and which deliberately excluded the actor from this list, thus confirming the lenient practice that had operated in Italy from the middle of the sixteenth century. In 1713 the ritual of Metz condemned anyone who contributed to the theatrical experience in any capacity whatsoever, from the man who swept the floor to the writer of the script.[70]

Even within the Jesuits, whom one might think well disposed towards theatre which was, after all, an indispensable part of their educational programme, stern opposition was to emerge to the public theatre. The reasons for this are in a sense understandable and stem from precisely the place of theatre in their teaching. Cressolles, from as early as 1620, even before the establishment of a fixed permanent troupe in Paris, raised the key issue of the relation of the actor to the orator, and more particularly to the sacred orator. Another Jesuit, this time Cellot, whose *Orationes* were written in 1631 but republished in 1641, also felt it necessary to attack the professional actor (he does not attack the theatre in principle).[71] The underlying problem is again one of frontiers. If theatre is legitimate for the Jesuits, why not for the public (a question raised by Samuel Chappuzeau in his staunch defence of the professional actor of 1674)? The resemblance between the two theatres needed therefore to be challenged: the

---

[69] Fumaroli, *Héros et orateurs*, pp. 456–7.
[70] See J. Dubu, 'L'Eglise catholique et la condamnation du théâtre en France', *Quaderni francesi*, 1 (1970), 319–49.
[71] Fumaroli, *Héros et orateurs*, pp. 462–4.

best opponents of the public theatre were those aiming themselves to create a Christian theatre, a rather striking suggestion when one considers that the principal complaint against the Society in the seventeenth century was its compromise with secularism. But the need for such a move within the Society was in itself a recognition of the power of the actor as a rival to the Church, in that the public and the sacred orator were appealing to the same Christian public.[72] However, they did not and could not share the same status.

But this distinction between orators is not as unproblematic as it seems. The Jesuits tended to reject the austerity of moral rigorism and opted for a 'softer' approach which did not necessarily compromise moral standards, despite many views to the contrary. The principles of their less confrontational approach to oratory included the Horatian synthesis of the 'utile' and the 'dulce' which formed the basis of moral instruction in literature and the theatre. The strategy of 'modération chrétienne' on the Italian model would then allow professional actors to lay claim to the status of 'tribuns du peuple laïcs', especially since the French lay state seemed content to tolerate the theatre in society. Such a situation, according to Cellot, could only lead to the seduction of the laity away from the teaching of the Church, and was the reason why he was so keen to deny any status at all to the actor on the public stage.[73] The adoption by a Jesuit of a predominantly gallican view of the theatre says much for the adaptation of the Society beyond the usual charge of their flirtation with the space of the world. It also illustrates the degree to which even the Jesuits disagreed on strategies in respect of the 'world'.

Interestingly, Corneille became the advocate, not of the Jesuit stance as represented by Cressolles and Cellot, but of the position adopted by Ottonelli. In his play-within-a-play, L'Illusion comique (1636), Alcandre symbolises the writer of plays for the 'comédien', that is to say the actor with his new-found status of teacher of morals. Corneille thus offers a polite remonstrance to his former teachers who, on the issue of the theatre, seem to forsake their 'douceur' for a position of rigour.[74] But is Corneille arguing for the theatre to represent the Church in the space of the world through the notion of Christian moderation as Fumaroli suggests, where the theatre would act as an extension of the Church's teaching in society? Is he arguing too that, if such a purpose is to be achieved, the position of the actor / public orator in society must be legitimated? This could only be possible if Corneille held to an idea of moral instruction or the transformation of society through the performance of plays. This is unlikely, it seems to me, from an author whose attachment to the notion of moral

[72] Ibid., pp. 472–3.   [73] Ibid., pp. 475–7.   [74] Ibid., p. 462.

instruction as the aim of theatre was never more than nominal, and, in the case of 'admiration', positively ambiguous. This is not to say that Corneille thought of the theatre as anything less than serious, but perhaps his conception of theatre is one that does not deny the Christian perspective but one which is happy to accept the space in which it exists as a secular one. The role of the theatre is quite simply different from the role of the Church in the way that it 'teaches', if it teaches at all.

That the existence of autonomous secular and religious spaces is an issue within the context of theatre is raised by Fumaroli himself who argues that the distinct nature, in its inception, of the Catholic as opposed to the Protestant Reform itself permitted the creation of an autonomous secular space. In the first place, it is the nature of the contract between actor and spectator which gives rise to that space, by contrast with the liturgical theatre based on 'actes sacerdotaux', where the secular theatre is performed by 'mercenary' actors whose connection with the spectator is purely financial. The space of the theatre is thus freed from any priestly mediation, and reflects a world where, in politics and in law, the secular space rivals that of the Church.

But this public is legitimated in another way and that is by the very separation that exists within the Catholic Reform between the priesthood and the laity. The Protestant Reform had sought to 'sacerdotaliser' the laity rather than to emphasise its purely lay status, thus laying the basis for a theocracy which, in the context of the theatre, allowed it to adopt more radical solutions. The problem with the Catholic Reform was that it created, in its implied division of the civil and the religious, and the sacred and the profane, a secular space with its own logic where the laity could lay claim to protection from its own powers once their position was threatened. Thus the king of Spain could protect actors in Milan from the Borromean reform of the diocese. The Church could no longer act against the laity once the latter had asserted its own identity, for it was the laity, including the Court, who built the theatres and courted actors. Princes and magistrates then ensure the continuation of the theatre's activities in the face of episcopal opposition. When the Church, after Trent, set out to reconquer the soul of the laity it had no choice but to accept the toleration of theatre.[75] It has to be said on the other hand that Spanish monarchs succeeded in closing the theatres for a time in both the sixteenth and the seventeenth centuries. Cromwell managed the same feat in England.

The *querelle du théâtre* in France is in fact a good example of the limitations of the powers of the French Church in the context of lay culture in our period. This is not to say that powerful influences in the

[75] Ibid., p. 453.

Church in France did not do all they could to eject the acting profession from the space of the Church by the threat of excommunication. Their action in that regard was never challenged by the French monarch. Louis XIV could only intervene in the case of Molière on a strictly personal basis. But the Church never managed to persuade the civil authorities to close the theatres. Despite Frain du Tremblay's attack in 1713 on the political argument that keeping the theatres open prevented the occurrence of greater evils in society – and he refers to the closure of theatres in England[76] – the Church simply had to accept that the conversion of the individual, and of quite a number of individuals at that, both actors and spectators, could alone diminish the need for such spectacles and reduce the personnel who serviced them. As Fumaroli has suggested, the enthusiasm of the laity for theatre, and of the most important members of that laity, was a major obstacle to the success of the Church. The space of society as a whole was immune to the powers of control that the Church exercised over individual conscience.

Books and literature

Many of the issues and arguments I have examined in the domain of art are not foreign to the area of books. As with the output of the artists of the period, the proportion of publications devoted to religion was substantial, and throughout the century it was around 50 per cent of the total. A good part of this percentage was composed of books of piety in small format which attracted those sections of the bourgeoisie favouring a more rigorous spirituality, particularly the jurists. At the end of the century the important works associated with Jansenism penetrated the libraries of this group of men, although the presence of these books may demonstrate more curiosity than a wholesale conversion.[77] In any case religious works represent yet another means by which the Church was able to occupy a part of domestic space.

Were there religious writers like there were religious artists? The situation is of course slightly different in that images had a more immediate and effective appeal in a kingdom where the overwhelming majority of the population was illiterate and where books, apart from the sort of popular literature of the blue books, had a limited audience. It none the less remains that a fair number of the works of piety were produced by laymen like Henri Lelevel, Frain du Tremblay and a host of other

[76] J. Frain du Tremblay, *Discours sur l'origine de la poësie, sur son usage et sur le bon goût* (Paris, 1713), (reprinted Geneva, 1970), p. 261.
[77] P. Deyon, *Amiens, capitale provinciale: étude sur la société urbaine au XVIIe siècle* (Paris, 1967), pp. 286–7.

little-known figures. The most spectacular recruitment of a layman in the service of religion was perhaps that of Blaise Pascal (1623–62) in the case of the *Provinciales*. His work of Christian apologetics, the *Pensées*, even in the incomplete version of 1670 published by Pierre Nicole (1625–95) at Port-Royal, had an enormous influence on thinkers like Nicolas Malebranche (1638–1715). Many more celebrated figures also wrote in the cause of the Church in a variety of forms. Boileau's twelfth *Satire* shows him to be a Jansenist sympathiser but it was never published during his lifetime.The lyric poet Saint-Amant wrote a religious epic entitled *Moïse sauvé*.

One must not forget Jean Racine (1639–99). His relations with his early mentors at Port-Royal were seriously damaged by his unmeasured response to Pierre Nicole's mistreatment of Desmarets de Saint-Sorlin, a fierce opponent of Port-Royal, as a playwright. Racine was later reconciled to them and eventually drafted a short history of Port-Royal. He also attended a funeral at Port-Royal at a sensitive time in the persecution of the Jansenist movement, a courageous act on the part of someone who is generally regarded as having been a careerist *extraordinaire*. He also wrote two biblical plays for Madame de Maintenon's girls' school at Saint-Cyr. But the performance at Court of *Esther* (*Athalie* was only ever rehearsed), when seats near to the king were at a premium, took place in circumstances which could only be considered worldly, a case where the frontier between the spaces of religion and the world was uncomfortably blurred, even during the king's pious period.

Within the literary world itself the Church did not find itself unrepresented. Much to the chagrin of more rigorously minded clerics, many 'abbés commendataires' and others found their way into the salons, even to the extent of becoming theorists in matters of worldly behaviour, such as l'abbé de Pure in the case of preciosity. L'abbé d'Aubignac was one of the foremost dramatic theorists of the period. The Jesuits were represented by two quite substantial figures who wrote on matters of literature and taste, Rapin and Bouhours. The former is the author of a series of *réflexions* on rhetoric and poetry, and the latter is one of the foremost theorists of what constituted good taste in language where the celebrated 'je ne sais quoi' played a key role. He even extended its domain to religion where it represented the ineffable in matters concerning the physical universe which science could not adequately explain.[78] Moreover, 'le *je ne sais quoi* est le fondement de notre espérance dans l'immortalité'.[79] Indeed, at times, in this mixture of the sacred and the profane it was sometimes difficult even to distinguish between sacred and profane love. At the level

---

[78] Busson, *La Religion des Classiques*, p. 357.   [79] Quoted in ibid., p. 360.

of the ideal woman, poems to the Virgin and to a loved one could sound strikingly similar in their imagery. Indeed Bouhours was himself accused of using a poem about the Virgin, expunged from later editions of his work, to illustrate a point concerning profane literary usage.

This confusion between the space of the world and the space of religion again derives, at least in part, from a shared tradition drawn from antiquity. On the side of the Church the strength of this tradition can be seen most forcefully in someone like Bossuet whose spiritual credentials are impeccable. We need only to refer to his description of Homer in the *Discours sur l'histoire universelle* to understand the deep respect that such a figure feels for the world of antiquity. Homer, along with so many other poets, whose works are no less serious than they are pleasurable, celebrates only the arts which are useful to life in this world: they are full of the public good and speak highly of their country and society, illustrating an 'admirable civilité'.[80] The poets of antiquity are therefore models for us all. The frontier is discreetly but clearly marked by Bossuet, for these poets are helpful only as far as 'la vie humaine' is concerned. They have nothing to tell us about the world beyond, a task only Christianity can truly undertake. This attachment to the culture of ancient Greece and Rome in fact introduces us to the more crucial relationship of the Church with the literary world concerning the use in Christian writing of forms and images which belonged firmly to antiquity. Writers often took sides on whether it was still appropriate to compose poems about the heroes of myth or whether these should be abandoned in favour of heroes drawn from biblical or modern history. The problem is that many writers, especially those who leant towards Port-Royal, felt that the boundary was too confused, and that pagan sentiment all too often found its way into Christian expression. And it found its way through the use of imagery from the pagan world. I have already touched upon this question in considering the world of art. But it is worth revisiting in the context of literature where it is clear that Tridentine severity had also penetrated to a considerable degree. Alongside a developed critique of pagan imagery, which in some ways went beyond that of their artist counterparts, writers elaborated in addition some quite radical solutions. However, the penetration of the Church's control could only be less effective, given that books did not adorn buildings in the same way as images. It is interesting therefore to discover that many writers clearly desired not only to police their own domain but also to reflect on the status of the writer in a Christian society.

Bossuet's praise of Homer was shared by a number of clerics in the

[80] Bossuet, *Œuvres*, XIV, 52.

seventeenth century and these include figures such as Rapin who praises the epic poet as being the source of, among other things, laws and science.[81] There arose, however, the question of what the source of inspiration for the epic should be, pagan or Christian. One of the central figures who saw no difficulty in promoting the epic as conceived by Aristotle in the *Poetics* is Le Bossu. For him, since the principal aim of the epic is moral, the central character must include characteristics and qualities which are common to all humanity and which are drawn from several originals. In this sense real historical characters will not do because the focus in terms of human qualities would be too narrow. He thus adheres to the preference for verisimilitude over truth, a classic Aristotelian position. Certainly, the epic would contain well-known mythological figures but their names are secondary to the prime purpose of writing a moral tale. In other words, the heroes of antiquity that a modern writer would imitate are, rather than characters, characteristic of the qualities one might desire to promote in humanity.[82] Le Bossu clearly regards his subject-matter as neutral and as conveying no particular value in itself. This view is shared by others, such as Rapin and Le Moyne. It is perhaps no coincidence that they all belong to the Society of Jesus, which had particular reasons for promoting the culture of antiquity.

The counter-position to that of Le Bossu is the rejection of antiquity in favour of biblical or historical subjects. The polemic on this issue was fuelled at one stage in the century by Boileau's assertion in Canto III of the *Art poétique* that the ornaments available from the myths and poetry of antiquity were better able to please than what would inevitably be the severe presentation of Christian doctrine. He also made fun of the sort of 'unpoetic' names which writers would have to accommodate in their verse. Many writers on the other hand dismiss the idea that religious subjects are unworthy of poetry or not susceptible to poetic effect. Le Laboureur laments the neglect of religious subjects on the part of poets who seem to prefer things which are either frivolous or dangerous.[83] Despite Le Moyne's adherence to Aristotelian principles he none the less points out that wars waged in the name of Christianity are of a different order to those waged over the golden fleece or Helen of Troy. Indeed, the space of temporal authority is thereby brought even more into the space of religion because, through such subjects, knights would learn that Christian and military values are not incompatible.[84] The reason often given for

---

[81] Le Père R. Rapin, *Réflexions sur la poétique* (Paris, 1674), pp. 16–17.
[82] Le Père R. Le Bossu, *Traité du poëme épique* (Paris, 1675), pp. 64 ff.
[83] Le Père L. Le Laboureur, *Sentiments de l'autheur sur la poësie chrestienne & prophane*, in *La Magdelaine pénitente* (Paris, 1643).
[84] Le Père P. Le Moyne, *Dissertation du poëme héroïque* in *Œuvres poétiques* (Paris, 1672).

the superiority of religious over profane epic is in part rooted in the nature of verisimilitude which cannot be the same in a Christian or pagan context. Cotin is not alone in explaining that the history used by the ancients in their poems is in fact myth and therefore devoid of credibility.[85] Some claim that the pagan gods in themselves destroy any notion of verisimilitude. In this case, Christian subjects, especially those from biblical sources, dispense entirely with these problems because our faith in the intervention of the Christian God is unimpeachable. God alone can validate the notion of verisimilitude in the epic. The rules and poems of the ancients are simply irrelevant in a contemporary context.[86]

Indeed to prefer antiquity is a slur on Christendom. For Frain du Tremblay Christian poets are wrong to invest pagan imagery with the authority they have,[87] thus creating a disregard for the law and for the Gospel,[88] and Charpentier argues that tolerance of the language and inventions of paganism could induce a dislike not only of one's own language but also of one's own religion.[89] In replying to Boileau, Desmarets even argues that to denigrate Christian poets is to denigrate Christianity. He states quite categorically that: 'il n'y a que les sujets de l'ancien et du nouveau Testaments, et des histoires de notre religion, qui puissent estre propres pour la dignité de la Poësie Heroïque'.[90] Frain seems to banish biblical subjects altogether but opts firmly on the other hand for resolutely modern heroes who are the only characters who can truly relate proportionately to us as human beings.[91]

So the subjects of French epic poetry in the seventeenth century include Saint-Amant's *Moïse sauvé*, Coras's *Jonas ou Ninive pénitente*, Le Laboureur's *Charlemagne*, Desmarets's *Clovis* and so on. Obviously the emphasis on subjects drawn from the history of the kingdom along with the specific choice of Christian heroes like St Louis is not without political significance. Indeed the emphasis on the link between the French crown from its beginnings and the defence of the faith possesses a clear contemporary message. Writers see themselves as exalting Louis XIV through his ancestors, thus suggesting (or desiring?) a continuity of the crown's status as a bulwark of the Church. Hence, for Desmarets, the king, as defender of the faith, requires a form of poetry which reflects his

[85] L'Abbé Ch. Cotin, *Poésies chrestiennes* (Paris, 1668), p. 4.
[86] J. Desmarets de Saint-Sorlin, *Discours pour prouver que les sujests chrestiens sont les seuls propres à la poësie heroïque* (1673), in F. R. Freudmann (ed.), *Clovis* (Paris, 1972), pp. 718–19.
[87] Frain du Tremblay, *Discours*, Preface.
[88] Ibid., p. 91.
[89] F. Charpentier, *De l'Excellence de la langue française*, 2 vols. (Paris, 1683), II, 718.
[90] J. Desmarets de Saint-Sorlin, *Traité pour juger des poëtes grecs, latins et françois* (1673), in F. R. Freudmann (ed.), *Clovis* (Paris, 1972), p. 94.
[91] Frain du Tremblay, *Discours*, pp. 69 and 72.

role in the Christian world rather than one borrowed from the Greeks.[92] The Christian epic also has a resonance outside the kingdom. Le Laboureur (a Jesuit) makes it quite clear that the point of his epic based on the reinstatement of Pope Leo by Charlemagne is that 'les Souverains de Rome' forget all too often the protection and other benefits they have received from the kings of France.[93]

Arguments over subject-matter were then complemented by arguments over the extent to which invention is permitted in a sacred subject. All writers without exception forbid the alteration of anything in the sacred text and the issue becomes one of additions to the text. Even the saints' lives present difficulties from this point of view. It is much safer according to Scudéry to take subjects from the history of Christianity rather than from Scripture itself.[94] Saint-Amant argues that some parts of the Bible are less important in their content than others and therefore allow for invention beyond what is written.[95] Cotin provides the general rule: 'l'invention peut avoir sa place dans une poesie sacrée, pourveu qu'elle ne repugne ny au motif, ny à l'evenement principal, non plus qu'aux moyens extraordinaires dont il a plû au ciel de se servir'.[96] But even in the biblical epic worldly drives require some satisfaction. Coras admits to having had to invent a love interest in *Josué*, explaining that he did not wish to produce a body without a soul.

Ornamentation too attracted widespread attention from writers of religious poetry. In general terms, Desmarets finds the legitimation of invention not only in the example of St Gregory but also in the parables and figurative expressions to be found in the Bible.[97] In any imitation of the ancient epic the sources of ornamentation would inevitably include examples of the gods who are necessary to the grandeur of the action. In fact Le Bossu regards it as a defect to omit 'la présence de la divinité'.[98] The problem is the relation of these gods to the Christian God. The ire of those who uphold the cause of religious subjects could only have been increased by the slippage from Christian to pagan culture that is evident in Le Bossu himself: 'Dieu est la premiere de toutes les causes en général: nous le mettons ici en l'auteur de la nature, et il dispose de toutes choses comme il lui plaît. Cette cause rend les moeurs d'Enée admirablement

[92] J. Desmarets de Saint-Sorlin, *L'Excellence et les plaintes de la poësie*, in *Esther* (Paris, 1670), p. 10.
[93] Le Père L. Le Laboureur, *Charlemagne* (Paris, 1666), Preface.
[94] G. de Scudéry, *Alaric* (Paris, 1654), Preface.
[95] M.-A. Saint-Amant (ed. J. Lagny), *Moïse sauvé*, in vol. v, *Œuvres*, 5 vols. (Paris, 1967–79), 141.
[96] Cotin, *Poésies chrestiennes*, p. 16.
[97] J. Desmarets de Saint-Sorlin, *Marie-Madeleine, ou le Triomphe de la grâce* (Paris, 1669), Preface.
[98] Le Bossu, *Traité*, p. 303.

bonnes. Il est superflu de dire combien ce Heros est cheri de Jupiter.'[99]
'Dieu' and 'les dieux' sit happily within the same sentence.

Some are, in contrast, content to exclude the pagan gods altogether since this would be a step towards the promotion of good morals especially in view of the often appalling image presented to us of supposedly divine beings. Another reason for their exclusion is that reference to the pagan supernatural suggests an equal status with Christian miracles. Moreover, the rejection of pagan imagery means the abandonment of certain literary practices like the invocation of the muses at the beginning of a work, presumably on the grounds that such an invocation is too close to prayer.[100] Not all poets were aware of the problem. As one might expect, Le Bossu saw no harm in it but again, alarmingly, he speaks in the same breath of the muses of the ancients and those of Christian writers.[101] Godeau, the poet bishop of Vence and Grasse, wrote of Homer and Virgil as the priests of the muses, and this in a devotional work.[102]

Like painters and art theorists, writers objected to the incongruity that might arise from the use of allegorical figures drawn from antiquity, especially in a sacred subject. Coras is adamant that the Christian poet must never use pagan images in a work of Christian inspiration. Pagan names can only ever be uttered by Christians if they are treated according to their merits, that is to say as the gods of an alien culture, although it would be appropriate for a pagan to utter their names with sincerity.[103] Charpentier, reasonably enough, objects to the god Bacchus being invoked in a description of the Last Supper.[104] Desmarets adds a political slant to the issue which he attacks the choice of pagan imagery to praise a Christian king like Louis XIV whose successes are thereby debased.[105]

Not all those who preferred to write on religious subjects shared the view of Banier, a member of the Petite Académie charged with finding appropriate inscriptions for commemorative medals, that allegory in ancient poetry was required in order to conceal the absurdities of myth and that it constituted in point of fact a disfigurement of truths which had their origin in earlier texts belonging to the sacred.[106] Cotin argued that allegory was in fact quite natural in religious subjects.[107] Certainly, Frain du Tremblay maintains that allegorical figures betray the origins of myth

---

[99] Ibid., p. 5.
[100] A. Phérotée de La Croix, *L'Art de la poësie françoise* (Lyons, 1675), p. 49, and M. de Marolles, *Traité du poëme épique* (Paris, 1662), p. 70.
[101] Le Bossu, *Traité*, p. 231.
[102] A. Godeau, *Saint Paul* (Paris, 1654), Preface.
[103] J. de Coras, *Jonas, ou la Ninive pénitente* (Paris, 1663), Preface.
[104] Charpentier, *De l'Excellence*, II, 734–5.
[105] J. Desmarets de Saint-Sorlin, *La Défense du poëme héroïque* (Paris, 1675), p. 94.
[106] A. Banier, *Explication historique des fables*, 3 vols. (Paris, 1715), Preface to vol. I.
[107] Cotin, *Poésies chrestiennes*, pp. 20–1.

in idolatry and in the passions, and as such will always be rejected by true believers.[108] But many writers follow the artists and plead for allegorical figures to be used in poetry. Godeau, in the preface to his *Saint Paul*, is less sure about wholesale rejection of the imagery of antiquity, arguing that it can be a fine ornament if it is well done. Saint-Amant pleads that what has been made by pagan hands is not any the less beautiful for that and can be converted to a sacred use.[109]

Some allow the two cultures to co-exist. Marolles permits the mixture of the sacred and the profane but only as far as the dignity of the subject will allow.[110] Others like Charles Perrault think that writers should be permitted to find Christian equivalents to the pagan gods. Angels and demons are a reasonable substitute, especially since they can command the belief of all Christians in a way that the gods could not do for the Greeks.[111] Frain du Tremblay will have no truck whatsoever with any substitutes for the ancient gods, for that would simply be playing their game. The use of angels simply demonstrates the lack of respect poets have for their religion since they are subjected to the whims of the imagination.[112]

The fact remains that many writers are able easily to inhabit both 'pagan' and Christian cultures as long as a clear sense of hierarchy and proportion is maintained. Godeau reveres those authors of antiquity who wrote within the bounds of decency and who have therefore much to teach us. But it is only right that idolatrous Rome and Greece should now yield to Jerusalem the Holy.[113] Marolles is content to protest against the extreme positions of both parties.[114] Even Desmarets, one of the most vociferous critics of the gods, cannot altogether abandon them. He chooses however to relegate them to subjects dealing with love, or they can find their place in the theatre and in gardens. It is clear that he regards love poetry as trivial and that those genres which can legitimately avail themselves of pagan imagery stand in contrast to 'serious' subjects. It is none the less odd that he, as a tragedian who wrote at the behest of Richelieu, should choose the theatre to reside on the margins of culture. At the same time, it is true that Desmarets is aware of a political problem in that the world of pagan imagery is drawn on by the most Christian king. Statues modelled on those of antiquity figure as decoration in palaces and

---

[108] Frain du Tremblay, *Discours*, p. 45.
[109] Saint-Amant, *Moïse sauvé*, v, 142.
[110] Marolles, *Traité*, p. 48.
[111] Ch. Perrault, *Parallèle des anciens et des modernes en ce qui regarde les arts et les sciences*, 4 vols. (Paris, 1692–7), III, 19.
[112] Frain du Tremblay, *Discours*, p. 85.
[113] A. Godeau, *De la Poésie chrestienne*, in *Œuvres chrestiennes* (Paris, 1633), p. 22.
[114] Marolles, *Traité*, p. 2.

gardens to signify the greatest powers of the land which even Scripture referred to as gods. Even here, however, the gods are not taken entirely seriously because in places which represent pleasure the presence of the sacred would be inappropriate, so that the gods of antiquity become objects of amusement.[115] It seems that paganism may be acceptable in what is interestingly regarded as a purely secular space.

The more fundamental debate addresses the legitimacy of imaginative literature. The notion of imaginative literature and its representation of the world as vanity was a commonplace revitalised in the seventeenth century by the rigorist elements among theologians and religious moralists and their allies in the secular space. Should this sort of literature be written by Christians at all? If so, what, within Christian culture, provides it with its legitimation? The case against literature is that many of its forms, as they were inherited from classical culture, served idolatry, and the use of those forms, such as theatre and dancing, were forever associated with veneration of the gods of antiquity. The very existence of the biblical epic is threatened by the implications of this position. In the case of theatre in particular a considerable number of patristic authorities can be called upon to decry its very existence, from St Cyprian to Tertullian, the most categorical critic of drama among the Fathers. But seventeenth-century writers know that the early Christian Church was not unanimous in its rejection of secular, that is to say, pagan forms of writing. Colletet, in order to justify his own interest in ancient poetry, generalises St Augustine's injunction that Christians should reappropriate those elements of ancient culture which either do not shock the principles of Christianity or which seem to have been taken from it.[116] The ultimate authoritative source for the justification for poetry is the Bible, even for the production of epic poems. For Le Bossu, perhaps the most important representative of the historical epic based on the myths of antiquity, the Old Testament is composed of allegories representing the doctrines and truths of religion.[117] For Desmarets, God is the ultimate model in the writing of epic poetry.[118] The most extensive defence of this position is found in Huet's *Traité de l'origine des romans* (1670) where he maintains that God communicated his will through parable.[119] Nor is it lost on writers that Christ himself spoke in this form.

Even if a case can be made for literature on these grounds, is it right that ordained members of the Church should themselves write it? What is the

---

[115] Desmarets de Saint-Sorlin, *Discours*, pp. 741–2.
[116] G. Colletet, *L'Art poëtique* (Paris, 1658), pp. 55–6.
[117] Le Bossu, *Traité*, p. 97.
[118] Desmarets de Saint-Sorlin, *L'Excellence*, p. 6.
[119] P.-D. Huet (ed. F. Gégou), *Lettre-traité de Pierre-Daniel Huet sur l'origine des romans* (Paris, 1971), p. 44.

legitimation of poetry within the immediate space of the Church? In the first place there are ecclesiastical precedents. Godeau, a bishop with a worldly career behind him, felt the need to defend his own practice by enumerating a number of them, some of whom were bishops like him.[120] Ménestrier protects his own corner, that of writing on ballet, by pointing to the example of those Fathers who had written on music, history and spectacle.[121] Some, however, draw the line at clerics taking part in literary discussions in a secular context. Barbier d'Aucourt, who was close to Port-Royal, condemned Bouhours for indulging in an activity which was unbecoming for a cleric. Page upon page of the *Entretiens d'Ariste*, he complains, are full of 'galanteries', love poetry and 'devises passion-nées'.[122] Barbier was particularly scandalised by Bouhours's mention of grace in his discussion of the 'je ne sais quoi'.[123] Frain du Tremblay, in similar fashion, is horrified at the thought that Le Bossu, a priest, could be so obsessed with profane poets to the extent of comparing them with sacred authors: we will be looking to the Koran for lessons next.[124] There was one voice of protest at least. Le Moyne states quite categorically that 'la Sorbonne n'a point de jurisdiction sur le Parnasse'.[125]

Conclusion

Opinion from within and outside the Church on art and literature is then extraordinarily varied. In art the rigorist position on a number of points was at times quite simply ignored or obeyed according to the circumstances the artist often found himself in. That is to say that the Church could not insist on the depiction of a subject according to the new rules if patrons wanted it otherwise, and patrons attached to the old ways came some-times from within the immediate space of the Church itself. Previous traditions were quite simply too embedded in the faithful for any wholesale change to take place. On the other hand some artists were sufficiently persuaded to internalise those rules and to produce works which were in harmony with the pursuit of an orthodoxy based on a much more literal reading of biblical texts in particular. In that sense the worlds of élite and popular culture were subject to the same rules and, in some cases, evinced the same sort of opposition.

[120] A. Godeau, *Poésies chrestiennes* (Paris, 1654), p. 15.
[121] Le Père C.-F. Ménestrier, *Des Ballets anciens et modernes selon les regles du théâtre* (Paris, 1682), Epître.
[122] J. Barbier d'Aucourt, *Sentiments de Cléante sur le entretiens d'Ariste et d'Eugène* (Paris, 1738), p. 207.
[123] Ibid., pp. 264 ff.
[124] Frain du Tremblay, *Discours*, p. 49.
[125] Le Père P. Le Moyne, *Peintures morales*, 2 vols. (Paris, 1643–5), I, 243.

Art was a much easier domain for the Church to control because so many images were produced for its own buildings. Books on the other hand presented a different sort of problem. If they were produced by clerics, as I shall demonstrate in another chapter of this book, the Church stood a better chance of overseeing their content, although this was not always the case. If books on religious subjects were produced by secular writers, control was much more difficult. For works of a secular nature, the control of the Church was non-existent, except in the case of heresy where the matter was covered by the law of the land. The Church thus depended on other sorts of influence, and it could do no more than this. The space of the world could be invested only by those the Church had itself prepared. Even then success could not be counted on. After all, Molière, whose *Le Tartuffe* directed attention to the dangers of allowing the domain of the Church to occupy domestic space, was a pupil of the Jesuits. But purely secular values, relayed by secular forms of literature over which the Church had no control, could be countered solely by educating the laity to reject those values and to espouse the cause of religion in all areas of life. Control had in this case to be self-control. Hence the importance of schooling and the involvement of the religious orders in forming the hearts and minds of the young who were eventually to inhabit and govern the space of the world.

3　The spaces of education

Introduction

If one of the working premisses of this study is the aim of the Church to occupy the space of the world to the extent that the Church's frontiers were conterminous with those of the kingdom, then education must be one of its success stories. Through schooling, the Church managed to embed itself in society in a way that it would never again be able to repeat. Apart from the academies attended by the nobility and a measure of private tuition, the Church, either in the shape of the religious orders or in the shape of episcopal authority, had the monopoly of education in the seventeenth century. Education was offered at one level in the 'petites écoles' which, originally the responsibility of the municipal authorities, came increasingly under the auspices of the bishops in the last quarter of the sixteenth century. They taught the rudiments of reading, writing and arithmetic, with an emphasis on civility. The colleges of the Jesuits and the colleges attached to the University of Paris taught in their own way courses in Latin and Greek grammar, the classical humanities and rhetoric, and also courses on Thomist/Aristotelian philosophy and science. The Jesuits added theology to the college curriculum. In both institutions a fluent knowledge of Latin was of the essence. The universities trained entrants to the liberal professions, including the clergy.[1] Alongside these institutions others were created in the course of the century with more or less specific aims of their own, but which often taught courses similar to those just described.

That the Church aimed to 'fill the space' with its educational establishments is evident in the geographical penetration of schools in our period. By 1710 the share of the religious orders in the establishment of colleges for boys was the following: Jesuits 117; Oratorians 72; Lazaristes 78; and the fathers of the Christian Doctrine 48.[2] In the north-east of France the

---

[1] See in particular L. W. B. Brockliss, *French Higher Education in the Seventeenth and Eighteenth Centuries: a Cultural History* (Oxford, 1987) and 'Richelieu, Education and the State', in J. Bergin and L. Brockliss (eds.), *Richelieu and his Age* (Oxford, 1992), pp. 237–72.

[2] J. de Viguerie, *Une Œuvre d'éducation sous l'Ancien Régime: les pères de la doctrine chrétienne en France et en Italie, 1592–1792* (Paris, 1976), p. 75.

Oratorians had twelve establishments in addition to those of the Minimes, Chanoines réformés and others. The orders also competed with each other in the same town such as in Reims, Metz and Pont-à-Mousson.[3] The schools of Jean-Baptiste de la Salle, the founder of the order of the frères des Ecoles chrétiennes, were established on an almost annual basis from 1679 to 1718, reaching from Paris, Reims and Troyes to Avignon, Grenoble and Marseille. A school established in Montreal in Canada was not a success.

Coverage, however, could never be complete. Charles Dupin's map of 1826 shows a north–south divide, with a greater participation in the north than in the south. But education tended on the whole to follow the centres of economic activity where the population was denser and, consequently, even in the south, schools became established in those areas where economic activity was high.[4] The Jesuits showed themselves to be motivated by more than reasons simply deriving from the struggle with the Protestants for the hearts and minds of the faithful, being just as anxious to implant their colleges where the Reformation had not taken root. They were particularly sensitive not only to local feeling but also to financial considerations which might affect the success of their schools.[5] An unevenness of schooling emerged therefore both between and within regions.

The relationship with the civil authorities was not always easy or even co-operative. As in all aspects of French life in the seventeenth century corporate hostility could not be ruled out. The status of the schools of the Christian Doctrine in particular became a problem because school-teachers did not constitute a 'corps de métier' and a school existed only by a contract established either with the municipality or with the Bureaux des pauvres. This eventually brought them into conflict with the maîtres-écrivains who regarded themselves as having a monopoly of the teaching of writing and the rudiments of arithmetic and accountancy.[6] Corporate hostility could be found within the Church. The University of Paris fiercely opposed the spread of Jesuit schools in particular and attempted to suppress schools which extended the curriculum beyond the rudiments and which retained pupils beyond the age of nine.[7]

Religion and order

The Church's educational programme should first be seen in its broad contribution. The schools provided the opportunity for a large measure of

---

[3] F. de Dainville, 'Collèges et fréquentation scolaire au XVIIe siècle', Population, 12 (1957), 467–94 (pp. 467–8).   [4] Chartier (ed.), L'Education, p. 16.   [5] Ibid., pp. 165–8.
[6] Y. Poutet, Le XVIIe siècle et les origines lasalliennes, 2 vols. (Rennes, 1970), II, 77.
[7] H. C. Barnard (ed.), The Port-Royalistes on Education (Cambridge, 1918), p. 5.

social control, a usefulness recognised by contemporaries. For the Protestant Barbeyrac, knowledge and letters remedy idleness, especially in those who, because of their wealth, do not need to work; because boredom would soon find an outlet in crime and debauchery, the pursuit of knowledge needed urgently to find a place of credit and honour.[8] On the Catholic side, Henri Lelevel identified the bad education of youth as the source of disorder in civil life, a point of view shared by Pierre Coustel, who had been associated with the educational experiments of Port-Royal.[9] Schools were popular with the authorities because at least the *internes* of the colleges were kept off the streets and were subject to the discipline of the school, although an element of disorder certainly remained.[10] At another level, schools provided a means of controlling mendicant children for whom they took on the shape of a sort of workhouse.[11] Charles Démia, founder of the charitable schools of Lyon, saw the schooling of the poor, increasingly seen as a threat, as useful to social order.[12] In that sense there was no frontier between the lay and religious sectors of society which were working to the same end.

The essential element of the schools' programme was, however, religious. Not that the role of religion in the schools could be separated in any absolute sense from the idea of social order. Education, Coustel claims, is necessary for the peace of mind of parents and families, the tranquillity of the state, and also for the glory and honour of the Church. A Christian education covers all the activities of the social space, and encourages a child in later life to be faithful to the institution of marriage, to be honest and dutiful in business, circumspect in the least of his actions and assiduous in his parish.[13] Religion and civility are inseparable.

The religious orientation of schools derived in part from the need to maintain the hegemony of Catholicism in French society. For that purpose pupils were required to be equipped with 'une solide doctrine propre à fortifier la foi et à nourrir la piété'.[14] In this perspective the struggle against heresy completely determined the educational ideology of the Jesuits which provided pupils in later life with the tools necessary for an adequate defence of the faith.[15] Arnauld complained that the bad education in the humanities received by Catholic theologians, along with

---

[8] J. Barbeyrac, *Discours sur l'utilité des lettres & des sciences par rapport à l'état* (Geneva, 1714), p. 15.

[9] H. Lelevel, *Entretiens sur ce qui forme l'honneste homme et le vray sçavant* (Paris, 1690), p. 29, and P. Coustel, *Traité d'éducation chrétienne et littéraire*, 2 vols. (Paris, 1749), I, 52–3.

[10] Brockliss, *French Higher Education*, pp. 93 and 100–2.

[11] Chartier (ed.), *L'Education*, p. 57.

[12] Ibid., p. 60.

[13] Coustel, *Traité d'éducation*, pp. 15–17.

[14] F. de Dainville, *L'Education des Jésuites XVIe–XVIIIe siècles* (Paris, 1978), p. 28.

[15] Ibid., p. 40.

the consequences for the knowledge of philosophy and theology, meant that they were so intellectually inferior to their Protestant counterparts that the honour of the Church could not be sustained, thus in turn encouraging error.[16] None the less the general theory was that if ignorance produced error and superstition, then in reverse, schooling and catechising could implant religion.[17] The school could eliminate the frontier between the secular and the religious.

Richelieu was particularly interested in the quality of religious education emanating from the institutions under the auspices of the Church. One of the small number of bishops of his generation who had received a religious training of any depth, he saw in the Paris Faculty of Theology an ideal opportunity to revitalise the French Church. Unfortunately the quality of its education left a great deal to be desired. Richelieu thus undertook to raise the social and intellectual status of theological studies by renovating the Sorbonne and taking a keen interest in elections to chairs.[18] Richelieu's educational aims in the field of religious training cannot be seen outside the context of the influence he brought to bear on the appointment of bishops who were increasingly better versed in theology.[19]

An adequate defence of the faith could not be divorced from questions of orthodoxy. Jesuit institutions regarded themselves as its guardians in all areas of knowledge and their attitude to orthodoxy was that it could not be seen to offer accommodation for different positions within itself. This was particularly true in the domain of scientific knowledge: while many pressures for change emerged amidst challenges to the Thomist / Aristotelian synthesis at the centre of their teaching, the educational programme the Jesuits offered could not start from a position of flexibility. It was impossible for the cause of orthodoxy to be furthered in an atmosphere of uncertainty or at least in an atmosphere where anything but a dogmatic truth could be asserted. Eventually Jesuit schools could not remain immune from those pressures. But Thomism and Aristotelianism survived much longer among the Jesuits than others. Even where the principles of the teaching of science may have differed from those of the Jesuits, as with many Oratorians of a radical Augustinian persuasion, the integral link between science and religion was just as firmly held.[20]

Naturally, a more direct education in the faith and religious practice

[16] A. Arnauld (ed. A Gazier), *Mémoire sur le règlement des études* (Paris, 1886), p. 5.
[17] Julia, 'La Réforme', 364.
[18] Brockliss, 'Richelieu', 252–6.
[19] See J. Bergin, 'Richelieu and his Bishops? Ministerial Power and Episcopal Patronage under Louis XIII', in J. Bergin and L. Brockliss (eds.), *Richelieu and his Age*, 175–202.
[20] See Robert G. Remsberg, *Wisdom and Science at Port-Royal and the Oratory: a Study of Contrasting Augustinianisms* (Yellow Springs, Ohio, 1940), p. 151.

was as important as, if not more important than, the practical aspects of the curriculum. For example, the aim of the fathers of the Christian Doctrine was firmly to inculcate a sense of good morals, sound doctrine and a knowledge of the articles of faith, with a particular emphasis for César de Bus, one of the founders of the order, on evangelising Protestants.[21] For this purpose the fathers elaborated what they called a 'théologie populaire' which enabled children of all social conditions and of all degrees of intelligence to gain an understanding of the faith proportionate to their rank and station.[22] In this respect the rural school was crucial in the way it supported other forms of instruction in the faith directed at the peasantry. School and catechism become inseparable notions in bringing young people to a greater familiarity with Scripture.[23] The teacher also had to take the children every day to mass. The link between the school and the church is further emphasised by the fact that on every religious feast day and on Sundays the children were to assemble at the school before attending divine office. Thus the children received an apprenticeship in piety and knowledge through catechism on the one hand, and an instruction in religious behaviour on the other.[24]

Although an introduction to proper religious practice through the school was particularly crucial in rural areas given all that has been said in another context, emphasis on religious practice was not limited to the poor and less privileged. In Jesuit and Oratorian schools no less importance was ascribed to the place of mass and prayers in the daily life of the schoolboys. Even at the schools for the *gardes de marine* established in the arsenal ports of Brest, Toulon and Rochefort by Henri IV for the purpose of providing a technological education, the cadets began the day by attendance at mass.[25] The two schools of Oriental Languages established by Colbert at Constantinople and Smyrna were run by Capuchins and one cannot imagine that instruction in faith and religious practice was neglected there either. Port-Royal was true to the position on the need for a sincere receptiveness to the spirit of the Eucharist in that the pupils of the *petites écoles* were under no obligation to attend mass on a daily basis: even on religious festivals it was an obligation only in the case of those who were thought worthy of receiving the sacraments.[26]

Indeed, we have already observed that the Church always had an interest in the behaviour of the faithful outside its own immediate space.

[21] Viguerie, *Une Oeuvre d'éducation*, pp. 45 and 67.
[22] Ibid., p. 400.
[23] Chartier (ed.), *L'Education*, p. 3.
[24] Ibid., pp. 124–5.
[25] James E. King, *Science and Rationalism in the Government of Louis XIV, 1661–1683* (Baltimore, 1949), p. 276.
[26] H. C. Barnard, *The Little Schools of Port-Royal* (Cambridge, 1913), p. 84.

The originality of the Counter-Reformation Church, drawing on the theories of Erasmus, is to have universalised a notion of civility which had previously been associated with models directed towards the Court and to social, therefore secular, differentiation among the élite. The sermon and the catechism, centred on knowledge of the faith, were complemented in the educational programme by an apprenticeship in moral conduct which, through the attempted control of dangerous behaviour and the sort of affectivity which produces it, acted as a means of policing a society still threatened by violence. A sign of this originality is La Salle's *Règles de la bienséance et de la civilité chrétienne à l'usage des écoles chrétiennes* (1703), the first book to include the religious reference to civility in its title, thus clearly merging the christianising intention of the school with a notion of social conduct.[27] The Counter-Reformation added to its control of belief a control of the body.

But ideally, the teacher assumed the policing of domestic space since domestic space was considered to be an extension of the school. This, as Chartier points out, is the reverse of the original intention of Erasmus's text of civility which was rather for use in the home and which was to encourage a new form of social life. The integration of an apprenticeship in behaviour along with arithmetic, writing and prayer was part of the surveillance of the child facilitated by the organisation of school space into group instruction.[28] This surveillance was in one school manual evident in the physical layout of the parish school where a screened window enabled the teacher to observe the behaviour of his children even out of class.[29] The presence and visibility of the school as a controlling mechanism for social behaviour complemented the visibility of the Church in terms of belief. The link between the two was the role of the school in encouraging appropriate behaviour in the space of the sacred, and as they passed from one space to another in procession through the streets.[30] In this sense the school was an extension of the church, but the space in between was also 'sanctified' by well-regulated behaviour, in turn the product of a teaching whose initiative came from the Church itself. The behaviour of the children would constitute a visible sign of its occupation of all social space. This worked in various ways. The school became 'une seconde demeure'.[31] At Port-Royal the school was not so much an extension of the home as a substitute for it. Pupils were accepted on condition that the school took total charge of the pupil, the family thus ceding its rights. At Saint-Cyr, family visits were very strictly regulated for fear that they might

---

[27] Chartier (ed.), *L'Education*, p. 138.
[28] Chartier (ed.), *A History of Private Life*, III, 178.
[29] Chartier (ed.), *L'Education*, p. 120.
[30] Ibid., pp. 124–5.   [31] Ibid., p. 145.

interrupt the atmosphere of the institution.[32] Whatever the case, education through the schools was meant to act as a control on domestic space by sending the children as examples back to the home, or by acting as exemplary 'homes' themselves.

The link between schooling and the control of social behaviour which I have examined here was not regarded as absolute in all cases. Certainly, many of the contracts of the schools of the Christian Doctrine made specific mention of duty and obedience to the king, and in this way reflected the Aristotelian conception of education as in harmony with the political order. Eventually, by the end of the Ancien Régime, mention of politically good intentions had disappeared in favour of education in belles-lettres rather than in piety, doctrine and good morals.[33] La Salle hardly ever insisted on the duties of the king's subjects, although he was shrewd enough to enlist the king's protection.[34] When, for purely anti-Protestant reasons, Louis XIV made schooling compulsory (even he could hardly discriminate between the two faiths on that score), La Salle made it quite clear to his brothers that in the case of absenteeism they should neither have recourse to the civil authorities nor even bring pressure of a religious nature to bear on parents, but rather emphasise the secular value of education.[35]

Indeed, Furet and Ozouf point to the tension between the secular and the religious which seems to emerge from La Salle's perspective on education. On the one hand the school with its religious finality sought to 'root orthodox Catholic piety in instruction'; yet on the other it embodied an instrumental way of thought which was 'concerned to normalise social behaviour through the internalising of a practical morality with a few simple rules'. They conclude that in all the 'normative' writings of the Ancien Régime 'one senses something like an anticipation of Victorian morality; a kind of socialised, secularised Christianity, reduced to the control of morality and behaviour'.[36] There are perhaps other implications in this conclusion. Accommodating the social space within the domain of the Church through education involved a risk. The two halves of the equation could never retain equal status while secular demands and aspirations, encouraged by the success of the institution of the school, grew in an increasingly more complex society. The 'need for an education' outstripped the need for religion. The success of the Church in education contributed towards weakening the influence of the school as a purely religious institution.

[32] See ibid., p. 243.   [33] Viguerie, Une Oeuvre d'éducation, p. 328.
[34] Poutet, Le XVIIe siècle, II, 41–5.   [35] Ibid., pp. 57–8.
[36] F. Furet and J. Ozouf, Reading and Writing: Literacy in France from Calvin to Jules Ferry (Cambridge, 1982), p. 61.

School and state

The presence of the Church as a force in society was greatly strengthened by its penetration of the world in the form of education which offered the ideal means to 'regiment the faithful'. Schooling acted not only as a means of control within the context of belief but also in the adaptation of that belief to all walks of life and in ways which benefited the secular powers. In an ideal perspective schooling was a totalising phenomenon within society. This would be equally if not more true of Protestant than Catholic education. The Church performed a signal service to society in providing it either with the future cadres of state government or with a workforce armed with the rudiments of reading, writing and arithmetic.

One might think therefore that, given the possible influence of schooling on the maintenance of social order, the state itself would wish to take a controlling interest in it. Royal authority did from time to time intervene, but not with a view to interfering with the internal organisation or curriculum of schools. In general, royal power held itself aloof from the creation of schools where the important transaction took place between the municipality and the religious orders. Indeed, the absence of direct state intervention led to a broad degree of lay involvement. In the Paris diocese predominantly lay initiatives contributed to the establishment of petites écoles.[37] The field was also left open for shadowy organisations such as the Compagnie du Saint-Sacrement which was involved in the establishment of the first school of Charles Démia (he was himself a member) in Lyon,[38] and which was also associated with La Salle in Rouen and Paris.[39] La Salle in addition had relations with the Aas, the secret Marian societies of the Jesuits.[40]

There was certainly no government policy in the sense that we would understand it today apart from occasional encouragement or reward, as in the case of La Salle who became responsible for the education of the Irish children who followed James II into exile.[41] There was not even an overall Church policy since schooling was in any case the prerogative of sections of the Church who owed their allegiance to different authorities. The Jesuits did not, for example, come under the jurisdiction of the bishops who, on the other hand, could influence education in their dioceses through the petites écoles in particular but only on a local basis. It is for this reason more than any other that schooling in the kingdom was uneven. But, apart from these considerations, a good deal of agreement existed on what the schools should teach, what they stood for and their role in society

[37] Ferté, La Vie religieuse, pp. 233–4.
[38] Chartier (ed.), L'Education, pp. 60–1.   [39] Poutet, Le XVIIe siècle, II, 295 and 302.
[40] Ibid., p. 355.   [41] Ibid., p. 43.

at large. Despite differences of emphasis a certain homogenisation of the space of education was achieved.

In fact royal authority, along with some individuals or corporate bodies, was concerned that the growth of schools in the seventeenth century would be detrimental in some way to commerce and agriculture in particular, as the representatives of the French clergy argued in 1614 and the University of Paris in 1624, but the latter was anyway anxious about the competition from the Jesuits in particular with its *collèges de plein exercice*. While Guez de Balzac too set out the commercial reasons in his complaint that the school population would only end up engaging in court cases, dialectic or poetry, Richelieu added a political consideration in his analysis of the problem in the *Testament*, where he asserts that indiscriminate access to learning would simply produce pride and disobedience.[42] Richelieu also wanted to reduce the number of colleges attached to the University, and succeeded.[43] The problem with a more educated population was that it was less easily controlled. Whether the subversive aspects of schooling were uppermost in Colbert's mind is in precise terms unknown, but under Louis XIV two inquiries were launched with a view to decreasing the number of schools, but the desire of the merchant and minor officer class to educate their sons proved too strong even for royal power.[44] At this level a clear correlation can be established between education and the groups who already had influence and power in society, and who wanted to keep it.

On the other hand, while it is true that there was alarm at the number of schools, the latter did provide the state with the manpower it required and the necessary mentality for the state's own survival. Brockliss argues forcefully in favour of the view that schools, in turning out lawyers and clerics imbued with an absolutist theory of power, were centres of orthodoxy which eventually helped create and support the monarchical conception of law which, before the Fronde, did not command universal consent.[45] Moreover, the colleges and the University constituted the predominant means of cultural exchange which meant that the influence of institutionalised education was of exceptional importance: 'at no time before the French Revolution was it possible for any but a few members of the intelligentsia to reject the cultural inheritance of their school days'.[46]

Schools thus provided an effective indoctrination of the élite through all aspects of the curriculum which conditioned the pupil 'in the belief that

[42] Dainville, 'Collèges et fréquentation scolaire', 475.
[43] Brockliss, 'Richelieu', 250.
[44] Dainville, 'Collèges et fréquentation scolaire', 475.
[45] Brockliss, *French Higher Education*, p. 449.
[46] Ibid., p. 4.

the path of righteousness lay in being obedient and subservient to his parents, the Church, and above all divinely constituted authority'.[47] The school replicated in its teaching the views of secular power. In a sense it is difficult to see how the situation could have been otherwise since, as Brockliss himself admits, exposure to alternatives, within the social order at least, scarcely existed. This 'indoctrination' was up to a point more likely to be reinforcement. Rather than seeing the situation as from the school outwards, Rabb links the school and social order from the outside in: 'the most striking evidence of the belief in knowledge as an agent of comprehension and thus of control was the extraordinary migration into higher education'.[48] It may well be that self-interest rather than indoctrination ensured that the educated would continue to support the crown and that alternatives would begin to have an attraction once the crown failed to serve those interests. School would then no longer have the same purpose. This is far from being the case in the seventeenth century where it seems inevitable that secular and religious space should in this perspective serve each other.

Another view of education in our period is, however, possible. It is precisely among the members of a cultivated élite that one might expect to find the seeds of discord, particularly in questions concerning orthodoxy. Evidence does not allow us to establish a dividing line between those who were orthodox or heterodox on the basis of where they went to school. In this sense Brockliss's model seems too mechanical and deterministic. As A. C. Kors makes clear in his discussion of atheism, the Church could not control the awesome consequences of its undertaking in education, and 'those who dissented from received culture and creed had been formed by received culture and creed'.[49] The very fears of Richelieu in fact. The education of a social élite outside the nobility itself turned out to be a double-edged sword.

Schooling and social groups

Within the limitations imposed by a way of life or by the geographical vastness of the kingdom, the Church managed in some degree to reach, through its various types of school, all sections of the French population, an especially crucial factor if schooling was to function as a form of social control. In addition, if the concern of the Church was with orthodoxy and,

---

[47] Ibid., p. 179.
[48] Theodore K. Rabb, *The Struggle for Stability in Early Modern Europe* (New York, 1975), p. 55.
[49] A. C. Kors, *Atheism in France, 1650–1729*, vol. I *The Orthodox Sources of Disbelief* (Princeton, 1990), 288.

as a consequence, with the homogenisation of social space, then the aim of schooling ought to be universal within that social space. To what degree was this the case? Which sections of the population went to school and what schools did they go to? The first point to make is that education was not compulsory in France of the Ancien Régime, except as an exceptional measure after the Revocation of the Edict of Nantes in 1685. While it is true that Démia may have recruited only a small proportion of children in Lyon by the beginning of the eighteenth century, he did succeed on the other hand in getting some of the poorest sections of the population into his schools. At the same time the efforts of La Salle testify to the immense effort put into reaching beyond the élite sections of society, far more than had previously ever been the case.[50]

As far as the colleges were concerned, the population of the schools was overwhelmingly bourgeois in the middle with a smaller percentage of sons of nobles and sons of artisans or *laboureurs* at each end, although regional variations prevent any secure generalisation.[51] A natural frontier therefore existed between this group and the mass of the population who remained illiterate, and between the highly cultured and those 'who had either not assimilated that [cultural] inheritance or had at best been casually introduced to its delights'.[52] The universalisation of education did nothing, and was not intended, to bridge that gap. The Church thus found itself, in a sense, helping to maintain a social status quo which was in any case built into its own ranks. It served perfectly the conservatism of secular society.

The education of the aristocracy was a rather more straightforward affair. It became apparent in the course of the century that the nobles required an education beyond music, dancing and fencing, which would equip them to carry out their public duties, particularly in the important offices they often held.[53] One contemporary Protestant writer, Crouzas, is particularly eloquent on the improvement of the nobles through education, in particular regarding their capacity to govern.[54] The impulse for the education of the nobility came from Henri IV himself who was happy to confide that education to the Jesuits of La Flèche whose less confrontational oratorical style would ultimately form a more docile court.[55] Again, education acted in the eyes of authority as a form of social control, a control through culture. In 1607, 500 sons of dukes, marquesses or counts accounted for 40 per cent of the school population of La Flèche. Later at

[50] Chartier (ed.), *L'Education*, p. 84.
[51] Dainville, 'Collèges et fréquentation scolaire', 478.
[52] Brockliss, *French Higher Education*, p. 7.
[53] Chartier (ed.), *L'Education*, p. 168.
[54] J.-P. de Crousaz, *Traité de l'éducation des enfans*, 2 vols. (The Hague, 1722), I, 326–7.
[55] Fumaroli, *L'Age de l'éloquence*, pp. 241–2.

the Collège de Clermont 300 of the *internes* belonged to the high-ranking nobility. But in the time of Louis XIII, nobles did not tend to remain long at schools of this sort. They went instead to academies where they learnt the physical skills associated with the nobility, but also elements of geography and mathematics which would be useful for their main role in life, the military defence of the kingdom. Three such academies remained at the end of the seventeenth century.[56] What is important here is that the academies constituted a separate space with a more directly secular aim. Within the universalising concept of education under the Counter-Reformation, the academies formed an enclave which escaped the direct control of the Church.

In their secular capacities, both Richelieu and Mazarin desired to bring a 'moralised' and less rough and ready nobility into the service of the state. To this end a constitution was drafted in 1636 for an Académie royale established for young nobles which would be situated in the rue Vieille-du-Temple in Paris.[57] Richelieu felt especially that the educational system of his day was wholly inappropriate for the nobility, and in 1640 founded an academy in the town of Richelieu. While it had a chaplain and chapel, the professors could not discuss religion in their courses. The institution aimed to educate pupils 'en la crainte de Dieu, en la fidélité, et en l'obéissance au Roy'. The academy folded at his death.[58] Mazarin was similarly motivated in founding the Collège des quatre nations in 1661. Although this was clearly a secular institution, religion was not neglected as one of the 'moralising' features. Again good conduct was associated with a knowledge of the faith in all its orthodoxy. The programme of the academy would have included the humanities as well as physical exercise, and here, inevitably, Mazarin ran into the opposition of the University which saw the state as encroaching on its domain.[59]

One category of the population which did not benefit from the same level of education as others was girls. This situation largely derived from a view of women as intellectually unable to take advantage of the sort of education offered to boys, and a view of the social role of the female as possessing a uniquely domestic vocation. An educated woman would be a source of disruption in the social order. Girls were thus in principle excluded from pursuing certain avenues open to their male counterparts. Only a few, and those of a particular rank in society, managed to cross the frontier separating 'male' and 'female' knowledge. That frontier, in itself a form of social control, was generally maintained by a theologically and socially driven ideology. Towards the end of the century attitudes certainly changed. Contemporaries were conscious of the shortcomings in

[56] Chartier (ed.), *L'Education*, pp. 169–71 and 179–81.   [57] Ibid., p. 183.
[58] Brockliss, 'Richelieu', 243–5.   [59] Chartier (ed.), *L'Education*, pp. 183–5.

female education. Poullain de la Barre, a champion of the cause of women, largely on the basis of the universal concept of intelligence contained in Descartes's *Discours de la méthode*, declares that the exclusion of women from study derives from ignorance and self-interest, especially since he has found nothing in the New Testament to support that exclusion.[60] But the traditional attitude remained strong and Fleury, for example, ranks women alongside the poor who would be provided simply with the most basic rudiments of knowledge.[61]

Some occupied a position in between which did not challenge the social role of women, but which held that within that role an education of a certain level was crucial. A major aspect of the education of girls remained fundamentally religious (including presumably lessons on the reasons for their own submission to male authority, including father, husband and Church). Instruction in religion almost to the exclusion of other subjects was the rule at Port-Royal where the girls were subjected to a particularly harsh régime.[62] A place was, however, increasingly assigned to subjects related to the role of the woman in the home. The most celebrated female educational institution was undoubtedly that of Madame de Maintenon at Saint-Cyr which was open to 250 daughters of the poor aristocracy who could prove four quarters of nobility. But the educational programme offered there reflected very much the limitations set on the education of women elaborated by even as enlightened a person as Fénelon, providing instruction in what was required for domestic duties, that is to say the rudiments of reading and writing, and the knowledge of arithmetic necessary to keep accounts and memoranda.[63]

But a fundamental problem arose with the education of girls. Who would teach them, especially if they needed to be sought out in order to be taught? The Church was after all overwhelmingly male. Moreover, it was strictly forbidden to teach girls alongside boys. These sorts of pressures eventually led to the breakdown of the hostility to new forms of female religious order I have already outlined. And indeed the proliferation of female teaching orders in the course of the century was quite astonishing. Their geographical base, in the first instance, was largely a function of the success of the Reformation in certain parts of France, and more particularly of the success of the Reformation among women. The Midi, then, was initially the principal arena for the implantation of these new orders in the kingdom. Some were local creations, such as the Filles de Notre Dame

---

[60] F. Poullain de la Barre, *De l'Education des dames pour la conduite de l'esprit dans les sciences et dans les moeurs* (Paris, 1674), p. 36.
[61] Fleury, *Traité*, pp. 109–10.
[62] Barnard (ed.), *The Port-Royalistes*, p. 33.
[63] W. Gibson, *Women in Seventeenth-Century France* (Basingstoke, 1989), p. 20.

who originated in Bordeaux. But in 1700 the Ursulines numbered 10–12,000 nuns in some 320 communities, thus adding greatly to the visibility of the Church throughout France.[64] Between 1660 and 1715 at least seventeen female teaching orders were founded. The occupation of the space of the kingdom undertaken by the Church in the hope of bringing orthodoxy to the whole population became both a male and female concern.

In essence the Church yielded to the need to teach girls an understanding of the faith, and the parish clergy could not shoulder that burden alone. But the teaching of religion was composed of more than just the truths of religion and addressed a way of life. The catechism was one element among others which was more related to the behaviour of children as Christians and citizens. Young girls would reform their families, their families would reform their provinces and their provinces would reform the world. In this perspective, the female teaching orders specifically proscribed teaching for the religious life.[65] Crouzas (in this instance his Protestantism is significant) extends this exemplarity to the education of women as acting as a control on the behaviour of men and of young children.[66] While Chartier on the other hand suggests that such a view was not universal in the schooling of young girls, since the whole pedagogy of the Visitandines was geared to the encouragement of vocations, a general view emerged in the course of the century that women should be taught because they were the teachers in the home. A place had therefore to be given to writing, grammar and arithmetic.[67] In any case the education of girls, and therefore of future wives and mothers, was for the Church the most effective way of extending its domain into domestic space.

The space of the school

So far I have considered the degree of presence constituted by the Church through its implantation in society by means of the school and the ways in which the aims of the school coincided with those of civil authority. I should now like to discuss how, in other ways, a predominantly religious institution saw its own space in relation to the world outside. What was the nature of that frontier constituted by the walls of the college or the school in terms of the life to be lived by the pupil? What did the school represent as a space?

One view of the school holds that the success of the educational programme lies in its isolation from the world, and this position is

[64] See Rapley, The Dévotes, pp. 42–3.   [65] Ibid., pp. 155–7.
[66] Crousaz, Traité, I, 58–9.   [67] Chartier (ed.), L'Education, pp. 236 and 232.

supported by the concept of childhood as in itself sinful rather than innocent, a concept which can be found in the works of the Fathers, notably St Augustine.[68] Such a concept indeed legitimates the school, especially from the religious viewpoint, as a means of control. What Snyders calls this 'pesanteur naturelle' of the child further legitimates cutting him off from the world and placing him in an environment which maximises the possibility of surveillance, for evil constantly threatens to insinuate itself into the child's soul.[69] One problem with this model is that the vast majority of boys in the colleges were *externes* and therefore lived in the world at home or in lodgings. Snyders maintains however that the *internat* was the model for the whole school, especially in view of the fact that those who lived in the school were selected and separated from those living outside for fear of 'contamination'. If this was indeed the case, then the pedagogic world was a closed world, where surveillance operated not only between teacher and pupil but between pupils to the point that delation was encouraged. In fact the *externes* themselves did not escape the watchful eye of the *préfet des études* who could surprise and inspect them at any moment in their place of residence.[70]

The closed nature of this institutional world extended even to aspects of the curriculum where the role of Latin as the medium of education, even in the pronunciation of French, contributed to the school as cut off from the world. But Latin had another function: in a pedagogy which was itself based on the surveillance of the pupil and which operated according to learning a set of rules, Latin prevented the spontaneous expression of the pupil.[71] In addition, the procedures of rhetoric, with its commonplaces and archetypes, were aimed at distancing the pupil from the real world he inhabited in order to place him in an ideal one.[72] This ideal world was created through a linguistic training which, in channelling the pupils towards a common and predefined goal, eliminated individual differences.[73]

Access to the works of authors was also strictly controlled and filtered through anthologies of extracts. Schools performed a sort of cultural screening process. But was this closed world not detrimental to the education of a child who had eventually to emerge from this cocoon? Not according to Snyders, who argues that the world outside the college demanded few technical skills of the pupils who were for the most part destined for offices which did not require proof of competence and which were acquired through purchase or inheritance.[74]

[68] G. Snyders, *La Pédagogie en France aux XVIIe et XVIIIe siècles* (Paris, 1965), p. 181.
[69] Ibid., pp. 42–4.   [70] Ibid., pp. 36–41.   [71] Ibid., pp. 68–71.
[72] Ibid., p. 118.   [73] Ibid., p. 122.
[74] Ibid., p. 145.

Snyders's model has its strengths as an analysis of the educational world of the seventeenth century. It possesses a certain accuracy as far as Jesuit education is concerned and by a strange paradox is true also of the attitude towards the pupils of Port-Royal. This is not surprising for a group which regarded the world as particularly hostile to the true Christian life. The small number of pupils in the *petites écoles* was meant in itself to facilitate their surveillance although, in contrast to the world of the Jesuits, punishments were relatively mild.[75] Moreover, the original location of the schools in the countryside was to remove the children from an urban environment where the dangers of the world were much to be feared. Indeed the emphasis on environment and example led some Jansenist educators to condemn travel as an educational agency.[76]

Other points of Snyders's analysis merit some attention. The teaching of orthodoxy as a universally valid set of beliefs could only be effective if they were seen as allowing of no deviation from a norm. The environment of an education which acted as the vehicle of that orthodoxy had therefore to reflect that universality. The encouragement of individual expression undermined the commonality so essential to the identity and strength of Catholicism of which the pupils were destined to be the articulate defenders. Subjects in the curriculum, especially as they were expressed according to the rules of rhetoric, were learnt rather than explored. Orthodoxy could only be handed down as an integrated whole with no possibility of individual interpretation being regarded as the starting point for discussion. In that context surveillance was essential, and in any case we have seen in other parts of this discussion how behaviour, even of adults, was closely watched over the whole range of social activity. Schooling thus became an apprenticeship in the realisation that one's actions did not escape, in one way or another, the eye of the Church. The school became what Foucault calls an 'observatory': 'The exercise of discipline presupposes a mechanism that coerces by means of observation; an apparatus in which the techniques that make it possible to see induce effects of power, and in which, conversely, the means of coercion make those on whom they are applied clearly visible.'[77] The knowledge that one was subject to control induced self-control.

But Snyders's model is defective as a universal description of the space of the school. Indeed its weakness is that it is mostly appropriate, and even then on a limited scale, to the colleges of the Jesuits where, for example, teaching in Latin for every subject and at all levels is applicable in their case alone. Port-Royal encouraged teaching in the vernacular, as did the

[75] Barnard (ed.), *The Port-Royalistes*, p. 26.
[76] Barnard, *The Little Schools*, pp. 76–8.
[77] M. Foucault, *Discipline and Punish: the Birth of the Prison* (New York, 1977), pp. 170–1.

Oratorians up to a certain point in the school when Latin then became the language of teaching and learning. Even in the colleges, the principal object of his analysis, it would have been impossible to insulate children from the world they knew and to which they returned. Parts of the curriculum were indeed turned towards aspects of the world, however limited these might have been in the context of our state of knowledge. The teaching of geography in the *collèges de plein exercice* transcended Europe and the Mediterranean, and teachers had to correct the mistakes of the old geography in the light of modern discoveries. They included in their analyses details about a country's government, mores, economy and religion, so that the geography course became a lesson in current affairs.[78] Lelevel thought it essential that the world, with all its fragility and ridiculous features, should be revealed to the child as quickly as possible rather than the curtain being drawn little by little.[79]

The impossibility of maintaining the closure of the system is revealed in the Jesuits' realisation that some public demonstration of their success with the boys would be the best publicity for their pedagogic methods. Pupils were therefore trained for performances of ballet. Plays were performed before parents and ecclesiastical dignitaries at the end of the school year, and performances were even open to the public at large, thus earning a rebuke from a variety of religious moralists in the course of the century. Many of these plays included references to contemporary events which spectators could not fail to miss.[80] Even Snyders has to admit that within the world of education a tension existed between enclosure and exercises which were rooted in the world. Quite simply the world could not be kept out of the school. The religious could not exist as an autonomous domain, and the frontier between the secular and the sacred had to be crossed. This, in the case of the Jesuits at least, was the price of continuing success. Indeed, on a more general level, the variety of models of education – and I have not mentioned those who were taught privately and not therefore removed at all from their home environment – do not allow for universal models of closure or of any other sort. La Salle's schools, admittedly of a different order from the colleges, were deliberately turned towards the world through work, since he became convinced of the value of manual work not only as a source of income but as a discipline. One Paris school was connected with a factory.[81] Nor was the intention of the brothers in any way to remove the child from his own milieu.[82]

[78] Brockliss, *French Higher Education*, p. 154.
[79] Lelevel, *Entretiens*, pp. 130–1.
[80] F. de Dainville, 'Allégorie et actualité sur les trétaux des Jésuites', in J. Jacquot (ed.), *Dramaturgie et société*, vol. II (Paris, 1968), 433–43 (p. 442).
[81] Poutet, *Le XVIIe siècle*, II, 22–6.
[82] Ibid., p. 78.

If the school reached into the space of society by sending 'new' pupils back into their domestic environment which would be changed by their example, the teachers generally speaking remained separate from the world they themselves set out to transform. While they were concerned to provide children with practical skills useful to society, teachers could be said to be acting in a world of which they were not fully a part, thus extending that frontier between the priest and his flock. This was particularly the case when the overwhelming amount of teaching was carried out by men and women in orders of some sort. This was not always so with the *petites écoles* which, in the rural areas in particular, and even in the towns, could be run by lay individuals. But it was usually stipulated, as in the case of Démia's schools, that they should most certainly be single, that is to say widowed without children, or unmarried.[83]

This perhaps holds the key to the more general conception of the teacher as protecting himself against a world which requires changing. Pupils cannot be taught by those who are tempted by the world which is as yet not the ideal space to inhabit. In any case the separation of the teacher from the taught reflected the degree to which the institution of the school was an extension of the space of the Church. Even in the person of the teacher, however, one can glimpse the tension between the secular and the religious which is so central to this whole study, and this tension derives from the different aspirations embodied in the institution of the school. At first the teacher was considered in his religious role, especially as the school was regarded as an instrument of christianisation. But from the other end, that is to say from the point of view of the community, the school represented the acquisition of important intellectual skills. Educational policy in our period possessed an inbuilt ambiguity: initially an aspect of Christian conquest, the programme of education undertaken by the Church became emancipated from its religious origins.[84] The seeds of a purely lay education were born, along with the concept of a teacher serving the needs of the community first and then, perhaps, the Church. Secular society would eventually occupy the space of the Church.

The curriculum

If the school is an instrument of christianisation through which orthodoxy can be disseminated, how precisely is this reflected in attitudes towards the curriculum? To what extent do secular and religious demands meet? Clearly, one aim of the school was to promote literacy which in itself could facilitate the absorption and penetration of an understanding of the faith.

[83] Chartier (ed.), *L'Education*, pp. 67–9.
[84] Ibid., pp. 34–5.

But within the general framework of literacy, reading and writing do not possess equal status: 'reading belongs to the domain of religion and morality, writing is an apprenticeship in utility'.[85] Reading is the mode of reception, whereas writing is a medium of expression and, as such, a more dangerous skill. On the other hand reading must be strictly controlled. A literate population has access to all sorts of material which could easily undermine the original purpose of a programme of literacy. This was the paradox at the centre of the Counter-Reformation desire to combat the Reformation through the printed word, by providing the faithful with pious works and catechisms as ways to implant sound doctrine. This is perhaps why the bishops' statutes and ordinances on education emphasise first and foremost the transmission of the content of the Catholic faith rather than the teaching of reading and writing skills.[86] This is yet again a reflection of the distinction between 'representation' and 'participation' that Julia identified in the domain of popular culture. The transmission of the faith involves reception rather than active reproduction. Reading and writing were to be strictly a function of religious instruction and not taught for themselves, in order at all costs to avoid the reading of the wrong sort of text, of either a religious or a profane nature.[87]

The rudiments of literacy constituted one stage, and probably the only stage, of the educational programme for the vast majority of the French population of our period. For another section of society, the more advanced stage of a high degree of articulacy in language was deemed important for the progress of religion in the state. Hence the importance of rhetoric, particularly in the colleges of the Jesuits, and the lesser emphasis placed on erudition which could encourage an introspection leading to moroseness or to excessive mysticism. In this sense, the Jesuits, in opposition to the model of Snyders, are 'tourné[s] vers le monde'.[88] The teaching of rhetoric reflected Jesuit spirituality in that it sought to create not only 'heroes' but 'héros de la parole' whose task it would be to mediate between God and the world.[89] Oratorical skills did not simply display the knowledge of a particular culture but were part of a theory of Christian action through the persuasive use of the word. It was also the means of social action, not only in the production of lawyers, magistrates and royal officials, but in the linguistic training of the nobility whose well-adjusted language would be the basis of brilliant conversation at Court.[90] Where was the point at which the religious initiative in the teaching of rhetoric

---

[85] Furet and Ozouf, *Reading and Writing*, p. 77.
[86] See Chartier (ed.), *L'Education*, p. 10.
[87] Lebrun (ed.), *Histoire des Catholiques*, p. 165.
[88] Fumaroli, *Héros et orateurs*, pp. 84–5.
[89] Ibid., p. 444.   [90] Ibid., p. 90.

served a purely secular usefulness in the eyes of those who availed themselves of this sort of education? Did the Jesuit initiative carry within it the seeds of secularisation, such a frequent reference point in the relationship between Church and culture?

Within the context of the Counter-Reformation, Ignatius of Loyola developed the concept of the conquest of souls through culture. More original was his desire not to confront the learning of the intricacies of the faith by beginning with theology, but to prepare minds for theology through the humanities, philosophy and science.[91] The remarkable aspect of this programme was the place that pagan civilisation was to have in its transmission, so that in schools which had a religious initiative as their foundation much of the content of the curriculum was non-Christian in origin. One of the remarkable features of the Jesuits in particular (they were not alone in this, however) was perhaps to assimilate what was on the face of it anti-religion in order to reinforce religion.[92]

The medium of the Greek and Latin languages posed no problems in itself given the origins of the primitive Church in imperial Rome and the fact that the native language of many of the Fathers was Greek. Greek did however pose one problem. It had to be part of the curriculum since, without it, the truths of the Christian religion would be inaccessible and Catholics would be unable properly to defend the faith against the Protestant heretics.[93] But precisely because a knowledge of Greek had led many into error during the period of humanism and the Reformation, the subject, on the advice of Loyola, had to be treated with caution.[94] There was no doubt on the other hand that the Protestants had been far in advance of their Catholic counterparts who felt the need to catch up.[95] Indeed in the colleges of the University, it was permitted to teach from the New Testament, the Fathers and almost any other text except Aristophanes and Aeschylus.[96]

Profane texts could therefore form part of the curriculum. The important question was how they were taught. From the beginning Loyola opposed the attempt of humanist education to encompass the whole range of ancient art and philosophy, preferring to extract from ancient civilisation only those values which could be considered universal. He arrived therefore at the notion of 'l'antiquité bien comprise', and the teachers

[91] F. de Dainville, *La Naissance de l'humanisme moderne* (Paris, 1940), pp. 21–2.
[92] L. Kolakowski (trans. A. Posner), *Chrétiens sans église: la conscience religieuse et le lien confessionnel au XVIIe siècle* (Paris, 1969), p. 92.
[93] Le Père J. de Jouvancy (trans. H. Ferté), *De la Manière d'apprendre et d'enseigner* (Paris, 1892), p. 2.
[94] Dainville, *La Naissance*, p. 25.
[95] Ibid., pp. 45–6.
[96] Brockliss, *French Higher Education*, pp. 133–4.

would therefore read the texts of ancient civilisation through a Christian teaching.[97] This sort of presentation was generally called 'prélection'. No attempt was made to deny the value of many of the moral teachings of the ancients which could quite easily be assimilable into Christian thought because they did not deny it. The task of the educators was rather to put the works of antiquity to good use and to avoid the excesses which humanist erudition had led to. In that sense the profane could become part of the sacred through a universal and therefore homogenised moral space. At the same time this could only be achieved through a number of exclusions. What was included had to be strictly controlled. The cultural heritage could not be handed down 'en bloc'.

One factor in the use of pagan authors was the teaching of Latin. The Christian sources from which it could be taught were difficult, since they would most often be the works of the Fathers, and too subtle in terms of meaning. The poets of antiquity on the other hand could be assimilated more easily by working on the imagination of the pupils and by offering simple and striking examples of vice and virtue, for at the same time as a linguistic formation, these texts could offer a moral one.[98] Lancelot, a teacher at Port-Royal, specifically states that the Fathers could only be approached after the pupils had been introduced to profane authors first.[99]

But the predominant emphasis on the teaching of the authors of antiquity was the link with the truths of Christianity. There was no way in which the teaching of these authors was in and for itself. That was precisely the problem with a purely secular erudition. The usefulness of the heroes of antiquity was that they often conformed to Christian teaching on mastering the passions and triumphing over adversity, and offered the picture of a world where self-control was essential.[100] By selecting from the texts of the ancients, teachers could point to passages which contained the premisses of Christian thought. The supreme nature of God and his justice, and the truth of the immortality of the soul, could emerge from these texts which illustrate the continuity of the human and the divine, of reason and faith, even of virtue and holiness.[101]

Not all educators stressed the positive use that could be made of the authors of antiquity, but neither did they deny their usefulness. The study of these authors was deemed to be necessary on several counts: to refute their errors, to compare the purity of Christianity with their paganism, to repossess a number of truths which were not rightfully theirs, and to return them to the Church to which they properly belonged.[102] The

---

[97] Dainville, *La Naissance*, p. 27.   [98] Snyders, *La Pédagogie*, p. 63.
[99] Ibid., p. 65.   [100] Ibid., pp. 76–7.   [101] Ibid., pp. 61–5.
[102] Coustel, *Traité*, pp. 10–11.

Oratorian Thomassin, one of the most prominent exponents of this way of thinking, insisted on the Christian nature of the instruction given especially in respect of the authors of antiquity and on reminding pupils of the words of the Fathers to the effect that all the human sciences were as the treasures of Egypt which had been removed so that they could be dedicated to God. Indeed a knowledge of antiquity was only licit in so far as it acted as a reminder of the false gods which had been deposed and of all the defeats that Christianity had inflicted on pagan antiquity.[103]

The ultimate justification for the study of pagan antiquity was that pagan myth probably derived from Scripture which had been subsequently corrupted so that it was no longer recognisable.[104] In this way, Saturn could be equated with Adam. The Jesuits also indulged in establishing anagogical meanings and were notorious for believing that a figure for the birth of Christ could be found in the fourth book of Virgil's *Eclogues*. What was known as figurism took a particularly controversial turn during the Chinese missions when some Jesuits composed treatises which attempted to find elements of Christian doctrine in the Chinese classics.[105] The profane was, then, founded on the sacred, at least in part.

Given this perspective of education, especially of Jesuit education, it could be argued that, contrary to the accusations often thrown at the Society by contemporaries and others, the thrust of their teaching did not cross the divide into the purely secular. Literature was no longer separated from life or from religion. The Jesuits reformulated the synthesis which had operated in the thirteenth century. In the face of a situation where more and more literature was pertaining to an order separate from that of the Church, the Jesuits undertook to prevent literature and science from becoming dechristianised.[106] How better to achieve that than through the teaching of the authors of pagan antiquity?

But not any authors. One contemporary educational theorist, Charles Gobinet, warns against poets in general, especially if they write about profane love, and Lelevel takes the hard line of recommending only devout poetry, since the rest simply inspires all the worst values of paganism.[107] School authorities too were careful to prohibit any text they felt particularly unsuitable. Jouvancy, in his *Ratio studiorum*, has an obvious distaste for Lucretius, and warns against the obscenity of

---

[103] Le Père L. Thomassin, *La Méthode d'étudier et d'enseigner chrétiennement et solidement les lettres humaines par rapport aux lettres divines et aux écritures*, 3 vols. (Paris, 1681–2), I, Preface.

[104] Coustel, *Traité*, pp. 44–5.

[105] D. P. Walker, *The Ancient Theology* (London, 1972), p. 228.

[106] F. Charmot, *La Pédagogie des Jésuites: ses principes – son actualité* (Paris, 1943), p. 509.

[107] Ch. Gobinet, *Instruction sur la manière de bien étudier* (Paris, 1690), pp. 187–8, and Lelevel, *Entretiens*, pp. 194–5.

Catullus, although his Latin is described as excellent . . . [108] On the whole it turns out that very few authors could be read in entirety, even at the level of individual texts, so that the recommendation was that selected passages should be the basis for teaching. Ironically Pius IV and Gregory XIII allowed expurgated versions of works when editions of the whole text had been placed on the Index because of problems arising from the notes of commentators.

As far as modern authors are concerned, Jouvancy is clearly suspicious, especially of poets, who might be detrimental to morality. He does not ban them completely, but suggests that a pupil consult with his teacher for guidance. [109] Snyders contends that modern texts were excluded on the grounds that they would be difficult to expurgate in quite the same way as the works of antiquity, and that such texts dealt with contemporary issues and were contrary to the enclosed pedagogic world of the school. [110] However, not all schools kept out the modern. The fathers of the Christian Doctrine allowed French texts into their libraries. At Tarascon, for example, Ronsard, Scudéry, Rotrou, d'Urfé and Corneille were represented, the latter by his comedy Le Menteur. [111] The number of profane works increased towards the end of the century. The library of the school at Saint-Charles contained 52 profane out of 3,500 books, including the sceptic and 'libertin' La Mothe Le Vayer. [112]

Conclusion

The world of education in the seventeenth century begins from a position of providing, with a certain degree of success, a wide range of the faithful with the necessary intellectual skills for an adequate understanding of the faith to be made possible. The space of the school, however, cannot be defined as what occurred within its walls. It reached out in a variety of ways into the world and particularly implanted itself in domestic space. Eventually, the Church was a victim of its own success and encouraged aspirations for an education whose emphasis had moved away from its original intention. A more educated population might be unlikely to accept the rigid controls that the Church attempted to place on personal belief, and a change in the balance of teaching from the religious to the secular was bound to lead to different attitudes towards the Church among the faithful. In addition, as we shall see in more detail later, new

[108] Jouvancy, De la Manière d'apprendre, p. 58.
[109] Ibid., pp. 18–19.
[110] Snyders, La Pédagogie, p. 108.
[111] Viguerie, Une Oeuvre d'éducation, p. 476.
[112] Ibid., p. 484.

ideas in the world of science and other areas of knowledge combined to place extraordinary pressure on the Church in the maintenance of its traditions and its expression of orthodoxy. Such novelties may only have reached a small intellectual élite, but they challenged fundamental principles which affected belief itself.

4   The spaces of dissension

Introduction

The previous chapters have outlined some of the spaces in which the Church attempted to implant orthodoxy at various levels of society and within its own immediate space. In the domains of popular culture and education, the general aims of all sections of the Church evinced a certain consistency in that it is clear that the space of the Church must occupy the space of society at large. What was at issue was the homogenisation of space. I should like now to take a step back into the concept of orthodoxy itself where more fundamental differences emerged as to the true nature of belief and the relation of belief to the authorities which were meant to underpin it. One of the issues at stake was the nature of 'the Church', particularly as it was manifest through Tradition, that is to say the transmission through time of a body of doctrine which could be referred to as 'orthodox' and as representing the universal Church. But the nature of Tradition turns out not to be the 'given' one might imagine. It becomes a significant space of dissension in itself. In other words the space of the Church turns out not to be necessarily homogeneous.

Institutions and rivalries

That the Church was in many ways a heterogeneous space or a space containing a number of points of divergence is obvious both within and between institutions. The Oratory, founded by Bérulle and generally associated with a neoplatonist and Augustinian theology, was not in itself a unified body. The differences between the provincials and other members of the congregation came to a head in the second half of the century when some of the great philosophical debates focused on the new system of Descartes and its relative merits in defence of the faith. The Oratory found itself divided among its 'Jansenists', its 'semi-Pelagians', its Cartesians and its scholastics.[1] This did not prevent inter-institutional

[1] P. Auvray, *Richard Simon, 1638–1712: étude bio-bibliographique* (Paris, 1974), p. 21.

100

rivalry between Jesuits and Oratorians being conducted according to the staunch adherence of the former to Aristotelianism, and the espousal of many members of the latter of Cartesianism. Nowhere was this rivalry of institutions more acute than in the domain of education where different teaching orders disputed the 'occupation of the space'. Rivalry was most acute where two schools of different orders existed in the same diocese or even town. Most often such rivalry involved the Jesuits and the Oratory, and for this reason the Jesuits tracked the content of Oratorian teaching, against which they did not hesitate to initiate proceedings of an inquisitorial nature. Intellectual positions and sectional interests in this respect came to the same thing.

The Jesuits not only came up against the Oratorians but also the University of Paris which was extremely jealous of its traditional and long-standing role in education. Except under duress, it refused to accept candidates from Jesuit schools for the *licence* or the *maîtrise* in humanities or theology.[2] At the beginning of the eighteenth century, La Salle's charitable schools experienced problems in their admission of elements of the lower middle classes not normally classified as poor. The clergy in general failed to come to the aid of such schools in the event of their experiencing difficulties, say, from the *maîtres-écrivains*. On the grounds that, by attracting pupils from a social class which normally filled the ranks of the parish clergy and by teaching them arithmetic and book-keeping rather than Latin, the schools of La Salle were accused of depriving the Church of good recruits.[3]

In addition, the regulars did not endear themselves to the parish priest who could see his normal functions of confession and preaching 'usurped' in his own space by those whose domain constituted an independent space within the diocese, especially as they owed allegiance directly to Rome and not to the bishop. Regulars such as the Capuchins also had a roving function and participated for example in controversies with Protestants whose temples Catholic clergy of the second half of the century had the right to enter without obstruction. Another complaint was that the regulars drew into their chapels members of the wealthy classes and deprived the parish of the material support it required to function properly. Moreover, in those towns where the Jesuit Marian societies were particularly strong, the control of certain sections of the faithful was such that their own organisation of liturgical discipline was found to be incompatible with that more appropriate to the parish.[4] All sorts of fraternities, particularly those organised by the laity, added to these problems. John Bossy comments that the secular élite was an ambiguous ally in the support of parochial

---

[2] Fumaroli, *L'Age de l'éloquence*, p. 245.
[3] Poutet, *Le XVIIe siècle*, II, 73.   [4] Châtellier, *The Europe of the Devout*, p. 140.

uniformity and order in the dioceses. Colbert, bishop of Mâcon, ruled in 1668 that attendance at mass in the parish church should take precedence over attendance at mass in the chapel of fraternities.[5] In some towns the fraternities came eventually under the control of the parish priest himself to avoid any conflict of interest.[6] The aim was clearly to achieve a unitary rather than a fragmented religious space.

The regulars were not necessarily always at peace with each other. Within the context of learning a dispute broke out within the Benedictine order over whether study should be permitted or not. A. Le Bouthillier de Rancé, provincial of the Trappist order in France, took a strict view of the notion of the contemplative order as involving the exclusion of the world, as a space free from the intrusion of obstacles to the order's main objective which was penitence and definitely not the pursuit of knowledge. There were exceptions celebrated for their doctrine but they did not constitute an example for others to follow.[7] Study is therefore quite simply alien to and destructive of the monastic state. The monk should restrict his reading to Scripture, the works of saintly monks, the lives of saints and exclude all that encourages curiosity.[8] No languages other than Latin should be permitted in the cloister, but most of all any form of 'critique' should be rigorously proscribed, especially as regards Scripture which would involve the study of Greek, Hebrew and Syriac texts.[9] Rancé puts his faith in manual work and regards study as idleness.[10] This anti-intellectualist stance did not on the other hand prevent Rancé from admiring the Oratory for its scholarly and educational work.[11] The dispute was strictly 'in house'.

Against Rancé, Mabillon, a Maurist of the abbey of Saint-Germain-des-Prés, saw the need to defend the activities of his own order which seemed to transgress the position of the monastic tradition according to St Benedict as Rancé had described it. Mabillon's defence rested on the exceptional nature of the abbey as the principal monastery of his order given over to study. Even then only a few of its members, some twelve out of fifty, were occupied in the pursuit of knowledge.[12] More generally, Mabillon is critical of the limited character of the sort of reading allowed monks which he does not deem to be in the best interests of the individual, the Church or religion.[13] Mabillon's own highly selective list includes

[5] J. Bossy, 'The Counter-Reformation and the People of Catholic Europe', *Past and Present*, 47 (1970), 51–70 (p. 60).   [6] Muchembled, *Culture populaire*, p. 257.
[7] A. Le Bouthillier de Rancé, *De la Sainteté et des devoirs de la vie monastique*, 2 vols. (Paris, 1683), 292.   [8] Ibid., pp. 295–8.   [9] Ibid., pp. 274–5.   [10] Ibid., pp. 293–4.
[11] Wright, *The Counter-Reformation*, p. 93.
[12] Dom J. Mabillon, *Réflexions sur la réponse de Monsieur l'abbé de la Trappe au Traité des études monastiques* (Paris, 1692), p. 333.
[13] Ibid., p. 18.

some poets and playwrights, but most importantly works relating to the human sciences (he excludes mathematics), philosophy and grammar which had always been considered necessary in the study of theology.[14] Mabillon clearly takes account of the historical circumstances of the Counter-Reformation Church which has, if it is to be successful in the transformation of the world, to enter into some – albeit controlled – negotiation with it. Mabillon was aware that the monastic orders could not stand back from developing the knowledge necessary for the defence of the faith. The Counter-Reformation Church was a Church of action, and even monks had their part to play in that. The traditions of the past had to yield to a new challenge.

The most virulent and the most famous theological controversy in the century concerned the concept of grace. The main impetus was given to this controversy by the publication in France of Cornelius Jansen's *Augustinus* in 1641. In this book, Jansen (Jansenius) advanced an interpretation of the works of St Augustine which rested on radically pessimistic assumptions concerning man's ability to contribute to his salvation, on his dependence on the unearned and gratuitous nature of grace, and on the fewness of the elect. This severe form of penitential theology was strongly opposed by the Jesuits who championed the theses on grace advanced by the Spanish Jesuit Molina. Molina emphasised rather man's freedom in the actions that could bring about his salvation, thus reducing man's dependence on grace and stressing the value of works and free will. Both positions were based on a view of mankind following the Fall, the Jansenists pointing to the fundamentally corrupt nature of our condition, and the Jesuits arguing that man had simply been deprived of supernatural gifts.

The nature of the dispute swiftly forced the Church to tackle problems which had not been resolved at Trent, partly because the issue of interpretation, especially of St Augustine and St Paul, was so fraught with difficulty that many probably thought it wiser to leave well alone. In seventeenth-century France the issue within the Church rapidly became political with Antoine Arnauld (1612–94), the foremost doctrinal expert of Port-Royal, eventually being expelled from the Sorbonne in 1656. The complex arguments on the forms of grace required for salvation, satirised by Pascal on behalf of Port-Royal in his *Provinciales*, led to the involvement of other orders, notably the Dominicans, and to the involvement of Rome.

Many within the Church, not only the Jansenists, held that Molina's theses on grace came close to the Pelagian heresy which focused on the

[14] Ibid., p. 143.

self-sufficiency of man and which had earned the condemnation of St Augustine. The gravest charges of heresy were levelled at the Jansenists who vigorously defended the positions on grace adopted by Jansenius in the *Augustinus*. An attempt was made to resolve the issue by extracting from Jansenius's book five propositions which were considered to be heretical. The Jansenists did not dispute the heretical nature of the propositions but denied that they could be found in the *Augustinus*. Thus was born the dispute over *droit*, which regarded the authority of the pope to pronounce in matters of faith, and *fait*, which addressed the pope's authority in matters of fact. Eventually all members of the regular and secular clergies had to sign what was known as the formulary, thus accepting the presence of the five propositions in the *Augustinus*. The controversy rumbled on at different levels of intensity during the whole of our period and beyond, according to many historians with grave consequences for the authority of the Church in general and the authority of St Augustine in particular.

Gallicanism

Not only did the space of the French Church contain spaces which were at odds with themselves, but significant sections of it maintained that it was in some ways an independent space in relation to the Church in Rome. Although the concept of gallicanism, the name given to the set of positions underpinning the theory of the independence of the French Church, was not universal within France, it played a significant role in the course of our period. The Church in France was defined to some extent by its national frontiers.

Gallicanism has been described at one level as a state of mind comprising an anti-Roman sensibility within Catholicism. At another it was a doctrine and a set of practices,[15] whose origins are mainly to be found in a number of privileges which were historically determined by the Concordat of Bologna in 1516 and which became known as gallican liberties. These seemed, however, to be reduced in significance and contradicted by the emphasis placed by the Council of Trent on the strengthening of papal power, and the kings of France and Spain were not pleased that the pope should in particular be declared 'bishop of the universal Church'. Thus the way was open for a series of disputes which severely tested the unity of the Church within France at various stages of the seventeenth century.

Gallicanism was entrenched not only in certain sections of the French

---

[15] Lebrun (ed.), *Histoire de la France religieuse*, II, 525.

Church but also in the lay structures of the state, especially in the world of the *parlements*. This was the gallicanism of the judiciary or 'gallicanisme judiciaire' which formulated the king's rights in relation to his own Church and Rome. His rights were in fact very broad. He was able to appoint to all higher posts in the Church of France, including 14 archbishoprics, and about 100 bishoprics. While the right of appeal by the clergy to Rome was severely limited, no bishop could be brought to judgement outside the kingdom. The king was also indirectly in control of the property of the Church and received the income from a see while it remained vacant. He had the right to oversee the exercise of the disciplinary and, to a certain extent, the spiritual authority of bishops. In this sense he was invested with a 'sacerdoce royal', that is to say a sort of priestly function in the defence of the faith. Indeed, the king stood in some ways between the Church and the laity in that not only could an individual appeal to the *parlement* or to the *conseil du Roi* against an episcopal judgement, but the monarch had the right to regulate and limit communications between his subjects and the Holy See. No papal bull or conciliar decision could be published without prior examination by the courts who would thus ensure that they contained nothing contrary to gallican liberties. The decrees of the Council of Trent never won legal status in France. Certainly, the Assembly of the Clergy of France made a declaration of reception of the decrees in 1615 but this was never validated by any French king.

So gallicanism set limits on papal power in France and effectively extended the boundaries of temporal power. This encroachment of the space of the secular on the space of the Church is further illustrated by the relative positions of Church and state in the question of censorship. The pope had the right to censor propositions contained in a book but no judicial moves could be made against the book or its printer until the civil power permitted it. Equally the pope could impose adherence on a point of faith but the judicial consequences of refusal to accept it, for example the deprivation of an ecclesiastical living, could only be decided by the temporal power.[16] Indeed, the pillars of gallicanism were the propositions that the king of France was sovereign in his kingdom, that he had no superior on earth, that the pope was unable to invoke any authority over temporal power, and that he had no personal infallibility, being subordinate to the Church in ecumenical council. These principles were enshrined in the *Cleri gallicani de ecclesia potestate declaratio* of 1682.

Episcopal gallicanism focused on the Church itself. Whereas in the secular domain the Church was in many ways subject to the power of the

---

[16] A. Adam, *Du Mysticisme à la révolte: les Jansénistes du XVIIe siècle* (Paris, 1968), pp. 15–16.

king, the bishops demanded autonomy in their dioceses. The importance of the status of bishops within the Church derives from the fact that their authority rests on the place they occupy within the apostolic succession. In other words they did not necessarily regard themselves as either the agents of the king or of the pope.[17] For bishops of Jansenist persuasion this could only strengthen their attachment to the idea of conscience as the ultimate guide, since they were in their person the continuation of a tradition which began with the Apostles. It is obvious that difficulties could arise from this interpretation for the Church as a body: 'Episcopal gallicanism made it especially difficult to establish doctrinal unity within the Church, because any bishop might reject any outside attempt to force his diocese to accept a theological principle with which he did not agree.'[18] Thus the very structure of the Church, irrespective of the opinions of individuals, created the potential for a space of dissension.

It is no surprise that gallicanism was extremely hostile to the regulars who owed no allegiance to the bishop but to Rome. This was especially true of the Jesuits who propagated throughout the century what are called ultramontane theses. In 1632 a work entitled *Petrus Aurelius* supported the bishops and the parish clergy against the regulars. The Assembly of the Clergy of France, as a sign of its approval, contributed towards the costs of publication, along with the Sorbonne who, as we have seen, were opposed to the Jesuits on other grounds.[19]

But it would be a mistake to paint a picture of the French kingdom as united in the cause of gallicanism. The kingdom was no more of a homogeneous space than the Church. Gallicanism did not have it all its own way, especially in the first third of the seventeenth century. In 1626 a Jesuit, Santarelli, published a work entitled *Tractatus de haeresi* in support of theses concerning the indirect power of the pope over kings.[20] It was immediately condemned by the Paris *parlement*, and provoked from the Faculty of Theology a forceful statement on gallican liberties. Rome's strong objection to these moves made the whole situation considerably embarrassing for Richelieu. The power of the ultramontanes inside the kingdom, notably at Court, and outside France was so strong at this stage that the *parlement* and the Faculty were ordered to cease their consideration of the work forthwith. During this period the French monarchy preferred to deal with the Holy See rather than with the *parlement* whose attachment to judicial procedures was a source of exasperation.[21] The gallican sympathies of the majority of doctors of the Sorbonne were countered on other occasions by an ultramontane group led by André

---

[17] Ibid., p. 24.
[18] Sedgwick, *Jansenism*, p. 10.   [19] Adam, *Du Mysticisme*, p. 99.
[20] See Brockliss, 'Richelieu', 258–61.   [21] Adam, *Du Mysticisme*, pp. 20–1.

Duval which, flying in the face of the independence of the French Church, aligned itself with Rome, the Court and the regulars.[22]

One incident in particular serves to illustrate the fact that not all gallicans supported the king. The affair of the *régale* which began in 1673 and ended in 1693, and which resulted in the publication of the *Cleri gallicani*, broke out when the king made it clear that he would extend his powers over the French Church to the appointment of all bishops, who would then hold their office directly from his nomination: 128 out of 130 bishops submitted to the king. The two who did not, Pavillon and Caulet, were well known for their Jansenist sympathies. The Concordat of Bologna may well have contained concessions to the French crown, but certainly not in an absolute sense and in the sense that the king was now imposing the redrawing of boundaries of the religious and secular authority in the affairs of the Church. At first sight papal power was set against the independence of the French Church, and the king was seen to encroach on a domain which was rightly that of the pope.

The Jansenist position was complex, addressing as it did the limits of both the pope and the king in the ecclesiastical domain. The Jansenists supported the gallican thesis that the Church in ecumenical council was superior to the authority of the pope as exercised in his person, and they of course had every reason to detest the Jesuits. They also believed in the immunities of the French Church. But they had no desire, either, to see the authority of the French Church pass completely into the hands of Louis XIV. Their support for Pavillon and Caulet was based less on support for the pope than on support for the principles of episcopal gallicanism. The Jansenists were prepared to support royal absolutism when it prevented the pope from exercising an illegitimate authority and when it defended the immunities of the Church against ultramontane pretensions. But the king had no right to encroach upon those immunities himself.[23] Towards the end of his life Arnauld, who had supported Caulet and Pavillon in his *Considérations sur les affaires de l'Eglise*, envisaged a national council of bishops which would protect the French Church against royal and papal interference. He further proposed that the election of bishops would be the responsibility of cathedral chapters, an extraordinary choice, for the canons of cathedral chapters seemed especially resistant to the Catholic Reform.[24] A further example of an unholy alliance of the Jansenists with the pope against the king, which in some ways prefigured the affair of the *régale*, was over a character they could not have thought of very highly except that he was a prince of the French

[22] Ibid., p. 46.
[23] Sedgwick, *Jansenism*, pp. 173–6.
[24] Lebrun (ed.), *Histoire de la France religieuse*, II, 521–2.

Church. Louis XIV wanted to dispossess the Cardinal de Retz, a major participant during the Fronde, of his ecclesiastical position but was opposed by Port-Royal and the Paris clergy who defended his ecclesiastical immunity. The pope refused to accede to the king's request. Retz finally resigned in 1662.

The affair of the *régale* took a very serious turn because dissension came close to schism, although Louis never allowed it to go that far. In view of Rome's refusal to ratify the king's appointments throughout the years of the dispute, thirty-eight sees remained vacant in 1688, thus endangering the pastoral life of a whole swathe of the kingdom. The remarkable thing is that the king did not ultimately gain very much from the dispute and indeed weakened the concept of gallican liberties. In an act of reconciliation Louis abandoned the prescription of the four articles drawn up by Bossuet which reaffirmed the independence of the French king from the pope, and a number of bishops apologised for having displeased the Holy See. It is true that the pope in return dropped his objection to the *régale*, but there is no doubt who was the loser.

Under Louis XIV, who gave a new impetus and strength to certain aspects of gallicanism, the crown was not always in conflict with the pope and sometimes found itself in conflict with the gallican position on the independence of the French Church. This was particularly true of Louis XIV's efforts to control Jansenism which, if they were to be effective, required a doctrinal judgement from Rome, the problem being here that the pope's authority was required, in contradiction of gallican liberties, to resolve a problem of royal authority. In the period following the publication of the papal bull entitled *In eminenti*, the civil authorities showed more zeal than the archbishop of Paris, Gondi, who simply urged obedience. The chancellor on the other hand demanded from the Sorbonne acceptance of the pontifical document.[25] In this case the secular arm took the lead in the imposition of a papal decision. In 1653 royal authority issued letters patent demanding the reception of *Cum occasione* throughout the kingdom. The bull of 1656 which definitively stated that the infamous propositions were indeed to be found in the *Augustinus, Cum ad sacram Petri sedem*, was received by the Assembly of the Clergy of France in 1657, following which Louis XIV demanded of an extremely reluctant *parlement* that they follow suit.[26]

The contradictions in the situation became even more complex when in 1664 Louis XIV wrote to the pope requesting a new judgement this time demanding signature of the formulary. In this case, since signature would be imposed by the pope and not by the king,[27] the latter would be

[25] Adam, *Du Mysticisme*, p. 162.   [26] Ibid., p. 205.
[27] Ibid., pp. 254–5.

accepting the jurisdiction of the pope over his subjects, something strictly contrary to gallican liberties. Instead of protecting the immunities of the French Church, the king was allowing a coach and horses to be driven through them, in addition to prompting opposition to the crown within the kingdom. Of course, the pope seized the opportunity and issued the bull entitled *Regiminis apostolici* in February 1665. But the issue did not stop there. Faced with four bishops who insisted on maintaining the distinction between *droit* and *fait*, the pope wanted them judged on his authority alone, a strictly non-gallican principle. Initially, Louis refused but was eventually caught by the logic of his own position and gave in, whereupon procedures were begun but not completed owing to the death of Alexander VII.[28]

The final straw was the papal bull *Unigenitus* which, it was hoped, would put an end to the affair of the formulary once and for all. In the period preceding the bull, it was suggested that the pope would issue a bull against Jansenism condemning in particular the position of respectful silence whereby individuals would not need to agree with the condemnation of the propositions on the basis of *fait*, but would none the less remain silent. The effect of the bull would be to indicate that it had been published at the request of the king, something which Clement XI had no wish to do, since it suggested that the papacy was not the supreme authority. Two years passed. Finally the bull was published in 1713. Its effect on the French Church was devastating. In its condemnation of Augustinian theses on grace it entrenched the Molinist position which was opposed by a wider spectrum of the French Church than just the immediate circle of Port-Royal. The bull also opposed access to the text of the Bible for all the faithful and rejected liturgical innovations. As Adam puts it, the Catholics of France now knew for certain that Rome did not accept the participation of the laity in the liturgy nor the personal reading of the Bible. The Church was not the union of Christians in Christ but a society whose prime duty was submission to the decisions of the hierarchy.[29]

The most important aspect of the bull was the implication of the pre-eminence of Rome over the French Church and the right of control of the Holy See over kings, thus reaffirming the medieval theses of pontifical theocracy.[30] While the bull was registered by the majority of bishops, its passage was afterwards far from smooth. The *parlement* was extremely hostile and the Sorbonne added its own form of obstruction. More significantly, far from burying Jansenism, it gave it a new impetus which carried its influence right into the eighteenth century. Once again certain

[28] Ibid., pp. 254–7.   [29] Ibid., p. 323.   [30] Taveneaux, *Le Catholicisme*, II, 326.

sections of the French Church had worked against their own interests, aided by a king who had in other circumstances risked schism in order to defend gallican liberties. Indeed, one might conclude that Louis XIV was less interested in defending the Church than promoting his own personal glory. The Church was on many occasions simply an instrument of secular power.

No account of gallicanism as one of the spaces of dissension can be complete without some further consideration of the Jesuits to whom gallicanism was anathema, although under Louis XIV they managed on the whole to stifle their ultramontane reflexes. They were regarded as the main proponents of the pre-eminence of papal authority, and attitudes towards them in France were partly determined by their attachment to their international networks and allegiances. Suspicion of the Jesuits as an intrusive force in the gallican milieu was inscribed in Henri IV's Edict of Rouen (1603) which stipulated that no new religious foundation could be created without the express permission of the king. Permission was also required for foreigners who wished to join the French branch of the Society. Moreover an annual oath of allegiance to the crown was demanded (although this stipulation was short-lived) and a Jesuit had to reside at Court to vouch for the loyalty of the Society.[31] The Jesuits were thus subject to an unprecedented surveillance. But the main significance of the appearance of the Jesuits in France is that they imported a culture which differed in many respects from that of the milieu which dominated French intellectual life at the beginning of the seventeenth century, that is to say the 'robin' humanism of the parliamentary milieu.

It is to Marc Fumaroli's *L'Age de l'éloquence* that we owe one of the most original analyses of the confrontation that was to emerge between a parliamentarian conservatism, rooted in a certain concept of Catholic tradition and which sought to affirm the pre-eminence of the Church of the Gauls, as the French Church was known, and the international culture of the Jesuits who felt the need to adapt tradition to new historical demands. Fumaroli follows the development of this confrontation in terms of the values each party ascribed primarily to language: 'avocats et théologiens contre régents de rhétorique et prédicateurs'.[32] Symbolic of these differences was the library of the two Dupuy brothers, pillars of the gallican milieu, which represented a sort of space of exclusion, in that it contained only books of erudition. It simply did not admit of the 'intrusion' represented by works of the 'beaux esprits "modernes"' and the works of Jesuit rhetoricians.[33] The *parlement* space was a 'pure' space uncontaminated by what was not gallican in spirit. In addition the essence

[31] Fumaroli, *L'Age de l'éloquence*, p. 239.   [32] Ibid., p. 234.   [33] Ibid., p. 577.

of Jesuit culture was oral and centred on the rhetoric of preachers. Gallican humanism engendered a mistrust of oral eloquence and put its faith in the written law. Its point of reference was not the 'bilan du savoir moderne finalisé selon les intérêts de l'Eglise tridentine', but the search for the truth on the basis of texts which had been either forgotten, falsified or wrongly interpreted.[34]

Fumaroli highlights two thrusts to the conscious attempt of the Jesuits to find a niche in the space occupied by the gallican humanists. In the first place, their role as teachers of oratory offered them the opportunity to educate courtiers and provide a form of Christianity tailored to the demands of the Court. At the same time, this space was too narrow, for the Jesuits aspired to the conquest of souls on a much wider social scale, and reached out to the 'public de robe'. They therefore decided to compete in the very world of erudition which was at the heart of gallicanism. As a consequence they needed to specialise and so divided their efforts on a 'geographical' basis. The professed house in the rue Saint-Antoine, in other words in a quarter populated by the court aristocracy, concentrated on preaching, spiritual direction and other tasks destined to diffuse their influence in the 'world'. The success of the Society was such that their spiritual direction was sought by the ladies of the *robe* as well as by the ladies of the Court. The king often visited the Collège de Clermont while never setting foot in the precincts of the University: 'l'esprit de Cour a désormais franchi la Seine'.[35] The Left Bank, however, was predominantly the space of the erudite *robe* with its schools, churches and law courts close to the centre of books and printing. The Jesuits were not slow to bring within their sphere of influence booksellers such as Cramoisy who imported or sold for the use of French scholars works printed in Rome or Roman works reprinted in Paris.

The degree of penetration of Jesuit culture was soon to be found in writers who embodied a new approach to the French language much less rooted in the erudition and gravity of gallican traditions. Their works did not pass without controversy. The letters of Guez de Balzac, one of the principal stylists of the first half of the century, became a battleground which pitted the partisans of the 'langage de cour' and of Jesuit-inspired eloquence – inspired in part by the courtly elegance of Italy – against the more severe adherents of the philosophical and oratorical authority of the language used in the magistrates' milieu.[36] This space saw itself invaded by a foreign and alien influence, where the likes of Balzac were cast as traitors in their midst who had to be expelled or at least against whom the space of gallicanism had to be protected.

[34] Ibid., pp. 685–6.   [35] Ibid., pp. 248–51.   [36] Ibid., p. 545.

But the walls had already been breached by the Trojan horse constituted by the Collège de Clermont, the Jesuit college established on the Left Bank in Paris and within the University, the Society's arch rival. Its pupils emerged with a culture more aesthetic than erudite and more rhetorical than philosophical. Indeed, even before the appearance of Balzac, Jean-Baptiste du Val, a parlement lawyer, broke ranks with the scholars of the Palais de Justice with the publication in 1603 of his *Eschole française pour apprendre à bien parler et à escrire selon l'usage du temps, et pratique des bons auteurs*, in which the principal point of reference had become the language of the Court.[37] What is more, the Court had come to favour writers like Théophile de Viau, Mareschal and Corneille, all originally from the milieu of the law, and young lawyers rushed to embrace the world of the theatre, the apogee of the rhetorical culture represented most strongly by the Society of Jesus. In a secular context, the space of the theatre turned this time into the rival of the law courts.

Encouraged by the model of the Court which exhibited a less morally inhibited life style than their own and by a language ('un bonheur d'expression') more suited to the less serious pursuits of life, the reaction of *robin* youth had been to leave the space of the family – that is, gallican humanism – in order to move closer to an alternative 'home', a Jesuit culture which offered the interesting proposition of a humanist education considerably more attractive than the learning associated with the law courts.[38] As far as the Jesuits themselves were concerned, the conquest of *robin* youth was important precisely because of the immense obstacle the *robin* milieu represented to the overwhelmingly Roman and Spanish elements of the culture identified with the Society. Hence the importance of the Court whose own culture was 'modern', expressed as it was not only in French, but in Spanish and Italian, the three major languages of the day.[39]

But the history of this transition from one culture to another was not without its complexities. Certainly, the nature of the space changed under the influence of the Jesuits but not ultimately to their sole advantage. The gallican erudite tradition was not supplanted. Rather it seems to have absorbed elements of the new culture to re-emerge triumphant in the second half of the century. The Court may have imposed its favourite genres – the novel, theatre and love poetry – on the literary world, but the literature of the Court was not its own work. It was the work of writers who had received a Jesuit education, and at the same time the moral and juridical imprint of the *parlement* milieu. The writer beginning to emerge in the course of the first half of the seventeenth century was at the frontier

---

[37] Ibid., p. 601.   [38] Ibid., pp. 592–7.   [39] Ibid., pp. 673–4.

of two worlds. He was a mediator and a 'passeur'. Moreover, erudition eventually combined with the metaphorical imagination of the orator in forming both the legal framework and the poetic and rhetorical presentation of absolute monarchy in the making.[40] The combination of the two cultures was designed to produce a more unitary space within the kingdom.

It was in these circumstances inevitable that some should have had regrets about moving too far into 'foreign' territory. Two figures stand out: Charles Sorel, who abandoned the uninhibited world of the *Histoire comique de Francion* (1623) – which satirises among other things the pedantry of the University colleges – for a sober form of criticism more in line with his 'caste'; and Guillaume Colletet, who, after the licentious anthology entitled *Le Parnasse satirique* – which was also in part the downfall of his fellow-poet Théophile de Viau – became the devoted agent of learned and devout humanism in Parisian literary life.[41] The traffic was not all one way. Former *dévots* who had initially adopted a hostile attitude to Richelieu, now moved over to his cause, especially on foreign policy. Such a case was the *cabinet* Dupuy to which Chapelain belonged. He in fact acted as a mediator between the spaces of official patronage of letters and the old world of Latin learning.[42] Indeed, under the influence of Richelieu, the 'doctes' regained their place in the world of letters through the institution of the Académie française. The Court was not allowed to become a purely 'Jesuit' domain since the king and the cardinal wished to retain their own control over it. The language of the Court was thus subjected to the control of men of letters issuing from the milieu of the *robe*. Under the influence of Richelieu, whose critical attitude to the Society was motivated precisely by the alienation from their milieu that a Jesuit education instilled in the youth of the *robe*, gallican learning became more youthful and less ponderous. Without making any concessions to vulgarisation and by agreeing to adopt a simple and clear style bereft of technical vocabulary, it regained the territory lost to a Jesuit culture which had always been considered foreign to the interests of France.[43]

While it is true that absolutism did not originally meet with the approval of the *parlement* milieu, one bonus which accrued from this 'inféodation' was that the role of the 'doctes' in the control of letters was considerably facilitated by the disappearance in the time of Richelieu of the *Grands* as patrons of writers who then had to seek protection from Richelieu himself. From being on the margins of society, writers, in dedicating their work to Richelieu and in supporting royal policies, moved to the centre of the stage, often in a quite literal sense, and assumed a sense of civic and

---

[40] Ibid., p. 244.   [41] Ibid., pp. 610–11.   [42] Ibid., p. 577.   [43] Ibid., pp. 683–4.

national importance. The price to pay for the control of letters was that the gallican milieu was itself constrained to participate in the praise of the cardinal and his works, and to construct an official poetics and rhetoric. Such a unitary view of language, bolstered of course by the designs set out for the Académie in the elaboration of an official rhetoric and poetics and in the production of a dictionary, meant that the Jesuits too had to conform to the new direction royal authority gave to culture.[44]

In this context the relationship of different elements of the Church to the cultural movements of the seventeenth century is an interesting and perhaps surprising one. It might be thought not only that Mazarin would succeed in reimplanting at the heart of French culture the Italianism associated among other things with Jesuit culture but that Louis XIV, in view of his eventual persecution of Port-Royal, might seek to hold at arm's length aspects of a gallican culture which led to such an independence of mind. Fumaroli argues that Mazarin, Richelieu's successor during the regency of Anne of Austria on the death of Louis XIII, succeeded only in delaying the monarchy's espousal of a new style which took account of gallican demands in the form of a 'simplicité chrétienne'. Thus Port-Royal contributed to the formation of classicism under Louis XIV by holding to a 'naturel', both French and Christian, in the face of the international and eclectic art favoured by the Jesuits, an art which was moreover 'pagan'.[45] In this way Louis hoped to draw to himself the allegiance of those who might otherwise have retained the gravest reservations about many aspects of his policies. Leaving aside what divided these various strands, what united them was the centrality of France as a source of cultural values. France was the graveyard of Jesuit internationalism.[46]

In the face of such a powerful alliance within the kingdom, the Jesuits could not fail to become absorbed within the space. But their presence could only function without tension so long as a political consensus existed and so long as the Jesuits were part of it. Indeed they could find their place much more easily within it when Port-Royal began to stand outside it, or at least when it was felt that Jansenism posed a serious threat to peace and order in the kingdom and to royal authority itself. There can be no doubt that the Jesuits seized the opportunity to reassert the pre-eminence of Rome in doctrinal matters, which could not fail to have implications for the political order. They thus attempted to regain the territory ceded in cultural terms through a theological controversy which was to be at the centre of discussions over the tradition of the Church.

[44] Ibid., p. 571.
[45] Fumaroli, *Héros et orateurs*, pp. 256–7.
[46] Fumaroli, '"Temps de croissance et temps de corruption": les deux antiquités dans l'érudition jésuite française du XVIIe siècle', *XVIIe siècle*, 131 (1981), 149–68 (p. 167).

Tradition, orthodoxy and authority

The Catholic Church defines itself in terms of an unbroken historical tradition of teaching which is first enshrined in Scripture and its interpretation by the Fathers of the early Church and then in the doctrinal decisions ratified by the councils of the Church in the light of reference to the whole of the Tradition. The Protestant Church by contrast is held to possess no tradition once it had broken with Rome. In abandoning the unity of Tradition, particularly in the interpretation of Scripture, Protestant religious space fragmented into the proliferation of sects and deprived itself of all useful criteria for the establishment of truth which Tradition alone can provide. In the course of the seventeenth century the unity that Tradition was supposed to ensure was severely strained, and the space of Catholicism too threatened to fragment, thus severely debilitating the efforts of the Catholic Reform. The argument focused not on the existence of Tradition, but rather on the exact nature of it. On the conclusion to that argument depended a whole range of issues regarding the legitimacy of one form of Christian practice as against another.

One of the reasons for the diversity of positions on Tradition is the status of the Fathers. It is the case that no individual Father of the Church in himself is deemed to embody the whole of Tradition. Fénelon reflects a perfectly orthodox notion when he states that the Fathers were fallible and could well have been mistaken or expressed themselves badly. Tradition is valid only on the points at which unanimity can be established.[47] Absolute homogeneity of space cannot in this sense be considered part of the heritage of the early Church. And here the difficulties begin. Theological speculation was encouraged, not to say rendered necessary, by the fact that vast areas pertaining to faith and to Christian practice remained unexplored by Tradition or at least were not given any definitive expression in Scripture. Principal among these are the trinitarian formula and the doctrine of child baptism. Hence attitudes to the authority of individual Fathers could not be unanimous. In the case of Tertullian, Malebranche's controversial view was that affected obscurities were not the equivalent of sacred mysteries and bursts of imagination did not constitute illumination.[48] Richard Simon, in the context of establishing the text of Scripture, adopts an independent line when he asserts that the true Christian should not be the unquestioning disciple of any individual, whether it be St Augustine, St Jerome or any other Father, since faith is founded on the word of Christ as reported in the writings of the Apostles

---

[47] Tavard, *La Tradition*, p. 229.
[48] N. Malebranche (ed. G. Rodis-Lewis), *De la Recherche de la vérité*, 3 vols. (Paris, 1945–62), III, 69.

and as they are enshrined in the tradition of the Church. If others had adopted this stance, many unnecessary disputes could have been avoided.[49] For Sainte-Marie no lack of respect is implied if the conclusions of the Church, which has ultimate authority in interpretation as a body, are preferred to the witness even of the Fathers.[50]

My discussion will focus on Augustine's three rules of faith: Scripture, Tradition and the teaching power of the Church. It is important to emphasise that these three sources of authority are not in opposition but complementary to each other, since neither can represent Tradition on its own. It is rather a question of what sort of authority can be ascribed to each and the points at which one supplements the other. Problems are compounded by the nature of the Old Testament as a written source, and therefore 'complete', and by the nature of the New Testament as being a record of what was spoken and therefore not constituting in any way in itself an exhaustive tradition.

The first problem to be resolved is the status of Scripture, the answer to which depends on what is being sought in Scripture. All interpretation has an end in mind, either a proof of the faith or of a particular practice. In these circumstances, Tavard explains Cardinal du Perron's position as being that the text of Scripture is insufficient in itself, the source of revelation and salvation being not so much the text of Scripture itself but a 'lecture comprise'. Interpretation of the biblical text is not therefore simply philological but also mystical, not literary but spiritual. But interpretation implies an interpreter. Who should this be? All or some? In Catholicism, if there is not to be schism or fragmentation, scriptural interpretations must carry the authority of the Church as a body.[51] No space exists outside this sphere of interpretation. The space of the text is in no way autonomous.

Indeed, the authority of the Church over time rests on an understanding of the historicity of Tradition. Is Tradition fixed in a particular historical time or can it evolve through time? If it can evolve, is it still 'Tradition'? The gallicans limited the tradition of the Church to the writings of the Fathers of the first few centuries of Christianity and to the councils before Trent, a council suspected as having been the work of the Holy See. It is this concept of a Christian antiquity, associated particularly with the ancient Church of France and its adherence to that tradition, which constitutes the foundation of the modern reaffirmation and regeneration of faith. Jansenists, who revered the authority of St August-

---

[49] R. Simon, *Histoire critique du texte du Nouveau Testament* (Rotterdam, 1689), Preface.
[50] Le Père H. Sainte-Marie, *Réflexions sur les regles et l'usage de la critique touchant l'histoire de l'Eglise* (Paris, 1713), I, 119.
[51] Tavard, *La Tradition*, pp. 38–45.

ine, took their inspiration from this gallican tradition.[52] As Owen Chadwick remarks: 'in the seventeenth century, the last quality desired by a Gallican theologian was originality'.[53]

The concept of Tradition according to origins as valid throughout history without variation stands in opposition to another interpretation whose most ardent supporters were the Jesuits. They saw in Trent a new departure for the Church in the light of which Tradition must be understood, even reinterpreted, in order to respond to the expectations of modern Christians. The emphasis on the cumulative experience of history with all its expressions of faith from which a form of truth can be drawn, and which takes account of the diversity of circumstances of an evolving history, provides a 'living' alternative to the emphasis on a point in time where Christian practice and morals existed in a pure state to which modern Christianity must return. Fumaroli, who identifies the Jesuit slant as deriving from their teaching of rhetoric where the explanations of faith are adapted to different types of audience and situation, regards Jesuit attitudes to Tradition as 'encyclopedic' rather than as representing a given truth, fixed for all time, as in the gallican tradition to which it is firmly opposed. The Jesuit stance, in its rejection of the replication or the straightforward imitation of behaviour of the Christians of the primitive Church implied by the gallican tradition, evokes the different ways in which humanity in history may seek salvation and builds on the richness of human experience, since clearly social conditions vary from one period to another. The same appeal cannot be made in the same way each time.[54] The Jansenist historical literalness inevitably led them to uncompromisingly rigid moral positions with no room for accommodation.

It is to Pascal's *Provinciales* that we look for the most coruscating attack on what he regards as the Society's position on Tradition. In its teachings on grace some of the terms they use, especially that of 'pouvoir prochain', have no grounding in Scripture, the Fathers or St Thomas and, as pure invention, only distort Tradition. Jansenist emphasis on the term 'grâce efficace' is on the other hand different since, in an unbroken chain of use, it was transmitted from the words of Christ through St Paul to St Augustine, and subsequently through St Bernard and St Thomas right up to Popes Clement VIII and Paul V. The implication is that the Jesuits have only themselves as a source in their claims to authority on grace, whereas those like the Jansenists ground their own understanding of the issue in words sanctioned throughout the history of the Christian Church. They

---

[52] Fumaroli, '"Temps de croissance"', 151.

[53] O. Chadwick, *From Bossuet to Newman: the Idea of Doctrinal Development* (Cambridge, 1957), p. 7.

[54] Fumaroli, '"Temps de croissance"', 152–4.

are the real guardians of Tradition. In Pascal's *Pensée* 871 the order of words reflects the order of history: 'Perpétuité – Molina – Nouveauté'.

The charge of novelty appears too in Pascal's discussion of the Jesuits' practice of casuistry as it is found expressed in the works of their authorities. Casuistry is the study of moral cases which provides the confessor with guidance on his direction of the penitent. The main problem within casuistry is probabilism which consists of opinions enunciated by 'grave' doctors who thereby carry authority. A 'probable' opinion could be used where there was room for doubt. The more controversial position was that of 'probabiliorism'. A potential problem could arise if, in the texts of two authorities, contradictory opinions could be found for the same case. Here the confessor could use his own initiative in choosing the most 'probable' opinion in any particular case. Leaving aside the selective nature and slanted translations provided in his letters, Pascal accuses the Jesuits of accommodating the penitent, of giving him the benefit of the doubt, rather than showing him the true path to real sorrow for his sins. Such conduct flies in the face of the straightforward concept of good and evil revealed by Scripture and the Fathers. The picture of Tradition presented by the Jesuits was again one of human invention, not the transmission of an immutable truth. One of Pascal's underlying concerns in this whole dispute was that human reason had replaced the divine as authoritative. This does not exclude reason as a necessary means of explanation or explication of the sacred since after all the Church is a human institution. But it is a reason which adds without justification; it is a reason which invents. Hence it was the Jesuits who placed themselves outside the tradition of the Church and not the Jansenists.

But significant nuances can be found even within what seem uncompromising positions on Tradition. One of the most telling examples is that of Arnauld himself. Arnauld certainly confirms the idea contained in the Jansenist and gallican perspective on Tradition that the Church was immutable and thereby retained an unchanging identity throughout time. Change can never be associated with an idea of progress, for the best of the Church was already complete in its beginnings and any change could only imply decadence. This decadence, however, is only superficial and in no way affects the existence of the Church in its fundamental principles.[55] Arnauld is adamant too that the works of the Fathers are on an equal footing with those of Scripture. Here he goes further than Trent for which the Fathers had an eminently privileged place. But the equation of the Fathers with apostolic doctrine, even where unanimity has been reached

---

[55] Tavard, *La Tradition*, p. 83.

on matters of faith and points of doctrine, is to forget their role in the evolutionary progress of the Tradition and their own efforts at developing theology and the need to adapt the Christian message to other times and other places.[56] Arnauld, however, regards their works as the literal 'translation' of the Gospels immutable through time. For Arnauld, nothing can be added to Tradition for it is not 'created' but 'received'. It is ready-made and only transmitted. The Fathers, the councils and the pope are not a part of Tradition in the sense that this is antecedent to them: they are only witnesses to it.[57] The space of the Church is defined in the Gospels, not subsequently. The role of the Church is as the guardian but not the owner of that space.

But the problem arising from the view of Tradition as simply 'received' is that, if taken literally, the words of the Fathers and of the Gospels need only be recited. It would turn out to be a rather dead tradition which would surely alienate the faithful deprived of any personal relation to it. Arnauld offers a way in which the faithful themselves can remain in contact with Tradition even as he has described it. The immutability of Tradition is not in doubt, but it is necessary to understand it as it has in its turn been understood by the 'sentiment commun du peuple chrétien'. Tradition remains unchanged, objectively speaking, even here. Subjectively it has become 'vie de foi'. Practice has varied over time, without ever leading to a substantial change in the faith, by the mysterious guiding influence of the Holy Spirit which has directed the faithful to what was most appropriate for the divine intention at any given time: 'le même sens commun du peuple fidèle a toujours reflété la constance de la tradition'. In the example of eucharistic practice this 'sentiment' is the means by which the faithful can know whether one biblical expression is to be taken literally or metaphorically and the means by which the faithful are able to reach into the true nature of Tradition. The individual conscience of the believer perceives this difference between two expressions: the next task is to explain exactly what the nature of that difference is. In this respect theology is guided by the 'sentiment' of the faithful. The true tradition is conveyed by the Christian faithful as a whole, as Tavard puts it, 'par un sentiment unanime et perpétuel', what Arnauld calls a 'consensus fidelium'.[58]

This interpretation of Tradition considerably widens it beyond the space of theological expertise. It is typical of Arnauld to envisage the space of the Church as existing in the conscience of the believers, and not in the ruling of a narrowly defined hierarchy. Tradition is truly the space of the Church in its entirety. Moreover, it is up to a point a participatory space,

[56] Ibid., p. 90.   [57] Ibid., p. 97.   [58] Ibid., p. 111.

and it is not surprising therefore that innovations in lay participation in the liturgy should have often been inspired by the Jansenists themselves. Arnauld is keen to underline the communality of the faith as it operates through the transmission of Tradition. The space of the priest and the space of the faithful may in some senses be separate, but they come together in a shared spirit which sustains the relevance of Tradition through time. It is also clear why so many of their opponents should have been concerned about the proximity of their theological position to Protestantism. The notion of this religious 'sentiment' is not quite the priesthood of all believers, because the true tradition is still a collective and not an individual phenomenon, but a malicious tongue could make much of it.

Arnauld is not alone in his explanation of a personally experienced relation to Tradition. Thomassin envisages a spirit shared by the Apostles and the faithful as the possible basis of an understanding of the faith, although his emphasis is placed rather more on the transmission of Tradition through the apostolic succession. He starts from the fact that Scripture was not dictated by Christ himself but written down by the Apostles, or by others in the line of the apostolic spirit who possessed a faith inscribed in the heart. So the law can only be understood by those who discover it in their own hearts, to the extent that the meaning of the Gospels, which can only be transmitted through a shared nature, is inscribed in the heart of the Apostles and the faithful together. The spiritual meaning of Scripture is certainly inscribed in Tradition and in the unanimous agreement of the Fathers, but also in the teaching of the saints of the past, the present and the future. Such a position also allows for the renewal of Tradition through the ages, for the interpretation of Scripture is the prerogative of bishops as the successors of the apostles: 'il faut donc dire de la tradition que la vérité réside à la fois, quoique de façons diverses, en son origine et en sa transmission épiscopale'.[59]

Bossuet very much represents the teaching power of the Church in the transmission of Tradition to the faithful through his role as a preacher. Two key spaces within the church identified specifically by Bossuet are the altar and the pulpit, for it is in the latter as well as through the process of the Eucharist that the power of God is experienced by the faithful. In other words Tradition is again not something received from outside but from within. Preaching is thereby placed on the same level as sacramental ministry, especially in a society where for the vast majority the spoken word constitutes the sole means by which an understanding of the faith could be reached. This form of transmission is in itself deeply historical

[59] Ibid., pp. 73–4.

within the Church because the non-written word is the first rule of Christianity. The preaching of the Gospel preceded its written transcription, which was in itself a simple record of what was already being taught orally.[60] It did not 'add' anything.

If, as we have observed, transmission is not simply recitation, what is it? Clearly, as Thomassin believed, Tradition requires explanation and a particular 'sentiment' which guarantees the conformity of that explanation with the truth as articulated by Christ and his successors. But what exactly is meant by explanation or explication if it is not to be invention? For Bossuet, preaching and the need to find explanations for the faithful of all intellectual levels, does not involve saying anything 'different'.[61] Bossuet did not reject the need to find new formulas of expression in terms of passing on an understanding of the faith to the faithful.[62] According to Chadwick, the explication of doctrine meant, for Bossuet, translation into clear language: 'Doctrine progresses not by Christians perceiving that it contains implications not hitherto known, but when more Christians receive it accurately.'[63]

Bossuet did on the other hand accept a space for theological speculation. Despite his hostility to novelty and his frequent invocation of the 'consentement unanime des Pères', Bossuet agreed that there were still points on which an understanding of the faith could be improved except where there was unanimity among the different patristic authorities. Theologians were able to pursue lines of enquiry which did not contradict established dogma. As long as these did not consist of 'rationalising' faith or bringing it down to a human level, the conclusions which emerged were acceptable provided they were clearly advanced as personal interpretations and not the interpretations of the Church as a whole. Bossuet desired rather a continual search for a better understanding of the faith, at the level of the faithful as well as of the Church as an institution, which was guided by the grace of the Holy Spirit.[64] What he didn't want was a theology comprising a purely rational science which accommodated human reason rather than the reverse.

Many issues of Tradition in relation to authority and orthodoxy came together in the affair of the *Augustinus*. In the beginning, unanimity – an essential ingredient in the perceived validity of Tradition from the time of the Fathers – was difficult to achieve even among those one might expect to be natural opponents of the Jansenists. The committed involvement of the French Jesuits in the polemic over the propositions extracted from the *Augustinus* was initially a subject of embarrassment for their Roman

[60] Ibid., pp. 158–61.   [61] Ibid., p. 163.   [62] Ibid., p. 194.
[63] Chadwick, *From Bossuet to Newman*, pp. 17–20.
[64] Tavard, *La Tradition*, pp. 166–72.

colleagues who were much less enthusiastic in their opposition to Jansenius's text, for they realised that, if Jansenius was condemned, problems would certainly arise in relation to St Augustine as a revered authority in the tradition of the Church. The papal nuncio Chigi felt that the Jesuits in France would have done better to remain silent on the issue and to have left Rome to sort it out, especially as some of the ideas which they attacked were eminently defensible. Several of the propositions of Jansenius that were brought to public attention (they originally numbered more than five) were regarded as perfectly orthodox.[65]

One suspects that the outcome of the dispute did not so much address correct interpretation as the authority of the Church as a body. It is certainly true that the affair of the *Augustinus* raised the fundamental principle of the precise domains of theological opinion in which Rome had authority. Arnauld, we recall, did not contest the heretical nature of the propositions and the right of papal authority to condemn them. He denied the facts of the case, namely that the propositions could be found in the *Augustinus*. Did the Church have the right to exercise authority on questions of fact? The argument turned then on the distinction between matters of faith and matters of fact, and, as a consequence, on the ways in which the Church reached decisions on doctrinal integrity. In matters of faith the infallibility of the Church was uncontested. But what view of the Church is meant here? Was the final decision on such matters for papal encyclical or was it the responsibility of the Church in council? If the latter, then theologians and others were free to express their opinion until a decision had been reached. This is especially the case in matters of fact where the Church might not even have the right to impose a respectful silence on those who disagreed on the interpretation offered by authority.[66] In the *Apologie pour les religieuses* of 1664, Arnauld wrote that in matters of fact reason was autonomous and that the pope's authority was no greater than that of historians.[67]

This whole argument was central to the issue of the formulary, imposed on the Church in general and on the nuns of Port-Royal in particular, which demanded submission on the question of the rights of the Church both in matters of faith and in matters of fact. The signing of the formulary fundamentally contradicted Port-Royal's concept of the limits of the authority of the Church over individuals. Whereas they most certainly denied the independence of reason in matters of faith, Arnauld and Nicole asserted the independence of reason in matters of fact. Nicole's argument takes on a perhaps surprising turn when he asserts that submission to authority on matters of fact would be tantamount to permitting the

---

[65] Adam, *Du Mysticisme*, pp. 158–9.   [66] Sedgwick, *Jansenism*, pp. 109–10.
[67] Ibid., p. 131.

proliferation of sects and thus destroying the unity of the Church which would end up like Protestantism with its Anabaptists and Socinians, since each bishop could set himself up as an authority and impose his views on the faithful of his own diocese. Disagreement among bishops – their judgement was after all fallible – could lead to a situation where the beliefs imposed in one diocese differed radically from another. Nicole further claimed that, if the model of papal authority on matters of fact were followed to the letter, authority could be extended to subjects like grammar, philosophy and history which belonged in the domain of reason.[68]

Pascal considers matters of fact in his eighteenth provincial letter where he distinguishes between the sort of knowledge required for determining facts and the sort of knowledge required for determining matters of faith. They are most decidedly not the same. In the first instance judgement passes through the senses. The authority of the senses even derives from faith, since it enters the soul through the senses in the form of the spoken word. Indeed doubting 'le rapport fidèle des sens' would be to destroy faith itself. The interpretation of Scripture falls into the same category as all things. First, we must apprehend the nature of the object under discussion in order to see which order of knowledge we are dealing with. Reason and the senses are entirely inappropriate to the consideration of things supernatural or divine. This is the domain of faith where Scripture and the decisions of the Church are paramount. On the other hand, where it is not a question of something revealed and if it is in proportion to natural reason, then reason itself can judge. If we are dealing with a point of fact, then we shall use our senses in order to decide.

Even in matters of Scripture, St Augustine and St Thomas argue that if the literal sense of a passage is in direct contradiction of what our senses tell us to be the case we should not disavow the senses but we must seek a meaning which accords with 'cette vérité sensible'. Pascal asks to be shown where the condemned propositions are in the *Augustinus* since this is simply a matter of using the senses. Papal authority too would in itself be damaged if a matter of fact were to be decided on the basis of authority alone: 'car il n'y a rien qui puisse faire que ce qui est ne soit pas'. The most famous example is that of Galileo's theory that the earth goes round the sun and that it rotates on its own axis. Rome's condemnation will not stop the earth from turning. The conclusion is that only a conference called to examine the *Augustinus* can ultimately decide. Pascal is certain of course that no delegate would be able to locate the propositions in the text, so they could not possibly have been extracted from it. Facts cannot be

[68] Ibid., p. 122.

decreed on the sole basis of authority. In this sense no papal bull that pronounces on the *Augustinus* which does not have the support of the Church in council is invulnerable.

Arnauld complicated things however when he slipped from a position of legitimate dissension in matters of fact to dissension in matters of faith. A single theologian had the right, according to him, to defend a doctrine which his judgement and his conscience proclaimed to be true. Arnauld affirmed that 'submission and obedience [of an individual] to legitimate authority does not mean that [he] has to fail in his duty to God and to his conscience'. The grounds for this judgement were that the Church in its earthly structure was composed of ecclesiastical officials who were human and therefore capable of error to the point that errors could not only be made in matters of fact but also in the construction of articles of faith by the pope, theological faculties and even councils. For Arnauld, infallibility in matters of faith could only be accorded to the Church in ecumenical council.[69]

Dissension over Tradition thus affected fundamental issues regarding the nature of the Church and its authority, particularly in the limits that are set to dissension itself and the tolerance that could be permitted within a body which ultimately rested on authority for its unity. Nicole seems to argue, almost paradoxically, that unity must be a function of argument and tolerance of dissension on matters of fact. Although Tavard argues that Arnauld's position must probably be accepted as correct on this matter, who is to decide what is a fact? Is it not possible that articles of faith and the construction put upon them can also be regarded as facts? Where are the limits to the notion of fact? This must particularly be the case where 'facts' involve an element of textual interpretation as in the case of the *Augustinus*. One wonders whether the defence of Nicole and Arnauld is weakened by their confusion of different sorts of fact.

Arnauld's position in particular seems to militate in favour of a boundless space of dissension. A defence based on individual conscience has no limits at all. In this sense what difference would an ecumenical council make if one still held its decision to be wrong? If the decision remained the same the error would be compounded at every stage. In human terms the highest authority becomes the individual, and the Church is bereft of authority save in the conscience of that individual. Again the line between this sort of argument and the Protestant position is a very thin one. Moreover, the rights of individual conscience must logically be extended to domains outside religion. It is easy therefore to see why royal power identified in Jansenism a significant danger to its own

[69] Ibid.

operations. The weakening of authority in one domain could act as a model for others. The space of the Church and that of the world ended up dangerously confused.

Any consideration of Tradition and interpretation raises problems of orthodoxy and authority. It goes without saying that the interpretation of Tradition depends on a notion of orthodoxy, on a body of doctrine to which all can refer and which acts as a bench-mark according to which any theological conclusion must be judged. But it is legitimate to ask whether any Church or body whose identity is based on a doctrine, and which arms itself with the means of disciplining those who no longer hold to it, can define in advance the boundaries of that orthodoxy. Dissension often seems to arise precisely from the Church's inability to fix stable limits to orthodoxy itself. Orthodoxy turns out to be retrospective since its points of vulnerability are unpredictable at any point in history. The space of orthodoxy of course presupposes a frontier with what is heterodox. The vulnerability of the orthodox is demonstrated not only through dissension from within, but in the way the space of orthodoxy relates to other spaces. The most obvious example is the establishment of Protestantism, which always held itself to be the guardian of 'orthodoxy', that is to say the 'real Church'. For some, orthodoxy is not a problem even in the face of the challenge from Protestants. Their own behaviour for Bossuet is a source of proof of the universality of the Church since they themselves recognise the historical validity of the primitive authority on which the Church is built. Leaving the Church can only be 'nouveauté' and therefore a break with a continuous history they cannot deny.[70] The only predecessors they can provide for themselves are those they share with the Catholic Church itself.[71]

The Council of Trent attempted to reformulate Catholic orthodoxy in the face of a clear challenge from without. Owen Chadwick describes Bossuet's position as implying that heretics help the Church to find new language to express belief. Ideas do not change, because the Church knows what it believes.[72] Leszek Kolakowski argues on the other hand that the orthodox is historically in many cases the product of the heterodox. Dogma appears because of the prior constitution of anti-dogma.[73] The periphery defines the centre. Heresy represents a visible frontier or limit beyond which it is impossible to go, but this cannot necessarily be known in advance since the exact formulations with which to combat heretical theses cannot yet be known. These themselves need to come under the

[70] Bossuet, *Oeuvres*, XIV, 376–7.
[71] Ibid., pp. 419–20.
[72] Chadwick, *From Bossuet to Newman*, p. 19.
[73] Kolakowski, *Chrétiens sans église*, p. 69.

closest scrutiny. This phenomenon was not, in seventeenth-century France, unique to Catholicism. Protestants too had their heretics who were measured against their own 'orthodoxy'.

The importance of orthodoxy in relation to Tradition is brought out by the degree to which it is permissible to interpret Tradition. As we have seen, doctrine, in so far as it is unanimously agreed by the Fathers and confirmed by the authority of the Church, is immutable. But this does not mean that new formulas cannot be found in the explanation of that doctrine. Hence in the mind of someone like Bossuet, a unified linguistic space exists where, ultimately, the frontiers of meaning are fixed. But these frontiers can only be fixed negatively in the same way that the frontiers of orthodoxy are fixed by what is heterodox. Rather than knowing what doctrine in its totality means in advance, we know what it cannot mean. But can the frontier between those two concepts be fixed in quite the way that the Church would like? What is certain is that orthodoxy and heterodoxy in Christian doctrine are in the end functions of language, which means that new explanations and novelty are never very far apart. The space in between is precisely the space of dissension.

Richard Simon and biblical exegesis

Within the tradition of the Church the text of Scripture was always bound to be a sensitive area, given the emphasis on the divine inspiration of the Old Testament and the direct witness of the authors of much of the New Testament. What brought renewed impetus to problems which had exercised the Fathers of the early Church or scholars in the time before the seventeenth century was the existence of rival interpretations of key texts by the Protestants. While it was clear that those interpretations needed a response, the answer, in the eyes of some, could not rest on the state of the biblical text as it existed. If the text was in some respects unreliable so must be the reply. But how far could individuals go in their criticism of Scripture? Simon's *Histoire critique du Vieux Testament* (1678) could be said to have come at a bad moment, following as it did the *Tractatus theologico-politicus* of Spinoza whose biblical criticism was motivated by a form of metaphysics considered by many as anti-Christian.[74] The very word 'critique' posed a problem in terms of its negative implications. In France, Simon's approach to the question concentrated minds on what was perceived as the challenge his work represented to Tradition.

Simon's work focuses on two levels of meaning in Scripture, the one literal and the other theological or mystical. The first might be in itself

[74] Auvray, *Richard Simon*, p. 42.

considered as of philological concern and the second involves interpretation leading to the establishment of doctrine. The literal sense, however, functions as a sort of control on the other because, as Simon reasons, the text could be translated according to theological prejudice: this would no longer be translation in the strictest sense but the imposition of personally held ideas on the word of God. On the other hand, the mystical meaning of Scripture is not the prime concern of that form of criticism which concentrates rather on grammar and history. The mystical meaning is addressed by theologians who must identify the way in which the witness of the past favours – in general terms or in a particular text – this or that spiritual sense, and the way in which it accords with faith. There is thus a tension between the priority to be given to a literal interpretation rooted in grammar and history, or a theological interpretation founded on the analogy with faith and the tradition of the Fathers. Simon is not opposed to theological interpretations, but he is opposed to those commentators who have abused an analogical interpretation and who pass off their work as the tradition of the Fathers. Serious theological interpretations should not be denied but they should be controlled in the light of the literal sense of the text.[75] The fixing of a literal interpretation establishes what cannot be the case and provides a yardstick by which to judge whether the Fathers themselves have got it right. It could therefore present itself as a control of orthodoxy.

Simon always maintained that, far from attacking Tradition, he saw himself as placing it on a surer foundation. His meticulous analysis of the conditions in which the text of Scripture had been handed down was meant to demonstrate the indispensable role of Tradition in any explanation, particularly in the light of the Protestant assumption that the Bible was a clear mirror which reflected a simple and self-evident faith.[76] One of Simon's principal arguments, which justified the concept of criticism, was that the Hebrew text of the Old Testament, while it preserved the substance of the Jewish tradition, was not 'fixed' in its details. The lack of clarity of its language had obvious consequences for its interpretation, precisely the reason why the text itself should be subject to close scrutiny along with the Fathers' own pronouncements which derived from that same Jewish tradition.[77] Simon's method was therefore to investigate commentators of all ages, to use all the tools of learning at his disposal, in order to ascertain the literal meaning of the text which would then ensure the soundness of the overall tradition.

One problem which needed to be resolved was the question of

[75] Tavard, *La Tradition*, pp. 126–31.
[76] J. Steinmann, *Richard Simon et les origines de l'exégèse biblique* (Bruges, 1960), pp. 97–8.
[77] Ibid., p. 103.

alterations and additions to the Hebrew text of the Old Testament. To what extent did these harm the authority of the text? The response of the Fathers was based on their conviction that the text was composed according to divine inspiration, the line followed by Simon in his reply to Spinoza who saw the changes as destroying the authenticity of the texts. These additions must have the same authority as the rest of the text, otherwise we would be forced to conclude that all that is contained in Scripture was not equally divine and canonical.[78] But how then are alterations to be defended at all? Simon here makes a distinction between inspiration and original authenticity which he bases on the concept of a global inspiration given by God to the whole body of scribes responsible for copying the text.[79] The same was true for Old and New Testament alike. Augustine himself had admitted oversights and confusions of one name for another by sacred writers. Whereas differences of order and expression could be found among the writers of the Gospels, matter and thought had been faithfully recorded.[80] Such a postulate threatened to dispense with criticism altogether, since a special providence might have led to the conservation of the texts. Simon denies this: quite simply the autograph manuscripts have been lost. In addition, Simon does not allow the fact of inspiration to stand against reason and experience. While those who handed down the texts were certainly the instruments of God, they were human. Certainly the Holy Spirit prevented them from making mistakes in what they wrote, but it cannot be assumed that everything they wrote was entirely divine and supernatural. Hence the necessity of a 'critique'.[81] But what is the exact order of error? A further distinction has to be made between inspiration and prophetic revelation. Inspiration is not the equivalent of a word-for-word dictation, but a form of assistance which prevents error in the choice of words and thoughts. The form of inspiration which can be regarded properly as prophetic reveals what is essential to faith, whereas the other sort of inspiration is concerned with what is properly moral and historical. Simon seems to hold to views expressed by others in the seventeenth century in which only doctrinal truths were guaranteed by inspiration: sacred writers were recognised as capable of error once they moved away from writing on the truths of faith.[82] The task of criticism was to distinguish between the results of the two forms of inspiration, otherwise articles of faith would lose their distinctive character in terms of belief.

[78] Simon, *Histoire critique du Vieux Testament*, Preface.
[79] Steinmann, *Richard Simon*, p. 100.
[80] E. Portalié (trans. R. J. Bastran), *A Guide to the Thought of St Augustine* (London, 1960), p. 122.
[81] Steinmann, *Richard Simon*, p. 209.
[82] Ibid., p. 266.

Crucial to arguments relating to Tradition is the status of Scripture itself within the entire corpus of texts which comprise Tradition. The complexity of the matter is apparent in Simon's assertion that the Fathers did not always resort to the Scriptures in disputes with heretics, but referred to the non-written word which had been preserved in the main churches founded by the Apostles.[83] Thus because a tradition existed prior to the writing of the Gospels and indeed because only part of this tradition has come down to us in written form, the Fathers' works relay a tradition parallel to the text of Scripture, so that Scripture is not sufficient in itself. This argument is again consistent with the views of Augustine: 'There are many things which the universal church holds, and which because of this are believed to have been commanded by the Apostles, even though they are not found in any written document.'[84] But here Simon clearly addresses the Protestants who have abandoned Tradition and who place their whole faith in Scripture alone. Irenaeus agreed that the sacred texts constituted a source for learning about religion but he also believed that they should be read through the successors of the Apostles who were the repositories of their doctrine.[85]

This has consequences for the status of the biblical text in terms of its correctness or otherwise. Simon attacks the Protestants and particularly the Socinians who consult the text as if it were the only version possible, irrespective of the state of the text through time. Hence the importance of Tradition, since it would be dangerous to seek the truth only in texts which had been subject to so many changes and which depended in so many ways on scribes.[86] For the Catholic at least, the traditions of dogma can be identified beyond Scripture through Tradition. In any case the Fathers had ruled that changes to the text did not affect faith or good morals, and, more importantly, did not affect the consideration 'en gros' (Simon's term) that must be given to the whole of Scripture.[87]

The text and therefore the status of the Vulgate raise more specific problems of orthodoxy. Is it the correct version of the Bible? It all depends on what is meant by correct. Certainly, the Vulgate, which antedates the Reformation, cannot, like more recent versions, be suspect. The Vulgate was also the version prescribed by the Council of Trent, and, as Simon agrees, the text juridically declared as authentic. That is to say that it is 'official' and 'recognised as having authority'. But it cannot be considered a text in exact conformity with the original text of the Bible. Simon affirms

---

[83] Simon, *Histoire critique du Vieux Testament*, Preface.
[84] Portalié, *A Guide to the Thought of St Augustine*, pp. 119–20.
[85] Simon, *Histoire critique du texte du Nouveau Testament*, p. 38.
[86] Simon, *Histoire critique du Vieux Testament*, Preface.
[87] Ibid., p. 6.

that the text of the Vulgate may be the least suspect but it is not free of error.[88] The Council of Trent's declaration of the Vulgate as the authorised version was intended to lead to conclusions on dogma but not to resolve questions of criticism.[89] For Simon, the debate surrounding the Vulgate did not in any case involve an article of faith.[90] The literal value of a translation is not a matter where Tradition is competent and is excluded from its domain. Theology is not the main concern but the exactness of language. Consequently, the authenticity of the Vulgate does not guarantee the exactness of the translation, only its religious and theological value.[91] Simon in this respect widens the space of competence to include trained critics rather than just theologians.

Beyond the actual text of Scripture what is the status of the Fathers' pronouncements upon it? Simon interprets the Council of Trent as establishing that one must never question Tradition or its authority in matters of faith. Whoever wishes to find faith in the Scriptures must read them in the light of the faith of the Church, which is also the faith of the Fathers. Such a position demonstrates the value of Tradition but also its limits. In the investigation of the text, where it is no longer a matter of faith, no-one is bound by prior opinion. The Fathers could not possibly have had the final word, since they had not had the benefit of more recent research techniques. In addition, their inevitable lack of long-term historical perspective deprives them of a privileged place among commentators.[92] In Simon's own words: 'Il faut donc mettre de la différence entre ce qui regarde purement la critique de la Bible, et ce qui regarde la créance reçue universellement dans l'Eglise.'[93]

In the space of criticism, it can happen that new interpretations which do not address articles of faith are to be preferred to the old, since the critic can draw on the discoveries of others like certain Protestants and Socinians, just as the Fathers consulted Greek versions of the Bible produced by the Church's enemies. In addition the Fathers neglected the Hebrew text of Scripture from which one must begin.[94] Simon interprets the Council of Trent as allowing that the interpretation of Scripture should not be linked to explanations provided by the Fathers but that one must interpret the biblical text as literally as possible, without being bound by their prejudices.[95] The opinion of a single doctor who proposed an

[88] Ibid., pp. 264–6.
[89] Steinmann, *Richard Simon*, p. 122.
[90] Auvray, *Richard Simon*, pp. 135–6.
[91] Tavard, *La Tradition*, pp. 147–8.
[92] Ibid., pp. 144–5.
[93] Simon, *Histoire critique du Vieux Testament*, p. 419.
[94] Ibid., Preface.
[95] Ibid., p. 419.

alternative interpretation of the text subsequently tolerated by the Church was sufficient to prevent persuasion simply by the authority of the greater number.[96] Simon's suspicion of some Fathers in their interpretation of Scripture extended to criticism of St Augustine who, he claims, sometimes accommodated Scripture to his ideas rather than the reverse.[97]

In the second half of the century opposition to the work of scholars working on the text of the Bible hardened both in France and in Rome to the extent that an independent space for scholarship became next to impossible. Simon's ideas were always bound to provoke controversy, especially if they raised the spectre of fallibility in St Augustine whose overall record on biblical exegesis, it must be said, has not fully stood the test of time. Simon's positions on biblical exegesis and his consideration of St Augustine within Tradition were virulently attacked by Bossuet (who had copies of the *Histoire critique du Vieux Testament* seized and burnt) in some of the strongest and most unyielding polemical texts of the century. Simon's work was no less than an attack on the authenticity of Scripture, the inspiration granted to those who wrote it, the providence which allowed its transmission to the faithful, Tradition itself, the authority of the Fathers and the uniformity of the Church's doctrine all at once.[98] His attitude to Simon was fiercely anti-intellectual. Bossuet did not deny that esteem was owing to those who possessed a knowledge of languages which led to enlightenment. But the rejection of abusive interpretations of texts could not possibly necessitate as much Hebrew, Greek, Latin, history or criticism as Simon implied in the body of his work.[99] He reiterates this prejudice in the *Défense de la tradition et des saints pères*, scornfully dismissing the idea that 'le fond de la science' and a knowledge of things sacred should depend so much on a knowledge of letters and of languages.[100] Bossuet simply does not question that there might be difficulties in such a 'science'.

Simon's eclecticism also provoked Bossuet's anger. References to contemporary critics, including the Socinians, in the establishment of the literal sense of the text, is seen to stand in opposition to the theological sense of the Fathers' interpretations which Simon despises.[101] Bossuet, ignoring the complexity of the case, seems to be arguing that Simon is establishing a clear-cut preference for one over the other, which is nothing short of plain distortion. Bossuet also claims, entirely without foundation, that Simon's reference to Socinian critics made of him a Socinian.[102] Guilt by association was enough, especially when assisted by a crude

[96] Quoted in Auvray, *Richard Simon*, p. 139.
[97] Quoted in Steinmann, *Richard Simon*, p. 113.
[98] Bossuet, *Oeuvres*, XXIII, 304.   [99] Ibid., p. 370.
[100] Ibid., XXIV, 168.   [101] Ibid., XXIII, 319.   [102] Ibid., p. 321.

deterministic view of the consequences of that association: because
Socinian criticism of the Bible was rational in nature and very hostile to
certain beliefs like the Trinity, Simon's recourse to their work in his own
research could not but mean that he came naturally to espouse their views.
Moreover, Bossuet believed that all those like Simon who drew on the
Hebrew tradition in the books of the rabbis could not fail to stray from the
truth.[103] Bossuet would have had no truck with Steinmann's modern and
liberal view that Simon's studies on Jewish culture had two aims: to enable
Christians to understand and above all to practise their religion better,
and to promote a truer understanding of the Jews who had hitherto been
the subject of gross lies and stupid prejudices.[104] Objective scholarship
simply destroyed the purity of Catholic space. Thus even the best of what
other sorts of religious space had to offer was excluded. Its inclusion
simply made frontiers dangerously unclear. Bossuet regarded Simon's
inclusive sense of scholarship as reducing everything to a state of
indifference and in so doing dissolving the frontiers of Catholic space.
Ironically Bossuet found himself in agreement with the Protestant
position that a special providence had presided over the survival of the
texts of Scripture, thus rendering any form of criticism irrelevant, a
position which Simon rejected.[105]

But the virulence of Bossuet's attack derives from his fundamental
belief that, in his criticisms of St Augustine and his conclusion that he had
in some ways parted company with other Fathers on the questions of grace
and original sin, Simon opened the door for the destruction of Tradition.
The most important consequences of Simon's position were, first, that
ownership of Augustine would be handed over to Protestants and, second,
that any suggestion of Augustinian innovation had the effect of relativising
tradition and introducing tolerance of different opinions.[106] The important conclusion that Bossuet arrives at is that the space of orthodoxy is
indivisible. One is orthodox in everything or nothing. If innovation occurs
or is suggested in one thing it can encourage innovation in others. In the
context of the text of Scripture, the orthodox commentator is guilty if he
does not support 'la plénitude du texte'. Simon sins, it would seem, in
preferring one or two Catholic authors to Tradition, to the Council of
Trent and to the unanimity of the Fathers.[107]

Bossuet was not alone in his criticism of Simon. Sainte-Marie's
approach in his work *Réflexions sur les regles . . . de la critique* (1713) also

---

[103] Ibid., p. 301.   [104] Steinmann, *Richard Simon*, p. 76.
[105] Ibid., pp. 208–9.
[106] A. Roumeliote, 'Bossuet gendarme de l'augustinisme face à Richard Simon et Jean de
Launoy', in P. Ranson (ed.), *Saint Augustin* (Giromagny, 1988), 398–405 (p. 400).
[107] Bossuet, *Œuvres*, XXIII, 332–3.

rests on textual fundamentalism: Simon's assertion that the commentator must be free to add vowel points and accents to the original text means that such changes are the result of a personal choice and that the text will no longer be the word of God. A part of the text will always have been of the editor's own invention. Since he will not have been able to speak and pronounce Hebrew as well as Jews themselves, it is to be feared that the translation will stray from the text and introduce new ideas. More than this, other commentators will appear who feel that their knowledge of Hebrew is greater and will change things further with the result that a pure text will no longer exist.[108] Commentators will then be working on each other's texts, and no longer on the original.

An equally bad idea is to put alternative translations in the margins of published editions or notes indicating that the real sense of the Hebrew is uncertain. In those circumstances, how will we be able to distinguish what is the real word of God? Not only does Sainte-Marie imply that giving the faithful a choice is dangerous and inappropriate but he asks how Catholics can then be different from Protestants.[109] Where, in other words, will it be possible to fix the frontiers of orthodoxy? Furthermore, if Simon produces a text according to the rules of his own method, who can be sure that his version is better than the next?[110] Where is the criterion for departing from the original? It can only be that we are talking about the end of Tradition. Sainte-Marie finds it impossible to reconcile Simon's adherence to the indispensability of Tradition and his deference to critical method.[111] He too takes Simon to task for preferring to the word of Christ and the Apostles the opinions of rabbis, Hobbes and in particular Spinoza who denied that Moses was the author of the Pentateuch.[112] Indeed Sainte-Marie homes in on what might be considered the real weakness of Simon, that is to say the distinction between the domain of criticism and that of faith. For Sainte-Marie the distinction does not hold because, if Simon is concerned with meaning and not with style, that is surely the business of tradition because meaning is related directly to belief.[113]

Simon has not lacked for defenders in the modern age. Tavard regards the way Bossuet distorts Simon's position as scandalous and his arguments as untenable. Particularly damaging was the false ascription of rationalism in biblical criticism to Simon. Certainly Simon wished to establish the literal sense of the text of the Bible, but at the same time he wished to preserve its religious and theological sense which was beyond the power of a criticism based on human reason alone, however grounded it may be in scientific method.[114] What is particularly galling is that

---

[108] Sainte-Marie, *Réflexions*, II, 112–15.   [109] Ibid., pp. 117–18.
[110] Ibid., p. 129.   [111] Ibid., p. 131.   [112] Ibid., I, 139.   [113] Ibid., II, 134.
[114] Tavard, *La Tradition*, pp. 149–50.

Bossuet denied Simon the freedom of exegetical and theological research, protected by providence, that he outlines in his *Explication de l'Apocalypse* and which would lead to 'une compréhension progressive des mystères'.[115]

Pierre Auvray rejects the charge that Simon was engaged in anything other than biblical criticism. Not only did he not begin from preconceived ideas, he expressly forbade himself to support one theological position against another. He did not engage in apologetics or counter-apologetics, like Spinoza or Bossuet, although he was not unaware of the usefulness of his work for his own religion which he wished not to challenge but to illuminate.[116] As Tavard notes, the notion of theological progress or progress in dogma is completely absent from the work of Simon.[117] In fact the need Simon felt to map out an independent space for criticism derived rather from the damaging and misleading results of criticism emerging from other quarters, especially from Protestants. Simon's impetus was determined by his perception that it would soon be too late to preserve a Christian France in the face of this assault from without.[118]

Unquestionably, however, Simon went quite a bit further than his predecessors. He wanted to elucidate the origins of texts, to investigate the conditions of production and transmission, to go beyond the answers provided by Tradition, although his analysis of the Pentateuch and its authors evinces a number of weaknesses, especially in his lack of precision.[119] In a period when the Church was attempting to combat deviant belief on so many fronts the audacity of Simon was clearly too much. Too many preconceived notions, especially of authorship, had to change: the possibility that the text of Matthew's Gospel had been translated into Greek by other than the Apostle himself, the conceivable inauthenticity of the Epistle to the Hebrews and other Catholic epistles, the mistaken attribution of the Apocalypse to John, and a host of other things. In a situation where belief in a text is all or nothing, the most effective critics came from outside the Church, like Hobbes and Spinoza.[120] Simon therefore exemplified the difficulties of establishing a tradition of criticism from within. How could you convince those in authority that orthodoxy and criticism are compatible? For his pains, Simon was expelled from the Oratory in 1678. Criticism was expelled from the space of the Church.

---

[115] Ibid., p. 173.
[116] Auvray, *Richard Simon*, p. 66.
[117] Tavard, *La Tradition*, p. 143.
[118] Steinmann, *Richard Simon*, p. 419.
[119] See Auvray, *Richard Simon*, pp. 58–62.
[120] Auvray, *Richard Simon*, p. 175.

5 The space of ideas

Introduction

If it is true that the Church constituted a space of dissension in terms of Tradition, orthodoxy and authority, how true must this be of the space of ideas during the age of the new science, or at least of the consolidation of that science? In many ways, the new (or not so new) discoveries were at odds with certain well-established ideas forming an essential part of the Christian tradition, and those who led the field in new developments showed themselves to be acutely aware of the difficulties of those discoveries for traditional explanations of the Christian faith. But they did not regard their scientific activities as destroying that faith. Scientists of the new sort did not see themselves in opposition to Christian orthodoxy. Many followed Descartes in explicitly affirming their allegiance to it. In addition, a number of thinkers within the Church itself accepted the new ideas which, they held, could be assimilated, if not by traditional teaching, at least by means of a reformulation of that teaching which did no harm to its fundamental principles.

The accommodation of new ideas to the space of religion could only be successfully achieved by establishing the distinction between what could properly be ascribed to explanations according to articles of faith, and what could legitimately be the role of reason in an explanation of the universe and the physical world. This did not entail the exclusion of reason from the religious space, especially in achieving an understanding of the faith; nor were matters of science considered entirely irrelevant to matters of religion. But it did entail avoiding confusion between the criteria to be used in different sorts of explanations. However, some awkward questions arose. Where exactly was the frontier between a religious and a scientific explanation, a problem which had in fact exercised the late medieval mind? What if the religious explanation for a particular physical phenomenon, originating in the text of the Scriptures, conflicted with the explanation of science?

Consequently, new explanations and new forms of thinking did not have it all their own way. In the course of the century, the new science was accused not only of falling short of Christian orthodoxy but of challenging the legitimacy of authority, so bound up with orthodoxy. What is at stake is the role of human reason in both the religious space and the space of the new ideas, and whether the use of human reason in either threatens faith itself. The safeguarding of the faith was not perceived only as the task of theologians. The new scientists were also conscious of the need to describe and explain their activity, not only in terms of its legitimacy in the study of the natural world, but of its importance in the space of religion itself.

It is impossible in one single chapter or even book to do justice to the complexity of ideas in seventeenth-century France. It is also impossible to adhere in any absolute sense to a black and white version of intellectual confrontations. It none the less remains true that fierce controversy raged in our period in defence of one intellectual tradition or another, and clear battle lines were drawn up. It is therefore necessary to proceed on the basis of some distinctions if we are to understand the issues at all clearly. Quite simply the principles of the new science and of Cartesianism in particular were rejected, with different emphases, by large sections of those involved in teaching either in the University of Paris or the Jesuit colleges, and we must ask ourselves why this was the case.

While Cartesianism does not represent the total space of the new science, at least that science which was opposed not only to the philosophy of the scholastic tradition but to various forms of 'occult' science, it must none the less constitute a major focus of interest in the intellectual controversies of the period. It is also unquestioned that, starting from a position within an established intellectual tradition, Descartes took seventeenth-century thinking in radical new directions by his perceived need to adapt that tradition to the perspective of a new form of scientific thinking endowed with a new set of tools.

Intellectual traditions and their adherents

What, then, were the intellectual traditions at the heart of seventeenth-century thought and philosophical controversy? Two major traditions confront each other in the course of the period: on the one hand the system of thought encapsulated in St Thomas Aquinas's synthesis of Christian thought with Aristotelianism, elaborated in the thirteenth century, known variously as Thomism or Thomism / Aristotelianism, and on the other, Augustinianism. The latter influenced not only the discussion of strictly theological issues but, in Augustine's opposition to Aristotelianism and his preference for the philosophy of Plato, also made its mark on discussions revolving around the principles of thought central to the pursuit of the new science as articulated in Cartesianism. It is often Augustine's preference for Plato which came between St Thomas and Augustine despite the constant reference of St Thomas to Augustine as an unimpeachable authority in so many areas.

The authority of Aristotle formed the basis of teaching in Jesuit schools and the colleges attached to the University of Paris, although a change began to be discernible in many minds from the 1660s. This was not of course an arbitrary choice. In the first place, the work of St Thomas gave intellectual and religious weight to it and in the second place, it was held to carry the weight of truth, especially in many (but by no means all) of its principles and descriptions, and in its explanatory procedures. Aristotelian principles were capable of explaining important aspects of the faith, like the phenomenon of the Eucharist.

Philosophical traditions are usually concerned with answering questions about how we acquire knowledge and then with establishing the status of the knowledge acquired. Seventeenth-century arguments over the processes of knowledge were central to an understanding of man's relation to God, and the relation of man's knowledge of the physical universe to what man could know of the divine. In the end any description of the universe came back to the Creator and the creation in one way or another, and what exactly we can know of each. It is important here to distinguish between forms of knowledge revealed in Scripture which cannot be the product of the human mind and forms of knowledge dependent on human reason, aided or unaided.

The basic principle of the Thomistic system in its purest form is that, in the realm of human reason, all knowledge comes first through the senses, the mind being initially a 'tabula rasa'. Knowledge is thus always determined by things and the active processes of the intellect extract from the data of the senses universals, that is to say the concepts by which we come to know species of objects. In this system all things are composed of matter and form, where form is the equivalent of the soul. The soul, of which the human soul is the prototype, is the principle of change in things or the principle which determines the activities of things. In human beings and in things body and soul cannot be separate entities in themselves. The importance of this view of matter in the universe, known as substantial forms, is the degree to which it determines the procedures of science as grouping things according to their qualities through what is universal in their activities and describing the behaviour of things according to those qualities. A famous illustration of this system of thought is Aristotle's explanation of acceleration. His theory that movement is at a uniform speed as it is imparted by the mover is contradicted by observation, since a stone thrown in the air visibly accelerates as it falls. Aristotle's explanation is that the stone being of the earth not of air, desires to regain its natural resting place because of a tendency within it.

This perspective on the acquisition of knowledge has repercussions for the thinking subject in relation to the physical world. Through the agency of the senses – and the senses are the means by which knowledge of things first enters the mind – the intellect becomes a prolongation of the physical world. The thinking subject has thus no direct intuition of itself. The human mind cannot apprehend the purely intelligible, and we have knowledge of the mind through its activity of knowing things in the same way that we come to know objects themselves through their own activities, especially in terms of the way they change. Even knowledge of God begins, at the level of human reason, with consideration of material bodies. St Thomas himself asserts that the knowledge of God gained by the human mind does not transcend knowledge gathered from sensible things. The human mind can have no direct intuition of God.[1]

Augustinianism, with its emphasis on aspects of Platonist philosophy, came to constitute the main rival to Thomism / Aristotelianism in the seventeenth century. Although St Thomas often referred to Augustine in his works, there are, since in any case Aristotle wrote against Plato, enough significant differences between them for individual thinkers, whether they did so explicitly or not, to describe themselves as Thomists or Augustinians. It is unlikely however that St Augustine would have considered himself primarily a philosopher and he showed little interest in human science as such. Augustine's principal orientation in his works is man's actual relation to God. His philosophy and theology revolve around the soul's orientation to God, and it is in this context that he deals with the objects of our perception in the natural world. Augustine took corporeal objects as a starting point in the mind's ascent to God, 'though even in this respect the soul is a more adequate starting point: we should return within ourselves, where truth abides, and use the soul, the image of God, as a stepping-stone to him'.[2] Augustine stressed inner truth, inner experience, introspection and self-consciousness. The nature of our thought has priority over its content in as much as it is more important to get our thinking right before coming to correct ideas about the objects of our thinking.

For Augustine the objects observable by our senses do not constitute

[1] I have, in this general discussion of the intellectual context of knowledge, drawn substantially on E. Gilson, *The Christian Philosophy of Saint Augustine* (London, 1961), *The Christian Philosophy of Saint Thomas Aquinas* (London, 1957) and Portalié, *A Guide to the Thought of St Augustine*.
[2] F. Copleston, *A History of Philosophy*, 7 vols. (London, 1958–64), IV, *Descartes to Leibnitz*, 55.

the proper object of the human intellect. This is because of the different qualities attainable in the truths of nature and eternal truths:

The rational soul of man exercises true knowledge and attains true certainty when it contemplates eternal truths in and through itself: when it turns toward the material world and uses corporeal instruments it cannot attain true knowledge. Augustine assumed, with Plato, that the objects of true knowledge are unchanging, from which it necessarily follows that knowledge of changing objects is not true knowledge.[3]

Augustine was certainly sceptical of a science which started from sense-data. The importance of St Augustine as a source of thinking was his promotion of a form of knowledge accessible to the human mind as a result of the process of inner contemplation at the level of intellect.

The influence of St Augustine in the relation of thought to a new sort of scientific thinking is exemplified in René Descartes (1596–1650) who, as we shall discover later, influenced Arnauld and, for a time, Pierre Nicole, another of Port-Royal's major thinkers and moralists. We shall also discover that many were of the opinion that Descartes used Augustinian propositions in a way for which they were not designed. In its fundamental principles, Descartes's philosophical system in its studied contemplation of the life of the mind rejects the dependence of thought on information received through the senses on the basis that it is not uniformly reliable. A more reliable foundation for the acquisition of truth about the world is thus found to be necessary. If a modern science was to provide an adequate description of the universe, mind had to be liberated from matter, in other words from the physical world, in the way that it was not in Thomism / Aristotelianism. Descartes achieves this in the *Méditations* (published first in Latin in 1641 and 1642) and, in shortened form, in the *Discours de la méthode* (1637), by conceiving of himself as having no body, rejecting the testimony of the senses and even the proofs of mathematical demonstrations in order to see whether something indubitable remains. His discovery is that, in thinking away all aspects of his relation to the physical world, he cannot think himself away as a thinking subject. In contrast to the Thomist perspective, Descartes has a direct intuition of the self at the level of pure intelligibility. Knowledge of the mind is not therefore determined by any content derived from outside the mind. Thought is not dependent on things. This leads Descartes to establish that the essence of matter is extension whereas the mind is unextended. Since the mind is unextended it is immaterial and, as a consequence, immortal. Knowledge of the exterior world cannot however rest on this level of inner contemplation. Although the *cogito* is what

[3] Ibid., pp. 55–6.

is known as a privileged idea in that it cannot be other than true, it does not in itself guarantee the truth of the contents of the mind since the thinking subject could have invented all the ideas contained in the mind. Descartes requires one true idea which he could not have invented and which would then guarantee, subject to certain conditions being met, the truth of all other ideas. This he finds in the idea of God whose existence can be proved in a number of ways. What is clear is that for Descartes there is no certain science without God.

Descartes's main target was the theory of substantial forms which, in their conjunction of the material and the spiritual, constituted an obstacle to a *quantitative* science which, using mathematics, offered a more accurate and self-correcting explanation of the universe, although Descartes's science itself was founded on arguments in themselves grounded in geometry. With Cartesian dualism the field was left open to scientific enquiry which could quantify the phenomena of the physical world without having to take into account any occult or 'spiritual' qualities in things. The scientist was separated from his field of enquiry and free to pursue knowledge of purely physical causes in the natural world. God guarantees the truth of mathematics without which the 'mechanistic' explanation of the universe is impossible. It is also the case however that Descartes, in relating the truth of mathematics to his idea of God, saw himself as making the case for religion as well as for science. The space of science was firmly rooted in, indeed depended on, the space of religion. Subsequent discussions in this chapter will attempt to explain why Descartes's departures from Thomism and other aspects of his philosophy fell foul of Thomists and Augustinians alike.

Ideas and authority

In the first four decades of the seventeenth century adherence to Aristotle as an authority in science carried with it adherence to a particular description of the universe. This was composed of a series of concentric, crystalline spheres which, moved by the outermost sphere of the *primum mobile*, revolved in perfect circles. The spheres were impenetrable and nothing could move from one to the other. The earth, whose moon was perceived as having a smooth surface, found itself at the centre of this universe and was alone subject to any form of change. Moreover, as the spheres progressed from the earth to the space of the prime mover, all things ascended in a hierarchy from the lowliest object through man to the highest form of intelligibility in what has become known as the 'great chain of being'. This description shows how easily it could be integrated within Christian thought, especially the linking of creatures with the Creator.

By the beginning of the seventeenth century cracks had already begun to appear in the Aristotelian scientific edifice. The nova observed in 1572 demonstrated that the heavens were also subject to change, and the comet of 1577 destroyed the notion that things could not pass from one sphere to another. Kepler calculated that the planets move, not in perfect circles, but ellipses, and, most important of all, Galileo destroyed the system of Ptolemy and discovered the moons of Jupiter, thus suggesting the existence of other earth-like systems in the universe. His telescope also revealed sunspots and the craters of the moon. How could the idea of authority, where the traditional teaching of science was, in the Thomist / Aristotelian system, so bound up with orthodoxy, withstand such a seemingly irrefutable onslaught? Equally, what could replace Aristotelianism as a more satisfactory guarantee of that orthodoxy? The complexity of the responses to the problems raised illustrate what might be perceived as a crisis or at the very least a challenge for the space of religion generated by changes in the space of science, especially when in the traditional forms of teaching the two were so organically linked through a single philosophical system.

In crude terms two responses presented themselves: accommodation to varying degrees and outright rejection. The response of the University of Paris and the teachers among the Jesuits is instructive. To suggest that Aristotelians remained static in their approach to science flies in the face of all the evidence which points to an 'eclectic tendency to accept new developments'. Charles B. Schmidt has demonstrated that they held a wide range of views from the outright conservative to the progressive.[4] But what in this context could 'progressive' actually mean? Brockliss, in his study of the collèges de plein exercice, rejects the idea that the institutions of higher education had absolutely no role in the dissemination of the new science and the scientific revolution. The processes of change were on the other hand slow. Few professors at the University of Paris ever accepted Cartesian ontology completely and most did all they could to reconcile Aristotle and Descartes. Substantial forms were rarely attacked or abandoned as a concept, particularly when such an abandonment affected the understanding of the process of transubstantiation. Those who did accept the Cartesian position offered no explanation of the process based on physics right into the eighteenth century and one who did (in 1700) was swiftly reprimanded for it.[5] Where Thomist proofs were not in doubt, they were supplemented by Cartesianism, as in the a priori proof of God.

[4] S. Pumphrey, 'Non-Aristotelianism and the Magnetic Philosophy', in J. Henry and S. Hutton (eds.), New Perspectives on Renaissance Thought: Essays in the History of Science, Education and Philosophy (London, 1990), 177–89 (p. 177).
[5] Brockliss, French Higher Education, p. 206.

Such a synthesis was first used approvingly by the Caen secular Pierre Cally, in 1670.[6] But innatism remained suspect until the end of our period and the discussion of the soul was dominated by the Thomist perspective.[7] There is no evidence of the teaching of dualism at the University of Paris until 1695.[8]

The attitude to authority in the University was not however uniform. In any case Aristotle was suspect on certain things, like the eternity of the world, which did not accord with Christian thought. As early as 1610 one professor maintained that Aristotle subjected everything to the scrutiny of reason. Another in 1629 suggested that at those points where Aristotle was found to be faulty 'we should embrace only what he ought to have thought', and in 1680 yet another affirmed that the veneration of authorities like Aristotle did not mean that 'we swear by the words of any man . . . since it is the task of the philosopher to strengthen his understanding by reason rather than authority'.[9] But there were limits to the direction that reason could take. Those limits were a function of the significance of the break that had to be made with ingrained patterns of thought. It was a question no less of changing a mentality in which supernatural and physical explanations had the same epistemological status. Such a change could only take place over a lengthy period of time.[10]

Of course professors of physics and medicine could not ignore scientific discoveries and from the middle of the century they informed their students of the latest news, despite the need on their part to find the right sort of explanation.[11] Mechanistic explanations were fiercely fought in the two decades following 1670, although occasional support for them is evident from the teaching of some professors.[12] Professors who were not necessarily wedded to the 'great chain of being' concept of nature could, then, be receptive to new explanations. They finally accepted the possibility of dualism once they were convinced of the mechanical explanations of the universe on offer. But their attachment to the Aristotelian idea of substance was such that they tended to play down the break with the past. Mind and matter, they continued to maintain, could only be known through their properties: thus 'Descartes's doctrine could not be metaphysically certain; its value was purely functional, and by transference its truth necessarily contingent.'[13] After 1690 the new philosophy definitely took root and in 1720 it was finally suggested that Cartesian mechanism should be adopted as the approved physical

[6] Ibid., p. 209.
[7] Ibid., p. 215.   [8] Ibid., p. 212.   [9] Ibid., p. 372.
[10] Ibid., p. 375.   [11] Ibid., p. 441.   [12] Ibid., pp. 348–50.
[13] Ibid., pp. 332–3.

philosophy in the University of Paris,[14] ironically at a time when it had been superseded by the Newtonian synthesis.

But for the greater part of the seventeenth century, the search among traditionalists was for a 'pure, reformed Aristotelianism that answered its critics'.[15] The enemy was certainly identified as Cartesianism, despite some softening of rigid positions, and special effort was put into refutation of his philosophy and into 'uncovering the illogicality, insufficiency, and impossibility of each part of his physics'.[16] It is clear that Thomist / Aristotelian science was for a long time on the defensive in the face not only of new scientific discoveries but also of new views of authority in science. This could only have repercussions for the space of religion. In departing from the authority of Aristotle, what were his opponents moving to? How could they justify rejection of authority in the first place?

Descartes's project, as set out in the *Discours de la méthode*, proceeded first according to an evaluation of the truths which he had inherited from his education at the Jesuit college of La Flèche. He concludes that the scholastic system on which the teaching was based could not, by its very nature, lead to a lasting and certain truth. All he had acquired was a diversity of opinion which at its very best achieved only the status of the probable. He had therefore to discover an alternative which satisfied the object of his quest, a firm basis for the mechanistic science which was clearly emerging from the new discoveries, particularly in its mathematical explanations of phenomena. This could not be based on the authority of the ancients when their thought and their science were found to be wanting in so many ways. Truth could only be established by the reasoning individual who would follow certain rules, including the so-called rule of evidence which stated that nothing should be accepted as true unless 'I' knew it self-evidently to be so. In the same way that knowledge could not be determined by things, truth in science could not be determined by others. It should not however be thought that Descartes invented opposition to authority in this period nor that he ploughed a lonely furrow in the pursuit of the new science. Galileo could not have advanced his system of the universe if he had sustained the authority of Aristotle. Nor was the influence of the English philosopher Bacon without influence on the rest of the continent of Europe. Descartes's prime objective however was to provide the principles which would bring order and certainty to the discoveries of the new science and to provide a firm foundation for its progress.

---

[14] Ibid., p. 354.   [15] Pumphrey, 'Non-Aristotelianism', 181.
[16] L. W. B. Brockliss, 'Aristotle, Descartes and the New Science: Natural Philosophy at the University of Paris, 1600–1740', *Annals of Science*, 38 (1981), 33–69 (pp. 46–7).

Descartes was certainly aware of the dangers of suggesting the abandonment of traditional authority in science. No doubt for this reason he was careful on the one hand to establish objective rules of evidence and a divine guarantee of clear and distinct ideas in his promotion of the individual pursuit of knowledge by the aid of human reason. The idea we have of God is the model for all our ideas. On the other he was careful to deny any implications of his position on authority in science for the authority of revelation. Throughout his life Descartes was careful to distinguish explanations according to faith, and the explanations of science which were limited to the physical world. There is no question that Descartes ever saw his method as contrary to the essential teachings of the Church which, we have no reason to doubt, he sincerely accepted. Descartes thought, however, that his system possessed the dual advantage of serving both science and the defence of the Christian religion. In this he was encouraged by Cardinal Bérulle. It was simply necessary that scientific activity legitimately secure its autonomy and its freedom from other forms of authority.

Disingenuously, perhaps, Descartes also asserted that his own project of enquiry was not directed at the authority of any social institution. This cut no ice with the Jesuits who were surely right to conclude that Descartes undermined the whole edifice of their education in which the authority of Aristotle played such an integral part. They saw the attack on substantial forms, along with the rejection of Aristotelian logic, as destroying a system which was so closely associated with the traditional defence of the faith. Because the thought of Aristotle was so integrated into this particular strain of Christian thought, the rejection of his authority in science was bound to be considered as spilling over into the realm of religion itself.

If, however, scientific activity was to be free of authority, how could the notion of authority be validated at all? What controls could operate in the space of science which were inappropriate in the space of religion? Arnauld was called upon to attend to the difference between the sorts of authority to be followed in science and religion when he replied, at the request of his niece, to a work by a Jesuit, Le Moyne, critical of Descartes's philosophical innovations. Arnauld not only attempts to defend a position in philosophy and therefore in the new science, but also to defend the authority of religious tradition. It is essential that the criteria on which the two are based should not be confused. His response rests on a distinction between the two antiquities, Christian and pagan. The latter is to be rejected in science because it is ridiculous to approach things which can be understood by using one's own judgement through the authority of someone who had lived two thousand years before. Arnauld identifies a serious confusion arising from the equation of any authority established on the basis of anteriority with the authority represented by Christian antiquity which is of a completely different order. In so doing, Arnauld dissociates the legitimation of the Christian religion from a philosophical tradition whose authority had been seriously undermined. Arnauld aims to clear up another confusion. While Protestants were utterly wrong to reject as errors what was universally believed by Christians for centuries through Tradition, the same does not hold for human judgement in the consideration of the natural world. A large number of opinions in this area can simply be wrong and the result of prejudice, even though they may have been commonly adhered to.[17] The false equation between what Pascal calls perpetuity in the Christian tradition and a centuries-old opinion in science can only harm rather than help the cause of religion. To argue according to a discredited authority in science runs the risk of devaluing the authority of religion.

In establishing different methods in the science of faith and the science of the natural world, Arnauld draws on the authority of St Augustine who himself drew the boundaries between the knowledge of natural things and knowledge of the mysteries of faith with the following principle: 'quod scimus, debemus rationi; quod credimus, auctoritati'. This allows us to avoid a further confusion. If I follow an opinion simply because the ancients have agreed upon it, I am convinced, not through reason, but because I adhere to their authority. In other words, I believe rather than know. It is a human faith attached to natural things, not a science. Augustine tells us that faith is appropriate only in divine matters. Nothing has made matters worse in philosophy and theology than to have used the wrong term in the wrong domain, that is to say, to have used 'believe' instead of 'know' and vice versa.[18] This not only enables us to avoid a serious category mistake, but it means that opposition to the scholastic perspective need not be anti-religious in itself. The legitimacy of modern scientific activity can be accommodated with a religious viewpoint, so long as the terms appropriate to each are not confused.

Philosophy and theology; reason and faith

The underlying problem in the discussion of authority in science rests on the relation of reason to faith. As we have observed, no philosophical system in the seventeenth century could be considered independently of Christian thought. Knowledge of the physical world had always to be seen

[17] A. Arnauld, *Examen du Traité de l'essence du corps*, in *Oeuvres*, XXXVIII (Paris, 1780), 92–3.
[18] Ibid., pp. 94–5.

in relation to knowledge of the divine. Indeed, controversies derived precisely from the exact nature of the relationship between the two forms of knowledge and over the precise limits of the claims that could be made for science and human reason. It was therefore urgent to define clearly what was appropriate to the spaces of religion and ideas. How could this be achieved if it was at the same time claimed that one was in the service of the other?

The two intellectual traditions of Thomism and Augustinianism had different emphases on the matter. For St Thomas philosophy and theology did not coincide and had different objects. Philosophy dealt with the essences of things and their proper causes, theology with the first cause of all things, God. Philosophy and theology did not however contradict or ignore each other, nor could they be confused with each other. Faith could not afford not to take science into consideration since consideration of creatures was useful for instruction in the faith. On the other hand, while God has seen fit to reveal truths necessary for salvation, he has not revealed all truths relative to creatures and the creation, and man is capable of learning these for himself. There is, then, a space of human knowledge outside theology, which deals with things considered in themselves and which is not necessary for salvation. Augustine could not reject a human reason which could be directed towards bringing man to faith, and once this had occurred, 'reason has its part to play in penetrating the data of faith'.[19] Nor did Augustine dismiss human science or its usefulness. But unquestionably he saw it as an inferior form of thought to wisdom which turns necessarily to divine ideas as the source of all things. Wisdom precedes human science in the order of thought and establishes its ultimate worth. Science can never equate to wisdom because it deals only with the temporal and the changing. We shall return to this position later in this chapter.

How was the relation of philosophy to theology perceived in the seventeenth century? This question has been answered in part by the fact that, in the traditional teaching of certain educational institutions, religious and scientific orthodoxy combine within the Thomist / Aristotelian perspective. What answer can be provided once this perspective has been abandoned? Descartes's arguments are particularly crucial in view of the claim that the principles of his philosophy provided important confirmation of the Christian faith at the level of human reason. Descartes believed that philosophy was prefatory to theology in that, in matters of faith, there is a need to persuade unbelievers for whom revelation means nothing. Equally, while it is important, the distinction between faith and

19 Copleston, *A History of Philosophy*, IV, 48.

reason should not be exaggerated. Philosophy can act as an auxiliary to faith by demonstrating the preambles to the faith, that is to say the existence of God and the immortality of the soul. Certainly the latter is a truth of faith, but philosophy can prepare us to receive it by demonstrating the distinction between extension as the essence of things and the mind as unextended.[20]

For Descartes the philosopher and the theologian did not necessarily exist in two radically different spaces. The philosopher could even be the rival of the theologian in the same space. According to Gouhier, Descartes uses the term 'theologian' in two ways: first he is a person who knows the teaching of the Church and whose authority is therefore unimpeachable because his teaching *is* the teaching of the Church. The theologian in this sense has a special competence which one must respect. But secondly the theologian deals at one and the same time with dogmatic truth and with philosophical truth. In that sense the theologian, outside his competence proper, is a human being whose opinions are subject to error and of no privileged value. It is here that the philosopher can feel free to contradict.[21]

It is true however that, whatever Descartes's relations with theologians, and whatever the usefulness of his philosophy to religion, he was not first a theologian but a philosopher seeking the proper foundation for scientific thinking. Certainly the idea of God is central to his whole system for without it science can have no certainty; the cause of science for Descartes is also the cause of religion, since ideas required to establish science on a firm basis can form the foundation of belief. But for Gouhier, Descartes's 'philosophie chrétienne' is not a 'philosophie religieuse'.[22] Philosophy is an adjunct to faith which, once some of its principles have been established, can be left for the activity of science, because in the end the principles of physics have their own autonomous domain. Scientific discoveries themselves do not reveal God, although they rely on the idea of God for their certainty. Descartes's major philosophical works are, in Gouhier's phrase, 'oeuvres laïques'. Amos Funkenstein offers a different emphasis in regarding Descartes as participating in the elaboration of a secular theology which was conceived by laymen for laymen, but where 'theological and physical arguments became nearly indistinguishable'.[23]

The relative place of reason and faith, and the limits of scientific enquiry in relation to faith, are reflected in the position of Marin Mersenne (1588–1648) who illustrates another way in which science can be accommodated within the confines of the religious space. The place of

---

[20] H. Gouhier, *La Pensée religieuse de Descartes* (Paris, 1972), pp. 214–16.
[21] Ibid., pp. 232–3.   [22] Ibid., pp. 168 and 179.
[23] A. Funkenstein, *Theology and the Scientific Imagination* (Princeton, 1986), pp. 3 and 72–3.

Mersenne in the history of ideas in the seventeenth century forces us to adopt a more nuanced view on the polarised model that might none the less be regarded as the dominant perspective on ideas in our period. Mersenne was in religious orders – he was a Minim – and a passionate devotee of the new science. But he also illustrates the tensions felt by many in the face of outright rejection of prevailing orthodoxy. He was a supporter of mechanistic science but kept his distance from many of the implications of Cartesianism in particular.

Mersenne firmly believed that science could play a part in the service of faith: while a little science could lead to irreligion, a more penetrating acquaintance with it could have the opposite effect. Only a proper science could allow us to define what was a natural phenomenon, and consequently what could rightly be called supernatural.[24] In this regard, where others might have felt that such an explanation would tend to damage the mystery of religion, he was much attached to advances in the mechanistic explanation of the universe and therefore opposed to much Aristotelian science, although not necessarily to the whole Thomist / Aristotelian framework. These advances safeguarded the notion of miracles which would only make sense if there was a natural order to which they could be compared. In any case, it was the role of religion to explain miracles, although Lenoble implies that Mersenne may have been more interested in safeguarding the notion of a natural causality which can be explained by human science.[25]

At this stage of the history of science, scholasticism was not the only enemy of the new thought. The mechanistic explanation of the natural world served to combat those like Campanella and his French followers who adhered to a view of the universe which could be variously described as naturalist, occultist or panpsychist, and which propagated the notion of a 'consciousness' in matter, of a 'soul' in the world. It included a notion of magic and a belief in the influence of the stars.[26] The Christian notion of miracle needed thus to be saved from this 'miraculous' nature.[27] Mechanistic science achieved this purpose by positing a natural world regulated by laws which allowed none the less for transcendence in the order of miracles. But there could be no confusion between the two orders as in naturalism. A new element was thereby brought to faith in the sense that belief in real miracles constituted as much part of the critical perspective of science, since false miracles could be discarded in the same way as inexact observations in the natural world.[28] Mechanistic science was in this way a Christian science.[29] Mersenne the scientist provided Mersenne

---

[24] R. Lenoble, *Mersenne, ou la naissance du mécanisme* (Paris, 1943), p. 94.
[25] Ibid., p. 121.   [26] Ibid., pp. 112–18.   [27] Ibid., p. 133.   [28] Ibid., p. 381.
[29] Ibid., p. 437.

the believer with a philosophy which safeguarded his cherished values. The science of a natural world of order, constant in its design, is what Mersenne particularly welcomed in Descartes.[30]

There is on the other hand a significant way in which Mersenne differs from the scientific perspective of Descartes. Mersenne could not accept the certainty of the transcription of the physical world that Descartes aims to provide in his method. The universe may be one of order, regulated by certain laws, but it could never be a transparent universe which yielded all its secrets to man. Mersenne can still project something of the mystery of faith into the physical world. Science for him is a gift of God which enables us to adapt to our world but to whose physical laws we could never pretend to give an exact translation in terms of ultimate reality. An absolute knowledge of the structure of the world remains God's secret. Mersenne particularly rejects the possibility of grounding a scientific system in metaphysics.[31] Science is but an efficient means of relating appearances to each other without being concerned with the nature of things beyond.[32] Only on this basis can laws be established. The principles of the physical world are hidden, and there can be no demonstration in the proper sense of the term.[33] We have no idea of things in their essence. Mersenne's idea of the usefulness of mathematics is wholly determined by this view. In this world we have a hold only on quantities, not on the founding principles of the universe, and mathematics, the science of quantity, is certainly indispensable. It must be clearly recognised that even mathematics can take account only of the 'outer shell' of things and has no explanatory role.[34] Mathematics is without ontological consequence, and it is here that Mersenne is the most critical of Descartes who, he felt, had exceeded his brief as a scientist in the metaphysics he constructed through science.

Even so, the pursuit of knowledge through mathematics could be endowed for Mersenne with religious inspiration. Mathematics with its concept of the infinite brings us to an understanding of the greatness of the human mind and its immortality, and at the same time lifts us up to God.[35] Mathematics can also play a part in Christian apologetics as an argument in favour of providence: one can show that nature is a perfect order, mathematics constituting the science of that order. The dignity of the soul is further demonstrated by its capacity to manipulate the infinite.[36] God for Mersenne is also venerated through physics in the sense that he has given us science to occupy ourselves with in this life in order to reveal the secrets of the universe as a reward in the next.[37] Heaven is a scientist's

[30] Ibid., p. 40.   [31] Ibid., p. 311.
[32] Ibid., p. 273.   [33] Ibid., pp. 312–13.
[34] Ibid., pp. 352–4.   [35] Ibid., p. 452.   [36] Ibid., p. 221.   [37] Ibid., p. 265.

paradise. Science is an activity which links us to God rather than cutting us off from him.

But Mersenne could not, despite his attachment to mechanism, advocate wholesale rejection of the past and he illustrates the difficulties that arose for many in the new climate created for science. It is apparent that Mersenne, who had none the less encouraged Descartes in his endeavours, was not prepared to align himself with a single direction. It was the individual's responsibility to evaluate the opinions of one philosopher or another to see if they were in conformity with 'nostre creance', with the result that a new philosophy might be born which accorded more with reason, experience and faith (in that order) than Aristotle or Plato. Philosophers were free provided their system or opinions did not conflict with Christianity.[38]

It was Mersenne's intention however to demonstrate through the whole of his work that being a good Christian and a good scientist was in no way incompatible. Hence his establishment of a link between religion and the study of mathematics, and Lenoble points out that none of Mersenne's published prayers are addressed to Christ, the Trinity or the Virgin but to the 'constructeur' of mathematics and physics, or to the guardian of social order.[39] The good scientist did not on the other hand necessarily indulge in the wholesale destruction of what had gone before. Mersenne was not a thoroughgoing critic of systems and St Thomas still provided an acceptable framework although he was not considered to constitute doctrine in a definitive sense. Mersenne could juxtapose with Thomism the proof of Anselm which St Thomas had expressly rejected.[40] Scholasticism remained important not so much for what it contained but for the way reason led to faith.[41] Science would not then be cut off from religion to which science itself pointed the way. Moreover, since science was about the use of reason, Aristotle could be referred to but not followed in a slavish manner. For Mersenne, Aristotelianism would be a stop-gap, useful in those parts which were situated between science and metaphysics, since science itself was unable to offer a definitive demonstration of the eternal laws of matter.[42] Mersenne used Aristotle as a point of stability, however wrong his science may have been, at a time when changes in thought were upsetting traditional explanations. For him, no clean break with the past was possible. He was concerned rather that opposition to Aristotelianism should not lead to questioning 'an established institutional structure to the defense of which he was largely committed'.[43] Despite moving away from Aristotelian orthodoxy in

---

[38] Ibid., p. 222.   [39] Ibid., pp. 536–7.
[40] Ibid., pp. 200–1.   [41] Ibid., p. 203.   [42] Ibid., p. 222.
[43] P. Dear, *Mersenne and the Learning of the Schools* (Ithaca and London, 1988), p. 4.

natural philosophy, he was still able to use the orthodox Thomistic account to undermine the claims of physics to constitute a genuine science.[44] The complexity of Mersenne's thought is contained in Dear's conclusion that important aspects of his science are grounded and often articulated 'in a pre-existing philosophical idiom suited to essentialism, and his ideas often display a borrowed rather than an intrinsic coherence'.[45]

Mersenne holds a sort of line in a changing intellectual world in occupying the space between the pure sceptic and the dogmatist, both of whom would be dangerous for Christianity, the one having no answers, the other having too many. As Wade comments: 'Scientific achievements . . . do not depend upon some unshakable metaphysical system. Both dogmatist and pyrrhonist can be wrong: between the two stands the constructive sceptic, or rather the Christian philosopher, doubtful of our abilities to find the essence of our knowledge, but in the meantime actively engaged in explaining the world.'[46] Mersenne none the less remains an example of a cleric who argues for a place for the new science within the space of religion. Lenoble arrives at far-reaching conclusions on Mersenne's scientific position which take us beyond Mersenne's hesitations between the old and the new: by emphasising in his attachment to mechanism the usefulness of a positivist science in the service of religion, Mersenne unwittingly led to a 'morale purement temporaliste et terrestre'. With Mersenne scientism was born.[47] Indeed Mersenne himself became less and less interested in theology which he was quite content to leave to others.[48] Paradoxically, therefore, the religious created the secular. It is not suggested that Mersenne was other than a sincere Christian with an attachment to his faith, but it was a faith perhaps devoid of a fundamentally mystical impulse.[49] His religion was not without mystery, but it was a mystery that would only be revealed once the individual encountered his God. The revelations of science could in those circumstances be prescribed only a limited role.

A limited role for science was the basis of Pascal's radical opposition to the claims made for science by those like Descartes whose unbounded optimism led them to believe that, in the words of the sixth part of the *Discours de la méthode*, men could be 'maîtres et possesseurs de la nature'. Pascal's position on science is not itself without complexity, especially because his arguments are those of a man of science who holds to radical Augustinianism. A further complexity is that Pascal seems to adopt

[44] Ibid., p. 53.   [45] Ibid., p. 230.
[46] Ira O. Wade, *The Intellectual Origins of the French Enlightenment* (Princeton, 1971), p. 145.
[47] Lenoble, *Mersenne*, pp. 238–9.   [48] Ibid., p. 244.
[49] Ibid., pp. 578–9.

contradictory positions in the preface to his lost *Traité du vide* and in the *Pensées*, Pascal's projected apology for the Christian religion. However, Pascal's position is different according to the primary perspective that he adopts, and the contradiction is in any case not as profound as it seems.

The preface contains Pascal's defence of science where the primary perspective is science itself. It is a defence which is also designed to distinguish clearly between the domains of faith and human reason. The context is that of authority and Pascal states quite categorically that reliance on the authority of antiquity in science is an obstacle to progress and inhibits the advancement of new ideas. But abandoning authority in our knowledge of science is not the equivalent of abandoning all authority in all fields of knowledge. Knowledge is divided into two separate areas, the one pertaining to memory (an idea borrowed from Jansenius) and the other pertaining to reasoning. The first includes history, languages, geography, law and, above all, theology. The second includes science where reason seeks to establish truths which are hidden from us. The first domain is composed of subjects to which nothing can be added by human reason, where there is in other words no concept of progress. This is particularly true of theology which is inseparable from truth and which points us to the Scriptures as the only source capable of enlightening us. The principles of religion are above nature and man can know them only through divine intervention. Science is on the other hand of an entirely different order and, because its domain is the sensible world and that of reason, the concept of authority makes no sense. Moreover, it is a domain where, because of experimentation, the state of knowledge at any one time can never be definitive or binding on future generations. But we must be careful. Just as it is wrong to hold to authority in scientific matters, so it is criminal to use reason alone in matters of theology.

This view of science, which in its reference to advances in ideas seems to lead to a concept of progress, cannot however be divorced from a profoundly Augustinian context. The scientist can make no exaggerated claims in a fallen world, and the changing state of knowledge has as its cause the changeable nature of the objects of science and the changeable nature of man. There can be no certainty in a context of instability. Certainty can be found in faith alone. And that is the emphasis of Pascal's pronouncements on science in the *Pensées* whose primary perspective is religion. It is in the *Pensées* that we see most clearly Pascal's opposition to Descartes who, he felt, made too many claims for human reason in the assertion that the human mind can reach certainty at the level of ideas. An essential part of Pascal's apologetic programme is bringing man to accept the limits of the conclusions that can be reached by human reason and that in any case those conclusions, that is to say the results of science, are irrelevant when faced with the problem of our salvation. Another aspect of Pascal's opposition to Descartes is his rejection as presumptuous of the possibility that the human mind can contain a clear and distinct idea of God. Indeed, it is also the status of that idea that concerns Pascal. Descartes only needs the idea of God, that is to say a sort of theorem and not the living God of the Old and New Testaments. Once he has established the truth of mathematics through this idea, Descartes can forget about God and get on with the job of science. It is possible that Pascal perceived the danger of aligning Descartes with the thought of St Augustine. It is not that Descartes was not Augustinian in some way, but that he was not Augustinian enough.

Pascal, in the very nature of the task he set himself, could not reject the use of reason in the service of faith. Reason was useful in bringing the unbeliever to accept, at an intellectual level (insufficient but necessary at this stage), the tenets of the Christian faith as a highly probable truth (a different version of mathematics in the service of religion – Pascal wrote on roulette), until the experience of faith – which Pascal could not provide – could make sense of the Christian religion as a certain truth. Pascal never demanded of his audience a blind and 'unknowing' acceptance of religion. But Pascal was simply not prepared to accept the demand that religion, in the light of the claims made for reason in the new science, be accountable to that same reason. Religion, while not contrary to reason, did not start from presenting itself as 'reasonable'. A Lockean perspective is out of the question. The Fall was in itself incomprehensible but man could not be comprehended without it. How in any case could religion be accountable to a fragile and unstable reason? Even his own attempts at proof, he avows, can go only so far, since achieving a proof of the Christian religion in a work of apologetics would say too much for human reason. Pascal has therefore to establish the limits of human reason in order to undermine any claims for its superiority in relation to religion. The truths of faith are simply of a different order.

Arnauld and Nicole take up a similar position in the *Logique* of Port-Royal, arguing that scientific reasoning must never be applied to those things we cannot hope to comprehend through reason. The finite cannot grasp the infinite. It would indeed seem that the utility of science lies not so much in its discoveries, which they describe as 'sterile' in themselves, but in the way science can point to an acceptance of what is incomprehensible. If we are unable fully to understand how matter can be divisible to infinity, we shall be less prepared to oppose reason to the truths of the faith on the grounds that they are incomprehensible.[50] Thus

[50] A. Arnauld and P. Nicole (ed. L. Marin), *La Logique ou l'art de penser* (Paris, 1970), pp. 363–6.

between science and religion there is a frontier which must not be crossed in terms of the use of reason. This does not mean that scientific activity need not constitute in itself a preparation for the reception of religious truth. Science can be appropriated for the cause of the truth in a sort of 'negative way'. Science can establish what reason cannot do.

The idea that Descartes was perhaps not quite Augustinian enough emerges in the new synthesis of faith and scientific thinking which was to bring Malebranche into conflict with traditionalists but also with other Augustinians like Arnauld. While interested in the concept of scientific truth, Malebranche was first of all a theologian, but a theologian anxious to demonstrate the continuity of theology and philosophy. Malebranche starts from the opposite end to Descartes. For him faith regulates the workings of our mind but it is reason which provides the mind with understanding. He argues that what faith reveals and what reason can discover are ultimately part of the same world of intelligibility, and consequently the objectives of both faith and reason are directed towards a knowledge of God and his creation. It is our infirmity which prevents us from having a real understanding of many of the truths of faith, but knowing them in any form is of benefit to man and science. Even an obscure knowledge of the truths of faith can illuminate the truths of reason, and the revelation of the unintelligible at the level of faith can render the universe itself more intelligible. Echoing Pascal, Malebranche holds that no operation of human reason can lead us to understand the Incarnation, but all sorts of solutions are provided by the fact of it. It is no longer reason which supports faith, but faith which supports reason, because at a time in the future faith will become reason. The difference between faith and reason lies not in the respective objects of their knowledge, but in the weakness of the knowing subject, so that truths of faith and truths of reason as separate entities exist only in the way man in his imperfect state represents the world as he sees it, but not in the world of the intelligible as it should more widely be understood.[51] There is no separation of faith and reason in God. This is a state to which man cannot aspire in this life, only as the result of divine revelation in the next.

Malebranche's model is Augustine, who never ceased to exhort us to acquire an understanding of what we believe. Reason alone cannot understand the truths of faith, but it can recognise their 'rationality'. Metaphysics and theology, while their starting point may be different, end up at the same place,[52] thus reflecting Pascal's principle that the truths of religion are not accountable to reason but they are not contrary to it either.

[51] H. Gouhier, *La Vocation de Malebranche* (Paris, 1926), pp. 148–50.
[52] Ibid., pp. 150–1.

Arnauld and Nicole too argue that faith presupposes 'quelque raison', and they refer to a point made on a number of occasions by Augustine that we could never believe what is above reason if reason had not first persuaded us that we should do well to believe certain things even though we were not fully able to apprehend them in terms of the human mind. This is true of faith since reason tells us that God cannot deceive us in what he reveals of himself and his mystery. Belief is not blind belief but 'une action raisonnable'.[53] It is not knowledge of the divine, but a predisposition of the mind to accept it.

The perception of Descartes has most often been that of a philosopher who, beyond any usefulness the conclusions of human reason may have for religion, established an autonomous domain for science which did not deny the Christian faith but left it to its own devices, in effect a perfectly Thomistic programme. Malebranche believed that Cartesianism could be modified so that the two separate domains became one. One of the problems that Malebranche identified in Descartes was the significance of innatism. Innatism represented the independence of thought in relation to matter since the mind was not dependent on things, and hence on sense-data, for its operations. For Malebranche innatism also seemed to affirm the independence of thought in relation to God who could be held to have provided us with, in Malebranche's words, a 'magasin d'idées' which then dispensed us from relying on God himself. Malebranche thought it necessary therefore to show the dependence of the mind in all its operations on God.[54] All systems of thought which did not take account of the union of the soul with God were to be discarded, since it was inadmissible that the soul should create its own ideas or that it should discover them in the consideration of its own perfections.[55] Indeed, Remsberg argues that Descartes was in danger of being understood as separating God and reason,[56] which would of course have legitimated reason as establishing an independent, 'secularised' activity. Malebranche set out to establish that the soul and all our ideas are inseparable from God.

This he attempted to achieve – and his attempt was not uncontroversial – by the notion of the 'vision en Dieu' in which our soul is united with a perfect being who contains all perfections of understanding, or all the ideas generated in the human mind. The process of this vision begins with a theory of ideas where in the first place to know an object is to unite oneself with it, and since the soul cannot unite with material objects, it can

[53] Arnauld and Nicole, La Logique, pp. 410–11.
[54] H. Gouhier, La Philosophie de Malebranche et son expérience religieuse (Paris, 1926), p. 275.
[55] Ibid., p. 300.
[56] Remsberg, Wisdom and Science, p. 155.

only know them by uniting with the ideas we have of them. The idea of an object 'inhabits' us and is always present to our mind. Malebranche did not contemplate the possibility that a real causal relationship could exist between extended matter and an unextended mind.[57] The second stage of the process is a theory of divine knowledge where God is the 'site' of all ideas. The third stage is a theory of man in which man is united with God through his will, which is defined as the love of God, and by his vision, which must be defined as the knowledge or vision of God. God is thus the source of all ideas.[58] Remsberg explains it thus:

Man was made to know and love God, i.e. man was intended to have true knowledge. Knowing consists of uniting an idea to our soul. Nothing can be known without the union of the soul to God. In and through God the soul can see all things.[59]

This had the advantage of ensuring the veracity of ideas and protecting them from sceptical attack.[60] In Malebranche more emphasis is placed on the divine will that we should know, whereas Descartes's innate ideas are there to be found. Malebranche thus brings Cartesianism back from the brink of dispensing with God in thought and consequently science.

There was one general point on which Descartes and Malebranche were in total agreement and that was the need to reject scholasticism. This is undoubtedly at the root of Descartes's dual use of the term 'theologian' I discussed earlier. Jesuit theologians could no longer sustain the link between Aristotelianism and religion: the former, discredited in its science, could no longer be relied upon for an adequate defence of the faith. The relation of philosophy to theology is even more clearly marked in Malebranche. If theology includes an attempt to make the dogmas of faith to some degree accessible to reason, and if it borrows the elements of its explanations from the principles of reason, and therefore philosophy, consequently the value of the theology depends on the value of the philosophy. Scholasticism has quite simply had its day and a new theology must be built on the new philosophy.[61]

Arnauld was to engage in a protracted, complex and not always polite polemic with Malebranche on the latter's interpretation of Cartesian philosophy. Arnauld was in fact keen to save Descartes from Malebranche. Arnauld was clear on what he thought of as the contribution of Cartesianism to theological problems and to religion: instilling correct principles of reasoning led to the possibility of clearing up a number of

[57] S. Nadler, *Arnauld and the Cartesian Philosophy of Ideas* (Manchester, 1989), p. 71.
[58] Gouhier, *La Philosophie de Malebranche*, pp. 234–5.
[59] Remsberg, *Wisdom and Science*, p. 155.
[60] Nadler, *Arnauld*, p. 72.
[61] Gouhier, *La Vocation*, p. 158.

problems in theology.[62] The *Logique* of Port-Royal, which drew heavily on Cartesian method, pointed the way to dealing with the human institution of the Church in so far as it was prone to error in the conflicts between theologians over Scripture and Tradition.[63] According to Arnauld, Malebranche takes Cartesianism in a dangerous direction by making God the immediate and direct object of perception: 'Arnauld's Jansenist sentiments are offended by the placing of God and man in [a] close, familiar and constant contact.'[64] Arnauld's criticism of Malebranche is, ironically, not far from Pascal's accusation that Descartes's idea of God claims far too much for the human mind. Pascal would not have looked too kindly on Arnauld's defence of Descartes.

St Augustine and seventeenth-century science

St Augustine's thought has been at the centre of much of the preceding discussion, especially in the way he may have influenced the thought of Descartes. But there were very specific ways in which the influence of Augustine progressed in seventeenth-century France. The espousal of St Augustine as an authority in science was not always received with unanimous approval or enthusiasm, and it is now timely to investigate in more detail the reception of Augustine in the context of ideas in our period.

Reference to Augustine was not unproblematic because Augustine's work could be used in different ways. Augustine was certainly sceptical of a science based on knowledge acquired through sensation and sense-data. The question is whether Augustine's scepticism extended beyond that to the establishment of a valid form of human science. On the one hand thinkers pointed to an Augustine who, in the works on divine illumination, maintained that the wisdom which is essential to all knowledge could lead to the construction of rational science. On the other, more radical thinkers like Pascal could find a reference point in the works on grace which underlined the vanity of science in the face of the most crucial problem, man's salvation. The problem was simply that Augustine offered no complete philosophical system: 'the "Augustinian" . . . is faced by an approach, an inspiration, certain basic ideas which are capable of considerable development, so that he can remain perfectly faithful to the Augustinian spirit even though he departs from what the historic Augustine actually said'.[65] The seventeenth century in France certainly offered an interesting picture of what fidelity to Augustine might mean.

The cutting edge of Augustinian influence in the space of science is, as I

---

[62] Nadler, *Arnauld*, p. 29.   [63] Sedgwick, *Jansenism*, p. 101.
[64] Nadler, *Arnauld*, pp. 136–7.   [65] Copleston, *A History of Philosophy*, IV, 50.

have indicated, to be found in the work of Descartes. This worked in two directions. Possibly Descartes implicitly, but certainly his followers explicitly, saw the advantage of espousing the authority of Augustine as a substitute for that of Aristotle. Arnauld saw the advantage of espousing the cause of Cartesianism as providing a popular exposition of Augustinianism adapted to modern times.[66] While we must not, like Nourrisson, exaggerate the number of those at Port-Royal who espoused Cartesianism, for some Jansenists it became a useful vehicle for the doctrine of grace. At the same time, in scientific terms, De la Forge, Clerselier, Régis, Rohault, all defend Descartes on Augustinian grounds, to the extent that Augustine is now quoted as Aristotle used to be.[67]

Did Descartes himself know Augustine well enough to borrow closely from his works? The suggestion is that perhaps he did not, although he was certainly acquainted with the Jesuit theologian Suarez who referred to Augustine's theory of innate ideas in his criticism of the Aristotelian theory of knowledge.[68] There is certainly no evidence that Descartes was ever interested in matters of grace. It would seem from his correspondence that Descartes was not much interested, either, in the parallels that could be established between his own work and the texts of Augustine.[69] Certainly, Arnauld did not presuppose that Descartes had read Augustine and thought it natural that two great minds should meet in matters of truth.[70] This did not prevent contemporaries from scouring the texts for parallels.

One of the areas of similarity which Cartesians attempted to establish was the theory of animal machines which Augustine certainly did not deal with independently of other matters. The first but not entirely successful attempt to link Augustine and Descartes in this question was made by Florent Schuyl in his edition of Descartes's work on the passions in 1662. Another edition in 1664, this time by Claude Clerselier (the attribution is contested by some), contains in its preface an explicit reference to St Augustine as the authority for Descartes's text. One of the aims of the preface was to show that Descartes's 'spiritualisme', which demonstrates the immateriality of the soul beyond doubt, was in accord with the Christian faith, and established the truths of reason required by the faith in a way that no philosophy had ever done before. In this way Clerselier sees in Descartes a reflection of the 'spiritualisme' of Augustine.[71]

Two years later Louis de la Forge published an edition of the same

[66] J.-F. Nourrisson, *La Philosophie de Saint Augustin*, 2 vols. (Paris, 1865), II, 207.
[67] Ibid., pp. 219–22.
[68] J. H. Randall, *The Career of Philosophy*, vol. I, *From the Middle Ages to the Enlightenment* (New York, 1964), 386.
[69] H. Gouhier, *Cartésianisme et augustinisme au XVIIe siècle* (Paris, 1978), p. 37.
[70] Ibid., p. 42.   [71] Ibid., p. 58.

work. No longer was it a 'recollection' of Augustine in Descartes's works, but a systematic textual comparison. In the light of this, two attitudes emerged. On the one hand, the Cartesians seeking to legitimate their philosophy were prepared to give loud acclaim to the similarities they found. On the other, while the Augustinians had no real need of Descartes – Augustine could defend himself – they none the less found in Descartes a confirmation of the truths to which they adhered.[72] An Augustinian like le Père André Martin, who taught at the Oratorian school at Saumur (his teaching was later banned), could never have offered such a precise analysis of Augustine's writings on animals and plants had the new physics not provided him with clear and distinct ideas on the nature of matter.[73] Cartesianism allowed a new reading of Augustine.

In the early stages of Cartesianism Mersenne and Arnauld could content themselves with the idea that Augustine and Descartes were of the same family. In his *Objections* Arnauld quotes four texts of St Augustine, none of which can be found to be in conflict with Descartes's arguments.[74] But in general, Cartesians who declared themselves 'on the side of Augustine' and Augustinians whose anti-Aristotelianism would lead them to declare themselves 'on the side of Descartes', in order to show that a proper understanding of Augustine did not contradict Descartes, chose to attenuate the differences rather than exaggerate the similarities.[75] But, as with the editions of Descartes's *Le Traité de l'homme*, some went further than this once the polemic shifted to an attack on the religious orthodoxy of Descartes. It was no longer a question of more quotations from Augustine and the juxtaposition of texts but of actually demonstrating the similarities from within.[76] A Christian impulse was as intrinsic to Cartesianism as to the work of Augustine. The space of science and the space of religion were one.

The main point about the relationship between Augustine and Descartes in the validation of scientific enquiry in the space of religion was that the authority of Augustine was in the process of being secularised and his works read as texts pertaining to the operations of scientific enquiry to the exclusion of their essentially religious significance. St Augustine's work was being turned into the work of a philosopher.[77] The fact was that St Augustine did not conceive of a philosophy without its theological component.[78] It is the philosophy of Descartes which is validated by Augustine. Indeed, du Vaucel, a supporter of Port-Royal, held that the metaphysical affinity between Descartes and Augustine rested on a small number of points of departure, and in order for the new system to benefit

[72] Ibid., pp. 88–9.   [73] Ibid., p. 96.   [74] Ibid., p. 37.
[75] Ibid., pp. 42–3.   [76] Ibid., p. 48.   [77] Ibid., p. 137.
[78] Ibid., p. 166.

from Augustine's prestige, the meaning of the Father's texts had to be considerably strained.[79]

The most ardent supporter of Cartesianism at Port-Royal was Arnauld who particularly welcomed Descartes's refusal to have anything to do with speculative theology and Descartes's avowed belief in the importance of revelation. Descartes was a solid Christian philosopher who revered the mysteries of faith and applied reason only to those things which were appropriate to it. He had pushed further than any other philosopher before him what could be discovered of the truths of nature with the aid of human reason, and Arnauld denied that such a philosophy could in any way be regarded as heretical.[80] But many other Jansenists of Arnauld's generation were positively hostile to Cartesianism. Nicole, Arnauld's collaborator on the *Logique ou l'art de penser*, a very Cartesian school text-book, may have praised him in chapter VIII of *De la Faiblesse de l'homme*, but was subsequently somewhat cool towards the work of the philosopher. Indeed, in one of his letters, he expressed the desire that in another life he would not wish to be counted among his followers. Even Arnauld's colleagues found him a little too inclined to defend Descartes's system instead of devoting himself exclusively to theological matters. Nicole would particularly have preferred that Arnauld refrain from an abstract philosophical dispute with Malebranche, where the interests of the Church became obscured, and limit himself to the correction of theological error.[81]

As my earlier discussion of Pascal has suggested, the root of the problem is to be found precisely in the affinity of Descartes to Augustine while at the same time Descartes, for some at least, seemed to be leading Augustine into areas very far from Augustine's original intentions. There was a danger in associating Augustine too closely with modern science. Pascal sets out therefore not only to defend religion from science but more specifically to defend Augustine. This involved a return to the first principles of Augustinianism which determined a view on the place of human science without any reference to its content. In this way it was possible to defend science and St Augustine who could clearly be found scientifically wanting in modern terms. Modern science could not then be turned against Augustine. These first principles centre on the importance of wisdom in Augustine's thought. The opposition of the wisdom into science paradigm to that of science into wisdom not only opposes Thomists and Augustinians, but in Pascal's articulation of the place of

---

[79] G. Rodis-Lewis, *Descartes et le cartésianisme hollandais: études et documents* (Paris, 1950), p. 181.
[80] Arnauld, *Examen*, pp. 90–1.
[81] Rodis-Lewis, *Descartes et le cartésianisme hollandais*, pp. 146–8.

wisdom in relation to science, it opposes those who seek in Augustine an authority for the new science and those for whom such a 'laicisation' of Augustine is anathema.

Wisdom into science is a position held by Augustinians, and science into wisdom represents the approach adopted by Thomists, in particular the Jesuits. The principle of each paradigm is related to the starting point of thought in relation to the world. Thomists begin with the nature of the world they find themselves in, whereas Augustinians begin and often end with an examination of the self and the relations between the self and God. This includes an examination of one's thinking before applying it to the world which derived from the emphasis in Augustine's early writings on the prior separation of the true from the false.[82] Thus 'wisdom' must be established before science.

For Aristotle the process was the reverse: science was essential if wisdom was to be found, and St Thomas was able to include this wisdom, which was for Aristotle an intellectual virtue, into Christian thought. By making science essential to wisdom, the Jesuits enhanced man's sense of responsibility and free will which, they taught, was the kind of freedom necessary if science was to become wisdom. Arguments on grace cannot be dissociated from arguments on knowledge. It was inconceivable to the Jesuits that man could possess the freedom to acquire knowledge without at the same time the power to apply it. The science into wisdom paradigm was thus the basis of a theory of human action.[83]

Some points concerning the Augustinian rejection of science into wisdom have already emerged, although here we must see 'science' in its broadest acceptance as 'knowledge through reason', a distinction not always clear in Remsberg's discussion. In the first place the sort of freedom essential to this paradigm is simply impossible in a perspective where the only true freedom is a divine gift of grace: 'Just as there is no natural freedom (no freedom without grace), so there is no natural science (no science without wisdom).'[84] Secondly, the science into wisdom paradigm, in placing science first, is defective in making wisdom depend on a study of the changing and the changeable world, the results of which are susceptible to sceptical attack. Augustine emphasises first and foremost the divine unchangeable side of the relation where attention is given 'to God's way with man, rather than to man's knowledge of God'. Wisdom may be essential to science but it is wisdom which has priority over science.[85]

The essential principle contained in the critique of the science into wisdom paradigm is that from man's interests and intellectual efforts

[82] Remsberg, *Wisdom and Science*, p. 12.
[83] Ibid., pp. 52–4.   [84] Ibid., p. 96.   [85] Ibid., pp. 28–9.

wisdom simply cannot be attained.[86] Nothing which is changeable can produce the unchangeable, and wisdom is a gift of God. Wisdom includes science and makes science true, but science cannot be necessary for the generation of wisdom, especially if that wisdom emanates from God.[87] The argument over the two paradigms in the realm of knowledge inevitably reflects the respective positions of the more optimistic current of seventeenth-century spirituality, Christian humanism, which limits the effect of the Fall to Adam's loss of supernatural gifts and the more pessimistic assertion of radical Augustinians that man was fundamentally flawed in the whole range of his activities and especially in the helplessness of the human will.

The fullest articulation of the wisdom into science paradigm is to be found in Pascal's *Pensées*. An essential part of Pascal's apology is the constant abasement of purely human reason. Pascal draws inspiration from the knowledge explosion of the seventeenth century in contrasting the infinite nature of what there is to know and man's limited capacity to know. This is paralleled by the inability of the finite human mind to comprehend the nature of the infinite, a clear attack on Descartes's claim that God's nature could be contained within the space of an idea in the human mind. Pascal's work of apologetics in itself could only operate at the level of human knowledge, and he rejected all pretension of being able to prove the existence of God through human agency. His attempts can only achieve the status of the probable. No knowledge of the divine which remains at the level of the intellect can carry the conviction of faith. Stopping there would encourage a sort of intellectualism which deprives the Christian religion of its mystery and depth, hence his dismissal of Descartes's God as the 'dieu des philosophes'. Pascal's science could not be transmitted to another as wisdom.

It is only once man has faith that 'probable' knowledge can become certain knowledge, since the believer can at that stage interpret that knowledge in the light of faith. The sort of proofs Pascal offers then carry their full conviction. It is only then also that man will be able to situate the activity of science in relation to the more pressing sorts of knowledge required for personal salvation. The science into wisdom paradigm encourages man to move from human to divine knowledge, which would also encourage him simply to consider knowledge of the divine in terms of human reason. Faith enables man to transcend that state since it is a form of knowledge completely separate from the operations of the human mind. Pascal therefore represents the position articulated by St Anselm in his maxim *crede ut intellegas* (believe in order to understand) rather than in

---

[86] Ibid., p. 73.   [87] Ibid., p. 30.

its opposite *intellege ut credas* (understand in order to believe). In fact Pascal seems to suggest that man should only undertake scientific activity once he is able to establish the right priorities. Those priorities cannot be established with the knowledge of human reason as a starting point. It is in this context that we must understand the seemingly anti-science statements of Pascal and his attack on human reason as a source of knowledge. Wisdom into science offers us a grasp on the global perspective in which science can be validated. Science will benefit from the global wisdom but it will not have pretensions to become the 'whole' wisdom which, in Pascal's view, would eliminate the need for faith altogether. Pascal's great importance in the seventeenth century derives precisely from his percipience in foreseeing the demands which would eventually be made on religion by reason and attempting to counter them.

Explanations old and new

One of the difficulties encountered, in different ways, by traditionalists and the new scientists alike was the compatibility of new scientific explanations or principles with Scripture, or explanations which seemed better to accord with faith. Again the two great intellectual traditions of the period are seen to conflict in the defence of traditional explanations or in the advancement of different types of solution. The authority of Augustine was invoked in a controversy which arose from the consequences of Cartesian physics for the Eucharist, one of the essential mysteries of Christianity. The process of the Eucharist seemed to admit of the transformation of the material substances of bread and wine into the body and blood of Christ, while the bread and wine remain ostensibly what they are. That is to say that the secondary qualities of the bread and wine, their colour etc., remain after transubstantiation. This confusion of the material and the spiritual is impossible if, as Descartes maintains, the essence of matter is extension, there being no 'occult' presence in things. How could the principles giving rise to a scientific explanation which contradicted the 'mystery' of the Eucharist still be accommodated within Christian thought? The change of philosophy posed certain problems for theology.

The issue turns essentially on a theological explanation being grounded in Thomist/Aristotelian principles deriving from the theory of substantial forms, Descartes's prime subject of attack if the new science was to be grounded in firm principles. If the theory itself was discredited, problems inevitably arose with providing a plausible explanation of the phenomenon of the Eucharist. Some felt that the scholastics discredited religion by hitching their wagon so uncompromisingly to a philosophy which had clearly had its day. Arnauld was one of the first to see the need to hitch theology to a new wagon, that of Cartesianism, which had the advantage not only of recognising the sovereignty of faith but also of proving beyond doubt those truths of reason which can be accorded with the truths of revelation, hence the interaction between an 'augustinianisme cartésianisé' and a 'cartésianisme augustinisé'.[88]

If Descartes's physics could be attacked on the grounds of 'res extensa' whereby the Eucharist cannot be a miracle in the way that it has been believed, and if the theory of 'res extensa' could be deduced from the work of St Augustine, could the same attacks be made against a Father of the Church that were made against Descartes? It was inconceivable that Augustine's thought, based on the same scientific principle of 'res extensa', should contradict the process of the Eucharist. By the same token Descartes's science could not be attacked for the same reasons. The urgency of breaking the link between the Eucharist and any philosophy or science made itself felt. Even if Aristotelianism was abandoned for another philosophy, a danger awaited theological explanation of a central Christian mystery on the basis of changeable human reason.

The problem was that Descartes kept digging the hole in his efforts at squaring his view of matter with the process of the Eucharist. The Cartesian Arnauld saw the difficulty and offered his own answer. He has no difficulty in accepting the Cartesian theory of 'res extensa' as a scientific concept and most certainly does not regard it as contradicting the mystery of the Eucharist. In the *Examen du Traité de l'essence du corps* he makes it quite clear, first, that defending the philosophy of Descartes does not involve following Descartes's own defence of his explanation of the mystery of the Eucharist, and second, that we do not need to accord the principles of Descartes's philosophy with the mystery of the Eucharist which he is quite happy to believe as a matter of faith, especially if Descartes accepts the mystery of the Eucharist on the grounds of positive theology (that is, an explanation according to Tradition).[89] If the experience of the Eucharist is disconnected from philosophical or scientific explanation, any argument after that must of necessity fall into the realm of speculation and Arnauld steers well clear of that. All sorts of problems arise if theological explanation comes to rest on science, the reason why Arnauld has nothing to do with Descartes's scientific attempts to explain the Eucharist.

Malebranche too refuses to contemplate a philosophical explanation of this mystery. It is something one has to accept and pressing reasons must exist to give a clear and intelligible explanation of something the Fathers

[88] Gouhier, *Cartésianisme et augustinisme*, pp. 131–2.
[89] Arnauld, *Examen*, pp. 123–4.

and the councils have never fully explained. Such novelty in theology would be suspect, and it is better to suspend one's judgement.[90] Malebranche, on the other hand, adheres to Cartesian principles of matter. The strategy of Arnauld and Malebranche is not without its own dangers. This separation of the domain of faith from that of reason legitimates the autonomy of the domain of scientific explanation which in itself could lead in an unfortunate direction for the maintenance of the space of religion.

The compatibility of the spaces of religion and science became an issue in the relation of Scripture to new sorts of explanation. The touchstone of this relationship was Copernicus's theory, confirmed by the observations of Galileo, that the sun is at the centre of the universe and that the earth moves on its own axis. How could the divinely inspired word of the Bible not represent what was clearly an observable reality? Many resisted the new theory right to the end of the seventeenth century. The position of Rapin, a Jesuit, is typical in that he does not disregard the new science but refuses to relinquish the principle that the Gospel is the rule in all things: the reputation of a philosophy, whether it be that of Descartes or Aristotle, depends on its contribution to the defence of religion.[91] The professors of the University of Paris were reluctant to discuss Copernicanism until the 1640s, although by 1690 outright hostility to this theory had all but disappeared. But its acceptance was mitigated by the perception of Copernicanism as a challenge to be met rather than as an explanation to be embraced, a perception underlined by the tenaciousness of biblical literalism. The Jesuits of the Collège de Clermont refused to abandon the traditional mechanics of planetary motion and continued to teach solid-sphere astronomy.[92] Le Maistre de Sacy at Port-Royal had no hesitation either in recommending adherence to Tradition, and believed that Moses possessed certain knowledge on the stars and the heavens that God preferred to conceal for fear of encouraging an unnecessary need to know among men.[93]

The status of the biblical text, if new explanations were to be convincing, had to be reformulated. The fact that in 1707 the *Journal des savants* felt it necessary to state that Genesis was not meant to teach physics and astronomy shows how far opinion had shifted. Earlier in the century Mersenne, while a supporter of Galileo in France, was, not unreasonably, quite cautious on the issue. As a basic principle, science

---

[90] Malebranche, *De la Recherche de la vérité*, I, 266–7.
[91] Le Père R. Rapin, *Réflexions sur la philosophie ancienne et moderne* (Paris, 1676), pp. 479–80.
[92] L. W. B. Brockliss, 'Copernicus in the University: the French Experience', in J. Henry and S. Hutton (eds.), *New Perspectives on Renaissance Thought*, 190–213 (pp. 193–5).
[93] G. Delassault (ed.), *La Pensée janséniste en dehors de Pascal* (Paris, 1963), p. 18.

and faith should avoid discord, and here, to a certain extent, his scientific scepticism came to the rescue. Neither science nor revelation can in fact tell us exactly how things have come to pass, and in any case it would make no sense to risk a schism over Galileo. But it would be equally unreasonable to reject an idea which was rapidly gaining acceptance, especially when the interpretation offered by the Bible was debatable and when the Bible had not been written for the express purpose of teaching physics.[94]

Pierre Gassendi (1592–1655), an anti-Cartesian who espoused atomist theories of matter, also rejected the idea of having recourse to Scripture in order to justify theses deriving from physics, but in doing so he had recourse to a strategy based on the 'agnostic' or sceptical approach to science he shared with Mersenne. Where a truth of reason clashes with a truth of faith, it is necessary to opt for the revealed truth, and simply to note the truth of reason or science which contradicts it. In the sphere of reason, scientific and philosophical truths are so uncertain that faith can then impose a truth on reason but without necessarily contradicting reason. The separation of the domains of science and reason would then leave us with the juxtaposition of two opposing statements, and we must always believe faith whereas we can never wholly believe reason. The possibility of holding to reason and revelation at the same time is explained by Gassendi's view of what Scripture represented. Scripture can be interpreted in two ways: literally, and symbolically or analogically. The Scriptures teach us faith not physics, and as such speak a language accessible to all men. But this language is not appropriate in the establishment of scientific truth.[95] In other words the Bible uses a language of accommodation – deemed unacceptable by many in the University of Paris[96] – which does not aim to depict things as they are. Thus the Copernicans and Scripture can be right in their own ways, since the text of the Bible can be interpreted as describing how things in the heavens *appear* to the human eye, not what is actually the case, whereas Copernicans do the opposite.[97]

This is not to say that Copernicans are of necessity right: their system cannot be demonstrated irrefutably to the extent of excluding other hypotheses. The same is true for the theory of the plurality of worlds which Gassendi can accept as a hypothesis but which he rejects at the level of faith. The sceptical position which can admit of a number of hypotheses leaves the field open to faith. Faith is the only constant, not, it could be

---

[94] Lenoble, *Mersenne*, p. 512.
[95] O. Bloch, *La Philosophie de Gassendi: nominalisme, matérialisme et métaphysique* (The Hague, 1971), pp. 324–5.
[96] Brockliss, 'Copernicus in the University', 194.
[97] Bloch, *La Philosophie de Gassendi*, p. 330.

said, necessarily in particular truths, but in the general way in which the Scriptures teach of the faith. On the other hand, religion does not prescribe an opinion on all things, and, where Scripture is silent, faith leaves the field open for reason. In this regard Gassendi denounced the methods of scholastic theology in which a defence of Aristotelian science was also a defence of the faith: starting from the truths of faith, those faithful to the schools deduced other truths which were sanctioned neither by Scripture nor by Tradition but which were necessarily linked to them.[98] Gassendi too therefore identified the difficulties involved in establishing religious truths on the basis of a discredited philosophy.

In 1691, Arnauld echoed the voice of earlier followers of the new science which asserted that canonical writers spoke of natural things in terms of commonly held opinions and that we should therefore not use Scripture to oppose demonstrable truths.[99] He was particularly hostile to the idea that the 'truths' of modern philosophers are no more certain than those of the past, because, being neither prophets nor apostles, their opinions are those of human beings rather than divine revelations. Arnauld saw the implications as being that, if one adhered to this view, either no science is possible or science must be based on canonical texts. Le Moyne seems to make another category mistake in suggesting that nothing in modern philosophy can be held to be certain unless it is always confirmed by the Church, since knowledge becomes more corrupt as the centuries progress. Arnauld, as we know, distinguished between the two antiquities, and while he would concede that the knowledge of positive theology could not now be more or less certain than at the time of the primitive Church, such could not be the case in science. We have immeasurably better astronomers and doctors now than before the flood, as one would expect, since human science perfects itself in time. He does not hesitate to praise Copernicus, Galileo, Huygens, Brahe, and to prefer Harvey over Galen.[100]

Indeed the assertion of Le Moyne that the only source of truth in all knowledge lies in Scripture or the works of the patristic authorities is actually prejudicial to faith in that attempting to persuade the *libertins* that nothing contained in Euclid or Archimedes, or in the geometry of Descartes is certain, or that the discovery of the four moons of Jupiter is false, simply exposes the faith to ridicule. What would the Church do in judgements of these cases: have recourse to Scripture which attests to three or four planets, or to the Fathers who admit to seven? All other discoveries would have to be regarded as nonsense in the absence of support for them in a biblical or patristic text. Even the Church reformed

[98] Ibid., p. 323.   [99] Sedgwick, *Jansenism*, p. 153.   [100] Arnauld, *Examen*, pp. 95–7.

its own calendar to take account of these discoveries. The sort of reasoning Le Moyne indulges in results from 'une piété mal entendue' which invents an authority which Christ himself never gave.[101] For Arnauld science cannot be a tradition in the same way as the truth of revelation because it is changeable through time. Equally the truths of Scripture in the total context of the faith are more important than the ways in which scientific explanations seem to contradict it. Science, as long as it does not attack the principles of faith, which in their turn cannot depend on the description of natural phenomena, can be left to pursue its independent enquiries.

Conclusion

It was inevitable that, once the authority of Aristotle was abandoned by some and eventually by most in the seventeenth century, the relation of the space of religion to the space of science would never be easy. Certainly the new science offered ways in which outright enemies of the Christian religion could be discredited at the level of their ideas. The new science, particularly mechanism, served the purpose of slowly but surely dealing a death blow to the theories of the likes of Vanini and Campanella. The problem of scholasticism was less straightforward. The abandonment of the synthesis of the material and the spiritual, possible through the theory of substantial forms, led from comfort to anxiety. Cartesianism, even though it reaffirmed a transcendent reality in the separation of the soul from matter in opposition to the concept of a soul in the material world, seemed in other ways to increase anxiety rather than remove it. Cartesianism, along with new discoveries which contradicted traditional teaching, moved in the direction of requiring serious reformulations of the status of certain explanations according to faith.

The new emphasis on mathematics did not help despite the enthusiasm of even those who were not unconditional Cartesians. On the one hand a new relation with God became possible through science. Lenoble identifies a quite radical departure in Mersenne's scientific thought. Physics is not the reflection of metaphysics but a means of making models based on the principles of mechanics which produce the same appearances as the creative act of God. Thus God provides us with a means of imitating him, in Mersenne's own terms, in 'la production extérieure'. The art of the engineer is endowed thereby with a spiritual component quite new to Christian thought.[102] On the other hand, the idea of knowing through doing or 'knowing by construction' was not without considerable prob-

[101] Ibid., pp. 98–9.
[102] Lenoble, *Mersenne*, p. 537.

lems. Malebranche believed that: 'the mechanical interpretation of nature could easily lead to the presumption that we know the making of the universe in the manner of the creator'. This threatened to 'erode the wall between human and divine knowledge'.[103] Malebranche's recognition of this danger is reflected in his systematic attempts to represent human knowledge as participating of divine knowledge rather than being a product of the human mind alone.

The anxiety constitutive of the need for new formulations is reflected in the conclusions of traditionalists who do not entirely reject the contribution of Descartes and others. Rapin recognised that some criticism of Aristotelian physics was possible, and that new experiments and new instruments could be of value. Rapin allowed that Descartes's system was subtle, contained 'de belles imaginations' and a body of doctrine more ordered than that of Galileo or the English. At least he was French and a Catholic. But Rapin could not bring himself to accept all the consequences of the new theories, especially when it was a question of the Eucharist. Aristotle was too much a part of important theological explanations to be jettisoned entirely, or even at all. The pursuit of scientific enquiry and the role ascribed to reason in that enquiry clearly had its dangers for religion. For Rapin physicists now reduced everything to nature, giving it more credit than it should have and extending its power beyond the limits the Creator had marked out for it. Any judgement on the operations of nature is a judgement on God.[104]

In the new perspective the most important quality of religion was at stake. Le Maistre de Sacy, whose views on astronomy we have already encountered, believed that the mechanistic explanation of the universe removed the mystery from God's creation and emptied the world of its theological significance. Many Jansenists felt that, despite his protestations to the contrary, Descartes did not sufficiently respect the distinction between faith and reason.[105] The rational optimism of Descartes and his sense of certainty were clearly seen to lead in an unwise direction. Du Vaucel thought that the reservations of thinkers like Descartes on the literal meaning of the text of Scripture were a mark of disrespect for Scripture as a whole.[106]

Many commentators argue that the seeds of a radical divorce between science and religion, which philosophers like Descartes would have regarded with horror, were already contained within the new philosophy and science. The Thomist / Aristotelian synthesis had the advantage of an

---

[103] Funkenstein, *Theology and the Scientific Imagination*, pp. 298–9.
[104] Rapin, *Réflexions sur la philosophie*, pp. 442–62.
[105] Nadler, *Arnauld*, pp. 19–20.
[106] Rodis-Lewis, *Descartes et le cartésianisme hollandais*, p. 176.

institutional cohesiveness which also worked to the advantage of an indivisible orthodoxy. Individual departures from it were relatively easily dealt with. The emphasis on reason as the basis of independent scientific enquiry seemed to legitimate such departures as a matter of course. In this context no orthodoxy and no institutional framework was possible once the authority which bound it together was of necessity disregarded. The anxiety generated by the need for radical reformulation transcended science itself. Descartes may well have emphasised his adherence to Tradition and the prevailing social framework. Would his followers adopt the same precautions? Self-control does not extend to the control of others. The original intentions of the masters may not be followed by the pupils, and the world of philosophical freedom can in time serve as a model for other sorts of freedom. Jesuit hostility to the teaching of the Oratorians must be seen in this light.

The challenge to the space of religion in the seventeenth century was ultimately its capacity to sustain seemingly incompatible positions and yet retain the validity of the space at all. The scholastics could be accused of discrediting religion by their adherence to a demonstrably obsolete system. The dangers of Cartesianism lay in the highly optimistic assumptions that could be made about the capacity of human reason, and ideas which challenged certain religious explanations while purporting to support them. Certainly, the space of science and philosophy was not in the eyes of the foremost seventeenth-century scientific thinkers necessarily a hostile space or even an exclusive space. They saw philosophy and science, within certain limits, offering a precious service to the faith, and had no difficulty in accommodating the space of science within the space of religion. But even for those who agreed that science should be undertaken from a different point within the religious space, the allowance that reason and philosophical conclusions were useful to religion inevitably resulted in a tension arising from the exact role that each would play. All of which goes to show that at this time two solutions presented themselves: either a fuller integration of science into religion (which made a critical method towards biblical texts supremely urgent), or the total emancipation of science from religion. The first position was on the whole that of seventeenth-century scientists, but the intransigence of certain sections of the Church to new ideas and, ironically, the more sympathetic position of those like Arnauld and Malebranche who separated explanations of science from those of faith, encouraged a movement towards the second.

6   The spaces of discussion

Introduction

Those interested in the development of new ideas in seventeenth-century France faced a dilemma. The traditional teaching of science and philosophy took place in the official spaces of orthodoxy located in the Jesuit schools and in the *collèges de plein exercice* depending on the University of Paris, where, with some modifications, the teaching of Aristotle was maintained and defended into the eighteenth century. In France the universities generally hotly contested any attempt to introduce the new system into any establishment under their aegis. Such institutions were by definition 'protected' and tightly controlled spaces. This defensive attitude was present even in the Oratory where one might expect and where one indeed found great sympathy for Cartesianism. The new science and in particular Cartesianism had overall no institutional framework within which to develop. Port-Royal, with its network of connections in seventeenth-century society, played its part in the public debate over Cartesianism. But the Jansenists who participated in promoting the new philosophy had their own sectional interests to look after, and in any case their confrontational stance in relation to certain religious matters made them doubly suspicious. In Holland, by contrast, Cartesianism was disseminated by university professors.

The exclusion suffered by Cartesians meant quite simply that other sorts of spaces had to be created if the new ideas were to reach a larger public. While not all these spaces were unconnected with members of the Church, the vast majority of them were of an overwhelmingly secular character and motivated by predominantly secular concerns. Certain consequences inevitably flowed from the way dissemination of the new science evolved in our period. Some of the spaces created were private in nature, that is to say gatherings of like-minded souls who wanted to keep up with and extend the new directions in scientific thought. But lectures and demonstrations too were a means of reaching not only those who might have had little contact with schooling in the formal sense, but those whose professional and confessional circumstances demanded prudence in the exercise of their official functions. But it would be misleading to equate new spaces for science entirely with Cartesianism. In any case new ideas for the organisation of science were abroad, culminating in the creation of the Académie royale des sciences. Cartesianism and its dissemination, on the other hand, inevitably constituted a major issue in the new direction science was to take.

The New Science and society

Descartes himself did not belong to and seemed not to encourage any permanent group to promote his scientific ideas. Descartes in fact led a fairly itinerant life, and it is almost typical that he should die in Sweden far from the country in which his philosophy was being developed. The account he gives of himself in the *Discours de la méthode* moves from a space where books were at first important to a space without books. These, he thought, made of one a historian of thought rather than a thinker, and he preferred to journey in what he called 'le livre du monde'. The stripping of his personal space is mirrored in the stripping of the space of the mind necessary to arrive at his first privileged idea, the *cogito*. He had need of little physical space given the individualist direction of his philosophical enquiry. For Gassendi too, philosophical freedom grew out of a personal freedom, itself based on the Epicurean precept of 'vivre caché'.[1] But Descartes was not so self-sufficient that he did not keep himself well informed through his voluminous correspondence, preferring this form of communication to a more collective one.

It was left to his followers in France to provide a solid foundation in society for the new system. Prominent among these were Clerselier and his son-in-law Jacques Rohault. Clerselier, a lawyer in the Paris *parlement*, whom we have already encountered as an editor of Descartes's works, was keen to advertise the cause of Descartes not only against Aristotelians but also against those who, like Gassendi, rejected scholasticism but did not accept the Cartesian system. In addition he desired to demonstrate a pre-established harmony between Christian thought and the new philosophy and in so doing to protect Descartes from those who attacked him on religious grounds.[2] Moreover, Clerselier sought to enhance the reputation of Descartes by promoting the sanctity of the philosopher's life and death. Sainte-Geneviève-du-Mont was apparently chosen for the reburial of his remains on the grounds that it was situated amidst the world of letters and of the University. The new science thus came to rest, literally, in the space of the Church.

[1] Bloch, *La Philosophie de Gassendi*, p. 36.
[2] Gouhier, *Cartésianisme et augustinisme*, pp. 48–9.

Rohault's Wednesday meetings, when he expounded on Cartesian physics, began in Paris in 1659 and over thirteen years became an institution. They attracted a wide audience, from Paris, the provinces and abroad. Another factor which made Rohault an interesting figure in the history of Cartesianism was that his audience was treated to experiments (virtually unknown in the schools) which confirmed aspects of Descartes's physics. Indeed, his interests were far from abstract since he paid some attention to technical matters and, drawing on his own ability to work with his hands, visited the workshops of artisans,[3] thus providing another way in which the new science became firmly rooted in a secular context. Paris was not the only city to benefit from the spread of new ideas. Rohault had also lectured in Amiens. Pierre-Sylvain Régis was another significant figure in the progress of Cartesianism and had been charged with a 'mission' by Rohault to spread the word across France.[4] In 1665, in the ultra-Catholic city of Toulouse, a female disciple of Régis defended Cartesian theses in public.[5] Régis himself lectured to a popular audience and gave private lessons to the marquis de Vardes, probably at Aigues-Mortes. After resuming public teaching at Montpellier, he returned to Paris where he gave lectures at the house of the chemist Lémery until, after six months, he was asked to desist by the archbishop of Paris, according to Fontenelle, out of deference for the old philosophy.[6]

Other spaces contributed to the spread of the new ideas in French society. For example the duc de Luynes organised a Cartesian academy in his château and lectures on Cartesianism were held in the hôtels of the Parisian-based aristocracy who were particularly keen to learn. Madame de Sévigné's daughter no doubt initially picked up her enthusiasm for the new ideas from the Cartesians who attended her mother's salon. Madame de la Sablière, La Fontaine's patroness, encouraged scientific debate in her salon where, as we know from La Fontaine's *Fables*, people were much exercised by the idea of animal machines. In the last quarter of the seventeenth century Desgabets continued teaching the philosophy of Descartes in the château of Cardinal de Retz at Commercy.[7] Talks on Cartesianism were also held at the residence of Bossuet on certain fixed days.[8]

The new science and Cartesianism were made known to the literate public in a number of other ways. In 1671, for example, Poisson concluded the *Avis au lecteur* of his commentary on Descartes with a list of

[3] Ibid., p. 71.
[4] P. Mouy, *Le Développement de la philosophie cartésienne, 1646–1712* (Paris, 1934), p. 112.
[5] J. S. Spink, *French Free Thought from Gassendi to Voltaire* (London, 1960), p. 200.
[6] Ibid., p. 207.
[7] Ibid., p. 195.
[8] Mouy, *Le Développement de la philosophie cartésienne*, p. 98.

places where Cartesian works could be bought.[9] Individual pamphlets also did their job in popularising new ideas. Before 1674, when he was called to England as surgeon to Charles II, J.-B. Denis published fourteen numbers of a pamphlet printed in quarto entitled *Mémoires et conférences sur les arts et les sciences*.[10] Indeed, such was the penetration of the new ideas that after 1690, scholastic works mentioned in the *Journal des savants* were treated as curiosities rather than as serious contributions to learning.[11]

It must not be thought that the space of the new science, especially as far as Cartesianism was concerned, was homogeneous. The anti-Aristotelian stance did not entirely unify all the individuals who adhered to the system as a whole. Régis's understanding of the physics was suspect, as was his personal reading of the metaphysics, which led him into theological imprudence.[12] Cartesians also differed over tactics. Clerselier, in the face of hostility to Descartes's philosophy, preferred to meet the attacks head-on whereas others thought it wiser to attempt to reconcile Descartes with Aristotle. In 1669, the Augustinian monk Le Bossu complained that disciples of Descartes, by letting their enthusiasm run away with them, were provoking censorship by publicising Descartes's views on the Eucharist before his physics had been better understood by the universities.[13]

The spaces of discussion created in order to debate the ideas which became current during the century did not belong exclusively to professionals. While it is true that the *Meditationes de prima philosophia* were addressed to professional philosophers, the *Discours de la méthode* was written in French for non-specialists. The metaphysics proper of the latter work are contained more or less in the fourth section only. The former work became the *Méditations* through the efforts of the duc de Luynes. Two comments arise from these facts. First, the new philosophy drew its adherents from a wide social spectrum and was notably well entrenched in the French aristocracy of the period. The young Condé princes, for example, were the private pupils of Rohault. Members of the royal family, it would seem, were never prevented from reading Descartes by Louis XIV who distinguished between a private Cartesianism towards which he was prepared to be tolerant, and a public Cartesianism which could sometimes threaten his political and ecclesiastical interests.[14]

[9] Kors, *Atheism in France*, p. 328.
[10] Harcourt Brown, *Scientific Organizations in Seventeenth-Century France, 1629–1680* (Baltimore, 1934), p. 200.
[11] Spink, *French Free Thought*, p. 195.
[12] Gouhier, *La Pensée religieuse de Descartes*, p. 131.
[13] T. McLoughlin, 'Censorship and Defenders of the Cartesian Faith in Mid-Seventeenth-Century France', *Journal of the History of Ideas*, 40 (1979), 563–81 (pp. 574–5).
[14] Ibid., 568.

Second, the lectures and demonstrations I have referred to were particularly well attended by women, some of whom became experts in a variety of fields. Madame de Galland was known as a mathematician, and Madame de Guederville and Madame de Bonneveau invited Christiaan Huygens (the Dutch scientist and astronomer) in 1660 to the sessions of scientific experimentation and philosophical discussion which they held every Saturday.[15] Through science, women were brought into a culture from which they were otherwise excluded, either by the extremely limited nature of the curriculum provided in girls' schools, or by the simple fact that they were excluded from the universities. The 'mondain' nature of the discussion of ideas is illustrated too by the works of Poullain de la Barre, largely addressed to women, who favoured Descartes over Aristotle. Fontenelle tells the marquise to whom his *Entretiens sur la pluralité des mondes* (1686) are addressed that he aimed to deal with philosophical matters in a way which was not philosophical, not too dry for the 'gens du monde', but not too chatty for the experts.[16] For Wendy Gibson, on the other hand, Fontenelle's attitude is suspect in that he equates his scientific explanation with a popular novel, in other words with the easy reading that is within reach of women's intellect.[17]

One possible reason for the apparent enthusiasm of aristocrats and women (sometimes the two together of course) for the new ideas is that they would have been relatively uncontaminated by the conservative teaching of the schools and thus constituted a particularly receptive and 'innocent' audience. In general they were removed from the world of the Latin language and were much more orientated to the vernacular. If Latin was the language of the Church, French was the language of the new science, and one cannot moreover dismiss the significance of this climate for the liturgical innovations discussed in an earlier chapter.

Another significant presence in the sorts of space I have discussed here is that of clerics. Rohault's lectures were attended by teachers from the colleges of the University, and it was at the Hôtel de Belingan that Marion, a philosophy professor of the Collège de Navarre and a disciple of Descartes, was able to escape his own milieu and hold a meeting every Thursday.[18] In this way the space of ordination was able to move into the secular spaces of discussion of the new science. But it was also a way in which science could make its way into the official spaces which tried hard to keep it out. An important feature of the secular spaces seems to be that they were inclusive rather than exclusive, in so far as social conditions allowed. It is as if science became a space in its own right which

[15] Gibson, *Women in Seventeenth-Century France*, p. 33.
[16] Ibid., p. 53.   [17] Ibid., p. 31.
[18] Spink, *French Free Thought*, p. 206.

superseded sectional divides. The spread of Cartesianism and the new science promoted a remapping of the cultural space in seventeenth-century France. A movement which began in the margins of official spaces had enormous consequences for the division between the secular and the religious in the period.

Scientific groupings

Mersenne found himself at the opposite pole to Descartes in respect of the space required for the discussion of the new ideas. He felt that the sort of discretion Descartes wished to maintain in the propagation of his ideas rendered a disservice to science.[19] Mersenne's view of the progress of science was a collective one, collaboration being even a duty, especially as science could benefit life and society.[20] Mersenne's moral approach to science was thus 'sociologique par essence, religieuse par accident'.[21] Mersenne accordingly gave the *Méditations* a wider circulation than Descartes himself had wished. Lenoble argues that Mersenne actually did him a greater favour by exposing him to a circle which included critics and not just sympathisers.[22]

The circle animated by Mersenne itself reflected the inclusive nature of the scientific space of discussion. It made light of differences within the Church and between the Churches. Hobbes, tutor at that time to the exiled Charles II, was most welcome in his capacity as a philosopher. He was one of those to whom Mersenne sent copies of the *Méditations* and he was, in his characteristic way, actually rather hostile to them. Interestingly, Pascal frequently attended scientific discussions in Mersenne's circle and was later active in that of the duc de Roannez before his spiritual crisis on 23 November 1654. Mersenne's cell was a meeting point of all kinds and, as a man in orders, he operated a space with no frontiers, paradoxically as it happens, from his monastic cell which moreover encouraged the coming together of representatives of the religious and the secular spaces. The eclecticism of Mersenne's thought – he at one time engaged with the problems of alchemy and Paracelsian science, a significant presence in the first half of our period – is reflected in the individuals he welcomed.[23] One is almost tempted to say that, with Mersenne, science found its church with Mersenne as its intercessor.

Mersenne's cell was in fact the nucleus of a much wider space which

[19] Lenoble, *Mersenne*, p. 45.   [20] Ibid., pp. 586–7.
[21] Ibid., p. 578.   [22] Ibid., pp. 47–8.
[23] For Paracelsianism in seventeenth-century France, see Allen G. Debus, *The Chemical Philosophy: Paracelsian Science and Medicine in the Sixteenth and Seventeenth Centuries* (New York, 1977).

extended beyond national frontiers for he maintained links with like-minded people on a European scale through his correspondence, one of the major means of scientific dissemination in our period. The most assiduous of correspondents in this domain was undoubtedly Nicolas Peiresc, another enthusiast of the new science. The network of his 500 correspondents extended across the whole of Europe and outside, including Damascus and Goa,[24] and provides us with further proof that the new ideas could not be contained within national or confessional frontiers. They could also rise above international strife. Gassendi corresponded with scientists in countries at war with France.

Théophraste Renaudot, a figure close to royal power in the first half of the seventeenth century, participated in the encouragement of open debate about philosophical and scientific matters. He was famous for his multi-purpose *Bureau d'adresse* and one of the facets of the bureau was the series of lectures held there on a variety of topics. The lectures, not limited to scientific topics, took place on Mondays from 22 August 1633 to 1 September 1642 without interruption. Again the emphasis was on the openness of debate, always in French, and all were welcome, thus underlining the essentially amateur nature of much scientific discussion of this period.[25] Again a very broad range of opinion was represented and the arrangements of the lectures were such that more than one speaker was chosen in order to offer a contrast of views on individual subjects, between for example scholastics and moderns.[26] Only matters of religion and state were banned. Five reports of the lectures, which included the demonstration of navigational methods and various devices, were published between 1634 and 1655.[27] The most popular subject was medicine, unsurprising on two counts: Renaudot was a physician and the Faculty of Medicine of the University of Paris was particularly conservative. Once again, the spaces of discussion in society provided an alternative to the official spaces. But Renaudot's success did not outlive Richelieu and was brought to an end by a vengeful Faculty of Medicine.

The involvement of others in royal government in spreading the new science is further illustrated by Henri Justel, a *secrétaire du roi*, one of whose duties included the licensing of publications. Justel inherited a large library along with collections of medals and manuscripts. He was also involved in the dissemination of English books on the rest of the continent of Europe, and he had correspondents in England and Ger-

[24] R. Mandrou, *Des Humanistes aux hommes de science, XVIe et XVIIe siècles* (Paris, 1973), p. 147.

[25] Howard M. Solomon, *Public Welfare, Science and Propaganda in Seventeenth-Century France: the Innovations of Théophraste Renaudot* (Princeton, 1972), p. 64.

[26] Brown, *Scientific Organizations*, pp. 21–2.

[27] Solomon, *Public Welfare*, pp. 70 passim.

many in particular. His conferences which began in 1664 were attended by a broad spectrum of French and European society, including the clergy from both confessions. Because he felt that theory should be subject to practice, the conferences frequently consisted of testing various, sometimes quite trivial, devices and inventions which he had picked up on his travels or from his correspondents.[28] His circle shows how wide-ranging 'scientific' interest was in the seventeenth century to the extent that science meant many things. But the presence of scientific discussion in a circle which maintained an interest in technological matters served to root science even more in a secular context. The abbé Bourdelot's academy began its life around 1648–9 and started up again in 1664, lasting until 1685, the year of Bourdelot's death. The predominant interest in the early period was medical, including a discussion of the transfusion of blood. The dissemination of science in the wider space of society, however, took a step further with Bourdelot, not only in the appearance of various publications but in the publicity given to meetings by means of posters. On 15 August 1674, 400 people were present at one of his meetings.[29]

The extent of public interest in scientific matters can be gauged by the proliferation of telescopes within the private spaces we are talking about here. Given that astronomy was one of the hot points of seventeenth-century science, such a facility encouraged even further the personal observation of phenomena quite outside the control of any official or unofficial body. In the provinces, too, interest in science was growing and academies were formed to pursue scientific discussion. They existed in Montpellier and Caen, the chief centre of experimental work outside Paris, especially in the practical problems of chemistry.[30] We shall return to Caen later.

Scientific groupings were not without their problems in the context of scientific debate. One of the features of the Montmor academy, which included among its members Clerselier, Cordemoy and Rohault, was the circulation and discussion of each other's books. It happened that, partly for this reason, the Montmor academy was not a place of harmony and light, since it was divided between those who preferred to talk and those who wished to proceed much more by experimentation. The temper of most of its members quite simply excluded 'doing'.[31] Pierre Petit, in a letter to Huygens of 1658, complained that the Parisian amateur was more eager to discuss than to work for the improvement of inventions.[32] Huygens himself complained in a letter to Boyle that French naturalists

---

[28] Brown, *Scientific Organizations*, pp. 168–71.
[29] Ibid., pp. 237 and 245.
[30] Ibid., pp. 209 and 216.
[31] Ibid., p. 142.   [32] Ibid., p. 86.

were talkers rather than experimenters.[33] Indeed the meetings often turned into acrimonious disputes over untested theories and conflicting authorities.[34]

The two main problems with the academies as constituted by people like Montmor were that, first, their nature as talking shops did not provide the initiative necessary for the advancement of science and its concomitant, technology. The leaders of the groups were amateurs more interested in books and words than action. Contemporary observers with a practical interest in physics argued that 'progress in the execution of their designs could only be made by separation of the social and discursive element from the experimental program and the concentration of each party on its particular interests'.[35] The other problem was that experimentation was costly and required space. This was especially the case with the construction of astronomical instruments and the purchase of raw materials for chemical and biological experiments. Only official intervention could lead to a more efficient science.

All these problems came together in a single example, the Académie de physique in Caen, which was in existence from 1662 to 1672. Before achieving a different sort of status the Académie was an informal group of 'savants' which was, however, transformed by the visit to Paris of one of its co-founders, Graindorge, an enlightened amateur, the other being the scholar and later bishop of Avranches, Pierre-Daniel Huet. Graindorge in particular envisaged a space for science not organised according to traditional natural philosophy but driven by an empirical approach.[36] In addition, Graindorge's vision was of scientific activity within a group dynamic where science progressed in a community. Science created its own space. In this new type of space a network of communication could be established and dissipation of effort could be avoided.[37] Graindorge's main inspiration was the circle animated by Thévenot, appointed royal librarian by Colbert, whose members made some contribution to the establishment of the new type of grouping which consisted of separating science as much as possible from metaphysical and religious controversies.[38]

This optimistic perspective did not last, and ironically the Académie's demise began at the point it achieved royal recognition in 1668. Un-

[33] R. Taton, *Les Origines de l'Académie royale des sciences* (Paris, 1965), p. 23.

[34] Brown, *Scientific Organizations*, pp. 76–7.

[35] Ibid., p. 119.

[36] See David S. Lux, *Patronage and Royal Science in Seventeenth-Century France: the Académie de Physique in Caen* (Ithaca and London, 1989).

[37] Ibid., p. 20.

[38] Desmond M. Clarke, *Occult Powers and Hypotheses: Cartesian Natural Philosophy under Louis XIV* (Oxford, 1989), p. 39.

doubtedly the real driving force (and source of funds) was Huet, a rather more substantial figure, intellectually and socially, than Graindorge. His presence in Caen at meetings of the Académie was crucial to its success. When Huet handed over patronage to the charge of the royal *intendant*, Chamillart, the enthusiasm of members waned and could not be sustained by Graindorge. Moreover royal funding 'raised the stakes for failure'.[39] The Académie was not up to the demands made on it and there were splits between the mathematicians and those interested in more practical activities like dissection.[40] It was also complained that the Académie spent too much on books and not enough on equipping the laboratory.[41]

Graindorge's vision of an autonomous space for science thus proved difficult to establish outside the structure of authority resting either on a charismatic individual or traditional institutions like the colleges of the Jesuits and the University of Paris where corporate and ideological interests formed the mortar which kept the bricks of the edifice in place. Science could not yet establish its own space, at least away from the centre, without a self-sufficient ideology of its own. But a separate space for science independent of traditional institutions under the auspices of the Church was precisely what the Académie royale des sciences was supposed to be. How did it fare?

The Académie royale des sciences

The scientific groupings we have encountered in Paris, however ineffective they may have been, undoubtedly prepared the way for the establishment of the Académie royale des sciences which set the seal on the implantation of science in an officially sanctioned and financed secular space, at a level of intervention the state had never imposed on education. The members of the various amateur groups could not entirely be excluded from the exercise of forming a different space for science, because they included many who had a direct interest in experimentation. In any case it may well have been that the Académie, before becoming an established organisation, was in its initial stages a casual association, rather like the Académie of Caen, before its appropriation by royal power.

Indeed two parallel plans existed for the Académie royale des sciences, one of which was drawn up by Charles Perrault and which would have included representatives of the arts. Moreover it would also have been involved in the discovery of the secrets of trade and commerce and would have recorded the practices of artisans so that the principles of chemistry

---

[39] Lux, *Patronage and Royal Science*, p. 83.   [40] Ibid., p. 93.   [41] Ibid., p. 159.

and physics might be given practical application. But, as in the case of the educational programme of certain sections of the Church, this sort of programme for the Académie crossed too many well-established frontiers and trod on the toes of corporate interest, including the medical faculty of the University of Paris and the Paris *parlement*.

The intervention of the Sorbonne resulted from its anxiety that religious problems might be discussed by an organisation not authorised and constituted by the Church.[42] In fact it was made quite clear that the Académie's discussions would not touch on religion or politics, or on any sort of controversy. Astronomers were therefore ordered to steer clear of theology, and chemists were under instructions not to indulge in alchemy.[43] To this end many members of the amateur circles were excluded because, as Chapelain put it, they were 'more concerned with cabals than making new discoveries'.[44] Montmor's academy among others had been particularly associated with drawing up battle lines between one philosophical tendency and another.[45]

Strict Cartesians were regarded by many as too sectarian and the prominent controversialists were excluded from membership, it is generally agreed, on the advice of Chapelain. This was equally true of those who adhered rigidly to Aristotle. It was considered that their prejudices and partisanship in terms of religious creed prevented them from possessing the open-mindedness necessary for the sort of scientific and technological progress envisaged as emanating from the Académie.[46] Indeed Statute XII of the Académie allowed only the honorary membership of priests. The Académie thus exercised its own form of control, or self-control. It would, however, have been impossible to exclude Cartesians altogether. Members included Cassini and Pierre Borel, the latter having written a biography of Descartes.

It was some time before the real status of the Académie, first established in 1666, became clear. Letters patent were issued only in 1713 and these confirmed the reorganisation of the Académie in 1699. The Académie thus had the status of a consultative body and not of a corporation. The first time that 'royal' was used in the title of the Académie was 8 February 1672.[47] Two of the most important aspects of the Académie were, first, that its members received pensions in exchange for which they had to give the whole of their time to the institution and, second, that the king paid the

---

[42] J. M. Hirschfield, *The Académie Royale des Sciences* (New York, 1981), p. 19.
[43] Ibid., p. 20.
[44] R. Hahn, *The Anatomy of a Scientific Institution: the Paris Academy of Sciences, 1666–1803* (Berkeley, 1971), p. 15.
[45] Brown, *Scientific Organizations*, pp. 67 and 72.
[46] Hahn, *The Anatomy of a Scientific Institution*, p. 15.
[47] Hirschfield, *The Académie Royale des Sciences*, pp. 20–1.

expenses for instruments and new inventions, and supplied the laboratory. A significant advance was made with the construction of the
Observatory in 1672, thus providing the landscape with a prominent and
visible space for science. In the same way that churches were a visible
reminder of the divine in the world, a secular activity, in other ways so
associated with controversy, was provided with its own cathedral.

Chapelain affirmed that the principal object of the Académie was to
banish all prejudices from science, 'basing everything on experiments, to
find in them something certain, to dismiss all chimeras and to open an easy
path to truth, for those who will continue this practice'.[48] This in itself
would have excluded strict Cartesians, with the exception of Rohault.
There was something of a paradox here in the sense that the Académie
recognised the Cartesian orientation towards mathematics but in a wholly
un-Cartesian way.[49] Pure reason was therefore mistrusted in favour of a
much more applied approach. 'Doing' thus avoided the speculative
controversies that were encouraged by simply talking or writing. The
ultimate nature of things interested less than their function, 'a type of
understanding that would allow the development of ideas and concepts
for the purposes of manipulation and control'.[50] Ideally science became a
space of action which fully emancipated scientific activity from the
tutelage of religion. But pure reason was not abandoned. Colbert was
keen to offer both the inducement of contributing on a practical level and
of examining problems from a generalised viewpoint.[51] The further
downgrading of pure research came with Louvois who had not himself
much interest in science and who '[groped] in the debris of older
pseudo-sciences'.[52] Despite the production of some machines of a trivial
order, we need, according to Briggs, 'to jettison [the] notion that the
Académie was seriously intended to play an active technological role',[53]
and its impact on industry was certainly slight.[54]

The Académie royale des sciences was a closed space, that is to say not
open to the public, and published only extracts of its minutes, although
Nicolas Lémery, who had abjured Protestantism in order to become a
member, conducted courses for large audiences. This is however the only
recorded instance of the Académie being involved in teaching.[55] One of
the advantages of Bourdelot's academy was in fact that people could not

---

[48] Hahn, *The Anatomy of a Scientific Institution*, pp. 15–16.
[49] C. Salomon-Bayet, *L'Institution de la science, et l'expérience du vivant* (Paris, 1978), p. 31.
[50] Hirschfield, *The Académie Royale des Sciences*, p. 112.
[51] Hahn, *The Anatomy of a Scientific Institution*, p. 17.
[52] R. Briggs, 'The Académie Royale des Sciences and the Pursuit of Utility', *Past and Present*,
131 (1991), 38–88 (p. 49).   [53] Ibid., 55.   [54] Ibid., 39.
[55] M. Ornstein, *The Role of Scientific Societies in the Seventeenth Century* (Hamden, Conn.,
1963), p. 158.

only learn of new discoveries but also penetrate the secrets of the Académie royale des sciences.[56] But within the Académie it was scientifically open. No party line was imposed, and the academicians were not committed to any scientific theory or authority. The Académie needed to believe it possible for minds to be changed. It was not opinion that was expected to be uniform but an approach or a way of behaving. The Académie demanded not the ostentation or the vanity of the individualist, but an earnest commitment to hard work and unadorned logic. The Académie was thereby justified in excluding the amateur, and elaborated 'behavioural norms that actually defined the scientific community'.[57]

The elaboration of a specific type of behaviour for the space of science, a phenomenon which, in general terms, was such a familiar part of seventeenth-century French culture, is emphasised by the manner of working in the Académie. Each scientist worked on his own particular area, but was expected to deal with matters which were brought to his attention.[58] It is clear therefore that the autonomy I have spoken of was not independence. Here the French Académie differed markedly from the Royal Society of London which grew out of the habits and interests of its members before it became an officially constituted body, remaining even then a 'free company of investigators': 'the veil of secrecy and the careful supervision under which they worked, the exclusion of doctrine, whether Cartesian or Jesuit, and the royal funds which provided salaries and expenses, speak of the high degree of regimentation and control which a successful public academy for the sciences demanded in Paris'.[59]

The activities of the Académie, while carefully organised within its own space, had their place in the more general intellectual climate of the period. Biological investigations were intended to provide proper scientific explanations which would counter the descriptions of folklore and reject the false ascription of qualities to animals.[60] Claude Perrault, in his studies of the chameleon and the salamander, was particularly anxious to dispel absurd popular prejudices.[61] One contemporary writer, Barbeyrac (not a member of the Académie), regarded ignorance of physics as responsible for superstition.[62]

The Académie royale des sciences created an original space for a number of obvious reasons. It was first and foremost a purely secular space in its emphasis on experimentation rather than on theoretical

[56] Taton, *Les Origines de l'Académie royale des sciences*, p. 28.
[57] Hahn, *The Anatomy of a Scientific Institution*, p. 31.
[58] Brown, *Scientific Organizations*, p. 149.
[59] Ibid., p. 160.
[60] Hirschfield, *The Académie Royale des Sciences*, p. 124.
[61] Ornstein, *The Role of Scientific Societies*, p. 150.
[62] Barbeyrac, *Discours sur l'utilité des lettres*, pp. 10–11.

speculation. The lack of a single scientific direction meant too that heterogeneity became legitimised. Such a retreat from the notion of orthodoxy could moreover only be legitimised in a secular space. But the overwhelming contribution of the Académie was its professionalisation of scientific space, although there were limits to the significance of its success. Indeed, we encounter some of the difficulties which led to the demise of the Académie de physique in Caen.

Professionalisation essentially meant bureaucratisation, since the scientist was dependent on royal finance and, ultimately, bound by royal priorities, especially in the military and economic fields. Royal appointment defined the professional rather than personal expertise. Again the status of science lacked its own internal drive. At the same time royal authority controlled the context within which scientific activity could operate, even if it did not define the intellectual basis of that activity. In a sense 'freedom from prejudice' was not necessarily an advantage in science since it inevitably led to a technological definition of science, rather than a science dealing with the frontiers of the subject. At no moment in its history did the Académie imitate the Royal Society in its defence and illustration of natural religion, nor did it follow the Academy of Berlin (founded in 1700) in setting side by side experimental and speculative philosophy.[63]

Royal patronage did not necessarily lead in itself to a stimulating climate for scientific research. Much depended on the individual protectorship at any given time. That of Chancellor Pontchartrain was, for example, uneven. He expanded the Académie and regularised its affairs, but he reduced its budget and the costs of research with the result that the research programme declined. Morale in the 1690s was at a low ebb and was not encouraged by the crown's failure to pay pensions for several years. The suggestion is too that the creation of the Académie did little to raise the status of science itself, and members of the Académie des inscriptions received their pensions more regularly than the scientists.[64] If the success and the status of science were wanting at the centre it is no wonder that societies at the periphery fared no better.

Despite all that, however, it remains true that the Académie represented an autonomous and official space for knowledge, or at least one which did not come under the aegis of the Church, and where a particular type of behaviour had a wholly secular function. For a time the private spaces had performed this role. It was now time for such a space to be created officially by royal authority. With the specific and deliberate exclusion of

[63] Salomon-Bayet, *L'Institution de la science*, p. 170.
[64] See A. Stroup, 'Royal Funding of the Parisian Académie Royale des Sciences during the 1690s', *Transactions of the American Philosophical Society*, 77, part 4 (1987), 1–167.

doctrinal controversy, which inevitably entailed the exclusion of certain individuals, 'real' scientific knowledge and activity was officially removed from the space of the Church. The Académie did not provide, however, a model of intellectual freedom, but a secular model of authority in the domain of knowledge. The emancipation from scientific authority, which was real enough, did not mean emancipation from all authority. The state's overwhelming interest in technical matters, however ineffective the results may have been, was a form of control.

Science and the space of the Church

One might expect the Church to control its own space more tightly than the spaces of discussion which were created outside its institutional boundaries. Officially the teaching in Jesuit schools stuck very closely to the traditional forms I have discussed in my chapter on ideas, and any obvious espousal of Cartesianism or deviations from the normal pattern of teaching were severely sanctioned. Even then it is impossible to adopt a simplistic view of Jesuit attitudes to Cartesianism. Some at least were receptive to Cartesian theses, although generally the Jesuits included in their ranks few who could be described as disciples in the strict sense of the term, and fierce opposition was mounted against the adoption of any elements of Cartesian metaphysics in particular. Indeed the Jesuits watched other teaching orders like hawks for the slightest deviation in this particular domain, especially when another teaching establishment, the Oratorians for example, was located in the same diocese. A more favourable attitude was however adopted towards the physics of Descartes, from which a number of professors borrowed in their teaching,[65] and it has been suggested that the further away from France they were, the more the Jesuits tended to forget constraints imposed in Catholic Europe. As early as 1643 le Père Fournier praised Descartes in a book entitled *L'Hydrographie*. In 1646 Descartes could be found side by side with, but not replacing, Aristotle, but a treatise of astronomy advocating the immobility of the earth could still be written in 1655, or even later. Officially the Jesuits remained staunch followers of Aristotle and of substantial forms until well beyond the end of the seventeenth century. The contribution of professors of the University of Paris to the dissemination of new discoveries, if not of new systems of thought, has been discussed in the previous chapter.

It is not surpising in view of earlier discussions, and in view of the place of St Augustine in any discussion of seventeenth-century science, that the

---

[65] G. Sortais, *Le Cartésianisme chez les Jésuites français au XVIIe et au XVIIIe siècle* (Paris, 1929), p. 86.

religious orders most favourable to the Doctor of Grace were also those who welcomed Descartes and, later, Malebranche. Among them were the Benedictines, within both the Congregation of Saint-Maur at Saint-Germain-des-Prés and the Congregation of Saint-Vanne. Mabillon in particular recommended professors of philosophy to include extracts of Descartes's works in their teaching, and singled out a number of works as permissible reading in philosophy: something of Rohault in order to become acquainted with the principles of Cartesian physics, even if one did not follow them; Huet's treatise against Cartesianism with the reply in French of Régis; and extracts from Malebranche's *De la Recherche de la vérité*.[66] Desgabets was a tireless follower of Descartes and even gave the new philosophy a more empirical inflexion.[67]

Some of the most ardent followers of Cartesian theses were undoubtedly to be found among the Oratorians who several times clashed with the authorities over the teaching of some of their number. The espousal of Cartesianism in the Congregation followed logically from the Platonist and Augustinian direction that Bérulle had initially given his theology. But the adoption of Cartesianism by the Oratorians was by no means straightforward. Certainly, the Collège de Notre-Dame-des-Ardilliers in particular adopted a more liberal attitude towards philosophical matters. Thomassin can be quoted as saying that nothing was more contrary to the spirit of the Oratory than for its members to be forced to take up one philosophical position rather than another. Differences are more about words than things, and it is less a question of opposing doctrines than of a diversity of opinions.[68] This may have obtained for individual opinion but a stricter policy was adopted towards teaching, and the superiors of the Oratory fixed limits to the content of courses which they did not expect teachers to transgress. Malebranche arrived in the order precisely at a point when Cartesianism was suspect.[69]

Gouhier warns against the consequences of identifying 'Augustinian' too closely with 'anti-scholastic' or even 'Cartesian'. For the Oratorians, following Plato did not necessarily mean mistreating Aristotle. Some anti-scholastics opposed Descartes, but not all anti-scholastics who were also Augustinians adhered to the new philosophy. Gouhier identifies two possible currents of thought within seventeenth-century Augustinianism. The first, as we have observed elsewhere, discovered in Cartesian theses the essential elements of a Christian philosophy. The second included

---

[66] Dom J. Mabillon, *Traité des études monastiques*, 2 vols. (Paris, 1691), I, 365.
[67] Mouy, *Le Développement de la philosophie cartésienne*, p. 100.
[68] Quoted in J. Prost, *La Philosophie à l'Académie protestante de Saumur, 1606–1685* (Paris, 1907), p. 71.
[69] Gouhier, *La Vocation*, p. 54.

those who, while disciples of Augustine, remained faithful to the teaching of the schools which they wished to rid of its excess baggage by returning to its source in St Thomas, himself a disciple of Augustine. If at the same time they encountered Plato, he already formed part of the synthesis. Any Platonist sympathies could then be accommodated with a slight but not thoroughgoing critique of Aristotle.[70] In this sense the Oratory cannot be confused wholly with Cartesianism. In 1664 the Oratory was in fact, with the arrival of le Père Bourgoing as superior, anti-Cartesian. He was very aware that mistakes in the relation of theology to the new philosophy could cost the congregation dear, especially in the links between Cartesianism and Jansenism. His hostility to Port-Royal is borne out in the way Bossuet referred to divisions within the Church in his funeral oration for Bourgoing. The symbol of Cartesianism at the Oratory, le Père André Martin, had already been penalised in 1652.[71]

For all that, the Oratorian college at Saumur was particularly interesting because it had existed alongside a rival institution, in the shape of the prestigious Protestant academy, which itself had a reputation for being more liberal in theology. Protestants went to Thomassin's lectures and Oratorians attended 'soutenances de thèse' at the academy. They even joined in friendly philosophical arguments with each other. Most importantly, however, the Oratorians were more advanced philosophically than the Protestants with the result that the Protestants themselves could not eventually stand out against the advent of Cartesianism in their own ranks.[72] Moreover, pressure on the Protestants was increased by a domestic public which had grown more and more aware of changes in the realm of ideas. In addition, Dutch and German students who knew what was going on in their own countries brought their knowledge with them to France.[73] The region eventually became a Cartesian milieu including the famous doctor Louis de la Forge. Some pastors proposed at the Synod of Baugé in 1656 that Plato should be substituted for Aristotle, or at least that there should be freedom to choose. The request was referred to an extraordinary council of the academy which, in the interests of unity, decided that freedom would bring confusion, although teachers could abandon Aristotle if he was considered to have strayed from the truth.[74] Finally, Cartesianism was brought lock, stock and barrel to the academy by Chouet who taught there from 1664 to 1669. One particular element of his teaching was that in matters regarding nature, the teaching of the Bible has no place, since the language it uses is a language of accommodation,

---

[70] Ibid., pp. 53–4.
[71] Ibid., pp. 51–2.
[72] Prost, *La Philosophie à l'Académie protestante de Saumur*, p. 69.
[73] Ibid.   [74] Ibid., pp. 76–7.

describing things as they appear, and not a medium for teaching physics or astronomy.[75]

Conclusion

Despite the gradual appearance of the new ideas in the world of education, the space of science as we might understand it in the modern sense was predominantly secular. The exclusion of the teaching of Cartesianism in particular and the slow progress that the new science in general made in the majority of teaching establishments in France meant that the dissemination of the new movement took place outside the religious space. One consequence of this development was that it tended towards the legitimation of a distinct secular space in the field of ideas from which the Church wished to exclude itself. Mersenne himself was conscious of the role of science in a secular context and what was required from secular authority if science was to prosper. He advocated the establishment of academies for the advancement of science, and he complained that writers and poets, who have only language, are supported by patrons whereas scientists are not.[76] Another significant factor of the secular context of science in the second half of the century in particular was that the emphasis was unquestionably on the purely scientific consequences of the new system. It was not in itself a place of religious controversy, only to the extent that a religious authority could be brought to bear in the support of a philosophical system. The secular place for science was consecrated by the founding of the Académie royale des sciences.

It is possible that the religious consequences of developments in seventeenth-century science might have been better controlled and explained had a greater number of the teaching establishments been less on the defensive and more welcoming of new ideas. Instead of ideas going to the schools (with honourable exceptions), the schools, in terms of particular individuals, had to come to the ideas with the loss of control that that entailed. Certain sections of the Church were directly responsible for the creation in people's minds of a purely secular space for the operations of the intellect, thus helping to weaken the relationship, which Descartes regarded as crucial, between science and Christian thought.

[75] Ibid., pp. 92–3.
[76] Lenoble, *Mersenne*, pp. 575 and 588.

7   The spaces of hostility: belief

Introduction

Much of the previous discussion in this study has involved hostility of some sort, arising for example from different positions over Tradition, from institutional rivalries within the educational system and from the abandonment of the old science in favour of the new. Some disputes led to a position where, from within the space of the Church, individuals like Richard Simon could even be described as the enemy within. In this chapter I should like to deal with two groups which existed in identifiable geographical spaces, one within the Catholic Church and one outside it, but within the space of belief.

Protestantism was a space in terms of a clearly differentiated form of belief disseminated in separate institutions: the temple and academies. The separate space for Protestantism was, moreover, enshrined in the Edict of Nantes of 1598. It was also a space geographically since adherence to the Reformed Religion was more widespread in some areas of France than others. Indeed Protestantism was a space to be defended from its confessional rivals in military terms, sometimes as a defence against invasion, as in Navarre and Béarn. The most spectacular event of this sort was the siege of La Rochelle whose consequences were so disastrous for Protestantism as a whole. On the other hand Protestants promoted the oneness of political space in the kingdom with many remaining fiercely loyal to the crown even at the height of their persecution. For the most part Catholicism constructed Protestantism as a hostile space, for the word 'heretic' automatically came to designate a Protestant. The Catholic hierarchy never accepted the existence of an autonomous space for a religious rival and from the promulgation of the Edict of Nantes sought to bring Protestants back into its own space.

The second religious grouping which could lay claim to the status of a hostile space was the Jansenist movement whose centre was Port-Royal, that is to say the Paris convent and the monastery of Port-Royal-des-Champs. Clearly, not all Jansenists in seventeenth-century France resided at Port-Royal, although there are interesting cases of society figures who resided as close to the Paris monastery as they could. Nor did all those who espoused Augustinian theses similar to the Jansenists express direct allegiance to Port-Royal. But Jansenism did constitute itself as a space at Port-Royal in the sense that some major figures in addition to the nuns of the reformed Cistercian order lived there, and for a short time it had its own school. It was also a space targeted by royal and ecclesiastical power.

There are certain ways in which the frontier between the space of Jansenism and other spaces cannot be drawn in any hard and fast way. Jansenists were gallicans and defended the same propositions regarding the extension of papal power as other sections of the Church. Their position on moral teaching, particularly in relation to confession and the Eucharist, could not be faulted doctrinally: 'practically every one of their individual views can be found in authors of unquestioned orthodoxy'.[1] The space of Jansenism was given more identifiable boundaries as the dispute over the *Augustinus* became more prolonged. Jansenist positions became more clearly defined as those of a specific group of people, especially as Arnauld came to espouse some quite radical positions on ecclesiastical organisation. In turn the Jansenists attracted the hostility of royal authority who saw their high polemical profile as a threat to order within the kingdom. No other set of individuals within the Catholic Church as a group constituted a target for persecution in the way Jansenists did. Their gradual isolation perhaps dates from 1657 when the Church officially hardened its own position on moral teaching by adopting Borromeo's *Instructions to Confessors*. The growing acceptance in the Church at large of a more rigorist line prompted many Augustinians to keep their distance from the leaders of 'le parti Janséniste'.[2]

The spaces of Jansenism and Protestantism are not unrelated in some ways. The Jansenists were acutely aware of the accusation that their theology resembled that of Calvinists and did all they could to distance themselves from it. One thing they share as groups however is the importance of individual conscience, for Jansenists and Protestants are in their own ways dissenters. In that sense we might be able to situate the two groups in the space of dissent.

Jansenism

While Jansenism had a sort of headquarters at Port-Royal, the space of Jansenism extended far beyond these boundaries. Jansenism was able to entrench itself within the space of the Church in individual dioceses

---

[1] R. Briggs, *Communities of Belief: Cultural and Social Tensions in Early Modern France* (Oxford, 1989), p. 341.
[2] Ibid., p. 352.

through the ecclesiastical status of bishops who were personally able to create 'manageable' spaces in which the full rigour of Jansenist spirituality could be installed. The two most prominent Jansenist bishops were Caulet in Pamiers and Pavillon at Alet. Pavillon, regarded as one of the Jansenist 'saints', is a particularly interesting case because it does seem that he went a long way in imposing discipline on what had previously been from a Counter-Reformation point of view an unruly community. Dancing and theatre were prohibited and a form of public admonishment was instituted. Pavillon himself led an exemplary and austere life which he devoted to his diocesan flock. The idea that such austere morals might alienate the faithful is usefully countered by the circumstances surrounding Pavillon's behaviour over the *régale* which incurred the wrath of the king. When Pavillon refused to obey the king's summons to the Court, Louis considered the idea of using force, whereupon he was advised that the people of Alet would themselves resist any attempt to remove their bishop against his will. But Jansenist influence among the Church hierarchy could be to a certain extent controlled by recruitment to the sees, and towards the end of the century in particular bishops were chosen who were greater supporters of an 'externalised' religion and who had little enthusiasm for a form of moral teaching which seemed to undermine the notion of privilege.[3]

Indeed, the spread of Jansenist influence cannot be seen as in any way totalising. Other sections of the French Church absorbed or resisted the influence of Jansenism to varying degrees. Brockliss has discovered no genuinely Jansenist courses in the colleges depending on the University of Paris. More support could be found in the faculties but on a small scale. His assertion that seminary courses followed the same pattern, however, needs nuancing.[4] A consequence of seminaries being under the control of the bishops meant that Jansenist bishops or their sympathisers would look at least to those of like mind to run them. Often the organisation of the seminaries was handed to the Oratorians whose *raison d'être* was precisely the education of the secular clergy and who remained on the whole of a more radical Augustinian persuasion than other religious orders. Briggs calculates that, taking into account seminaries not directed by a specified order, a quarter were run in the early eighteenth century by clerics heavily influenced by Augustinianism.[5]

Jansenist influence on the religious orders varied a great deal, even within a single order. The Oratory is a good example of the complexity of the situation, especially in the light of the situation of the order at the time

---

[3] Ibid., p. 232.
[4] Brockliss, *French Higher Education*, p. 251.
[5] Briggs, *Communities of Belief*, p. 354.

Malebranche joined it, as we have seen. The Oratorian authorities were extremely sensitive to the consequences for their survival as a rival teaching institution to the Jesuits of any accusation which might align them with the Jansenists, for example in discussions on Cartesianism where Cartesianism could be associated with Augustinianism, particularly through the abandonment of the concept of substantial forms. That the Oratory could be considered a hostile space was proved by the prohibition in 1674 of the course of positive theology taught by le Père André Martin at Saumur. The General Assembly of the Oratory held in September 1678 specifically forbade the teaching of Cartesian ideas.[6]

Other orders were not immune from the confusion of Cartesianism and Jansenism. Taveneaux relates that in the Benedictine congregation of Saint-Vanne the first was the vehicle of the second, and that Desgabets and the Benedictines of Saint-Mihiel made the very close association between the impassioned commentary of Cartesian theses and Jansenist polemic.[7] The fathers of the Christian Doctrine were not untouched by issues deriving from the Jansenist controversy. In the first place there was an Augustinian base to their spirituality which made them receptive to influence, and they eventually became embroiled in the whole affair surrounding Port-Royal. In 1683, the king took the superior of the order, Thomas Chevallier, to task for 'nouveautés en matière de doctrine'. Louis had to repeat his dissatisfaction, exhorting Chevallier to take firmer action. The matter dragged on until 1689.[8]

Jansenism was highly influential in Lorraine, and particularly at the abbeys of Hautefontaine and Orval. In this region real frontiers were of considerable significance. Chaunu argues that a clear distinction emerged between the Jansenism of what he calls the 'frontières de catholicité' and that of the 'interior' of the kingdom of France. The influence of Jansenism was strongest therefore where it was in contact with a strong Protestant minority, as in Metz where its influence was felt as early as 1623. Moreover, it was a strictly theological form of spirituality which dominated to the exclusion of matters of ecclesiastical administration. Chaunu recalls that as individuals Jansenius and Saint-Cyran were in close contact with Protestants, the first in the majority Calvinist Utrecht and the second in Bayonne where there existed a strong Huguenot minority.[9]

Chaunu further asserts that the desire to reunite the Churches was particularly strong on the frontiers of Catholicity where it was understood

---

[6] Gouhier, *Cartésianisme et augustinisme*, pp. 85–7.
[7] R. Taveneaux, *Le Jansénisme en Lorraine, 1640–1789* (Paris, 1960), p. 123.
[8] Viguerie, *Une Œuvre d'éducation*, pp. 422–3.
[9] Chaunu, 'Jansénisme et frontière de catholicité', 135–7.

that the reconquest of the Protestant north could only take place 'au prix d'une marche convergente dans le sens d'un radicalisme chrétien'. In other words Chaunu holds that the similarities between Jansenism and Calvinism did not diminish the desire for reconquest but enhanced it since the nearer Calvinism was theologically to Jansenism, the more the representatives of the latter considered as unacceptable a hasty and badly led reform.[10] Consequently the sort of Jansenism found on the frontiers of Catholicity was a purer form of Augustinianism than elsewhere in France since its appeal to the other side was based precisely on its purity. A further implication of Chaunu's argument is that the reconversion of Protestants was hardly likely to be achieved through Molinism. The Catholic Church had therefore to provide a space in which Protestants could feel theologically at home.

This aspect of the question is enlarged upon by Kolakowski who enumerates precisely those elements of Jansenist spirituality which might appeal to Protestants: the importance for religious life of the Fall and the emphasis on the corruption of humanity with its corollary of the strong opposition of grace and nature; a mistrust of natural processes leading to salvation and the critique of sacramental and ritual automatism; the rigorism directed to Christian behaviour and a heightened consciousness of the risks involved in any concession to nature and the world.[11] One might add that it is Pascal who points out in *Pensée* 900 that Jansenists resemble Calvinists in the desire for the 'réformation des moeurs'. What is interesting in the thesis of Kolakowski, and what relates it in some way to that of Chaunu, is that a better understanding and promotion of one's own space depends on crossing a frontier and 'inhabiting' the other side with all the risks of assimilation involved. The implication of the arguments advanced by Chaunu and Kolakowski is that the Counter-Reformation could only be really effective where there was a competition for space, but a competition which started from an element of common ground.

Not all saw the influence of the moral austerity of Jansenism in the overall space of Catholicism in France as positive. Olier, the founder of the seminary of Saint-Sulpice, writes of the Jansenists as turning people away from the Church, while the preacher Massillon's complaint against the Jansenists was that, by encouraging women and the laity to discuss and dispute delicate matters of faith, they helped to spread irreligion, since for the laity little distance separated disputation and doubt, or doubt and unbelief.[12] Even priests of Jansenist persuasion saw the dangers of

[10] Ibid., 137–8.
[11] Kolakowski, *Chrétiens sans église*, p. 356.
[12] Adam, *Du Mysticisme*, p. 182, and Briggs, *Communities of Belief*, p. 363.

imposing too harsh a penitential practice on their parishioners.[13] Chaunu claims that in the 'interior', as opposed to those areas on the frontiers of Catholicity, Jansenism was destructive of faith and Christian practice, particularly in the Paris basin where Jeanne Ferté herself notes a certain resistance to the Catholic Reform, especially in the low number of priestly vocations.[14] Chaunu is quite categorical: 'Le Jansénisme, là où il s'est implanté durablement, a stérilisé la pratique.'[15]

The hesitations of Jansenist priests leads to a consideration of the degree to which, given the austerity of Jansenist moral teaching, a proper religious and spiritual life can be led in the space of the world. Pascal (in *Pensée* 693) spoke for many Jansenists who held that the temptations of the world were too great for the successful pursuit of a spiritual life:

Les conditions les plus aisées à vivre selon le monde sont les plus difficiles à vivre selon Dieu; et au contraire: rien n'est si difficile selon le monde que la vie religieuse; rien n'est plus facile que de la passer selon Dieu. Rien n'est plus aisé que d'être dans une grande charge et dans de grands biens selon le monde; rien n'est plus difficile que d'y vivre selon Dieu, et sans y prendre part et de goût.

Pascal pursued this theme in a manuscript entitled 'Comparaison des chrétiens des premiers temps avec ceux d'aujourd'hui', where in a manner typical of Port-Royal he compares the conduct of contemporary Christians with that of the primitive Church. In the latter the practice was to enter the Church having first left the world, whereas now one enters the Church at the same time as remaining in the world. The world and the Church were considered as two opposing entities and two irreconcilable enemies. Birth into the Church in fact constituted then a second birth which substituted for the first. In our time, birth into the world is confused with birth into the Church with the consequence that: 'On fréquente les sacrements et on jouit des plaisirs du monde.' The two worlds are no longer distinguishable.

The overall result of the degeneration of behaviour since the time of the primitive Church was that the Church of the Saints now found itself sullied by the presence of the wicked. Their children, nurtured from birth in the world, bring into its very heart, even while participating in its sacred mysteries, the cruellest of the Church's enemies, that is to say the spirit of that world with all its impurities. Hence the importance of baptism and the declaration of godparents, especially in its reference to the renunciation of the world and Satan. Children must above all be protected against the 'contagion du monde' and Christians must submit to a form of

[13] Briggs, *Communities of Belief*, p. 333.
[14] Chaunu, 'Jansénisme et frontière de catholicité', 134, and Ferté, *La Vie religieuse*, p. 313.
[15] Chaunu, 'Jansénisme et frontière de catholicité', 122.

penitence which involves an austere mortification. The seventeenth-century Christian must return to the mores of the early Church.[16] The Christian was under siege in the space of the world. Indeed the strong feeling of disjunction between the spaces of the world and religion, in part derived from Augustine, which one finds in the *Pensées*, leads almost to the conclusion that they never can be one.

This is not to say that the Jansenist movement championed the monastic way of life. It has been argued that the Jansenists, in their conception of the religious life in relation to the space of the world, reduced the distance that the Counter-Reformation as a whole desired to establish between the priesthood and the laity. Many of the *solitaires* were not themselves ordained and in any case harboured considerable suspicion of life in orders. One of the implicit conclusions of the radical Jansenist view on the corruption of nature was that the monastic life bore the mark of nature because vows were of human origin. Consequently, monastic life did not carry with it any idea of 'extra' holiness in the sense that no holiness can derive from a human source.[17] The decision to live apart provided the context in which it might be possible to lead a more properly religious life, but that separation was not in itself sanctified.

The relation of Jansenism to the world outside its own space was not always easy. Certainly, la Mère Angélique re-established enclosure in 1609 and broke immediate links with the world, marking this change on the celebrated *jour du guichet* when her father was refused admission to the interior of the convent and was received instead in the visiting room. However, after the move from Port-Royal-des-Champs in 1625, the Paris convent became a considerable worldly success, offering a magnificence of spectacle which attracted 'les gens de qualité' to its precincts and chapels. The first spiritual director of Port-Royal, Sébastien Zamet, bishop of Langres, with his love of intellectual refinement and ceremony, wanted an ordered Church but one whose prestige would impose respect on Protestants as well as *libertins*. He also aspired to creating a Church which maintained intimate links with the monarchy and the aristocracy. Accordingly Zamet encouraged a socially determined recruitment of novices with substantial dowries in order to bring a certain elegance to a place where he considered it natural to find 'le beau monde'.[18]

For Wendy Gibson the presence of a number of prominent aristocratic figures gave the Jansenist movement 'the appearance of a select club, membership of which distinguished the fashionable penitent from the flock'.[19] Despite the social grounding of Jansenism as predominantly in

[16] See B. Pascal (ed. L. Lafuma), *Œuvres complètes* (Paris, 1963), pp. 360–2.
[17] Kolakowski, *Chrétiens sans église*, p. 357.   [18] Adam, *Du Mysticisme*, pp. 110–11.
[19] Gibson, *Women in Seventeenth-Century France*, p. 229.

the *robe*, there is much evidence for this view. Jansenism always attracted significant elements of the traditional aristocracy. Madame de Sévigné's adherence dates from the early 1670s and Madame de la Sablière was a convert to its cause. Madame de Sablé had an apartment in the Paris convent and the marquise d'Aumont lodged there in her capacity as a benefactress. Other supporters included the comtesse de Maure, Madame du Plessis-Guénégaud, Madame de Guéméné, not to mention the duc de Luynes (the translator of Descartes's *Meditationes*) and the marquis de Liancourt who was a supporter of the *solitaires*.[20] Adam adduces as one element of the persecution of Port-Royal precisely its entrenchment in the upper elements of society,[21] and Louis especially disapproved of the gatherings of Jansenists in the Hôtel de Longueville.[22] The comtesse de Gramont found herself excluded from the select group invited to the king's hunting lodge at Marly after she had gone on a spiritual retreat to Port-Royal-des-Champs.[23] Indeed the anxiety of the king and those around him derived from the fact that the space of Jansenism should have spread beyond the limits of Port-Royal into the space of the Court itself. This fear might have been compounded by the favourable description of Port-Royal-des-Champs in Mademoiselle de Scudéry's novel, *Clélie*, where the *solitaires'* existence is promoted as leading to a form of wisdom not alien to the world but which is only possible in the life they have created for themselves away from it.[24]

Port-Royal is certainly associated with the notion of withdrawal, although the precise nature of that withdrawal is open to question. Arnauld can hardly be seen as a shrinking violet when it came to the defence of the cause, participating, much to the chagrin of others in the group, in some of the major philosophical debates of his time. Equally, the Jansenists, who started from the position of wisdom as essential to science, did not abandon science: they had a programme based simply on a different approach to the subject from their Jesuit counterparts.[25] All this was proof of an engagement with the world at least to some degree. On the other hand, the movement, especially in the material production of many of its pamphlets, was forced into a form of clandestinity, thus symbolising its uneasy and ambiguous relation to the world.

Interestingly Jansenism was conceived in a sort of solitude since, shortly after the death of Henri IV, Saint-Cyran (1581–1643) and Jansenius

[20] Adam, *Du Mysticisme*, p. 177.
[21] Ibid., p. 222.
[22] Ibid., pp. 276–7.
[23] Gibson, *Women in Seventeenth-Century France*, p. 230.
[24] See A. McKenna, 'Madeleine de Scudéry et Port-Royal', in A. Niderst (ed.), *Les Trois Scudéry: actes du colloque du Havre (1–5 octobre 1991)* (Paris, 1993), 633–43.
[25] Remsberg, *Wisdom and Science*, p. 74.

(1585–1638) spent some years working and meditating together in the south-west of France. An alternative and habitable space was already in the making. Indeed, the Augustinian emphasis in philosophy on intro-spection seemed too to determine the nature of the movement, even in a way with Descartes, who cannot be regarded as a Jansenist. Introspection was precisely the means for the penitent to come to a consciousness of his own corruption and to recognise the presence of grace.[26] Clearly, the best conditions for such introspection were to be found in solitude, the virtues of which were, for Saint-Cyran, the condition of a true love of the Church in the avoidance of coming into contact with the passions of those who dishonoured its sanctity.[27]

Sedgwick however would seek to nuance the meaning of solitude for Saint-Cyran as described by Adam. Solitude meant not necessarily a refusal to participate in the world but a refusal to be governed by its standards. This would of course explain the stand made by Saint-Cyran along with others in the *parti dévot* against the alliance of France with Protestant powers in the war with Spain. The Christian determined first that his vocation came from God after which he was obliged to fulfil the responsibilities attaching to his social function. These responsibilities were based on charity and not self-interest: 'the proper performance of one's duties was a means by which the Christian was able to learn whether his actions were indeed a manifestation of God's grace working within him'. This is not without its own dangerous implications. Introspection precedes the acceptance of one's responsibilities to the extent that a tension might be created between those responsibilities and the spiritual needs of the individual. In a hostile society 'the dedicated Christian might well be forced to choose between active resistance to worldly ethics or complete withdrawal into the self'.[28] Seventeenth-century French society did not turn out to be terribly congenial to this definition of 'participation' and, as Sedgwick notes, Richelieu's view was that continuous solitude and contemplation were an obstacle to activity for the public good.[29]

The inclination to place the spiritual needs of the individual above the needs of society came to constitute a significant alienating factor in Jansenism, and had significant political consequences. In the context of obedience to the Church, emphasis on the responsibility of the individual Christian to make a decision on his worthiness presented problems in that Jansenist ethical principles could lead to a conflict 'between an individual entirely committed to God's purpose and ecclesiastical authority tainted by earthly considerations'.[30] In addition this need for private and perhaps prolonged meditation seemed ill-suited to the continuity of public life as

[26] Sedgwick, *Jansenism*, p. 34.   [27] Adam, *Du Mysticisme*, p. 122.
[28] Sedgwick, *Jansenism*, pp. 37–8.   [29] Ibid., p. 39.   [30] Ibid., p. 82.

conceived in our period. Certainly, throughout the century, no private space could be accommodated within the political space. It would have been a space beyond the control of authority and as such inherently suspicious.

Marc Fumaroli advances an argument on the choice of solitude by the figures associated with Port-Royal centred on the development of eloquence and its values in the first half of the seventeenth century. The dilemma of the Arnauld family in particular was identical to that of the *parlementaires*. The influence of their civic tradition, itself founded on eloquence, had been severely weakened by royal absolutism which itself became the focus of all eloquence. This secular appropriation of values previously associated with a religious tradition thus imposed a choice: to embrace the 'world' under the auspices of Richelieu and as a consequence the emerging literary public, thus effecting the betrayal of their own values, or to 'transfigurer l'éloquence des "grandes âmes" en éloquence de l'exil et de la fidélité chrétienne, et c'est alors la retraite, retraite éloquente toutefois'. They chose the latter, thereby creating a foyer of resistance and private witness, away from the temptations of the Court, where the flame of gallican erudition and faith could be kept alive.[31]

All this crystallised around the recruitment of Le Maître as a *solitaire*. His departure from public life was considered to be truly a scandal and, in the eyes of some, nothing less than pure seduction. Port-Royal thus became perceived by others as a space in opposition to the world which could attract those who in fact had most to give it. What would happen if a significant proportion of the élite followed suit? Le Maître's was truly a choice of nonconformism, a choice to live in the margins of a society which others more properly motivated were trying to organise around absolutist royal power. This sort of misguided heroism implied a rejection of those 'vertus moyennes' without which life in the state could not function. Some wondered whether society and the state had any meaning if Christian life consisted of refusal and withdrawal.[32]

For Fumaroli, the withdrawal from public life of Le Maître in 1637 and the entry of Patru into the Académie française in 1640 represent the two directions chosen by those who claimed to be the repositories of the values associated with the gallican rhetorical tradition. Saint-Cyran exhorted the last of the real faithful to make of the French language 'le dépositaire de la foi authentique des premiers siècles de l'Eglise', whereas Richelieu invited all 'bons Français' to serve the state and to help adorn a Court which would be the proper heir in Europe to the grandeur that was Rome.[33] These two spaces, so irreconcilable in their differences, simply could not

---

[31] Fumaroli, *L'Age de l'éloquence*, pp. 625–7.
[32] Delumeau, *Le Catholicisme*, pp. 176–7.   [33] Fumaroli, *L'Age de l'éloquence*, p. 647.

co-exist. One had to occupy the other. Jansenism did not have force on its side. So it eventually chose isolation.

This isolation, necessary for adequate and effective meditation on one's moral condition, was constitutive of the nature of penitence in Jansenist spirituality with its demand of withdrawal from the sacraments until a renewed state of worthiness could be achieved. The perception that the ability to cope with such a harsh personal régime was accessible only to a few, further marked out the boundaries of Jansenism as a separate space, considered as élitist within the Church: a few arrogated to themselves a moral and spiritual superiority over others, thus giving the impression that only they were the chosen few mentioned in Matthew 22:14. This position could even be hostile to the moral authority of the Church as an institution. The importance of a profound sense of individual responsibility in penitential obligation seemed to limit the redemptive powers of the Church which encouraged the sinner to take advantage of its healing power by frequently taking the sacraments.[34]

The Jansenist space was further defined by the preference for contrition over attrition, another factor which brought the group into conflict with Richelieu who had himself written a work on attrition. Attrition demanded less of the sinner and certainly not the sort of meditative process involved in contrition. In the case of the latter, the role of the priest was more limited because, in the eyes of Saint-Cyran and others, a sinner's inability to overcome self-interest and mend his ways could not be dealt with simply by the power of absolution. The demand for contrition contributed therefore to the perception of Jansenism as a separate, almost 'purer' space, especially in the promotion of the primitive Church as a model of Christian behaviour for the modern world within the Church as a whole.

It has to be said, however, that the frontier within Catholicism between Jansenism and other sections of the Church was up to a point fairly mobile. During the contrition versus attrition controversy, at its height in the first half of the seventeenth century, no evidence was ever forthcoming that the rigorist position was in any way doctrinally heretical and could of itself place the Jansenists outside the space of orthodoxy. On the other hand, as a practice it was sufficiently visible to isolate individuals and to act as a distinguishing mark in their relationship with the main body of the Church. It contributed to a concept of difference, and a willing and willed difference at that. A difference, moreover, which in many ways, at least in the first half of the century, ran counter to a more universalist view of orthodoxy in the Church, especially in terms of the sorts of behaviour

[34] Sedgwick, *Jansenism*, p. 82.

bishops and episcopal visitors were trying to impose on parishes through-out the kingdom. In these circumstances doctrinal subtleties became something of an obstacle and Jansenism therefore appeared as a predomi-nantly 'intellectualist' movement without a true universalist vocation, especially in view of the burden imposed on the individual by its penitential theology, and despite efforts to bring the meaning of the liturgy closer to the laity.

The differences between Jansenists and the rest of the Church on moral teaching, and its consequences for confession and absolution, are less clear-cut later in the century once the Assembly of the Clergy of France had prescribed Borromeo's *Instructions to Confessors* in 1657 and adopted a more rigorist attitude. Briggs has convincingly shown how in reality the new rigorism in the gallican Church produced a tension between educated clerics from the urban bourgeoisie, who reflected the concerns of the élite, and those who had to implement this harsher moral teaching in a wide diversity of circumstances. Briggs believes that the Church as a whole 'overreached their strength, by producing an impossibly demanding manifesto', a manifesto which 'was completely at odds with the social and mental universe of all but a small segment of the population'. Moreover, the policy was undermined by a clergy 'many of whom found it more attractive or simply easier to concentrate on the innumerable external aspects of the faith'.[35] In this perspective the wider Church, in its official positions, joined with the Jansenists in reducing severely the universalist function of religion and belief. Along with Jansenism the Church as a whole, in its own terms, narrowed the confines of its own space, or made that space less accessible or less habitable.

It was the implications of Jansenist rigorism for its relation to the state that put the survival of the space so much at risk. The view of Port-Royal as a politically critical and therefore hostile movement occurred early in its history with the circulation in France in 1637 of a pamphlet entitled *Mars gallicus* and written by Jansenius, known to be a friend of Saint-Cyran, which opposed Richelieu's alliance with Protestants against Catholic Spain. The position of Saint-Cyran, who had included injudicious political references in his *Vie d'Abraham*, was not improved by his acceptance of a see on the Day of Dupes. Saint-Cyran was eventually arrested and confined in the château of Vincennes. Political difficulties continued to dog Jansenism at the time of the Fronde although accusa-tions of opposing royal authority seem to have been unjust. Again, certain appearances were against them in the shape of the rebellion of the duc de Luynes, a Jansenist sympathiser, under the influence of his mother, the

[35] Briggs, *Communities of Belief*, p. 336.

duchesse de Chevreuse. At the same time, friends of Retz were themselves Augustinians.[36] The grounds were laid for Jansenism as a space of opposition.

The attitude of Jansenists to political authority was in itself not entirely straightforward. Although Augustinian theology promoted obedience to civil power on the grounds that a world corrupted by sin must none the less be ordered, Jansenist support for civil power did not turn out to be unconditional. Augustinians were bound to think of themselves as 'philosophes chrétiens' who could not remain indifferent to a régime whose principles were overwhelmingly of this world: 'il est évident que Port-Royal . . . juge sévèrement le régime de la France monarchique et lui refuse, non pas certes sa soumission, mais du moins son adhésion'.[37] This was not enough for a government which was seeking to homogenise space through the imposition of a single political orthodoxy. Jansenist ideas on the relation of religion to politics stem from their more general view of wisdom. Augustinians argued that knowledge on how to govern is divinely inspired and has God as its direct source. The wisdom of faith precedes that of the world with the result that 'the king should give greater recognition to the hand of God in the affairs of the state'.[38] It is only on the achievement of faith which becomes the guiding light of our actions that 'science', in whatever form, can find its proper place. Just as science into wisdom placed a disproportionate emphasis on the achievements of the human mind, the promotion of the 'expert' in politics, as reflected in the Jesuit position which emphasised action according to principles that derived from experience of politics in the world, started from the wrong end and could lead to all sorts of error.

Sedgwick argues that in any case the Jansenist mentality would have been quite at home in the context of the Fronde, given *dévot* opposition to the government's war policy, to Mazarin's personal power and given their support for the rights and struggles of the priests in the parishes. In addition: 'this Frondeur mentality contained a philosophical attitude that firmly maintained the rights of the individual against any authority which might suppress them',[39] although we should certainly be careful in interpreting the Jansenist position in terms of a universal theory of human rights. In practice a link between the Frondeurs and *dévot* principles, which opposed putting the aggrandisement of the state above the welfare of the king's subjects, could be established from the letters of la Mère Angélique concerning the condition of the poor and of the countryside during the hostilities.[40] Her remarks echoed Jansenist opposition to the

[36] Adam, *Du Mysticisme*, p. 190.   [37] Ibid., pp. 191–2.
[38] Remsberg, *Wisdom and Science*, pp. 81–2.   [39] Sedgwick, *Jansenism*, p. 106.
[40] Ibid., p. 64.

cult of luxury which Richelieu and others regarded as the mark of a great king. Marandé's pamphlet of 1654, entitled *Inconveniens d'estat procedans du Jansénisme*, attacked Jansenist views on the economy and affirmed the principle that 'the opulence and splendor of the great families assures the prince against popular turmoil and disorder'.[41]

In any case the theology of the Jansenists tended to distance itself from the idea of monarchy as divinely instituted. At the very least the more pessimistic perspective of radical Augustinianism on original sin could hardly except one individual among others. Jansenist attitudes towards the legitimacy of power and authority in society derived much more from acceptance of the political system of France than belief in its status as providential. The *Trois discours sur la condition des grands*, usually attributed to Pascal, deconstruct this theme of the legitimacy of power.

The position of the nobleman in the social hierarchy has nothing in itself which makes it superior and is, in its origins, a matter of chance. The inheritance of position, however, has been transformed into human institutions by law-makers whose reasons for doing so, while sound, convey no natural right. Possession of a title is not a 'titre de nature' but an 'établissement humain'. Pascal extends his argument to kings. He presents us with the image of a man who is mistaken for a lost king and who decides to keep his real identity quiet. Implicitly the 'chance' of being king is identical to the chance involved in possessing the riches of a nobleman. But it would clearly be an act of folly for this king to forget his natural condition and to believe that his position was a natural right.

Pascal is led to make a distinction between what he calls 'grandeurs d'établissement' and 'grandeurs naturelles' which in their turn command different forms of respect, and recall Pascal's division of different types of knowledge and what can properly be ascribed to each. 'Grandeurs d'établissement' reflect the arbitrary origins of the nobleman's position in that they have no intrinsic legitimacy but, once established, acquire force of law. 'Grandeurs naturelles' on the other hand comprise real and effective qualities of mind and body, including knowledge, intelligence and virtue, which have intrinsic worth. Each set of 'grandeurs' is due different sorts of respect according to their worth. It is necessary to pay homage to a duke by virtue of his social position but recognition of esteem is not obligatory if it is not earned by the possession of 'real' qualities. Were he to oblige me to show esteem without reason he would be acting unjustly. It is important therefore to avoid category mistakes. Even if a king or a nobleman can achieve the respect due to 'grandeurs naturelles', that respect is not a given and can presumably be forfeited. What Pascal

41 Ibid., p. 72.

seems to allow for here is an inner space where we recognise the arbitrary origins of power while in the world we must respect it as lawful.[42]

Pascal extends the domain of this inner space in his consideration of law in the *Pensées*. We can have little respect for human laws once we discover how they have come about. But the most dangerous thing in the world would be to think that we are able to change them for the better by means of revolution. We would soon find that we would not gain in the exchange since they would still be human laws, produced by a corrupt humanity. On the other hand we must obey them as 'good' laws and persuade the people, or even fool them into thinking, that they are good. Pascal again argues for an inner space where we maintain an awareness of a divine order superior to the order to which we give our outward respect. Since the social order has no intrinsic merit, we would be wrong to invest in it a value which it does not possess. The social order is an 'exterior' phenomenon whereas the essential religious order is an inner space, a 'knowing' space, what he refers to as a 'pensée de derrière'. One has to conclude from Pascal's analysis that, in the end result, adherence to the political order has no grounding in essential principles, only in practical ones. This surely allows for a space of dissent although no-one is more fearful of social disorder than Pascal whose memory of the Fronde is clearly determinant.

Obedience to royal and ecclesiastical authority became a reality in the matter of the formulary. Here Arnauld attempted to draw a distinction between temporal and ecclesiastical power: the former was based on utility and might from time to time sacrifice the interests of the few for the public good as a whole, whereas the power of the Church was grounded in the interests of the Christian community as a whole. Arnauld believed that the Church was confusing its own power with that of the temporal domain, another category mistake, by expecting bishops to enforce a course of action which did not accord with the laws of God or nature. Hence the Church, in seeking to impose the formulary on those who had some qualms about signing it, was guilty of the heresy of domination.[43] The implication of Arnauld's argument is that if the Church had not acted beyond its powers in the affair of the *Augustinus* there would have been no need for any intervention by the temporal power. In practice the distinction was impossible to maintain. Resistance to ecclesiastical authority became political opposition once the personal authority of the king was called upon. The two powers combined. The Jansenists could not inhabit the space of one but not the other. Or they set themselves up in a space outside that of ecclesiastical and royal authority, in other words a hostile space.

[42] See Pascal, *Œuvres*, pp. 366–8.   [43] Sedgwick, *Jansenism*, p. 132.

But it would be wrong to think of the space of the Jansenists as homogeneous even if they were united in opposition to the content of the formulary. No single tactic could be agreed upon. For example, la Mère Angélique would have preferred silence to the *Provinciales*, and Martin de Barcos favoured signing the formulary and keeping clear of intrigues and discussions.[44] Barcos defended his position with the explanation that: 'All this suffices to say that obedience and submission do not signify interior consent and acquiescence.'[45] The party of silence strongly disapproved of Arnauld's attitude, although Arnauld himself abstained for four years from publishing anything against the bull entitled *Cum ad sacram Petri sedem*. Arnauld and Nicole, who proposed signing with reservations – there were two views even then on the precise nature of how these should be expressed – did not share this detachment, believing in the importance of clearly stating their position.

Which of these two camps entered the space of the enemy? Was it la Mère Angélique and Barcos, or were they protecting their inner space, while recognising an 'external' and legitimate order (with also perhaps the fear of schism, that is of rending the space of the Church to which they none the less belonged)? Or was signature the violation of that very inner space? Or again was even participation in discussion accommodating the space of the enemy within one's own inviolable space? Argument was a sort of engagement with the world. Eventually the space of Jansenism split into two: those nuns who signed unconditionally occupied the convent at Port-Royal in Paris. Port-Royal-des-Champs became the unconditional space of opposition.

For this of course the Jansenists paid heavily. Their immediate space had already been violated on a number of occasions. In 1664 Péréfixe, the archbishop of Paris, entered the Paris convent which was surrounded by armed men, and instituted a reign of terror. Those who refused to sign were eventually removed from the convent and placed elsewhere. The *petites écoles* suffered a similar fate. The groups at Le Chenais and Les Granges were broken up – de Beaupuis still held out with seven pupils in the former – although smaller groups were formed in the house of the marquis de Guivry at Perchai and others were placed under the protection of Monsieur de Buzenval, bishop of Beauvais. By March 1660 the dispersal was complete. The girls' schools were revived in 1669 but closed again in 1679.[46] The fragmentation of Jansenist space was followed, significantly, by the wholesale destruction of the buildings of Port-Royal-des-Champs in 1710. It was only on the intervention of Pomponne that the remains of prominent figures including those of the Arnauld family,

[44] Adam, *Du Mysticisme*, p. 239.   [45] Quoted in Sedgwick, *Jansenism*, p. 116.
[46] See Barnard, *The Little Schools*, pp. 39–49.

the duchesse de Longueville and the princesse de Conti were transferred to other places. Those of the nuns, of some *solitaires* and friends of Port-Royal, were thrown into a common grave.

Jansenism occupies a somewhat paradoxical position within the space of the French Church during the seventeenth century. It was unquestionably rooted in the Catholic Reform and in the Counter-Reformation proper, especially in its emphasis on sacramental practice. Even in the course of the long doctrinal quarrels where certain groups like the Jesuits had a clear interest in promoting the 'difference' of the Jansenists, no substantial evidence was produced to suggest that Jansenist views stood outside the space of orthodoxy. Indeed, from 1657 the gallican Church as a whole appropriated many aspects of the movement's moral teaching.

The Jansenists themselves however set up their own frontiers, especially in the aggressive attitude many of them adopted towards other sections of the Church. They displayed a sense of moral and spiritual superiority in the belief that their own form of sacramental practice was correct above all others, and they saw themselves as guardians of the space of orthodoxy in their positions on Tradition. In regarding attacks on themselves as attacks on the authority of Augustine and therefore on the authority of the Church, they pushed the Church to the limits of its ability to remain a unified body. Ecclesiastical authority in a formal sense lay elsewhere, but spiritual authority was theirs. Moreover they were highly visible, especially in their establishment of centres in Paris and its environs which acted as a focus for French society of the time, either in terms of support or hostility.

It is unquestionably their attitude to authority which counted most against them, for their argument with ecclesiastical authority became an argument with royal authority. The political sins of the second half of the century simply compounded the sins of the first in the eyes of the king and his ministers. Royal power could not create its own visibility and at the same time accommodate another which belonged to a space of opposition. In this sense the treatment of the Jansenists was the religious equivalent of that meted out to Fouquet (although Vaux-le-Vicomte was, interestingly, never destroyed). Jansenism in fact, in its uncompromisingly high profile, turned out to be a sort of Catholic Quakerism. In a hostile environment, witness was more important than survival.

Protestantism

The scandal for many Catholics, and certainly for the Catholic hierarchy in seventeenth-century France, was that there existed a space for Protestantism at all. And that space was also a highly visible one where the nature of the community and to some extent the behaviour of the occupants were significantly different from the space of Catholicism. Ironically, a form of religion which promoted the concept of the invisible church was all too visible. One of the most obvious aspects of that difference was the temple itself, a prominent challenge to the existence of the church. While they were certainly subjects of the same king, Protestants manifested their desire to worship in a different place and in a different way. The Edict of Nantes, not the first act of toleration in France but certainly the most important, officially established another religion in the kingdom on what looked like a permanent basis. The Catholic Church could never admit to the legitimacy of the Protestant religion which was known as the 'Religion Prétendue Réformée'.

The spread of Protestant communities, which were 60 per cent rural, was not uniform across France. The majority of Protestants were largely concentrated in Languedoc, almost a quarter in fact of the somewhat controversial total of 850,000. The six northern provinces numbered some 150,000. While the north contained fewer Huguenot communities, that centred on Dieppe numbered some 10,000. In the south the space of Protestantism was more pronounced: cities like Nîmes, Uzès and Montauban contained a majority of Huguenots while in addition some cities, the most celebrated being La Rochelle, had, until the Paix d'Alès, their own fortifications. This led to the complaint in some quarters that Protestantism constituted a 'state within a state'.

Space was certainly an issue for Protestants in a real sense because under the provisions of the Edict of Nantes, Protestant worship was permitted in some places on the basis of certain strict rules and in others prohibited completely. Protestant worship was forbidden in Beauvais, Toulouse, Alet, Dijon, Lyon and Agen. In these circumstances Huguenots had to travel to the nearest temple. This was the case with the most prominent city in which Protestant worship was banned, Paris, whose Huguenot citizens were forced to travel out to Charenton where the river crossing was not without its dangers (Casaubon, the Greek scholar, drowned while going to the temple). Worship was permitted in 'lieux d'exercice' where the establishment of a temple had to be prior to the base-line year fixed as 1596–7, or in 'églises de fief', that is to say temples on the land of 'seigneurs haut-justiciers', or of lesser noblemen if the congregation was not more than thirty. In the case of the property being sold to a Catholic (or obviously conversion to Catholicism), that right ceased automatically.

The importance of Protestantism as a space of particularism, and by definition of hostility, is that it involved a culture of choice.[47] Reaching

47 Lebrun (ed.), *Histoire de la France religieuse*, II, 468.

adulthood and remaining a Protestant in the face of the rewards for conversion, especially for the nobility, constituted an act of deliberate self-exclusion. From a position within the Catholic space, that exclusion was not considered as absolute and might even be regarded as self-deluding. The Protestant's baptism as a Protestant marked him or her as belonging to the Christian community, hence the special duty of the Catholic Church in bringing that person back. That a Protestant should himself abandon a confession he had previously professed or that this confession should have excommunicated him meant that the heretic was a rebel who had flouted the authority of the Church. It is then legitimate that the mother Church should use sanctions and call on the secular authorities to use force against him 'pour ramener dans son giron celui qui ne peut pas plus cesser de lui appartenir que les liens du sang ne peuvent être abolis: membre gangrené de l'Eglise, l'hérétique reste cependant un membre de l'Eglise'.[48] Despite the Edict of Nantes, therefore, the status of Protestant space was only ever temporary.

Adherence to Protestantism can be distinguished in another way. Elisabeth Labrousse argues that Pierre Bayle (1647–1706), as a result of his journey of conversion to Catholicism and reconversion to Protestant-ism, regarded a degree of subjectivism and individualism as self-evident in his own feeling of religious belonging. Some of his texts seem to imply an equivalence between religious affiliation and the express personal adher-ence to a set of beliefs, whereas in Catholicism the second is the most developed, if not an exceptional, form of the first. For Bayle it is not the simple fact of belonging to a Church through baptism which accords that Church any rights over the individual, but the latter's acquiescence at the level of personal conscience, and that is subjective in nature.[49] The Protestant space is thus a constructed one but not constructed once and for all time. Each individual adherence constructs it again. The space of the Church is not a given as in the case of Catholicism. In the course of the century the continual reconstruction or renewal of construction was reinforced by reaction to the existence of a hostile environment where the immediacy of different types of choice was apparent and pressing. Hostility helped maintain the space in its active existence.

Earlier remarks on the temporary nature of Protestant space and on the consideration of Protestants as albeit rebellious members of the Church are reflected in the numerous attempts in the course of the century to bring the two Churches together. There were always those on both sides who considered the distance between them eminently bridgeable. The first flirtation with a rapprochement between the two confessions took

[48] E. Labrousse, *Pierre Bayle*, 2 vols. (The Hague, 1963–4), II, 532–3.
[49] Ibid., pp. 535–6.

place under Richelieu whose idea of a gallican Church with the cardinal as its head attracted some Protestants but repelled others. A number of occasions arose subsequently, particularly from 1666, when attempts were made to come to an agreement on what could constitute a common body of doctrine. Arnauld suggested that Protestant and Catholic differences on the Eucharist could be reconciled.[50] The more subtle interpretation of Tradition offered by Arnauld as a sort of 'sentiment' common to all Christians in whatever historical period was in fact elaborated in the light of a possible reconciliation of the two faiths.[51] The space of the Church defined as an inner space but as part of a common framework of tradition could transcend some important differences. Arnauld seemed to promote a sense of 'living within' through a consensus of faith. All these attempts, like the discussions between Bossuet and Ferry, one of the great pastors of the century, came to nought.

Attempts to bring the two Churches together also took place around the translation of the Bible. Richard Simon believed that an interconfessional project could avoid all tendentious translations and exclude partisan notes, thus constituting as exact a reflection of the original as possible.[52] Such a hope can be attributed to Simon's concern for the literal sense of the text as a control on any doctrinal interpretation. In this way, perhaps, common ground could be found between the two faiths. It was the fault of both sides to interpret the text according to their respective prejudices. As Simon wrote himself: 'Il ne s'agit pas de décider en controversiste.'[53] Many in the Church were most alarmed at this development. The Benedictines complained that an agreed text in its translated version would lead to 'l'indifférence des religions'.[54] The dissolution of frontiers implied by such a text would reduce the specific identity of the Catholic faith. Hence a doctrinal reading of the text was paramount. In any case the Protestants failed to see eye to eye with Simon over the Septuagint which they considered to be divinely inspired and without error whereas Simon did not. For the Protestants it was a matter of faith: for Simon it was a question relating to 'critique'.[55]

While certainly separated doctrinally, to what degree did Protestants and Catholics inhabit different social spaces? Elisabeth Labrousse argues forcefully that, if there were differences at all, they were differences of degree. The complaints about moral behaviour emanating from Catholic preachers were replicated in the sermons of Protestant pastors. Huguenots did not refrain from playing cards, from going to the theatre or from

[50] Tavard, *La Tradition*, pp. 102–3.
[51] Ibid., p. 111.
[52] Steinmann, *Richard Simon*, p. 92.
[53] Quoted in Steinmann, *Richard Simon*, p. 95.   [54] Ibid.   [55] Ibid., p. 234.

dancing. Indeed the Huguenots resembled in this sense more their Catholic brethren than their English, Genevan or Scottish co-religionaries. In this context Elisabeth Labrousse quotes the words of Lucien Febvre: 'Les Réformateurs n'avaient pas reproché aux romains de mal vivre mais de mal croire.'[56] A greater degree of moral austerity may very well have marked those communities or individuals associated with Jansenism or other sections of the Catholic Church. Moral rigour was not the monopoly of one sect or another.[57] In time, however, exhortations to their flock by Protestant pastors to adopt a greater moral rigour were based on the need to keep a community together under pressure. In a situation where individuals were subject to persuasion to convert, pastors clearly understood that aping the behaviour of the majority community was the first form of assimilation. The survival of the Huguenot communities depended on a distinctive visible identity, especially as temples were gradually being closed and destroyed.[58]

There is no question however that the Protestant Church could also be closely identified with a social vocation, a vocation marked from its beginnings by closer integration of the community with the organisation of the consistory of the temple and the wider Church, although again differences must not be exaggerated. The system of elders ensured very close contact with members of a particular community and it is certain that care of the poor, for example, was well developed, as the Huguenot exodus to England and the support given to the indigent in the London churches continued to illustrate.[59] But respect for the moral demands of the *Discipline*, the regulatory document of the Protestant Church, seems to have been stronger in those areas where Protestants comprised the majority of the population and where the civil and religious authorities combined to underpin the authority of the consistory. Where Protestants formed a slender minority, discipline was harder to keep.[60] Protestant space was geographically fragile in more than one sense.

A much discussed difference between the two communities centres on the respective degrees of literacy among Catholics and Protestants. It has been assumed almost as a matter of course that personal possession of the Bible and familiarity with its texts (particularly the Psalms often produced in pocket-sized versions) implied a higher level of literate skills among the

[56] E. Labrousse, *'Une Foi, une loi, un roi?'*: *la Révocation de l'Edit de Nantes* (Paris, 1985), p. 81.

[57] See ibid., pp. 77 ff.

[58] See H. Phillips, 'Les Chrétiens et la danse: une controverse publique à La Rochelle en 1639', *Bulletin de la Société d'histoire du protestantisme français* (1977), 362–80.

[59] See R. Gwynn, *Huguenot Heritage: the History and Contribution of the Huguenots in Britain* (London, 1985), especially pp. 107–9.

[60] Labrousse, *'Une Foi, une loi, un roi?'*, p. 80.

Huguenots. Some historians are highly sceptical of this view. Frijhoff calls it 'une mythologie culturelle favorable aux protestants', while Delumeau argues that it is impossible to oppose 'un protestantisme qualifié de lettré et de citadin à un catholicisme réputé ignorant et rural'.[61] Other historians are supportive of a significantly different perspective. Labrousse comments that Protestants were on the whole probably more literate but with variations from community to community, most significantly in the contrast of urban and rural.[62] What is certain is the relation of linguistic competence to a profound biblical culture. In Languedoc even the most humble Protestants had at least a good passive knowledge of French, the language after all of their Bible, liturgy, sermons and consistory records. Knowledge of French among Catholics was, it is advanced, correspondingly less secure.[63]

Such a view finds an echo in the work of Dominique Julia who claims that the Protestants in the Cévennes succeeded in achieving a greater degree of acculturation of the faithful. French was the read and sung language as opposed to the spoken dialect of everyday life. The learning of French would have been reinforced by the *ABC des Chrétiens*, the catechisms of Calvin and Théodore de Bèze, and Clément Marot's translation of the Psalms. Thus the Protestants of the rural areas became 'des bilingues d'un statut particulier puisque chaque idiome a sa fonction spécifique'.[64] A ruling of 1622 actually forbade the use of patois in the academies of Montauban and Die and ordered the use of French from seventh to fourth grade at which point Latin was, from 1660, the recommended language of teaching.[65] Even Protestant French, however, tended to mark out the particularity of Huguenots, since, heavily influenced by their translation of the Bible, it was somewhat archaic and full of Hebraicisms, and became known in the nineteenth century as the 'patois de Canaan'. Huguenots would also have been instantly recognisable by their tendency to quote from the Gospels and their recourse to a significantly different vocabulary in describing their religious milieu. In that sense the space of Protestantism maintained its visible – or audible – particularity.[66] Moreover, the pastor and his congregation shared a common language for every aspect of their spiritual life: they were not

[61] W. Frijhoff, 'L'Etat et l'éducation, XVIe–XVIIe siècles: une perspective globale', in *Culture et idéologie dans la genèse de l'état moderne* (Rome, 1985), 99–116 (p. 103), and Lebrun (ed.), *Histoire des Catholiques en France*, p. 134.

[62] Labrousse, *'Une Foi, une loi, un roi?'*, p. 49.

[63] Lebrun (ed.), *Histoire de la France religieuse*, II, 464.

[64] Julia, 'La Réforme', 364.

[65] P.-D. Bourchenin, *Etude sur les académies protestantes en France aux XVIe et XVIIe siècles* (Paris, 1882), p. 359.

[66] Lebrun (ed.), *Histoire de la France religieuse*, II, 465.

separated by a liturgy in a language accessible only to the privileged few. The space of Protestantism was essentially participatory, again reinforcing its perception as hostile.

A consciousness of cultural difference was evident in the approach that some sections of the Catholic Church felt was necessary in any pastoral contact with the Huguenot community. In the diocese of La Rochelle, the Catholic clergy needed re-education in the matter of speaking to Protestants, but priests versed in the divergences between Protestants and Catholics were thin on the ground. In a pastoral letter of 1686, Bishop Henry de Laval forbade the use of the word 'heresy' in teaching 'Nouveaux Catholiques' and made a particular point of the use of Scripture. For this purpose, Godeau's translations of the New Testament and of the Psalms became absolutely crucial. On the other hand, the bishop made it clear that the Bible was for reading and not for discussion, significant enough in itself. It was important to offer an interpretation of Scripture strictly according to Catholic tradition. Laval also preferred the obviously more subtle teaching of the secular clergy rather than the more aggressive behaviour of the missionary orders in his efforts at conversion, since the latter simply put Protestants off the idea altogether.[67]

What particularised Protestant space most starkly, however, was the relation of the pastor (who might be married) to the congregation. One of the major elements of the Counter-Reformation was precisely the separation of the priest from the faithful, where the vocation of the priest was invested with a quality of the sacred distinct from that of the laity. Protestantism on the other hand was the Church of the priesthood of all believers which dispensed with the necessity of intercession and where the responsibility of the individual, whose sole authority was the Bible, was paramount. The Protestant Church could not dispense entirely with a clergy which was certainly more learned and articulate than many of the faithful. But, while the pastor was in many ways a teacher and a focus in the temple, the status of the Protestant clergy was not one of superiority on the level of the sacred. Pastors and professors of theology were not therefore priests, 'des hommes à part', and Protestant congregations did not hesitate frequently to remind them of it. For this reason the expulsion of pastors at the Revocation of the Edict of Nantes in 1685 did not have as damaging or as immediate an effect on the Protestant Church in France as the ban on Catholic priests, necessarily trained abroad, in England.[68] An inner space of religious conscience was a vital part of the maintenance of Protestant space beyond or even before the existence of Protestantism as an institution.

[67] Perouas, *Le Diocèse de La Rochelle*, pp. 330–3.
[68] Lebrun (ed.), *Histoire de la France religieuse*, II, 461.

Education of the Protestant faithful, an essential component of Protestantism as a separate space, was one of the permanent concerns of the consistories. The need Protestants felt for a separate educational system obviously derived from the preponderance of the religious orders and more generally the Catholic Church in the schooling on offer. Moreover, higher education was closed to Protestants – universities admitted only Catholics – who therefore had to set up their own academies notably at Die, Montauban, Saumur and Sedan. Although religious instruction formed an important element of the curriculum in Catholic and Protestant schools, the orientation of the teaching of the two confessions was significantly different. In Catholic schools the explanation of Christian doctrine took precedence over familiarity with the Scriptures, the interpretation of which took place only on Sundays during the sermon or in a lesson given by a professor of Scripture. Knowledge of the Scriptures was a much more fundamental aspect of teaching in Protestant schools through the reading of the text or the singing of Psalms. Moreover, much of the teaching relating to particular aspects of Protestant worship took place in the temple itself, thus tightly linking the school and the community.[69] The Protestant school prepared pupils for the participatory role they could play in the life of their Church.

Moreover, in the same way that Jesuit schools sought to produce Catholics capable of articulating the faith in a variety of circumstances, Protestant schooling was, in a hostile environment, crucial in reinforcing the traditions of faith in the community and of producing competent pastors. Protestant schooling perhaps demonstrates the degree to which the visible space was important for the invisible Church. One can then understand the consternation of pastors who saw Protestant children attending Catholic schools, particularly those of the Jesuits (in Nîmes for example). The motives of the parents addressed perhaps the quality of the teaching, but their social aspirations, shared with their Catholic neighbours, could not have been far behind. Social assimilation was perceived by the pastors as a prelude to the dissolution of religious particularity, to the disappearance of a distinctly Protestant space.

But the history of Protestant schooling in the seventeenth century is largely the history of its progressive erosion by the civil and religious authorities. The importance of education in the maintenance of Protestant space was recognised by the fierce determination of the Catholic Church's assault on Protestant schools and academies. Education was a means of reconquest of the space. In some instances it was simply the case of a Catholic takeover, as in La Rochelle after the capitulation. Jesuit

[69] R. Chartier (ed.), *L'Education*, p. 161.

participation was particularly notable in Nîmes, Die, Sedan, Orthez, Castres, Montpellier and Montauban. In the first half of the century, the situation remained relatively stable. The process of reconquest through the schools accelerated more rapidly in the second half of our period with the advent of the personal rule of Louis XIV. In any case, the Edict of Nantes had restricted the establishment or continued existence of Protestant schools to the 'lieux d'exercice', themselves based on the restrictive guidelines relating to temples. The only Protestant schools to have a legal existence were those established before 1598, but their right to exist was not necessarily safeguarded. Such schools disappeared at Coulié and Nérac in 1647 and 1648 respectively. Increasingly, as with the temples, written documents became important for survival. While the demand of the Assembly of the Clergy of France in 1665 for the suppression of all Protestant schools was not met, those schools which after this date could not provide duly registered letters patent came under Catholic control. The Edict did not formally allow the establishment of new schools.[70]

The curriculum of Protestant schools, which included religious instruction, reading, writing, arithmetic, and sometimes Latin and philosophy, also came under attack. The authorities adopted an increasingly legalistic form of harassment: nowhere in the Edict of Nantes, they argued, was the teaching of Latin expressly permitted. An *arrêt* of 1670 limited teaching in schools to reading, writing and arithmetic, a limitation already in force in Languedoc from 1663. As early as 1645 the head of a school was prosecuted for employing a teacher of Latin. The attacks on different elements of school activity made no educational sense and were simply directed at the confessional nature of Protestant education. This was clear from the 'Grands Jours de Nîmes' in 1666 when the king was asked if he wished to put an end to Protestant teaching of Latin and philosophy. The danger of the proposition that emerged from the same body in 1667 was that prohibiting the teaching of more than the basic subjects of reading, writing and arithmetic implied prohibiting the singing of the Psalms and any teaching of dogmatics. Moreover, given the nature of the reading manuals employed, this more or less meant the suppression of the schools altogether.[71] Their *raison d'être* in creating a space distinct from Catholicism was removed.

Even the traditional opposition of *maîtres-écrivains* to the teaching of writing in schools took on a religious significance with Protestants. In 1662 the arguments of the masters directed against three Protestants of

[70] A. Th. Van Deursen, *Professions et métiers interdits: un aspect de l'histoire de la Révocation de l'Edit de Nantes* (Groningen, 1960), p. 40.
[71] Ibid., pp. 40–2.

Rouen were that the models through which writing could be taught contained dangerous materials, including what were considered blasphemous statements against the pope and the Church, or at the very least the basic principles of the Protestant faith. Even the teaching of horse-riding was forbidden to a Protestant in 1665 on the grounds of faith. Restrictions were imposed on the permitted number of Protestant schools and teachers, an *arrêt du conseil* of 1671 authorising only one master per school and one school in each 'lieu d'exercice'. This ruling was slow to take effect but it affected Aunis in 1678 and Saintonge in 1679.[72] Residence of pupils was addressed in 1669 when pastors could house only two *pensionnaires*,[73] a ruling which clearly disadvantaged those who did not live near a temple. This fragmentation of the space of Protestantism was compounded by the prohibition of contact between local synods.

Effectively, what Protestants witnessed in the years leading up to the Revocation was the constant invasion of a space which was essential to the survival of the faith in real terms. Nor could families hope to supply all the teaching necessary for a full understanding of that faith. From 1681 Catholic teachers were appointed to schools even where Protestants were in a majority. However, Protestants were not slow in attempts to protect their own space. This became particularly crucial when in the same year the declaration of 17 June accorded to children of seven years the right to enter freely into the Catholic religion even against the will of their parents. The Huguenots of La Charité-sur-Loire felt no longer able to leave the education of their children to Catholic teachers, and in Poitou Protestants set up small schools run by dissident teachers after the *dragonnade* of 1681 had seriously depleted the number of their co-religionaries.[74] One interesting case reported by Van Deursen involved teachers in Poitou in 1681 instructing either from the Protestant or the Catholic catechism, which earned the rejoinder of Louvois: 'il arrive que les enfants se confirment dans l'opinion que l'une et l'autre religion sont également bonnes', a clear case of indifferentism, this time in education. Such teaching became impossible after 1685.[75]

What in education was left for the Revocation to do? In the first place, it forbade all Protestant schooling, and it ordered that all children born after 1685 be brought up in the Catholic religion and that they attend Catholic schools. The situation did not turn out entirely to the satisfaction of the government because it was found that converted Protestants, *Nouveaux Catholiques* (NC) as they were called, still taught the principles of the religion they were supposed to have left. Such masters escaped detection either because the bishop who had to approve them discovered too late,

[72] Ibid., pp. 42–4.   [73] Chartier (ed.), *L'Education*, p. 11.
[74] Van Deursen, *Professions et métiers*, p. 49.   [75] Ibid., p. 51.

usually on the occasion of the (sometimes irregular) episcopal visit to the diocese. In these cases, a school might suddenly find itself without a teacher. Or the teachers did not turn up to be inspected.[76] These developments had a number of consequences. The Church was not convinced by the sincerity of conversions, and had to recognise that the fusion of the two Churches had given rise to disorder and uncertainty within the Catholic Church. From the position of having an enemy without, the *Nouveaux Catholiques* constituted an enemy within. In November 1685 Louvois had to issue an order that no NCs could be authorised to teach. More time was needed for them to acquaint themselves sufficiently with Catholicism before they could be entrusted with it in schools. This measure, intended to last two years, was extended to 1692.[77]

Those Protestants who had not managed to send their children abroad – this was forbidden as early as 1681 – were in general reluctant to allow them to enter what was now a uniquely Catholic space, and preferred to keep them in the space of the family where some sense of integrity at least could be preserved. To this end 'écoles buissonnières' and other forms of clandestine teaching were instituted. In 1693 the law punished absentee-ism with fines, and four years later in Languedoc Bâville, the *intendant*, imposed the billeting of troops as a punishment. How generally effective the sanctions were is open to doubt because a register of absentees was not kept. Some Protestant communities kept the stipend of the Catholic master so low that he left. In 1698 new measures had to be called for.[78]

The decree of December 1698, which stipulated compulsory schooling for Huguenot children, had important and interesting repercussions on schooling for Catholics. For a moment it seemed as though at last the state had taken a direct interest in education and, as such, it was praised by Catholic historians of the eighteenth century. We must not however be misled. The prime aim of the declaration was to wrest Protestant children from the influence of their parents. It not only referred to schooling but also to compulsory catechisation in the Catholic faith and to the obligation of daily attendance at mass for those still at school. An interesting dilemma arose which highlighted conflicting interests in the space of Catholicism. Should this exceptional measure apply to Protestants only or should it be extended to all children regardless of confessional allegiance? The clergy were certainly in favour of catechising the maximum number of children, Catholics 'anciens' or 'nouveaux'. The needs of Protestants, as perceived by the civil and religious authorities, intruded on the space of Catholicism. But this universalism ill accorded with earlier governmental

[76] Ibid., p. 50.   [77] Ibid., p. 53.   [78] Ibid., pp. 55–6.

reservations about the extension of schooling and met with the opposition of parents who needed children to work on the land (not, incidentally, a Protestant view). Bézons, the *intendant* of Guyenne, agreed that the period of work should be five months, but parents insisted on nine, and even excused their children from the remaining three on the grounds of bad weather or wolves.[79]

The measure was a failure in both cases since in 1712 the bishop of Gap observed a 'manque d'éducation'. He ordered that masters should be found who would take the children under their charge to Holy Offices on all Sundays and feast days. It is little wonder, writes Van Deursen, that in these circumstances Protestants preferred to live without education. Eventually, royal power renewed its indifference to matters of schooling in general and legislation just dried up. It really had been an exceptional measure which had simply served its short-term purpose. Indeed this educational crusade collapsed partly as a result of the failure to provide adequate financial support, since in the absence of a school the local population had to pay up, and frequently couldn't – or wouldn't. Or, when the clergy, as in La Rochelle, invoked the law of 1686 which allowed for children to be removed from parental control, the reply of the civil authorities was: who will provide the cash?[80] The alliance between the crown and the Church in France had never been unconditional to the same degree as in other countries, either Catholic or Protestant.[81]

If the school was a visible affront to the Catholic clergy in our period, then so was the temple. In the course of the century permission for the existence of temples came under closer and closer scrutiny. Communities which could not prove with the aid of documents that worship took place in their temple during the period prescribed by the Edict of Nantes as the base-line (1596–7) found their temple closed. Temples allowed on the land of noble converts to Catholicism were shut down. By a royal decree of 1663 invasion of the space of the temple was made official when Catholic preachers were allowed to interrupt services by challenging the pastor. In order to prevent conversion or reconversion to Protestantism, a decree of 1679 ordered the destruction of any temple where a pastor had made a profession of faith before a Catholic or a former Protestant. In addition mob violence against temples was not unknown, as in Dauphiné in 1683.[82]

Protestants also had to suffer the indignity of the occupation of their domestic space when, during the notorious *dragonnades*, soldiers were

[79] Ibid., pp. 61–2.   [80] Ibid., pp. 62–3.

[81] Frijhoff, 'L'Etat et l'éducation', 102.

[82] J. Garrisson, *L'Edit de Nantes et sa révocation: histoire d'une intolérance* (Paris, 1985), p. 209.

billeted in Huguenot households in order to encourage the abandonment of the Reformed Religion. As access to temples was made more difficult, particularly in sparsely populated rural areas, the domestic service which took place each evening and which was a long-standing Protestant custom assumed a far greater importance than before. The authorities did not let up in their persecution even here and raided houses in order to confiscate Bibles in French, psalters and books of prayers.[83] Eventually the Protestant Church had to find an alternative space of worship and became a Church of the Wilderness – 'l'Eglise du désert' – where services were held in the open air, in secret and at night. This was however not without immense risk and carried severe penalties, like imprisonment or the harsh régime of the galleys. Finally, the Protestant Church became the Church of the Refuge in exile. Many Huguenots emigrated to England, Scotland, Holland, the Dutch provinces of South Africa, and America. In England, however, the distinctiveness of the community did not survive many generations and its membership dissolved largely into the Anglican Church.[84]

The particularity of the Protestant space in terms of faith, belief and way of life should not lead to its construction as hostile in a political perspective. Here Huguenots might be considered less suspect than Jansenists. Indeed many members of the Reformed Religion served the governments of the first half of the century, and Huguenots were prominent in the officer ranks of the French navy. Along with their Catholic counterparts, the majority of Huguenots accepted the system of monarchy as a given and saw no reason to change it for any other: they even espoused the views on despots that were to be developed by Bossuet in the second half of the century, notably that obedience must be given to the authority of kings in whatever circumstances. Moreover, the monarchy was the only protection available to the Protestants against both the Holy See and the Catholic Church within the kingdom. In addition, the concept of divine right was believed to function as protecting Protestants against the abuse of power.[85] One event in particular reinforced these positions. During and after the English Revolution French Protestants desired above all to distance themselves from their regicide co-religionaries.

Huguenots could also relate to the space of Catholicism in their attitudes to the origins of power in the state. Protestants were unconditional gallicans to the extent that, if Catholics were gallican, Protestants

---

[83] Ibid., p. 263.
[84] See Gwynn, *Huguenot Heritage*, pp. 91–109.
[85] See E. Labrousse, 'La Doctrine politique des Huguenots: 1630–1685', *Etudes théologiques et religieuses*, 47 (1972), 421–9.

were, as Elisabeth Labrousse puts it, 'hypergallicans'. In this respect they were more anti-papist than anti-Catholic. It is in this area where the greatest hopes of an unenforced merger between the two Churches might have been entertained. Protestants could look only favourably upon gallican belief in the superiority of councils over the personal authority of the pope and total rejection of papal interference in the affairs of the kingdom. Protestants even congratulated themselves that their legal existence in France encouraged the French Catholic Church to adhere to the purity of the Christianity of the primitive Church rather than follow in the less surely directed footsteps of the Italians and Spaniards.[86] Huguenots found many reasons why they could live happily in the political space of the kingdom rather than in the margins to which they were assigned by others.

But deeper cultural reasons prevented this cohabitation from being a persuasive reality. The Catholic space, with its emphasis on hierarchy and on the special place of the priest over the faithful, was in many respects a perfect mirror-image of political power invested in the special nature of the king, who was also defender of the faith. The relation of the Catholic faithful to the priest was a model for the relation of subjects to the king. Neither the political nor the religious space was participatory: things were 'received'. The Church and the king were spectacles to behold with awe. Despite their protestations of absolute loyalty to monarchy, the organisation of Protestant space or the nature of their theology did not reflect royal power in the same way. This is no doubt why Protestants in their submission to the young Louis XIV in 1657 advanced the thesis that, in politics as in religion, 'un sujet ne peut jamais rien mériter de son souverain et qu'après lui avoir rendu les plus signalés services dont il est capable, il ne pourrait qu'avec insolence prétendre à la moindre de ses faveurs sinon comme à une pure grâce'.[87] Such a thesis seems to transcend any form of organisation and reflects a direct appeal to the king as to their God. Protestants conceive of the king as part of their own religious space. It may also be for these reasons that, despite Briggs's assertion that the Catholic hierarchy did not request the Revocation of the Edict of Nantes and that it was therefore a secular act,[88] royal power and the Catholic hierarchy, most of whom raised little or no protest at the *dragonnades*, combined to weaken and to damage irrevocably the place of Protestantism in the kingdom.

Two factors in particular contributed to suspicion of the Huguenot community. First, the organisation of the consistories and synods, where

[86] Labrousse, *'Une Foi, une loi, un roi?'*, pp. 68–9.
[87] D. Ligou, *Le Protestantisme en France de 1598 à 1715* (Paris, 1968), p. 174.
[88] Briggs, *Communities of Belief*, p. 219.

the laity held more power than their Catholic counterparts, seemed to demonstrate republican leanings which ill suited the monarchic ideal. It is no accident that Protestants found republicanism in the nineteenth and twentieth centuries more congenial to them than many Catholics. Second, their association with 'the enemy' outside the kingdom, notably in Geneva and England, added to the perception of them as a 'foreign' element inside the kingdom. English intervention during the siege of La Rochelle was not easily forgotten. Some Protestant pastors came from outside the kingdom, notably Scotland, and many of the others had been trained outside France.

All protestations of loyalty were ultimately of no avail and the English Revolution simply increased the horror of many for the Reformed Religion. As in the case of Jansenism, particularism and nonconformism were problematic in a kingdom where the development of royal authority rested on at least the ambition of homogenisation of space under a single political orthodoxy which, in the course of the century, became the ambition for a single religious orthodoxy as well. In any case the Revocation provoked many, but by no means all, Protestants into rethinking their relation to royal power, particularly along the lines of the principle of freedom of conscience. The solidarity of the Protestants with the crown, in other words their attempt at a sort of political assimilation within which they could live in their own religious space, had to yield to a more complex relationship which truly enshrined a notion of pluralism in French political theory, an idea so much at odds with the notion of absolutism they originally supported. Such a move could only really happen outside the space of the kingdom, in exile.

One individual who went into exile and who was concerned to reformulate the position of French Protestantism in relation to royal authority, especially when the fully repressive measures taken by the authorities against his faith became clear, was Pierre Bayle. Bayle was not an unconditional opponent of the régime which forced him to leave France and in this he stood in often stormy opposition to Pierre Jurieu who took a much more radical stand in the reaction to the Revocation, including advocating deposing Louis XIV for having broken the contract with his Protestant subjects as constituted by the Edict of Nantes. Bayle's views on the relation of subjects to monarch was more conciliatory and pleaded for a religious tolerance which could be accommodated to the political demands of the régime. Despite this air of compromise, Bayle's theories on the matter of tolerance represent a milestone, especially in the way they are argued, in the concept of civil rights for minorities.

Bayle believed that, in the political space as a whole, it was the proper right of government to suppress heresy, but he believed that this right should be exercised only in the case of heresies which were politically or socially subversive. In this he admitted to the concept of 'délit d'opinion'. On the other hand the visible political space of the kingdom concealed the 'inner' space of conscience, over which it had no jurisdiction and which was inviolable, 'qu'il s'agisse de l'expression "modeste" d'opinions spéculatives ou de la célébration discrète et paisible de cultes particuliers'.[89] In other words, Bayle argues that repressive legislation should be based not on the falseness of any particular opinion but on whether it was contrary to 'la tranquillité publique'.[90] Almost as a consequence of the 'délit d'opinion', Bayle even envisaged the legitimation of censorship in the strictly limited cases of outrageous and scandalous pamphlets, and it is noteworthy that Bayle denounces the excesses of the Dutch press more often than he praises its freedoms.[91]

Bayle's attachment to the monarchical system, as we have seen an essential part of Protestant political culture, did not waver with the Revocation. He denounced the Edict of Fontainebleau as an iniquitous abuse of a power which none the less retained its legitimacy. Indeed he regarded the system in place as the most favourable, within certain limits, to religious freedom of the individual. Where else would Bayle have been able to look for such a guarantee? For this reason he attempted to create a space for toleration within the political and religious space. In this Bayle distinguishes himself from the Jansenist view of inner conscience which was much less discreet, not to say positively confrontational. It was rather Jurieu who looked forward to the French Revolution whereas Bayle 'reste pourtant tributaire de la structure de l'Ancien Régime'.[92] Bayle wished to preserve Protestantism from the charge of being a space of hostility, which it certainly became under Jurieu.

The issue of religious toleration as articulated by Bayle brought together a number of factors which crystallised around the practice of enforced conversion of Protestants. This practice can easily be dismissed as abominable in human terms but defence of such a practice was legitimated by following literally the words of Christ in Luke 14:23: 'Go out into the highways and hedges, and compel them to come in, that my house may be filled.' This became known as 'Contrains-les d'entrer' or the *Compelle intrare*. Rejection of the practice rested in turn therefore on rejection of the literal meaning in favour of a 'spiritual' one, or at least in a demonstration that Christ's words could not of themselves permit violence. We have already encountered the immense difficulties experienced by those who sought to promote 'critique' in biblical exegesis and the chances of the introduction of tolerance into Catholic space in this way

[89] Labrousse, *Pierre Bayle*, II, 555.   [90] Quoted in ibid., p. 547.
[91] Ibid., p. 549.   [92] Ibid., p. 555.

were by definition slim. But Bayle also attacked the Church's recourse to state violence in addressing religious claims to rightness as a tyranny. Because I believe this, others must be forced to believe it too. If such claims, which do not address the 'correctness' of belief as such, could be found wanting in some way, then the state could truly become the arbiter of religious freedom within the limits Bayle outlined in my earlier discussion.

Bayle addressed in detail the question of religious toleration and inner conscience in his *Commentaire philosophique sur ces paroles de Jésus-Christ: 'Contrains-les d'entrer'* (1686). For Bayle this exhortation could not possibly be taken literally. Bayle did not address philological issues but introduced into the interpretation of Scripture a judgement according to 'lumière naturelle' which, in this case, led to the conclusion that: 'tout sens littéral, qui contient l'obligation de faire des crimes, est faux'.[93] To justify figurative interpretation Bayle invoked the authority of St Augustine: any literal interpretation of the type represented by the *Compelle intrare* could not be a revealed truth, but would only represent the 'visions', passions and prejudices of the person who advances it. The essence of Bayle's argument is that the words of Christ simply cannot mean what Catholics make them say.

Bayle's 'lumière naturelle' is not human reason acting independently: his position is essentially Augustinian in that the source of 'lumière naturelle' is God, is a 'révélation naturelle', and 'nous fait contempler dans son essence les idées des vérités éternelles, contenues dans les principes, ou dans les notions communes de métaphysique'. In this way there are axioms 'contre lesquels les paroles les plus expresses, et les plus évidentes de l'Ecriture, ne gagneraient rien', such as the whole is greater than the part and that two contradictory statements cannot each be true at the same time. However much you tried to establish a doctrine contrary to the universal maxims of common sense, man would prefer to believe that Scripture communicated in metaphor than to believe that 'la lumière naturelle fût fausse dans ces maximes'. Crucially: 'tout dogme qui n'est pas homologué . . ., vérifié, et enregistré au Parlement suprême de la raison, et de la lumière naturelle, ne peut qu'être d'une autorité chancelante'. Bayle's conclusion is that, in the case of the Catholic treatment of Protestants in the context of conversion, it is thoroughly opposed to good sense, to 'lumière naturelle', to general principles of reason, 'à la règle primitive et originale du discernement du vrai et du faux, du bon et du mauvais', to use violence in order to persuade others of a religion they do not profess.[94]

[93] P. Bayle (ed. A Niderst), *Bayle: Oeuvres diverses* (Paris, 1971), p. 104.
[94] Ibid., p. 111.

Bayle also draws attention to consequences of a moral kind if the Catholic interpretation of Luke's text is correct: with the lifting of all barriers which separate vice and virtue, there is no action so infamous that it could not be considered an act of piety and religion, if such acts are committed in the name of extirpating heresy. It would also be an own goal, Bayle implies, because, if every religion believed that it is the true religion, all violence to all other religions is thus legitimised when this sort of conversion is thought of as a service to God.[95] No space is safe in these circumstances, since any space could thus be constructed as hostile.

Bayle substantially contributed to the modern notion of tolerance moving from a position of 'putting up with' to one of respect for the conscience of another in his *Commentaire philosophique*, where he argues according to the principle of reciprocity and against persecution on the basis of a tyrannical claim to rightness. It seems appropriate therefore that Bayle should begin from a position of historical relativity. If toleration is rejected on the principle that one religion overturns the fundamentals of another, pagans were surely right to be intolerant to those who preached the Gospel.[96] The pagans' claim to rightness stands as their defence. Contemporary Catholic behaviour towards Protestants legitimises Roman violence in the persecution of Christians. If Catholics find this a disagreeable argument, then they must as a logical consequence reject violence to Huguenots. The claim to rightness cannot legitimise persecution. Bayle, in going beyond the circumstances of his own century and the situation of his own faith, argues on the basis of a principle he would hold as universal. Bayle discerns the existence of a logical necessity 'qui oblige, si l'on prétend condamner une persécution et une manifestation d'intolérance, à condamner toute persécution et toute intolérance'.[97] True reciprocity can only work if both sides renounce their claim to rightness as a tyranny, although each can still continue to believe it is right. Then there is no such thing as the space of religion or belief. It is a space of religions and beliefs, a truly plural space. Indeed Bayle mentions as a case in point the world of Islam which tolerates the existence within its own space of other religions. Intolerance is essentially a Christian practice.[98]

The claim to rightness is also reflected in interpretation of the Gospel. In reality Bayle is pleading for an interpretation of Scripture which, when Scripture is taken as a whole, is coherent. The interpretation given by Catholics to *Compelle intrare* was so contrary to the rest of Christ's teaching that it could not be correct. Catholics were thus guilty of a partisan reading. Their claim to rightness was based on an error. Partisanship is a major theme in Bayle's treatment of history across all

[95] Ibid., pp. 116–17.   [96] Ibid., p. 120.
[97] Labrousse, *Pierre Bayle*, II, 523.   [98] Ibid., pp. 521–2.

religious confessions where he points out that it is ridiculous for one party to pass over arguments or facts that the other party has alluded to, which leads him to argue in some cases for a 'pyrrhonisme historique'. Partisan history simply perpetuated a spirit of intolerance. He calls for what Labrousse calls 'un effort de critique sereine . . . pour ramener l'opinion à moins de sectarisme persécuteur'.[99]

Whatever the principles of the matter, false conversions work to the disadvantage of Catholicism since they pose more problems than they solve. Conversions secured for purely political reasons do not reach the souls of the converted. The latter bring with them all their previous beliefs and they import into the new space the content of the old. Bayle invokes an argument familiar in the rest of his work when he asserts that the situation could simply be reversed: Catholics, if they had been forced to convert, would have retained their belief in the Virgin and saints' relics, and would not have rid themselves of 'la pieuse credulité qui leur avoit été inspirée dès le berceau pour les miracles, pour le Purgatoire, et ce qui s'ensuit'.[100]

The importance of belief as occupying the inner space of individual conscience is explained by Bayle in an argument which emphasises in a particularly Augustinian way the importance of knowledge and love of God. The instruction of man is useful in persuading us of the truth, but we can be persuaded of this truth without loving it. So it is not through other men that we come to love the truths of the Gospels. This is the work of God alone who adds to the illumination of our soul 'une disposition de coeur qui nous fait trouver plus de joye dans l'exercice de la vertu, que dans la pratique du vice'.[101] Enforced conversion, even if those thus converted are persuaded of another truth, is only ever external. It affects the outer not the inner man. Only individual conscience can make that truth a truth of the soul. Bayle's argument is one of free assent. For Bayle, there can be no compulsion to embrace a particular sort of faith. If an individual does not wish to give his free assent to the Catholic faith, he is free to remain within his own, and that freedom cannot be denied without seriously damaging the nature of the alternative faith. In any case if the Church rules only over souls and if its weapons are by definition spiritual, then its use of force is an abuse of power: it constitutes 'une ingérence inadmissible', for the Church 'prétend décider de questions qui ne sont pas de son ressort'.[102]

But we must be careful not to overinterpret Bayle's position on freedom

[99] Ibid., pp. 22–3.
[100] P. Bayle (ed. A. Prat), *Pensées diverses sur la comète*, 2 vols. (Paris, 1984), I, 227.
[101] Ibid., II, 67.
[102] Labrousse, *Pierre Bayle*, II, 511.

of conscience. The nature of the space he envisages is not the complete fragmentation of individual sects or Churches into one space composed simply of a multiplicity of individuals all thinking different things, or individuals being allowed to express any opinion within their own sect or Church. If Bayle exhorts churchmen to be tolerant, he does not plead in favour of 'la tolérance ecclésiastique'. That is to say that a Church has the perfect right to excommunicate any of its members for good cause. This could only work in a situation where there was a civil tolerance which neutralised the effects of 'l'intolérance ecclésiastique'. In Holland, for example, after the Synod of Dordrecht, individuals could be excommunicated for doctrinal reasons without any detrimental social consequences, whereas this was far from the case in those countries in Europe with a single state religion.[103] Bayle thus achieves the position of safeguarding the rights of Churches and the rights of the individual. The space of society can no longer be defined in terms of a religious space. But we must be clear. Bayle's promotion of tolerance of different opinions does not mean that they are all equally valid: 'l'erreur qu'il tient pour innocente est celle de l'homme de bonne foi qui a réellement, bien que peut-être très maladroitement, cherché la vérité. Il ne s'agit pas d'avaliser toutes les positions à la fois, en vertu d'une indulgence niaise, qui supposerait une confiance a priori dans la nature humaine.' This leads Labrousse to the interesting and perhaps surprising conclusion that Bayle does not promote tolerance so much as freedom of conscience. Bayle's position is emphatically not that one dogma is worth another.[104]

But the space of tolerance was never to materialise in France of the seventeenth century. It would be wrong, however, to exaggerate hostility. Elisabeth Labrousse properly warns that overstating the differences between Protestants and Catholics conceals what they shared, especially at the level of the community where they had a number of common interests.[105] In many areas of France relations with Catholics were family relations, either from a time before conversion or as a result of mixed marriages. Professional relations too were important and in this sense it is impossible to think of Huguenot communities as 'ghettoised'. The space of Protestantism was properly the invisible Church of inner conscience. Elisabeth Labrousse maintains that, were it not for religious particularism, the Reformers would have been easily absorbed into the mass of the Catholic population.[106]

On the other hand, as Labrousse readily admits, peaceful co-existence was precarious.[107] In the end result, it was the profound attachment to

103 Ibid., pp. 538 and 541.   104 Ibid., pp. 582–4.
105 Labrousse, 'Une Foi, une loi, un roi?', pp. 77 ff.   106 Ibid., pp. 80–1.
107 Ibid., pp. 89–93.

their own religious particularism which distinguished Protestant and Catholic subjects of the kingdom of France. For the Catholic authorities, both religious and civil, the space of Protestantism remained a space of reconquest. Bossuet held that it was the duty of kings to destroy false religions and that there were plenty of biblical precedents for such a principle. Also it is an error of impiety to believe that religion can be free, as Bossuet makes clear in his *Politique tirée des propres paroles de l'Ecriture sainte*: 'Autrement il faudroit souffrir dans tous les sujets et dans tout l'état l'idolâtrie, le mahométisme, le judaïsme, toute fausse religion: le blasphème, l'athéisme même, et les plus grands crimes seroient les plus impunis.'[108] For Bossuet the space of religion is the space of a single orthodoxy and as such is indivisible. Bossuet believed too that universal tolerance led to indifference to religion, which in turn became unbelief. But the principal error on the part of prelates like Bossuet was to underestimate Huguenot attachment to their particularism to the extent that they believed that conversion from one faith to the other could be easily accomplished. Nobody in the Catholic hierarchy imagined that there could be a problem of conscience and they regarded Protestant resistance as sheer obstinacy.[109]

Yet again, with some honourable exceptions, those on the Catholic side made a major miscalculation. After the Revocation Protestantism, through the Church of the Refuge, attracted attention on a geographical scale that had never been envisaged. The diffusion of the French language in northern Europe meant that those who had been marginalised in their own space had a ready-made audience who were keen to read authors whose works were prohibited in France.[110] This was certainly the case when Huguenots found asylum in England (emigration to America was less significant). In general, the Catholic Church contributed to the emptying of its own space, either by the failure of the NC to attend Catholic offices, or by disgusting its own flock by the awful treatment Protestants were subjected to. Indeed many of the latter could not have left the kingdom without some help from the Catholic population. The Revocation of the Edict of Nantes simply led to dechristianisation in certain of the French provinces. In seeking to destroy the space of Protestantism the Church succeeded only in damaging its own.

---

[108] Bossuet, *Œuvres*, XVI, 305–6.
[109] Labrousse, *'Une Foi, une loi, un roi?'*, pp. 92–3.
[110] Lebrun (ed.), *Histoire de la France religieuse*, II, 501–2.

8   The spaces of hostility: unbelief

Introduction

In the France of our period groups can be identified who saw themselves as hostile to the Church in some way or who were constructed by others as hostile groups, but this time outside the realm of belief as it can be understood within Catholic or Protestant orthodoxies. Unsurprisingly, atheists constituted such a group, although the term itself was not always used in the seventeenth century to designate unbelief in a modern sense. Whether atheism existed at all at this time continues to be a historical problem to the extent that it has been argued that the 'complete' atheist was the creation of the Church itself.

In addition, the *libertins* clearly have their place among groups consider-ed hostile to the Church. 'Libertinage' too constitutes a problem, especially since the founding principles of René Pintard's monumental work on the subject have now come to be challenged. Much controversy surrounds the precise definition of the term, and the degree to which it accurately reflects a position hostile to Christianity itself. The problem of 'libertinage' has been compounded by the view of hostility to belief as the natural bedfellow of loose sexual mores. Some recent commentators have suggested that 'libertinage' as an atheistic stance has been unduly confused with a position critical of certain aspects of dogma, and one which was clearly suspicious of religion as it was organised in the seventeenth century, but not of all belief. A space thus existed between orthodoxy and heterodoxy.

Those within the Church in seventeenth-century France did not doubt for a moment that the *libertins* constituted an organised group who set out to destroy the beliefs of others, particularly through an easily identifiable behaviour. In terms of mores this group created one sort of counter-space centred, according to some, on the tavern, a symbol of moral disorder already familiar to us. Another sort of counter-space was the library where groups of individuals who were linked by friendship or like-mindedness met to discuss their ideas.

Towards the end of the century, we can add a further group of individuals to the atheists and *libertins*, the deists, who are less closely defined as a group. The space they occupy is a shared one of beliefs outside orthodoxy but, as we shall see, not necessarily outside belief as such. This did not prevent them from being construed as a group hostile to the Church and its teaching.

Libertinage

The concept of *libertinage* has given rise to great controversy over the years. The *libertins* as a group have been reckoned to constitute a space hostile to Catholicism and to Christianity as a whole. One problem in the study of *libertinage* has been distinguishing between description and attitudes loading the description. For this reason it is important to look at Pintard's work, *Le Libertinage érudit dans la première moitié du XVIIe siècle* (1943), which remains the most important reference point in this domain, in some detail. We have to begin with attitude.

Nobody familiar with their alarming audacity, Pintard writes, can fail to conclude that a conspiracy had been mounted against the Church by those of independent mind and loose morals: 'pour la première fois l'édifice immense de la Chrétienté chancelle'.[1] Pintard never manages to conceal his contempt for the *libertins*, regarding their fideism, a concept by no means heterodox in itself and found to some degree at least in Pascal, as a subterfuge for the free expression of 'pensées impies'. These, we discover, combine to form a rationalist interpretation of nature and man, 'et continuent de ruiner ce qui restait de philosophie chrétienne'.[2] Fideism is quite unequivocally used to draw a veil over unbelief.

This subterfuge, according to Pintard, takes a variety of forms. In the first place attacks on the Trinity, the existence of angels and demons, or on attributes of the nature of the divine, are couched, as in the works of Gabriel Naudé, in terms of separating the truths of faith from those of reason.[3] In this way, one gradually undermines the other. Secondly, an exclusive and unconditional attachment to Greek and Roman culture imported the alien concepts of paganism into the Christian world of the kingdom.[4] The attractions of the ancients ultimately led to an anti-Christian philosophy which in some cases amounted to no less than 'un acte de foi païenne'.[5] The *libertins* operated within the space of orthodoxy as a whole by adopting a thoroughgoing religious and social conformism, of which Pintard obviously disapproves.[6]

---

[1] R. Pintard, *Le Libertinage érudit dans la première moitié du XVIIe siècle* (Paris, 1943), (new edition Geneva, 1983), p. 32.   [2] Ibid., p. 47.
[3] Ibid., p. 465.   [4] Ibid., pp. 56–7.   [5] Ibid., p. 285.
[6] See ibid., p. 34.

One of the questions Pintard broaches is the precise location of the frontiers in the *libertins*' critique of what is sacred and what is profane. For thinkers like Naudé and La Mothe Le Vayer there were no frontiers: they may, in pointing to the absurdities and contradictions in historians and philosophers, claim to stop short of religious belief itself, but in reality faith itself is shown to be bogus because, given the sort of programme they set themselves, their own religious protestations ring false,[7] as in Naudé's 'war' on the supernatural on the basis of scrutiny of historical witness.[8] Jean de Launoi was no doubt right to question many accounts of the saints' lives but he went too far in the case of Notre Dame de Lorette, and advanced dangerous views on the form and substance of the sacraments. But even legitimate criticism of certain aspects of traditional beliefs or accounts provided a pretext for the *libertins* to promote doubt in the certainties of faith.[9] Criticism in one space offered a model for criticism in another. The two spaces were too close for comfort.

For Pintard, the *libertins* undermined belief precisely by not confronting beliefs head on. Naudé encouraged a denial of providence in his criticism of 'destiny' on the basis of explanations according to chains of natural causes and not theological explanations. Naudé did not deny miracles or the actions of demons but certainly denied the processes by which miracles and these actions could be effected. Naudé drew so many parallels between true and false religion that what he imputed against pagan philosophy could also be turned against Christianity itself. Naudé's method was insidious in its approach to the extent that all sorts of truth figured in the domain of criticism, irrespective of whether they belonged to Christian truth or not.[10] Naudé thus brooked no distinction. No frontiers could be established between the space of criticism and the space of orthodox belief. Criticism inevitably amounted to heterodoxy.

Gassendi was another member of this conspiracy against the Church. He is held to have adopted an escape route whereby he justified by faith what he condemned through reason, either by drawing a demarcation line between faith and reason, or by superimposing one on the other without any attempt to reconcile them as contradictory propositions.[11] Gassendi, through naivety or cunning, acted as if his scientific curiosity had no implications for revealed truth.[12] Pintard thus suspects Gassendi of claiming an autonomous space for science, now opposed to religion, which would offer alternative – and better – explanations than those according to faith. In his early works Gassendi marked his intention as one of reasoning 'en penseur libre'.[13]

---

[7] Ibid., p. 163.   [8] Ibid., p. 450.   [9] Ibid., p. 279.   [10] Ibid., pp. 467–75.
[11] Ibid., p. 153.   [12] Ibid., p. 488.
[13] Ibid., p. 150.

François de la Mothe Le Vayer (1588–1672) is excoriated for his seeming hypocrisy. He developed a theory of knowledge and of life containing not an ounce of the Christian doctrine he professed, and elaborated for himself a philosophy quite independent of any inspiration of the Gospels and the Fathers, and without asking whether it posed problems for theology and moral systems. In his writings on religion his only refuge was in incoherence.[14] Pintard is convinced that La Mothe worked assiduously to undermine the space of orthodoxy in his writings, even in his promotion of accommodation with custom whose absurdities and incoherences he does not hesitate to demonstrate. His appointment as tutor to the young Louis XIV is no proof in his defence: either he managed to conceal his true spiritual identity or the queen's preferences yielded to those of Cardinal Mazarin 'fort peu embarrassé de scrupules religieux'.[15]

In more general terms the hostile space of *libertinage* was populated by doctors who were often charged with being irreligious. In the area of mental illness, they preferred natural explanations to the idea of possession favoured by many members of the Church. In the main, then, doctors opted for atheism and unbelief.[16] This accusation was denounced by the royal physician, Charles Lussauld, in 1663. One particular example of an 'impious' doctor was that of Gui Patin who, in addition to finding the whole incident of Loudun highly suspect, also doubted truths in the lives of the saints, doubted miracles related to relics and held to a 'political' view of religion,[17] that is to say, religion as purely a necessity for a well-ordered state.

The main problem with Pintard's analysis is that all too often he uses a vocabulary and expresses attitudes which take the orthodoxies of the seventeenth century as the orthodoxies – or what should have been the orthodoxies – of his own age (a charge he makes against others in the essay prefacing the 1983 edition of his work). Pintard clearly has little time for what he regards as the anti-Christian views of his authors. One of the most bizarre of his judgements, given the aggressive environment of the Catholic Reform in the first half of the seventeenth century, is that such writers and thinkers very largely kept their subversive thoughts to themselves or expressed them in a coded way, rather than being honest and open about them. He is particularly scathing about 'les mécréants en soutane', presumably those in orders like Gassendi, who, unlike the 'clergé honnête' in their 'école de sainteté', preferred their 'école d'hypocrisie'.[18] Pintard has no understanding either that it might be a legitimate position to wish to live in a space on the margins of the orthodoxies of the day, or that survival depended at the very least on the

[14] Ibid., pp. 509 and 520.   [15] Ibid., pp. 143–5.   [16] Ibid., pp. 80–2.
[17] Ibid., p. 317.   [18] Ibid., p. 83.

creation of an inner and more habitable space at the expense of seeming to acquiesce with the rights of the more dominant space. Taking the side of the Counter-Reformation in this uncritical way leads to the most absurd conclusions, as with Busson, who regrets that heliocentrism was most of all associated with the *libertins* among whom, incidentally, he seems to include Bayle.[19] A case of the right idea in the wrong hands.

The position Pintard and Busson adopt towards *libertinage* has since come under much scrutiny. Richard Popkin's interpretation of *libertin* thinking advances an alternative theory, dismissed out of hand by Pintard in the preface of 1983, which emphasises almost perversely the Christian, or religious, content of their thought. In this perspective, *libertinage érudit* comes to represent a certain type of liberal Catholicism, opposed to either superstitious belief or fanatical Protestantism, which did not therefore set out to destroy or undermine Christianity as a whole. Popkin of course starts from the assumption that scepticism in itself was, in the sixteenth century, more anti-Protestant than anti-religious. In these circumstances the *libertins* could be held to adopt a position against the credulity of simple men and perhaps even to despise the religious organisation to which they belonged rather than condemn the core of Christian belief.[20]

Ultimately, interpreting *libertinage* is a matter of determining adequate standards for evaluating sincerity or intent. We must try to avoid using criteria or standards which are not appropriate to the period in judging seventeenth-century figures by what articles of faith they assert. La Mothe Le Vayer, for example, is then no more ironical or anti-Christian than other major Christian thinkers. La Mothe Le Vayer's work is neither critical nor theoretical but rather illustrative. To those critics who argue that the logic of La Mothe's assault on rational standards meant that no basis existed for choosing to be a Christian, Popkin replies that this would be equally true of the entire history of sceptical Christian fideism. In addition, Popkin doubts that Naudé merited the description of a 'learned unbeliever', being as he was simply wary of superstition and any type of fanatical dogmatism. In fact it is almost impossible to pin down exactly what the religious views of the likes of Naudé and Patin were. Naudé, if he was really hostile to religion, would have had to succeed in concealing his place in the conspiracy against the Church from a whole host of cardinal employers.[21] It could on the other hand be supposed that some of those in ecclesiastical authority were rather more liberal in their acceptance of less orthodox positions than we might think.

Popkin is particularly keen to defend Gassendi: 'it most strains the

[19] Ibid., p. 109.
[20] R. Popkin, *The History of Scepticism from Erasmus to Spinoza* (Berkeley, 1979), p. 96.
[21] Ibid., pp. 89–96.

limits of one's credulity to consider him as completely insincere', especially in view of the testimony of friends and associates who regarded him as a sincere Christian.[22] Bloch too identifies points where Gassendi's philosophical views are determined by Christian orthodoxy as in his evaluation of Gassendi's Epicureanism.[23] His philosophy is modern, containing as it does elements of eclecticism, compromise, circumspection and relativism, but it is not 'une pensée libertine'.[24] Bloch admits however to a difficulty. While he does not deny the sincerity of Gassendi's belief, the balance of profane and spiritual learning remains a problem: the little interest Gassendi the priest paid to the spiritual or intellectual aspects of his religion 'nous paraît bien manifester une surprenante rupture entre l'homme et le penseur, qui a de quoi laisser perplexe sur la profondeur de l'intérêt porté par le philosophe aux problèmes métaphysiques que pose sa foi'.[25]

Even here Bloch is pointing to the complexity of Christian thought in an age of great challenges and changes, a complexity ignored by the rigid divisions established by Pintard's model, although for his part Popkin perhaps makes light of some of the real critical issues raised in the context of the fundamentals of faith. Is it not none the less the case that the *libertins* were negotiating a space, a space of critical belief, they could inhabit between the strictly delimited spaces of orthodoxy in their own time? They were not prepared to accept a religion which was simply received, and wanted room for manoeuvre. Given the unconditional orthodoxy of Catholic reformers, no negotiation within the space of religion itself was possible, at least in any open form. Critical belief was too vulnerable. Lebrun understands the rise of irreligion in terms of a more demanding and more exacting form of Christian orthodoxy which forced thinkers out of a space where fideist compromises were once possible.[26] Spink contrasts the *libertins*' lack of aggression and dogmatism with their aggressive and violent enemies who had power on their side.[27] Internal exile was all that was open to them.

How did the enemies of the *libertins* think of the space the latter occupied? Louise Godard de Donville is highly critical of Pintard for having more or less adopted the critical optic of seventeenth-century opponents of *libertinage*, in particular the confusion of loose morals and thought.[28] This aspect of the *libertins*, despite the example of the poet

---

[22] Ibid., p. 94
[23] Bloch, *La Philosophie de Gassendi*, p. 300.
[24] Ibid., p. 76.   [25] Ibid., p. 298.
[26] Lebrun (ed.), *Histoire de la France religieuse*, II, 433.
[27] Spink, *French Free Thought*, p. v.
[28] L. Godard de Donville, *Le Libertin des origines à 1665: un produit des apologètes* (Paris–Seattle–Tübingen, 1989), p. 27.

Théophile de Viau, perhaps the most celebrated object of accusations of loose morals (in his case homosexuality), seems not to have dominated contemporary writings critical of the *libertins* as a group. Godard de Donville's analyses of texts have revealed that 'libertinage' and 'libertin' are rarely found outside the context of religious controversy, and that Christian apologists addressed the specificities of deviant belief among the freethinkers rather than conduct.[29] While at one moment moral accusations may have intensified, the notion of sociability or pleasure became less and less marked.[30]

The term 'libertin' itself points to a problem of parameters. 'Libertin' in the seventeenth century, as Godard de Donville indicates, is a reductive term alluding to an all-embracing 'space' with no attempt to distinguish between different moral or philosophical positions: the *libertin* is quite simply the enemy of religion,[31] one who fails to correspond to the model of the perfect Catholic as conceived by the Council of Trent. As one who does not think 'like us', he automatically becomes a persecutor of the faith.[32] The suggestion is that the Jesuits were responsible for the reappearance of, or at least the new vogue for, the term in the seventeenth century, Richeôme using the term even for Protestants. The extensibility of the term is marked by its use in the context of gallican Catholics who, despite the fact that they are not actually accused of unbelief, find themselves lumped together with atheists.[33] The unlimited space of *libertinage* constructed by the controversialists meant that defending oneself against such accusations was more or less impossible. It may be easy enough to defend someone against specific allegations of atheism or debauchery, but much more difficult to find a reply to the simple charge of 'libertinage' which covered all actions or thoughts which did not conform to the strictest definition of orthodoxy.[34] Since the Jesuits confused the interest of religion as a whole with their own sectional interests, the term 'libertin' was used for anyone, for those who were irreligious or simply anti-Jesuit. Precise definition gave way to plain denunciation.[35]

One real consequence of the constant denunciation *libertins* were subjected to was that their opponents managed to confuse the spaces of belief and critical belief. More than this, the Church actively contributed to the creation of a space that had not hitherto existed in real terms, that is to say, 'une future jonction, jusque-là impensable, entre tous ceux à qui l'Eglise du Concile de Trente refusait toute concession en matière de foi et de moeurs'. This is perhaps why apologists in the second half of the century played down the concept of 'libertinage'.[36] They had begun to understand that the effect of their tactics was not entirely to the advantage

[29] Ibid., pp. 94–6.   [30] Ibid., p. 343.   [31] Ibid., p. 70.   [32] Ibid., pp. 90–1.
[33] Ibid., pp. 106–9.   [34] Ibid., p. 330.   [35] Ibid., pp. 106–7.   [36] Ibid., p. 372.

of the Church: 'Le personnage auquel le Jésuite avait si magistralement rendu vie et qui s'était imposé à quelques autres défenseurs de la foi, était bien fait pour exercer une fascination dangereuse sur les esprits faibles.'[37]

This charge has often been levied against the Jesuit Garasse who publicised theories that few people would otherwise have had access to. In fact Garasse constructed the *libertin* that Théophile was to become by reading the text of his poems as a magistrate might interrogate a witch. By stitching together isolated lines completely out of context, the controversialist more or less dictated the text to the poet,[38] a tactic in fact used in the interrogation of the poet by his inquisitors after his arrest.[39] But the prominence given to Théophile backfired in that he provided the image of 'un libertin "exemplaire"'.[40] In the context of 'libertinage' as a whole, Garasse managed to give weight and importance to the phenomenon, and moreover to give it a structure it had not previously possessed.[41] What we have observed as a diversity of views within the space of critical unbelief in the form of a society of individuals took on a coherence as an autonomous space, this time both for the Christian apologists and for the public at large. A construction focusing on Théophile and his entourage was, as it were, necessary in order to clarify the boundaries of orthodoxy. You are in one space or the other: you cannot have a foot in each. At the same time it is almost as if those who defended the space of orthodoxy had some realisation of its fragility. They had to create a homogeneous space for the enemy of the faith which in turn created their own. Heterodoxy, or the image of it that was projected, was an *absolute* distortion of an orthodoxy which was absolute in its turn. The controversialist could never recognise diversity in the space of the opposition for fear of opening the way to diversity in the space he himself occupied.

If the space of *libertinage* was in the minds of its detractors necessarily homogeneous, then one sole *libertin* could stand for them all. Through the work of Garasse, Théophile 'se démultiplie dans les reflets anonymes du groupe indifférencié, non chiffré, des "beaux esprits"'.[42] Théophile was pure metonymy. No attempt was made to substantiate the existence of others, so that any resemblance whatsoever of another individual to the central model immediately associated that individual with the space created by the poet who was its leader. That space was, in this case, unequivocally the tavern, an 'école d'impiété' if ever there was. A group who existed outside the space of orthodoxy inevitably required a location

[37] Ibid., p. 409.
[38] Ibid., p. 154.
[39] See F. Lachèvre, *Le Procès du poète Théophile de Viau*, 2 vols. (Paris, 1909).
[40] Godard de Donville, *Le Libertin des origines à 1665*, p. 410.
[41] Ibid., p. 264.   [42] Ibid., p. 123.

and that location had, it seems, to be visible. In that the *libertins* indulged in a shared comportment: the tavern commanded a certain type of behaviour. Moreover the world of letters came to be associated with the tavern.[43] This image is not surely deprived of some legitimacy, which of course would have helped in making it stick. It was important for Garasse that the tavern was recognised as co-extensive with the frontiers of this world. Even the Court was brought into this space because there the *Grands* invited Théophile to drink with them on a familiar basis.[44]

Garasse was not alone in identifying *libertinage* with a particular and visible space, for spatial imagery extended to biblical analogy. Cotin, a famous preacher of the period, in his *Discours à Théopompe* (1629), modelled his description of Paris on Babylon, thus allowing for all manner of metaphorical extravagance.[45] Zacharie de Lisieux, in his *Relation du pays de Jansenie* (1660), stretched the boundaries even further by speaking of a country 'dont les géographes n'ont point parlé jusqu'icy', that is to say 'la Libertinie' which is itself confused with the space of Jansenism.[46] All these writers, and others, experienced a clear need to be able to identify and to situate their enemies. Their own space was defined by their construction of other spaces.

To the society coterminous with orthodoxy, the *libertins* opposed a 'counter-society' which was regarded of necessity as aggressive in that it negated entirely the values of the other. It could never be accepted that a portion of society could live without those values because that would throw doubt on the need for the authority which upheld them.[47] If the *libertins* could be constructed as a sect, with a leader and a doctrine signifying a sort of army against the Church, it was easier to marginalise them.[48] But it was also important that the *libertins* placed themselves outside the space of orthodoxy, since orthodoxy does not, from within its own perspective, produce victims. The *libertins* were in a similar position to Protestants. Toleration of another religion might suggest an equality, a possibility of integration. The space of orthodoxy would then be deprived of real meaning, certainly when authority in the seventeenth century was considered to be indivisible and where royal power associated itself with the Catholic Church. The space of society would no longer share the same frontiers as the space of belief, thus creating a concept of secular autonomy, a space where living in a particular space, or even moving from one to the other, was a matter of individual responsibility or choice. Any hint of accepting pluralism, however minimal, destroyed the space of orthodoxy. It lost its role as 'orthodoxy' to become one space among others.

---

[43] Ibid., p. 176.   [44] Ibid., p. 161.   [45] Ibid., p. 349.   [46] Ibid., p. 397.
[47] Ibid., p. 200.   [48] Ibid., p. 244.

What sort of space did the *libertins* create for themselves as opposed to that created for them by others? For Spink, French free-thought was defined by its sociability.[49] But it was an overwhelmingly masculine society, unlike the world of the salons which were very much organised around women and the integration of an ideal of womanhood into élite culture. The space of the *libertins* focused on learning based on the culture of antiquity, an area of learning which excluded women until towards the end of the century when Madame Dacier, a Latin and Greek specialist, still remained something of an exception. Certainly the *libertins* all came from the educated élite of the kingdom and mostly from the intellectual circles of the capital: some like Gassendi had strong regional connections as well. The *libertins* were largely from the gallican milieu of the magistrates and included in their ranks, as has been evident, a sprinkling of clerics like Gassendi and Michel de Marolles (we have encountered the latter in his contribution to literary and artistic debates). The space of the *libertins* did not therefore divide along the frontier separating the sacred and the profane. This suggests that in critical terms they identified a number of problems common to both domains which they could discuss without an aggressive authority intervening on either side. The space of critical belief allowed for the comfortable co-existence of clergy and laymen so that, to a certain extent, it overlapped with other spaces. Montmor, a key figure we have discussed in the context of science, kept company with those who most certainly did not share his own piety. He was close to the Compagnie du Saint-Sacrement, contributed to the endowment of a monastery at Notre-Dame-de-la-Miséricorde and was 'marguiller de sa paroisse'.[50] Indeed, the most notorious of the *libertins* from the point of view of moral behaviour, or so the tradition has it, Théophile de Viau, enjoyed good relations with some members of the clergy, including Coëffeteau, Cospéau, bishop of Nantes, and Camus, bishop of Belley. He also had friends among the Capuchins and, so Adam claims, the Jesuits.[51] Even Pintard has to admit that Patin's ideal of living was to maintain good relations with one's neighbours 'sans méchanceté, sans hypocrisie, sans fanatisme, dans l'obéissance à la loi de la nature, dans l'amour des bonnes lettres'.[52] Given that clerics along with laymen met in the same space to share views on matters of mutual concern, Jean Beaude is in a sense right to conclude that no absolute space of *libertinage* exists. No straightforward opposition can be advanced between a 'monde dévot' and a 'monde libertin': 'Gassendi est-il libertin ou un bon prêtre? Il n'y a sans doute pas de réponse à cette question parce qu'elle est mal posée.'[53] On the other hand

---

[49] Spink, *French Free Thought*, p. v.   [50] Pintard, *Le Libertinage érudit*, p. 403.
[51] Ibid., pp. 293–5.   [52] Ibid., p. 320.
[53] Godard de Donville, *Le Libertin des origines à 1665*, p. 19.

the increasing rigidity of the French Counter-Reformation Church perhaps drove a number of clerics into a space which could then be defined as 'libertin', since it certainly wasn't 'orthodox'.

Pintard, whose descriptive work remains powerful in its breadth and depth, identifies as the core group of *libertins érudits* the Tétrade, as they were known, composed of La Mothe, Gassendi, Naudé and Diodati. The group itself went through a variety of phases in the course of the first half of the seventeenth century, ending in around 1630 and reconvening in 1642. The private space of critical belief had its own way of behaviour and even its own language. The group around Naudé formed a sort of secret society with its pseudonyms and half-spoken thoughts: its deliberations were clear to initiates but not to outsiders.[54] We should however be careful not to overvalue the secret nature of this world since its members did publish quite extensively.

The space of critical belief was in one sense inclusive. This was the result of its fundamentally heterogeneous nature, and Pintard is right to emphasise this. How, by its very nature, could it be anything else? Between them they had no common programme as such and in fact found fellowship in their difference from each other. After all, it was a fellowship in critical belief which could hardly exclude according to any orthodoxy. The space of critical belief simply had to be the space of diversity. But they shared a common fund of sources in, for example, Cicero, Seneca, Montaigne and Charron, and a common direction in fending off the 'intrusion de l'incontrôlable', that is to say Christian metaphysics or occultism, in matters of science.[55]

But, interestingly enough, even the society of critical belief had its limits. Those *libertins* whose space was a relatively fixed one, stabilised to a certain extent by the offices they held in the houses of the great, needed to act with great circumspection. Consequently they were not above defending their own space against those who might attract unwelcome attention. With very few exceptions no alchemists, astrologers or cabalists were admitted to their circles where an exact study of nature was the order of the day.[56] This is not so surprising for a group who rejected any form of 'superstition', popular or otherwise. Nor did the likes of Naudé share the appeal of extravagance which seems to have affected those individuals Spink identifies as 'the wanderers', more or less of no fixed abode, 'resentful of authority, unsubmissive in spirit'.[57] Throwing caution to the wind, they risked imprisonment or worse. Vanini, for example, with no fixed employment and having no real social status, was executed for his

[54] Pintard, *Le Libertinage érudit*, p. 176.
[55] Ibid., p. 174.   [56] Ibid., p. 438.
[57] Spink, *French Free Thought*, p. 12.

opinions in Toulouse in 1619. This did not prevent some from within the space lending their support to dissension a little nearer home, a stand which at times divided the *libertins* themselves. While others attempted to dissuade him from doing so, the Dupuy brothers defended the decision of Saumaise to publish an anti-papist work, even at the expense of his departure from France.[58] The space of *libertinage*, often rooted in the gallican milieu, tended to support particularly those who for intellectual reasons had fallen foul of Rome. The space of critical belief was intimately connected with the space of dissension within Catholicism itself.

In another way *libertinage érudit* was exclusive. The *libertins*' own perception of their space was one of positive differentiation. Not only did its members feel themselves, by virtue of their intellectual positions, excluded from the space of orthodoxy as defined by the Church, but they valued their own beliefs as quite distinct from those of the 'common herd'. La Mothe expresses their sense of themselves as an intellectual élite in these words: 'Il y a fort peu de bons esprits au monde: et les sots, c'est-à-dire le commun des hommes, ne sont pas capables de notre doctrine; et partant il n'en faut pas parler librement, mais en secret et parmy les bons Esprits, confidans et cabalistes.'[59] Secrecy was required therefore not only to avoid unnecessary trouble with the authorities, but in order not to devalue the currency of intellectual discussion. It was above all a space of intellectual fellowship and for that reason alone a space of exclusiveness.

Intellectual fellowship required none the less a physical space where those who shared the perspective of critical belief could meet with like minds while for the most part outwardly acquiescing in the larger space where their ideas would not be welcome. A number of erudite societies, not all of them to be confused with *libertinage*, flourished in the first half of the seventeenth century and into the 1650s, some of which we are already familiar with. One of these was formed around the président de Mesmes and it is here that we encounter the typical space of the *libertins érudits*, the library. The Dupuy brothers held the post of librarians to the président de Thou and convened meetings in the library at his hôtel in the rue des Poictevins, close to Saint-André des Arts. In 1645 Pierre Dupuy replaced Rigault at the Bibliothèque royale in the rue de la Harpe, and all his scholarly companions followed him there. Naudé was the librarian of Mazarin, and La Mothe of Richelieu. The library is appropriately symbolic of *libertinage érudit* since this was essentially a book culture. Moreover, the library provided all the books no individual scholar could

[58] Pintard, *Le Libertinage érudit*, p. 97.
[59] Ibid., p. 177.

afford to supply for himself. Libraries also constituted a very private space since they were in the houses of the big bourgeois or aristocratic families. These houses represented an independent space free of the sort of surveillance that the space of orthodoxy was increasingly subject to. It may well be that their owners turned a blind eye or a deaf ear to some of the things that happened there.

Given the private nature of *libertin* circles, how did the individuals composing them fare in the wider space of society? Despite the privacy and freedom sought by the *libertins érudits*, the frontier between the space of critical belief and the world at large was by no means hard and fast. Priests, doctors and above all those in the employ of public personages still played their part in the general social function. For example, La Mothe la Vayer straddled the world of the independent intellectual and that of official spaces, in his case the Académie française. Pierre Dupuy went on missions for Richelieu and his vast expertise was drawn on in the composition of *Droits et libertez de l'Eglise gallicane*. Naudé, as Mazarin's librarian, had the responsibility of building up the collection, and also performed other semi-official duties. Gassendi supported Richelieu's policies, notably his alliance of Protestant princes against Spain, and La Mothe also wrote texts at the cardinal's bidding. Many of the *libertins érudits* thus moved freely in the space of the world. In their lives outside the library (and even in it) they were well integrated in the mainstream of public activity. While on the one hand their intellectual 'reclusiveness' offers another example of inner space in our period, they did not on the other necessarily have to elaborate a theory of solitude or withdrawal.

Was there not however a certain paradox in occupying a private space of critical belief in which independence of thought was possible, while supporting and working for political institutions which did not encourage that independence? Pintard suggests that the resolution of this apparent conflict lay in their attachment to order and to a 'political' view of religion, inherited from Machiavelli, as contributing to the maintenance of order. In this way conformism served at one and the same time to preserve their inner space and to preserve a régime which protected the peace within which they themselves existed. Pintard also claims that they desired to achieve this independence of spirit for themselves rather than 'convert' others to it.[60] They did not wish to lose their mark of distinction.

As Françoise Charles-Daubert points out, as an intellectual élite even within the world of learning, the *libertins* were conscious of their political weakness. The dissemination of their own critique of oracles, miracles and the relativism of morality would itself threaten an order based on

[60] Ibid., pp. 563–4.

custom.[61] The right ideas had not to fall into the wrong hands. In this way the *libertins* perpetuated the fear of the populace endemic in educated circles of the seventeenth century. After all, who was to know whether, even as the instigators of novelty, they would not find themselves on the wrong end of the forces novelty unleashed? But Charles-Daubert sees their position not as timorous but as a clear understanding of their political responsibilities in not allowing critical ideas to undermine the system.[62] It seems none the less difficult to conclude, as Charles-Daubert does, that *libertin* independence of thought was the harbinger of the Enlightenment.[63] This is part of the attempt to see a 'modern' consciousness in a century where the conditions for its appearance were largely absent. Naudé's scepticism with regard to the legitimacy of royal power she describes could very well be seen in the same light as the views of Pascal on the same subject. As Charles-Daubert herself admits, the *libertins'* sceptical position, especially with regard to the relativism of political systems, led them to opt for the system which had proven efficacious.[64] Naudé did not see the system of monarchy as a matter of theoretical concern and limited himself to advice on its good functioning.[65]

The space of critical belief eventually fragmented in a variety of ways. The Fronde interrupted proceedings and split the fellowship among its various political factions. Ménage and the Dupuys opted for Retz, Naudé obviously for Mazarin. Others like Sarasin, Bourdelot and Lapeyrère threw in their lot with Condé in Holland and Bordeaux. The space was dispersed geographically. While intellectual heterogeneity could keep them together, political division could not. The space of the library itself did not survive. At Pierre Dupuy's death, a 'stranger', wet behind the ears at that, was appointed to the post of librarian at the Bibliothèque royale. Another major blow was the sale of Mazarin's library and the invasion of the hallowed sanctuary by the 'other' in search of a good commercial deal. In the second half of the century scientific gatherings, as we have seen, became more open affairs. Scientific discussion also penetrated the salons, like that of Madame de la Sablière. But the introduction of an element of 'galanterie', and the presence of nobles and women, dissipated the atmosphere of scholarship, learning giving way to manners.[66] With the accession of Louis XIV who held in suspicion all private gatherings, the space of critical belief, as it had been organised in the first half of the seventeenth century, would never reconstitute itself in quite the same way.

---

[61] F. Charles-Daubert, 'Le Libertinage érudit', in H. Méchoulan (ed.), *L'Etat baroque: regards sur la pensée de la France du premier XVIIe siècle* (Paris, 1985), 185.
[62] Ibid., 183.   [63] Ibid., 194.   [64] Ibid., 186–7.
[65] Pintard, *Le Libertinage érudit*, p. 548.
[66] Ibid., pp. 432–3.

The space of *libertinage* was at one and the same time simple and complex. It was held to be the enemy of faith through an amalgam sincerely or cunningly constructed by those who regarded themselves as the guardians of the strictest orthodoxy from which under no circumstances was it legitimate to depart. *Libertins* exiled themselves from the space of orthodoxy either through their outrageous behaviour, be it sexual or blasphemous, or through their unwillingness to accept uncritically all the beliefs that unconditional adherence to the space of orthodoxy implied. The 'wanderers' did not last long, and the trial and subsequent condemnation of Théophile induced a caution which was evidenced in the changed ways of his friend, the poet Saint-Amant, who ended up writing religious epic poetry.

Matters are much more complex with the narrower category of the so-called *libertins érudits* who have not always been separated from the other group. Irreligion and loose morals have often, rightly or wrongly (mostly wrongly), been associated. This group did not on the whole exhibit its personal views openly and members created for themselves a space where they could discuss with like minds their hesitations about, and criticisms of, religious and, sometimes, political orthodoxy. In doing so, they satisfied their desire for an inner space of independent thought free from the constraints of institutions, free from intellectual authority. Their sense of conscience did not, as in the space of Protestantism, require an open organisation. They were freethinkers but not dissidents (nor were Protestants), and the private nature of much of their intellectual existence prevented it from constituting a universal theory of freedom of thought. The elaboration of the latter is surely the true mark of the modern intellectual. From the point of view of the state, *libertinage érudit* could not be considered a space of hostility. But that, for many in the Church, was precisely one of its problems: it seemed to separate ideas from religion. In refusing an adherence to the Church from a position of unconditional belief and in regarding religion as a necessity in the state from the point of view of order, it denied the Church as the source of its own authority. It was instrumental in a secular programme. For the Church such a position could not be more hostile.

Atheism

Atheism is quite simply unbelief, and the behaviour of atheists, reflecting their unbelief, will of necessity be sinful and debauched. Such might be the position of the Christian apologist like Garasse who adheres to the strictest version of orthodoxy as it became defined in the seventeenth century. The atheist's exclusion from the space of orthodoxy is immediately apparent from his behaviour. He is a visible sign of his own exclusion. Such a simplistic and straightforward view was not destined to survive the seventeenth century. Atheism, like *libertinage*, is a problem of definition. The contemporary components of atheism included the diminution of the role of God in the creation, a belief in the spontaneous generation or the eternity of matter, and the denial of Christ's miracles as natural phenomena. Atheism might be attached to one or more of these components although, as Nicholas Davidson remarks, holding one or more of these positions would not necessarily preclude belief in the existence of some sort of God.[67] Atheism, like *libertinage* (the two sometimes go together in our period), confer a spurious unity on a range of heterodox ideas.

The problem of atheism is further compounded by the question whether an atheist could in reality exist in the early modern period. Lucien Febvre thought for example that the conceptual tools for such a position were simply not available. The deviations from orthodox belief which could be found did not resemble atheism in the modern sense. More recently, A. C. Kors has argued that atheism was the creation of or was given credibility by theologians themselves, irrespective of the existence of real atheists. But a considerable body of thought has now emerged which challenges the idea of atheism as the figment of the theologian's imagination and which actively encourages us to think of atheism as a real phenomenon in sixteenth- and seventeenth-century Europe, especially in Italy where all the problems surrounding atheism were discussed extensively in print.

For many orthodox theologians in France, atheism represented a position which was intrinsically absurd: it was no more than an aberration within the space of belief possessing no real content at the level of ideas. There was widespread insistence that sincere atheistic belief was an impossibility because persuasion of the existence of God was: 'an "instinct" in all men, a "light independent of their reason", which was why it could be universal even among the unlettered; it was so irrefutably demonstrable'.[68] Atheism was thus a perverted act of will, not a belief as such. Hence the emphasis placed by so many commentators on the immoral behaviour from which they inferred 'atheism': comportment was the external sign of this willed unbelief and was influential because it 'was deemed to give rise to objections, doubts, and ways of thinking that in some sense "removed" God from the world'.[69] The atheist was in other words a greater threat in his behaviour than in his ideas.[70] Paradoxically

---

[67] See N. Davidson, 'Atheism in Italy, 1500–1700', in M. Hunter and D. Wootton (eds.), *Atheism from the Reformation to the Enlightenment* (Oxford, 1992), 55–85.

[68] Kors, *Atheism in France*, p. 34.   [69] Ibid., p. 25.

[70] Ibid., p. 33.

atheists were irretrievably part of the space of belief. They could not exist outside it, even though they so placed themselves, because unbelief was simply impossible. It can only be the case that atheism constituted therefore a hostile space in the way it was perceived. Moreover, if the cause of belief and society were coterminous, then atheists, as enemies of belief, were also enemies of society, the enemy within.

At length certain developments led to the modification of the view of atheists as enemies of society by virtue of their unbelief. Pierre Bayle, in his *Pensées diverses sur la comète* (1683), was the first Frenchman to argue extensively in print that atheists could find their place in society without necessarily endangering the structure of belief by their behaviour. His arguments could perhaps have evolved only in the particular circumstances of a Protestant in exile and outside the space of Catholic orthodoxy which held to the traditional view of the atheist. In fact his defence of the atheist is very much bound up with his defence of the legitimacy of Protestantism, including a criticism of Catholic behaviour, to the extent that the two are sometimes difficult to separate absolutely. Bayle's views were not uncontroversial, nor were they welcome in his own space. Some have placed a question mark over Bayle's sincerity of belief and his treatment of atheism has contributed to the suspicion that he was inclined towards it. Certainly Jurieu, his arch-opponent, was disgusted by the leniency of his views. A more recent commentator, Kolakowski, also seems to accuse Bayle – in the way Bayle relies on a fideistic position and in his determination to list all the positions hostile to religion in his *Dictionnaire historique et critique* (1696) – of joining forces with the Renaissance sceptics and the *libertins* in encouraging impiety in the period of the Enlightenment.[71] The veracity or not of Bayle's attachment to his religion is not my immediate concern, although it seems to me that his perspective on atheism can be accommodated with the relentless logic that he brought to other discussions, notably religious tolerance.

It is interesting and unquestionably significant that Bayle should choose the superstition and fear aroused by celestial phenomena such as comets for, among other things, a discussion of atheism. Is the fear of atheism in the same way baseless? Or can we indeed talk of a homogeneous space for atheism which allows for outright condemnation without any form of distinction? Bayle shows himself to be quite aware of the traditional representation of the unbeliever. Attitudes to the atheist are determined by those who, because they willingly stifle belief in God through sheer malice, are the most debauched and determined sinners. But Bayle establishes an important difference between the abominable atheist who

---

[71] Kolakowski, *Chrétiens sans église*, pp. 277–8.

wills himself so, and the 'Athée de naissance' or the 'incredule sans dessein et de bonnes moeurs'.[72] In this case we might then ask how we proceed if atheism is not willed but simply an absence of belief. The answer is implicit rather than explicit. If, as Bayle seems to suggest, we may be born without belief, the ineluctable conclusion must be that entering the space of religion is an act of choice. Bayle's consistency is quite remarkable and audacious here, and we see why a 'just' approach to atheism could only come, initially at least, from a Protestant who affirmed the need for free assent to belief. Without justifying atheism in itself, it turns out that a certain form of atheism can be adduced to legitimise the choice of being and remaining Protestant. Bayle's tolerance has its limits, however, since he suggests at the same time that leaving the space of religion remains a perverse act of will.

What can we make of the assertion that an atheist may be 'de bonnes moeurs'? What consequences does this possibility have in the context of belief? Is immoral behaviour a necessary corollary of unbelief? Bayle compares the atheist to the idolater. Before affirming anything of atheistic societies whose customs we know little about (as we shall see, not at all the case), we must say that idolaters could have committed all the crimes that have been imputed to atheists.[73] In other words, immoral behaviour is not exclusive to atheists. In a sense, we might think that idolaters are superior to atheists in their adherence to a belief, however false. It turns out that they are not. For Bayle, not to believe in God is less outrageous than believing God to be what he is not and cannot be.[74] Moreover, the idolater, who knows but does not follow the will of his god or gods, will be more severely punished than the atheist ignorant of any divinity.[75] The example of the idolater may not be all that sound, but the atheist none the less emerges well from the comparison. It removes the absoluteness from the argument. It might be added that no reference to idolaters could possibly be innocent in the confessional context of seventeenth-century Europe.

Bayle in fact launches a frontal assault in the *Pensées diverses sur la comète* on the correlation between immoral behaviour and unbelief, and brings the argument nearer home. A visitor from another world who observed the actions of Christians would conclude after a short time that 'on ne se conduit pas selon les lumières de la conscience'.[76] This must be a clear reference to the *dragonnades*. Christians who fail to live in accordance with the principles of their religion cannot at the same time be charged with a lack of conviction in respect of the mysteries of their faith, as perhaps in the case of idolaters, since that would simply increase the number of

---

[72] Bayle, *Pensées diverses*, II, 121–2.   [73] Ibid., I, 337.
[74] Ibid., p. 307.   [75] Ibid., p. 311.   [76] Ibid., II, 8–9.

hidden atheists: 'qu'y a-t-il de plus insoûtenable que de ranger parmi les Athées tous ces soldats chrétiens qui commettent des desordres inouïs ...?'[77] If such actions, by implication, take place within the space of belief and in the name of belief, and are not the work of atheists, the deterministic correlation between immoral behaviour and unbelief does not apply. The logic of Bayle in defence of the behaviour of atheists thus rests on actions within the space of belief. The actions of Catholics now imply a defence of the behaviour of atheists.

If it is true that crimes are not a necessary consequence of atheism and can be committed by believing Christians, then good does not necessarily follow from knowledge of God. Bayle almost offers a 'naturalist' rather than a cultural, much less a religious, explanation of our behaviour in society when he argues that, if good is the result of our temperament strengthened by education and self-interest, then this is true of atheists as well as of others: 'Ainsi nous n'avons aucun droit de soûtenir, qu'un Athée doit être nécessairement plus déreiglé qu'un Idolâtre.'[78] The passion predominating at any given moment determines our actions. Debauchery does not depend on opinions concerning the nature of God, but on the corruption of our body and on the pleasure we find in 'l'usage des voluptez'.[79]

What do we in fact find if we look at the behaviour of atheists? Since we have no record of the mores and customs of an atheist nation, we cannot refute a priori the conjecture, in any case uncertain, that atheists are incapable of moral virtue and / or that they are at the level of beasts.[80] Hypothetically, then, in the same way that ignorance of God would not prevent members of such a society from experiencing the passions common to all men, we would find among atheists those of good faith in commerce, those who would help the poor, stand up against injustice, be faithful friends, renounce the pleasures of the flesh and do no harm to anybody.[81] This is so of individuals in the past: not all atheist pagans were distinguished by their debauched actions, nor were the Sadducees who denied the immortality of the soul.[82] Nor is debauchery at the origin of heresy. Indeed, Bayle throws doubt on the possibility of isolating atheists in space, a tendency we have observed with the likes of Garasse, when he asserts that 'ceux qui ont l'esprit d'incrédulité en partage, et qui se piquent de douter avec raison, se soucient peu du cabaret'.[83]

Moving one stage further, Bayle doubts that religion is sufficient in society to remedy on its own the effects of vice.[84] Otherwise, how could it be that Christians, who are aware that happiness depends on the

---

[77] Ibid., p. 18.   [78] Ibid., p. 36.
[79] Ibid., p. 33.   [80] Ibid., p. 36.   [81] Ibid., p. 103.
[82] Ibid., p. 108.   [83] Ibid., p. 116.   [84] Ibid., I, 342–3.

renunciation of vice and who have so many excellent preachers, so many directors of conscience and books of devotion to exhort them to virtue, can still live in such dissolution?[85] The members of any society are regulated by civil laws. There is nothing to suggest that other societies would be regulated any differently, so that a society of atheists would resemble a society of pagans on the level of mores and social action: the rule of law would in both cases be necessary to punish crime.[86] In this way, 'l'Athéisme n'est pas l'origine de la méchanceté'.[87]

The first conclusion to draw from this presentation of Bayle's opinions on atheism is that atheists are not instantly recognisable from their behaviour, so that, unless they have made an open confession of their unbelief, they may very well be integrated in a variety of ways within the space of orthodoxy. On the basis of behaviour alone Christians and atheists cannot be told apart. The space of society can be defined as homogeneous without the need to refer to religion, and certainly not to a single religion. A further implication is that, even if atheists declare themselves to be so, society itself, as an organised entity, is not at risk. Atheists are just as capable as others of defending the integrity and justice attaching to social space, especially in view of the fact that the law is, in preventing or punishing crime, more effective than religion. Bayle again separates the space of orthodoxy from the space of society. It is possible to live properly in the latter yet reject the former. Bayle does not seem to be concerned that unbelief can 'set a bad example', and this is primarily because Catholic behaviour in the conversion of Protestants does not itself set a good example. Atheists do not persecute those who hold other beliefs. The space of unbelief need not therefore be worse than the space of belief. The worst conclusion from the point of view of orthodoxy is that, according to Bayle, a Godless but ordered society is possible. At the very least the space of society for Bayle is one of diversity, and, beyond that diversity, almost as a consequence of it, one which is held together by a common adherence to the secular power which guarantees the freedom of belief, or unbelief, of those who occupy it. From Bayle's confessional point of view, his argument is of the most supreme importance for Protestants, even at the price of the tolerance of atheism within the space of religion, for if unbelievers are acceptable, so must believers be, despite their difference.

Another development occurred in the context of atheism which considerably influenced attitudes to unbelief. A. C. Kors has produced an excellent analysis of the way in which the detailed refutation of atheistic propositions created a space of unbelief. The idea of atheism as a possible

---

[85] Ibid., II, 13.   [86] Ibid., pp. 77–8.   [87] Ibid., p. 40.

and conceivable position, absolutely denied by theologians, eventually came to represent a greater threat than the behaviour of so-called atheists. The starting point for many theologians, we remember, was that atheism constituted an aberration in that it was willed unbelief in the face of all that revealed God. The foundation of the theologians' assertion that atheism could never be a sound position to hold is that of universal consent to the existence of God. God was manifest in the exterior world and to the senses (an argument Pascal was careful to avoid in his own apologetics), and was internally manifest to the mind or soul. How could the existence of God be denied when all men believed it and when all things taught it? If the atheist could deny such things: 'to imagine him, one would have to imagine alternative explanations for putative universal consent'.[88]

Universal consent as morally persuasive faced a number of challenges, not least in the discovery of atheistic peoples recounted, from the sixteenth century and early in the seventeenth, in the reports of travellers, hence the disingenuous nature of the remarks of Bayle I quoted earlier. Examples of atheism among the Canadian Indians and the Turks were crowned by accounts of the Siamese in 1678, 1688 and 1691. Real geographical knowledge thus led to a modification of the geography of knowledge. Perhaps the most striking example illustrating the possibility of conceiving of an atheistic society was China. China in fact became a battleground within the space of orthodoxy in the controversy over Chinese rites, when the Jesuits were accused of making concessions to or accommodating certain indigenous practices with Christian worship in order to secure more easily the conversion of the Chinese people. The argument turned on whether Confucianism could be determined as atheistic or not. The Dominicans believed that it could, an opinion supported by the Church in Rome and the Faculty of Theology. The Jesuits took the opposite line, asserting that Confucianism revealed a concept of the deity. One of their number, Le Comte, attempted a reconciliation of the two positions and warned that, if Confucianism was condemned, the argument from universal consent would be in grave danger. The warning was not heeded. Le Comte was censured by the Faculty, and Louis XIV removed him from his post as confessor to the duchesse de Bourgogne.[89]

The importance of the dispute was that public attention was alerted to the idea that a society of atheists could exist. Between 1660 and 1714 more than 130 books were published on the subject in France alone, and this number does not include illegal imports from Amsterdam and Cologne. Unintentionally, therefore, the reading public was regaled with

[88] Kors, *Atheism in France*, pp. 74–5.   [89] Ibid., p. 172.

subversive views of atheism and educated minds were, on a wider scale than hitherto, introduced to its 'thinkability':

In the heat of the polemic . . . positions lost their nuances, and a concert of voices insisted that what most educated French took to be the most learned minds of the most civilized nation outside Europe were 'atheists' pure and simple . . . Its own Church would come to insist that this was not a theoretical possibility, but a historical fact. If one accepted the widely circulated view of the excellence of Confucian ethics and the official determination by both Rome and the Faculty of Theology at Paris that Confucianism was atheistic, this conclusion followed ineluctably.[90]

Discussion within the Church publicly created a habitable space outside it.

The Church's case against atheism as conceivable did not rest solely on the notion of universal consent. The Church held that the existence of God could be demonstrated by argument. Despite quite respectable medieval theologians advancing arguments contrary to the official view, the eighth session of the Fifth Lateran Council of 1513 declared that 'knowledge of the existence of God, while it could be legitimately derived from faith alone, did not depend on faith alone'. In France, this was upheld explicitly by the Faculty of Theology.[91] Proofs of God thus constituted a 'preamble' to the faith. Moreover, belief in God was also part of the preamble to the faith and not an article of faith since 'belief in a God who revealed was logically prior and in that sense prefatory to belief in the content of revelation'. Bernard Lamy claimed that 'to believe by faith that God exists would be to accept the word of a being whom you did not yet know to exist, which would be absurd'.[92]

In this perspective it rapidly becomes clear that arguments surrounding the problem of atheism could not ultimately be separated from the philosophical and theological controversies in respect of ideas. Whether the preamble to the faith was convincing or not came to rest on an attachment to one philosophical tradition or another. The traditional teaching on the validity of sense-data as a starting point acted as a natural focus for debate since demonstrations according to natural lights – and this demonstrability must obviously be evident in the natural world – were considered by the Church as compelling and therefore a matter of faith. Philosophical proofs had a central place in the intellectual presentation of belief, one 'that, ironically, would contribute mightily to the possibility of atheistic belief'.[93]

This was so for a number of reasons. The central place of philosophical

[90] Ibid., p. 162.   [91] Ibid., pp. 115–16.   [92] Ibid., p. 125.   [93] Ibid., pp. 117–18.

arguments raised the possibility of disagreement on the validity and strength of the different arguments available, since they were subject to objections and doubt. Not having the right and compelling arguments meant implicitly that one might as well be a speculative atheist.[94] The problem was compounded by those, like Campanella, who exposed the objections of atheism and replied to them only weakly, the worst of all worlds. The strength of the Christian position depended in these circumstances, not on the compelling nature of the arguments in their most general terms, but on human skill in deploying them.

The absolute nature of contrary positions in the domain of Christian philosophy did not help either. The mood was not one of overwhelming mutual support. Lamy produced four atheistic objections: there can be no unproduced first being; there were only material beings, and matter was eternal and necessary; the first cause necessary to physics is nature; and educated Chinese believed matter to be eternal. He added that only Cartesian philosophy could provide efficacious replies to these objections while Aristotelianism would be helpless in the face of them.[95] The debate involved two conflicting visions of philosophical language, conception and demonstration, and arguments over which of them was the most appropriate to the cause.[96]

The major difficulty is in fact a familiar one, the association of Christian apologetics with Thomism / Aristotelianism and reliance on the primacy of sense-data. Bérulle's enthusiasm for Descartes may have lain in his realisation that the philosopher advanced a 'sounder' alternative, and an Augustinian one at that. Descartes offered three proofs of God's existence which were necessarily prior to proof of the existence of the external world. Descartes's position that knowledge of what God was had to precede knowledge that God was might be regarded as reasonable, especially since it had the authority of St Augustine behind it.[97] Moreover, Desgabets, a pupil of Descartes, taught that a posteriori proofs could never convince a rigorous atheist since such proofs or demonstrations presupposed the reliability of the senses and the induction on which they depended.[98] Descartes's philosophy provided therefore a perfect solution. The weaknesses of Cartesianism on the other hand were variously listed as the difficulties encountered in Cartesian physics over the Eucharist, and the suggestion that demonstration should proceed from methodological doubt to conviction by clear and distinct ideas. The problem here was that the Christian was called upon to suspend belief in God while awaiting the outcome of the demonstration. Others rejected the idea that during this suspension of belief Descartes could have recourse to proof of God from

[94] Ibid., p. 294.   [95] Ibid., p. 105.   [96] Ibid., p. 269.   [97] Ibid., p. 338.   [98] Ibid., p. 344.

the idea of the infinite in view of 'the manifest inadequacy of any human conception of the infinite to be a source of any certain consequence',[99] a position shared by Pascal and Malebranche.

Refutations of atheism thus moved firmly into the space of dissension. In the Cartesian / Aristotelian debates that ensued, Jesuits fought Oratorians or Benedictines; the University of Paris came up against provincial universities, or groups of philosophers and thinkers who did not belong to any institution.[100] The consequences of the debate over atheism for the Church were thus enormous. Who needed freethinkers when each side, with the same aim in view, was so convincingly refuting the arguments of the other?[101] Before the largest reading public the Western world had ever seen: 'the refutations employed or indeed generated by that great fratricide became the preamble of early-modern atheism in France'. Atheism could not have emerged 'without a belief that the demonstrations arrayed against it were not compelling'.[102] If the demonstrations of God were not compelling for Christians, who were they compelling for? The collapse of the space of orthodoxy in the face of the refutation of challenges to it seemed to be complete when the five ways of St Thomas himself were all regarded, at least by some who rejected even a priori proofs, as vulnerable to refutation themselves. The situation was reached where a theologian, the abbé Armand de Grérard, could, in 1680, only offer St Thomas's arguments as illustration for those who already believed, asserting at the same time that 'both Aristotelian Scholasticism and Cartesian innovation stood condemned by their manifest inabilities to prove the God known by authority'.[103]

One other major contribution to the 'thinkability' of atheism emerged however in the pedagogical system which was supposed to equip future apologists with the arguments necessary to defend the faith. Aquinas's imagined objections to his own demonstrations, themselves based on the Fathers' study of Greek philosophy, had the effect of offering 'the essential portrait of the hypothetical atheist'. Of course, Aquinas had inherited from Aristotle recognition of the need to anticipate the fullest objections to one's own position. This was all right in the thirteenth century, before the age of the printed word when one was talking to a few theologians who might possibly come into contact with the non-Christian world and require a stock of natural arguments to deal with it. The portrait offered by Aquinas assumed rather different consequences in a world containing new schools of thought and new information on non-European societies.[104] The process of argumentation in the schools and universities became a subject of criticism in some quarters. Spanheim,

[99] Ibid., p. 311.   [100] Ibid., p. 266.
[101] Ibid., p. 356.   [102] Ibid., p. 262.   [103] Ibid., p. 372.   [104] Ibid., pp. 106–7.

Brandenburgan ambassador to France in the second half of the century, thought that school exercises were themselves responsible for the production of real atheists since disputation has two sides. It was possible that the feigned arguments of unbelief were found by some to be more convincing than what was supposed to be the right answer.[105] Most important of all, perhaps, was that, with greater access to information, all who passed through higher education, all who read works of formal theology and philosophy, either in their learned or vulgarised form, were able to familiarise themselves with the arguments of the theoretical atheist.[106] Education was a double-edged sword.

But knowledge of the atheist was not confined to the world of education and there can be no doubt concerning the wealth of information available to the 'general public'. Many alternatives, not to say contradictions, of the official perspective were contained in books, such as classical and patristic works, which were by no means esoteric for the learned culture of the period.[107] These texts were more or less explicit in the ways they dealt with atheism. The works of the Fathers more than hinted that atheism was widespread in the ancient world.[108] Another genre of increasing importance, found particularly in English and German culture, was the history of atheistic thought. Thomas Stanley's *History of Philosophy* was known in France and a Latin translation of the work could easily be procured.[109] Above all, the last third of the seventeenth century saw an increase in travel literature, especially regarding the French colonies, which gave an account of very different sorts of societies where the absence of the Christian religion did not lead to cruelty or the decomposition of society. On the contrary such accounts stressed the sense of fraternity and equality among these peoples and the 'republican' nature of their social organisation. Wade claims that the travel literature of this period, in whatever form it took, prepared 'for a reform of man through knowledge of man in a medium where free-thinking is more understandable than systematic philosophy'.[110]

In view of all this, serious questions could be asked about the official view of atheism. If belief in the existence of God was so compelling, and if its denial was an act of will and not an act of mind, why did we need so many books to refute it? And if it were answered that such a plethora of apologetics was necessary to anticipate atheistic objection to Christian belief in the less learned and to 'strengthen shaken minds', or to convince the learned too, the retort might be: 'What "shaken minds", if the etiology of atheism were in the will alone? What "doubts", let alone what "positive

---

[105] Ibid., p. 67.
[106] Ibid., p. 107.   [107] Ibid., p. 197.   [108] Ibid., p. 193.   [109] Ibid., p. 230.
[110] Wade, *The Intellectual Origins*, p. 391.

and confirmed doubts", if belief in God were so ineradicable that it required a positive action of perversity to cast any shadow on it at all?'[111] It might also be asked why, if all these things are the case, the concept of the speculative atheist was needed in the first place. If the objections of the atheist were inane, why take them seriously?

In any consideration of the space of unbelief one therefore has to start from whether or how it existed. Historians are now prepared to argue that real atheists, both learned and less learned, could be found in European society from at least the sixteenth century, although the extent of unbelief will never accurately be established. The space of unbelief must also be looked at from the point of view of contemporaries, especially from that of Christian apologists in the new aggressive era of the Counter-Reformation when the Church was attempting to impose a strict version of orthodoxy as defined by the Council of Trent. For these Christian thinkers, utterly convinced of their own positions and persuaded that they were the only positions, atheism as a reality was in the most literal sense 'unthinkable'. The space of unbelief could simply not exist.

But, as we have already observed, the identity of the space of belief could emerge fully only in relation to another or an 'other'. Kors is surely right to claim that:

Early-modern thinkers who denied that there could be any genuine 'speculative' atheists knew that there nonetheless had to be an 'atheism' in the form of atheistic argumentation, whether or not there were any minds who actually held to or proselytized for such a point of view. It did not require an atheistic mind to conceive of an atheistic objection to claims of theistic proof. If atheism in that sense did not exist, the members of the learned world would have had to invent it.[112]

The speculative atheist was transformed into 'an intelligent, sincere thinker as yet unconvinced by such proofs or unable to overcome specific objections to them'.[113]

One of the conclusions of this discussion of atheism is that the guardians of the space of belief imported into that space the elements which would provide the basis for the establishment of a more extended space of unbelief. Where unbelief had perhaps been sporadic, it could now become more widespread with the increased attention given to atheistic argument and with the ever-growing number of works which created a systematic look to atheistic thought. That systematicity was brought about by the need to provide the foundation of systematic belief. Educational establishments encouraged this through their methodology.

[111] Kors, *Atheism in France*, pp. 42–3.
[112] Ibid., p. 81.
[113] Ibid., p. 62.

In putting pupils or students in the position of adopting the stance of the other in such a convincing fashion that the replies would be more convincing still, one ended up creating 'others'. Establishments whose primary purpose, within the space of belief, was to strengthen Christianity thereby helped to weaken it. This led to another expression of the paradox Kors explores, namely that 'a believing culture generates its own antithesis, disbelief in the principles of its own belief'.[114] Affirmation of the space of belief required the creation of a space of unbelief, in the same way that a construction of a space of *libertinage* was necessary for a clarification of the frontiers of the space of orthodoxy.

There can be no argument that atheism, however it may have existed or been created, remains, from the point of view of belief, a space of hostility. Atheism and atheists of necessity undermined faith because they offered an alternative to the space of belief. They advanced the cause of another 'habitable' world. The space of unbelief, however, lost some of its force as a space of hostility in the light of the disputes which raged over the best way to defeat it. The hostility within the space of belief, the space of dissension I have explored in another part of this study, failed to provide an adequate example of living in a harmony the atheist and the *libertin* were supposed to destroy.

Deism

In a sense there is a clarity about atheism which is intellectually comforting one way or the other. Atheism simply denies the existence of a deity and theology ceases to exist as an important agency in the direction of human life. The atheist is thus spared the problems involved in facing different definitions of the grounds for belief. Equally, believers have a 'simple' position against which they can argue. Unbelief is unacceptable, and this can still be a gut reaction even in the face of the failure of others to provide a sufficiently convincing rationale for it. Deism is a different matter, for its proponents accept the existence of a deity but deny any divine intervention in human action or, after the creation of the universe, in the material world. Why should deism, then, be included among the spaces of hostility?

The first reason is that deists are vehemently opposed to the consequences that organised religion have for the organisation of human life, especially in the area of individual conscience. Theirs is therefore a position of arguing against. This does not exclude a homogeneous space in questions of belief, for deism is composed of a much reduced structure

[114] Ibid., p. 79.

of belief which can only be seen as encouraging homogeneity. What deists oppose is a space of orthodoxy imposed by authority. The second reason is that, while deists do not deny the existence of God, those who oppose them argue that their simplification of belief is likely to lead to irreligion or at least to indifference to religion, which for them comes to the same thing. Deists are therefore weak defenders of belief in the struggle against unbelief. The third reason is the deists' emphasis on a view of human reason which excludes the sort of speculation at the root of theological controversy. The fourth reason is that many deist views were articulated through accounts of non-Christian societies.

It is really in the last third of the seventeenth century that metaphysical rationalism was identified as a threat since, as Christopher Betts remarks, 'in the mid-century free-thought of any kind is rare, more so than for many years before or after'.[115] Indeed in the second half of the century deism was more common than atheism as a term describing certain types of heterodox belief, although there are works earlier in the century which can be identified as deist in nature.[116] As with atheism the content of the term is unclear and the positions of those who were 'anti-deist' equally so. It might seem strange that Mersenne who denounced the first 'deistic' poem in French should have regarded at all favourably Herbert of Cherbury, generally regarded as the first of the English deists. Even at the end of the century, works of rationalist Catholic writers appear not to have been tarred with the deist brush. Contemporary accounts, albeit without much supporting evidence, suggest that: 'there was an unidentified body of opinion resembling Enlightenment deism in the 1620s, but it was not then called deism. Conversely, the author of the *Anti-bigot*, who does call himself a deist, professes views which seem typical of early seventeenth-century free-thought, but are not much like the deism of the Enlightenment.'[117]

So what was the typical content of deism? It emphasised a secular perspective, a morality based on reason, an indifference to doctrine and hostility to the Christian religion.[118] In general terms, Bossuet regarded deism and anti-trinitarianism as one and the same thing,[119] which also explains his hostility to Simon's use of Socinian biblical exegesis. Needless to say, deism, recognised as subversive and dangerous, was used as a pejorative term, especially since it also smacked of anti-clericalism.[120] These component elements were in fact articulated in a number of utopias towards the end of our period, and I propose to look briefly at two of them.

---

[115] C. J. Betts, *Early Deism in France from the So-called 'déistes' of Lyon (1564) to Voltaire's Lettres Philosophiques (1734)* (The Hague, 1984), p. 33.
[116] Ibid., p. 55.   [117] Ibid., pp. 27–9.   [118] See ibid., p. 57.   [119] Ibid., p. 90.
[120] Ibid., p. 139.

The first, *La Terre australe connue*, is by Gabriel de Foigny and dates from 1676; the second, *Histoire de Calejava: ou De l'Isle des hommes raisonnables*, was written by Claude Gilbert in 1700. The latter received his education from the Jesuits in Dijon and the former, who had entered the order of the Cordeliers de l'Observance, seems to have led an uncertain spiritual life between Catholicism and Protestantism to the end of his days.

Of particular note in these utopias is the space given, especially in Gilbert, to reason. One of his characters underlines the need for belief in God, the immortality of the soul and the penalties and rewards of an after-life, but this belief must be founded on 'raisons solides et naturelles' and not on reasons of authority.[121] Belief, it is suggested, must be intellectually grounded and based on free assent. Echoing the opening statement of Descartes's *Discours de la méthode* concerning the possession of reason by all men, Gilbert asserts that 'il n'est difficile de trouver un esprit qui ne se puisse pas gouverner par lui-même avec un plus ou moins de peine'.[122] Indeed clearness and 'évidence' in the Cartesian sense occur frequently in the text. The Gospel, equated with natural law, accords too with the dictates of reason rather than simply being a revealed text which must be taken on its own authority.[123] The Gospel is subject to assent, not simply to belief.

The importance of reason is substantiated further when other religions or belief systems are taken into account. Gilbert's Avaïtes are a non-Christian community who live according to the precepts of a morality to which one can take no exception, and Foigny's Australians are even, implicitly, morally superior despite not having been enlightened by the grace of God.[124] Reason is also, as a divine gift, above the 'vaines institutions de l'homme'.[125] It is clearly at this point that we can see the erosion of differences between men since reason provides us with the principle of universality which transcends religious differences. The division between different sorts of spaces of belief, especially as determined by the space of Christian orthodoxy, dissolves. Christians might say that Moslems are profoundly ignorant of Christianity and have received only the rules of reason from God. Moslems can argue in the same way about Christians. The conclusion to draw from this is that: 'c'est à la raison, que Dieu a confié la conduite de ses créatures'.[126] The space of belief becomes the space of reason and is inclusive. For this reason, any history which identifies one people, or set of individuals, as receiving any

---

[121] C. Gilbert (ed. M.-S. Rivière), *Histoire de Calejava: ou De l'Isle des hommes raisonnables* (Exeter, 1990), p. 10.

[122] Ibid., p. 12.   [123] Ibid., p. 66.

[124] G. de Foigny (ed. P. Ronzeaud), *La Terre australe connue (1676)* (Paris, 1990), p. 98.

[125] Gilbert, *Histoire de Calejava*, p. 15.

[126] Ibid., p. 16.

special protection from God must be regarded as false.[127] In addition, the concept of deity is in essence uncomplicated and seen only as a universal cause.[128] God is an eternal being and the prime mover of the universe.[129] As a consequence the belief system on offer here is radically simplified: articles of faith are reduced to a minimum. The one article of faith necessary for salvation is that Jesus the son of Mary is Christ or the Messiah.[130]

But the context in which this article of faith is discussed is the important thing: 'Faut-il pour une heresie nous brouiller les uns avec les autres; qu'importe à Dieu & aux hommes si Arrius croit que Jesus-Christ est fils naturel ou adoptif de Dieu?'[131] If the principle of universality is to be maintained, theological controversy as an important determinant in establishing orthodoxy becomes a disruptive force. Universality as conceived here also dispenses with the notion of heresy, and hence with orthodoxy. In Foigny's imaginary society it is a crime to expound on religion, on the Incomprehensible, for it follows that such exposition can only be undertaken 'avec beaucoup de diversité'.[132] God is treated with respect but young people are brought up to adore God without talking about him, and to believe that it is impossible to speak of his perfections without offending him: 'D'où suit qu'on pourroit dire que leur grande Religion est de ne point parler de religion.'[133]

Another consequence of this position is the reduction in importance of ceremony. The Australians believe that prayer actually offends God.[134] Gilbert's Avaïtes too are reported as investing little in prayer: they pray only for those things which it is in their own power to acquire.[135] Nor do the Avaïtes have a special place for prayer since spiritual substance has no one place. More than this, the Avaïtes are discouraged from thinking in terms of 'l'existence locale'.[136] The principle of universality requires a oneness of space. That division between the church and what surrounds it dissolves. There is no place for a priest who is different from others, especially as he has no special ceremonies to perform. God's independence places him above everything and he has no need of incense and 'sacrifices' (a common term for the Eucharist).[137]

The dissolution of the organised space of religion, from which public (and therefore official) theological speculation and division are excluded,

---

[127] Ibid., p. 40.
[128] Foigny, *La Terre australe connue*, p. 120.
[129] Gilbert, *Histoire de Calejava*, p. 22.
[130] Ibid., p. 64.
[131] Ibid.   [132] Foigny, *La Terre australe connue*, p. 119.
[133] Ibid., p. 113.   [134] Ibid., p. 127.
[135] Gilbert, *Histoire de Calejava*, p. 61.
[136] Ibid., p. 46.   [137] Ibid., p. 36.

has a further consequence, perhaps the most important of all, namely the sanctity of inner conscience, freedom within the confines of an inner space. Both our utopian texts are adamant. The prohibition of any discussion of the attributes of God means that each individual is left 'dans la liberté d'en penser ce que son esprit lui en suggere'.[138] Gilbert is also unequivocal: if we force people to act 'contre leurs sentiments ou contre leur conscience', we force them to sin and we sin ourselves; we must therefore in conscience allow individual freedom of opinion, so long as it does no harm to the state or lead to crimes against civil order.[139] This inner space is contrasted with the external features of religion when Gilbert defines baptism as being possessed of an 'interieur éclairé' by which we are able to judge our actions; we are then in a position to do 'tout ce qu'on jugera en conscience être obligé de faire aprez un bon usage de sa liberté'. That is to be, as Gilbert puts it, implicitly Christian, a state to be preferred to an exterior attachment to ceremony and 'superstition' which is 'sans réflexion & sans connaissance'.[140] This underpins even more the notion of a space of assent.

The views encountered in Foigny and Gilbert were of course more widely held by writers in the last third of the seventeenth century. D'Huisseau wished to distinguish between essential and inessential doctrine but at the same time had to come up with an answer to the objection that such a restricted version of Christianity could lead to indifference and even irreligion.[141] The importance of individual conscience is encountered in the famous manuscript of the *Militaire philosophe* (1710), in which the author regards his salvation as his own affair and not that of any authority. His entrance into the space of orthodoxy was, as a child, not his own doing, so that he feels himself free to abandon Catholicism if he finds it wanting.[142] It is a space one must not only be free to enter but free to leave without sanction.

But the significance of deist texts in the seventeenth century and their insistence on the oneness of space cannot be divorced from the pressing problems arising from the persecution of Huguenots. In this sense, as Betts notes, Gilbert's utopia 'appears as a form of wish fulfilment, an ideal, universalist religion which is compatible with the New Testament, and therefore acceptable to all Christians, but more especially Protestants'.[143] The unification of believers is only possible through the dilution of belief, through the dissolution of the frontiers between the two spaces. Hence, presumably, the dismissal of the importance of ceremony which eliminates the problem of the Eucharist.

[138] Foigny, *La Terre australe connue*, p. 119.   [139] Gilbert, *Histoire de Calejava*, p. 65.
[140] Ibid., p. 66.   [141] Betts, *Early Deism in France*, p. 76.
[142] Ibid., p. 140.   [143] Ibid., p. 127.

One cannot begin to write a section on deism, let alone end it, without saying something about Fontenelle (1657–1757). Writer of many parts, a member of the Académie française and the Académie royale des sciences of which he was secretary from 1699 to 1740, he remains a difficult character to categorise. This derives from the number of options open to thinkers at the end of the century, and from their need to adopt protective strategies in varying circumstances and uncertain times. In any case different texts of Fontenelle seem to offer different perspectives, and it is impossible here to do justice to the complexity of this interesting figure whose intellectual career stretched from the beginning of the last third of the seventeenth century to the middle of the eighteenth. One of the themes we have encountered so far in our discussion of deism is the anti-clerical stance of writers, implicit or explicit to varying degrees. This anti-clerical stance is not just a hatred of priests and religious, although one cannot exclude such feelings. It is a consequence of an intellectual attack on certain aspects of belief itself, particularly the supernatural.

It is interesting to approach this theme through the position that Fontenelle adopts in his *Histoire des oracles* (1686). This text was in fact an adaptation rather than a translation of an erudite but rather indigestible book by a Dutch doctor, Van Dale, written in 1683. The question of oracles became an important one, especially after Bossuet had stated as fact in his *Discours sur l'histoire universelle* that pagan oracles had ceased to be uttered by demons at the birth of Christ. This was not a new belief and, though not a dogmatic truth, came to constitute an integral part of belief in proving the effectiveness of divine influence on the course of history. Fontenelle's version of Van Dale's text, made much more accessible (and therefore more dangerous), was an attack on this version of events but transcends historical interpretation to embrace the status of organised religion in society.

One of the main purposes of the *Histoire* was certainly to deny the black and white, then and now picture given of the passage from the pagan world to the world of the Christian era by many Catholic thinkers. Fontenelle believes that our confidence in Christianity should be such that we should not need to avail ourselves of strategies of this sort or any other false advantage.[144] While Fontenelle seems to be defending Christianity whose credibility, he implies, should not come to depend on an erroneous version of history, separating the decline of oracles from the advent of Christianity meant that Christianity itself was deprived of the deterministic force ascribed to it by such as Bossuet. History was not directed by providence.

---

[144] B. Le Bovier de Fontenelle (ed. L. Maigron), *Histoire des oracles* (Paris, 1971), p. 5.

The real reason for arguing for the existence of oracles even after the advent of Christianity is apparent when Fontenelle explains that oracles were in decline for reasons independent of the influence of Christianity and would have in any case died out.[145] Why should this have been the case? The insolence of priests, and the trickery, falseness and obscurity of oracles themselves, would have been enough to bring oracles into disrepute even if paganism had not been superseded by the Christian religion.[146] The role of the priesthood in pagan times was of course underpinned by the disposition of humanity to believe. Give me half a dozen people, he says: if I can persuade them that daylight is not the result of the sun's rays, I would expect to be able to get whole nations to adopt the same view: 'Quelque ridicule que soit une pensée, il ne faut que trouver moyen de la maintenir pendant quelque temps, la voilà qui devienne ancienne, et elle est suffisamment prouvée.'[147] Chapters XII and XIII of the *Histoire* list all the ways that priests (pagan, of course) have played on people's credulity. He then asks a telling question: 'si les Prestres ont si bien fourbé pendant quatre cents ans, pourquoy ne l'ont-ils toûjours fait?'[148] The adverb 'toûjours' could of course refer to the time-span before the cessation of oracles. It doesn't however need an enormous shift of the imagination to make the adverb refer to the future as well, when it can be made to reflect on the organised religion and belief system of Christianity.

If we accept the possibility that emerges from Fontenelle's account, namely that what is true of paganism can be true of any religion, a number of obvious conclusions can be drawn. The space of orthodoxy is a space of power or abuse of power through the agency of belief. If the priests of paganism exploit the gullibility of their flock, why should this not be the case with other religions? Such a position inevitably leads to the question: what special status is possessed by Christianity which excludes it from similar considerations? If we cannot so exclude it, why should it have such an exclusive right to occupy the space? The more compelling conclusion concerns the long-term future of Christianity itself: if paganism died of its own accord, thus suggesting that Christianity did not necessarily have the telling effect that has traditionally been thought, why should the same thing not happen to Christianity? Are religions therefore to be analysed not in respect of their foundation in one truth or another, but in respect of the evolution of mankind? As Alain Niderst remarks: 's'il existe en ce domaine un progrès, c'est le progrès même de la raison'.[149] In that sense, any religion at all is denied special status. Fontenelle's position seems therefore one of hostility to belief.

[145] Ibid., pp. 179–80.   [146] Ibid., p. 196.   [147] Ibid., pp. 97–8.   [148] Ibid., p. 146.
[149] A. Niderst, *Fontenelle à la recherche de lui-même, 1657–1702* (Paris, 1972), pp. 295–6.

The position adopted by Fontenelle in the *Histoire des oracles* is, according to Niderst, typical of a more general and later view of the relation of Christianity to myth. In Fontenelle's comparative writings on religion, he was not concerned, like some others I have mentioned in another part of this book, to ascribe an allegorical meaning to myth, but to show how a mythical status can be ascribed to Christianity.[150] This is carried over into Fontenelle's more general conception of history where he attempts a laicisation of the subject in contrast to the providentialism of Bossuet.[151]

Fontenelle's personal position in relation to religion and authority is, however, by no means clear. Even at the end of the century, and into the next, difficulties attached to the translation of alternative beliefs into behaviour. It was still necessary to negotiate a *modus vivendi* with the space. Fontenelle provides us with an example of a thinker wrestling precisely with this sort of problem. At the very least Fontenelle kept his options open, criticising the Revocation of the Edict of Nantes in the *Relation de l'Ile de Bornéo*, yet composing later a *Triomphe de la religion sous Louis le Grand*. Fontenelle was a social and intellectual 'déraciné' who simply could not discover a firm identity within the space,[152] possibly because he did not know what the precise limits of the space were. The centre was everywhere and the circumference nowhere.

The space of deism aims at maximum consensus, not through the establishment – and certainly not through the imposition – of a systematic orthodoxy, but through the recognition of, and free assent to, a small number of seemingly unexceptionable beliefs. An important aspect of deism is, furthermore, not so much the beliefs in themselves but the promotion of reason as the means by which we come to assent to them. This may be the reason why Fontenelle took refuge in science. Knowing the physical laws of the universe is a way of knowing God whose designs on the other hand are unfathomable: 'Que ce Dieu soit celui des chrétiens ou des déistes, c'est un autre problème.'[153] Such a position would not necessarily require a pronouncement on the nature of God.[154] In general terms, the emphasis has firmly shifted from the divine end of the spectrum, which is effectively emptied of its interventionist power, to the human end. Humanity is responsible for its own space without the active mediating agency of orthodox Christian belief.

Undoubtedly, as the text of Gilbert tends to show, one factor in the establishment of deism, although it took time for its true effect to be widely felt, was the influence of Cartesianism, with a particular influence coming by way of Malebranche:

---

[150] Ibid., p. 215.
[151] Ibid., p. 227.   [152] Ibid., p. 614.   [153] Ibid., p. 560.   [154] Ibid., p. 356.

Descartes's approach and ideas become an intrinsic part of a comprehensive Christian system of thought, instead of being a separate philosophical adjunct or preliminary to faith. In the apologias, although reason is ostensibly at the service of revealed truth, reason has pride of place, the universal rational truths being 'proved' first, and with greater confidence, than the particularities of Christian revelation. The early deists, after 1700, accept the basic rational truths, but reject the elaborate apparatus of proofs constructed in order to bring the Bible and Church traditions into harmony with reason. Catholic faith and the facts of the history of Christ both become liable to critical examination. The development of reason in religion means that the idea of natural religion develops simultaneously, one of the tenets of rationalism being that reason is 'la lumière naturelle'.[155]

It can only have helped these developments that Cartesianism established itself outside the strictly regulated space of orthodoxy. If Betts is right, the worst fears of Descartes's opponents seem to have materialised.

The genre of the utopia is invested with a particular importance in the sense that it can construct the idea of a homogeneous space, based on the principle of universality, from which religious controversy and organised religion have been evicted. In it the social space can exist in its own right. In addition, the sanctity of the inner space of conscience loads the dice even more on the human side, for, implicitly, adherence even to the reduced system of belief is not compulsory. A social identity has a right to autonomy. This is not to say that deist writers condoned atheism. But Gilbert at least refuses the necessary correlation of unbelief and immorality, 'car sans religion on peut vivre moralement bien'.[156] One could add that atheists are also endowed with reason, therefore they are not separated from their brethren in the organisation of society. Since the content of deist belief is slight, so is the difference between the atheist and the 'believer'. This is no doubt what led to the charge of indifferentism against deists who could quite easily accommodate atheists within whatever space of religion they constructed.

Deism is ultimately hostile to the space of orthodoxy because it dispenses with the need of the institution of the Church, especially its mediating role in moral teaching. The deists might well have paved the way in France for the 'affirmation of ordinary life' which Charles Taylor identifies as one of the driving forces of English reforming theology.[157] The Avaïtes, for example, adore God by adoring his attributes and greatness, after which they review their actions and examine their faults in order to correct themselves.[158] In all this there is no mention of external

---

[155] Betts, *Early Deism in France*, p. 77.
[156] Gilbert, *Histoire de Calejava*, p. 22.
[157] See Charles Taylor, *Sources of the Self: the Making of the Modern Identity* (Cambridge, 1989), especially pp. 211–302.
[158] Gilbert, *Histoire de Calejava*, p. 61.

moral guidance in the form of confession or penance or preaching. The Avaïtes are endowed with an internal sense of moral obligation. All men in this regard are the same. No privileged knowledge or status is claimed. It is in fact vigorously denied. Such a version of humanity unquestionably has its difficulties, since one could surely argue about the proper content of a strictly human morality. The foundation and legitimacy of values outside the space of religious orthodoxy were to become essential elements in the intellectual debate of the eighteenth century. But the sense of personal commitment in the idea of assent, so prominent in Bayle's Protestantism and the utopias, seems to have had a more crucial and lasting effect on the evolution of French society than the 'received' religion of the space of Catholic orthodoxy.

9 The space of the word

Introduction

The space of the word was truly a space in all senses. First, various powers could, in a variety of ways and to varying degrees, intervene in order to change what was on the page and between the covers. The book itself was a space which needed to be controlled. Second, the print shop where the book was produced was gradually subjected to increasing regulation in the course of the century along with all those who worked in it. Third, the wider but immediate space of the book trade, that is to say the concentration of booksellers and printers, as far as Paris was concerned mainly in the University quarter, needed to be policed. Fourth, the circulation of books in the kingdom came under close scrutiny, and fifth, attempts were made to control the entry of books from abroad. Within the overall attempts at control, Protestants were a particular target for special regulations, some of which had already been enshrined in the Edict of Nantes.

The book trade in France attracted the attention of the civil and religious authorities because royal power needed to protect itself from adverse comment both from within the kingdom and from without, and because the Church needed to protect itself from the propagation of error and heresy. These were not however separate and independent interests: many of the problems faced by both types of authority in the seventeenth century coincided with major religious polemics. The overriding concern of each was with the suppression of 'mauvais livres'. One of the major features of the history of the book in our period is the often problematic but increasingly necessary conjunction of the secular and religious spaces in terms of control. Royal power too had a stake in the maintenance of a space of orthodoxy. But this did not always work to the advantage of the Church.

The space of the word was truly all-embracing, encompassing the whole range of issues I have dealt with in this study. The space of dissension within the Church, the space of ideas and the spaces of hostility all led to the publication of works which at one time or another troubled the

262

authorities. All these spaces were therefore subject to control within the space of the word.

The spaces of printing

The space of printing in Paris had from its origins been associated with the Church. First, the vast majority of books produced at the installation of presses were religious; second, as a consequence, presses were installed in close proximity to the University. It became an aspect of the control of books in Paris that printers and booksellers (who were of course often the same person) were obliged to establish their commercial premises in the Latin quarter. This remained a requirement right into the seventeenth century. The traditional area of booksellers, still a feature of present-day Paris, was the area around the Eglise Saint-Séverin and the rue Saint-Jacques, between the Chapelle Saint-Yves and the rue des Fossés-Saint-Jacques. The rue Saint-Jacques itself housed something like seventy-one bookshops at the end of the sixteenth century, Jesuit and Jansenist booksellers later existing more or less side by side. The seat of the Confrérie des libraires et des imprimeurs was moved to the Eglise des Mathurins in 1582.

Control of printing and bookselling in geographical terms soon presented problems. An increasing demand for books placed such a strain on the official space of the word that the authorities had to concede the right to booksellers but not printers to establish themselves in other parts of the city. In fact it had been a long-standing practice for bookselling to take place outside the narrowly determined official space, especially in the Galerie du Palais, but also around Notre-Dame. After the fire of 1618 which damaged the Palais, booksellers asked that, notwithstanding the regulation confining them to the University quarter, they be allowed to continue plying their trade there. Accordingly, those who could prove their rights of occupation before 1618, and who were not at the same time printers, received authorisation to stay. This did not prevent others from implanting themselves illegally. Books were sold not only in the Palais de Justice, but in the Galeries des Merciers, the Galeries des Prisonniers and even on the steps of the Sainte-Chapelle.[1] Later La Reynie, the first lieutenant of police in Paris, had also, under force of circumstances, to extend the official space of bookselling to the rue Dauphine, and in 1686 to include the approaches to the Pont Saint-Michel and the Quai des Augustins.[2] In 1649 booksellers were forbidden to sell at fairs, one of the

---

[1] J. Duportal, *Etudes sur les livres à figures édités en France de 1601 à 1660* (Paris, 1914), p. 52.
[2] H.-J. Martin, *Livre, pouvoirs et société à Paris au XVIIe siècle, 1598–1701*, 2 vols. (Paris, 1969), II, 696.

regulations more honoured in the breach, because it had to be reiterated in 1665, 1666 and 1686.[3]

Many publishing enterprises were established near to the colleges and were positively encouraged by the Jesuits who often preferred to see them run by their former pupils. These sold or produced grammars and text-books for use in the schools. But in 1686 it was quite clearly stipulated that printers and booksellers could under no circumstances either live or set up shop inside the colleges or communities 'tant régulières que séculières, lieux prétendus privilégiés et renfermés'.[4] This did not prevent the growth of clandestine printing by tutors and pupils in the colleges. In the room of one of the former at the Collège de Cambrai the police discovered in 1701 a cache of 301 prohibited and pirated books, mostly comprising anti-Jesuit letters of Jansenist inspiration, copies of an anti-Fénelon satire, and two indecent oil-paintings. The problem was seemingly endemic in the world of education, where there grew up 'a veritable academic counter-culture' at the colleges of Navarre, Plessy and Harcourt.[5]

Colleges were not the only premises on which the authorities discovered forbidden books, which, as in the previous example, invariably included works of religious polemic. Not surprisingly, the Palais was another, but more interestingly also châteaux, including Versailles. Again, in Paris itself, one purveyor of 'mauvais livres', Joseph Huchet, stored his merchandise, pornography alongside religious works, at the personal residences of Sully and Condé.[6] In 1694 Cordelier and Jacobin monks in Lyon had managed to hoard 21,000 items.[7] Jansenist texts were stored even in one of the towers of Notre-Dame.

Controlling the space of the word was not limited to Paris. The production of 'mauvais livres', often clandestine, took place elsewhere in the kingdom. One prominent centre was Lyon, but Rouen and other cities were also involved. Indeed, in order to cover their tracks, many provincial printers put foreign places of publication, like Frankfurt or Cologne, on the title page, or published under the universal name of the fictional and ubiquitous Pierre du Marteau. Within the kingdom the authorities had some success in suppressing this activity. But one of the greatest threats was the production of 'mauvais livres' from outside which then made their way into France.

[3] E. Tromp, *Etude sur l'organisation et l'histoire de la Communauté des libraires et imprimeurs de Paris, 1618–1797* (Nimes, 1922), p. 92.

[4] Ibid., p. 89.

[5] R. Birn, 'Book Production and Censorship in France, 1700–1715', in K. E. Carpenter (ed.), *Books and Society in History* (New York, 1983), 145–71 (p. 148).

[6] Ibid., 148–9.

[7] R. Birn, 'La Contrebande et la saisie de livres à l'aube du Siècle des Lumières', *Revue d'histoire moderne et contemporaine*, 28 (1981), 158–73 (p. 163).

Jansenist and Protestant works, along with pamphlets hostile to royal policy, were imported at certain key points, a process which accelerated towards the end of the century. Pontchartrain complained at the very beginning of the eighteenth century that Champagne was the source of much seditious literature, particularly such towns and cities as Sainte-Menehould, Troyes, Vitry-le-François and Châlons. But the practice had developed much earlier during other periods of political and religious controversy. At the time of Marie de Médicis Catholic pamphlets were prepared in Paris, sent to Flanders and Bavaria, and printed at Augsburg or Ingolstadt.[8] Many imaginative ways were found to smuggle books in, to the extent that well-known personalities, whom simple guards would be reluctant to stop, themselves accompanied the books on their journey. In this way, in 1667, Monsieur de Pontchâteau managed to get a cart laden with Jansenist books into Paris through the Porte Saint-Antoine. Forbidden books were even packaged in crates of jam. Any parcel of books coming from outside the kingdom, instead of going straight to the receiver, went first to the offices of the Communauté des libraires et imprimeurs for inspection. No conception of a private space existed. Under legislation passed quite early in the century private libraries could not be sold until they had been inspected by representatives of the Communauté. The library in the secular world was officially a potential space of subversion.

The *colporteurs* both in Paris and the provinces added to the problems of controlling the space of the word. In the course of the century the authorities targeted them once they realised the potential for the wider dissemination of heterodox ideas. Those with a permit (numbers were officially at least strictly regulated) were authorised to sell ABCs, almanacs, small books of hours, and prayer books of not more than two sheets, although legislation was more flexible in the provinces. Rulings dating in fact from the time of Henri II, when it was noticed that *colporteurs* were the purveyors of works emanating from Geneva, were consistently flouted. This led to a tightening of the law in 1686 when it was recognised that the *colporteurs* were still a major source of religiously and politically seditious works of all sizes. Eventually it was not only stipulated that they should wear a distinctive badge around their neck but (in 1711) that they should also be able to read and write: they could not then plead ignorance of what they were selling.[9]

Problems of controlling circulation increased at the beginning of the

[8] C. Bellanger, J. Godechot, P. Guiral and F. Terrou (eds.), *Histoire générale de la presse française*, 5 vols. (Paris, 1969–76), II, 75.
[9] P. Brochon, *Le Livre de colportage en France depuis le XVIe siècle: sa littérature, ses lecteurs* (Paris, 1954), p. 14.

eighteenth century with the production of hand-copied, clandestine manuscripts containing ideas contrary to orthodox political and religious belief. In 1698 a search subsequent to the arrest of one carrier revealed among his papers titles such as 'La Croyance des matérialistes' and 'Doutes sur la religion proposés à Mss les Docteurs de Sorbonne'. Between 1697 and 1748, 102 treatises were circulated, 14 of these before 1710. Wade argues that the number of clandestine manuscripts actually increased with the severity of censorship between 1710 and 1740.[10] Yet the time of Pontchartrain and Bignon from 1700 is regarded by many commentators as being more severe than at any time previously in the seventeenth century.

During the century a large body of legislation was put together in order to control printing. Elements of reform, especially at the time of Colbert, included registration of printers' marks and fonts so that those who flouted the law could more easily be traced, and regulation of the sale of any printing materials. But policing the space of the word could not work without police. Who could the authorities rely on to watch over the book trade in Paris and the provinces? Between 1610 and 1618 a number of moves were made to reorganise the printers and booksellers with a view to making them more responsive to the needs of royal power. These moves culminated in 1618 in the formation of a 'chambre syndicale' of printers and booksellers (Communauté des libraires et imprimeurs), the first general regulation of printers and booksellers in the kingdom, with a syndic and *adjoints* who would be primarily responsible for controlling the activities of their peers. The régime of printing was further tightened in the second half of the century when the post of *lieutenant de police* was created and occupied by the proactive La Reynie, who had charge of the surveillance of the press in Paris, including that of the 'corps et métiers'.

The Communauté was closely watched by the crown which did not hesitate to organise the results of elections to its offices. In the provinces printers and booksellers had traditionally formed corporations and held similar functions to those which operated in Paris. The problem was that nowhere could the officers of these self-regulating bodies be relied upon to perform their responsibilities efficiently or obediently. They were reluctant to act against or inform on their peers, and, in particular cases, they followed their own religious allegiances rather than the rules of the Communauté or corporation. The difficulties of their situation in respect of their colleagues were in any case compounded by the absence throughout the century of any list of forbidden books to refer to.

Personal religious affiliation of printers and booksellers by no means

[10] Ira O. Wade, *The Clandestine Organization and Diffusion of Philosophic Ideas in France from 1700 to 1750* (Princeton, 1938), pp. 263–4.

constituted the sole reason for the wide-scale production of 'mauvais livres'. The worsening of the economic state of the trade tempted many in and outside the capital, especially in Lyon, to turn to the production of either scandalous or religiously and politically suspect works simply to make a living. Financial hard times meant looking for alternative outlets. The response of the authorities was to make drastic reductions in the number of printers. In 1667 it was ordered that the number of printers in the capital should be reduced from eighty-six to thirty. A major advance on the previous régime of censorship occurred in 1700 when a much more rigorous regulation of the industry was extended to the provinces with the census of l'Abbé Bignon, an officer of several academies and royal librarian, and the activities of his uncle, Chancellor Pontchartrain.

Church, state and censorship

Royal intervention in the regulation of the book trade was ominous in the sense that it signalled the growing interest of the secular power in a domain which traditionally, although not exclusively, was that of the religious space. Indeed, almost symbolically, the space of the word had in geographical terms already outgrown the University quarter to spread to other parts of Paris. The connection of the censorship régime with the Church had an obvious historical origin in the sort of books produced in the early years of the development of printing and bookselling. Indeed in most decrees on censorship religious heresy occupied a privileged place along with sedition and personal libel (the latter being the particular province of the *parlement*): 'the laws protected the Church, the monarchy, and the individual's reputation'.[11]

The Church's direct role in the space of the word was enshrined in statute. Under the Edict of Châteaubriand of 1551 the *parlement* could not give permission for any book until it had received approval from the Faculty of Theology. Volume IV of Fontanon's catalogue of the *Edits et ordonnances des Rois de France* of 1611 which dealt with what he significantly called 'la police sacrée' seems to indicate that no books could be printed 'sans la visitation des docteurs en théologie et prélats de France'.[12] Even in the regulations of 1618 which reformed the Parisian industry reference is made to the 'syndic et gardes de nostre dite Université', thus reinforcing the organic link of the trade with the space of the Church. Prior to the 1620s books of religious content were submitted directly to the the Faculty of Theology, by which means the Church had the authority to control its own space. Even royal power could not in

[11] D. T. Pottinger, *Censorship in France during the Ancien Régime* (Boston, 1954), p. 7.
[12] Duportal, *Etudes*, pp. 4–5.

principle allow a work to be printed which included faulty doctrine. Authors had to obtain the approval of five doctors for permission to publish to be granted. These were not necessarily official appointees: any doctor, whether an active member of the Faculty or not, could act. The system was therefore open to corruption: doctors either did not read the text properly or sold their signatures.[13] Even some of Vanini's works (he was burned, we remember, as a heretic) managed to find the necessary signatures. The Faculty also had the right to intervene after the publication of a work, or at least to register a protest, as it did more frequently after the death of Henri IV.

Almost certainly as a result of the spate of religious controversies and the disorder in the publication of religious pamphlets under the Regency, the state was no longer prepared to allow the independence of the Church to continue in the domain of printing, even for religious books, and from 1623 efforts were made by the secular authorities to take total control of the censorship régime. In 1623 it was the *conseil du Roi*, encouraged by Cardinals Richelieu and La Rochefoucauld, which appointed four official censors from among the theological doctors in order to try and impose some order on the system. The Faculty of Theology, however, along with the *parlement* which was hostile to such a monopoly, resisted vigorously, complaining that the decision constituted a slur on the intellectual capacity of all other doctors and contravened the long-standing tradition that a doctorate in theology accorded an automatic right to censure or approve books pertaining to doctrine. In any case there were too many books for only four censors to read.[14] This attempt, and another in 1624, failed. The four nominees renounced their appointment before the Faculty in full session in 1626.[15]

Royal authority returned to the charge in 1629 with the Code Michaux, article 52 of which stipulated that the manuscripts of all prospective books must be submitted first to the office of the chancellor who would then arrange for them to be examined. Enough specialists must have been available among both the secretaries of the king and the entourage of the chancellor for the required number of censors to be found. It seems also that by 1633 royal power had at last succeeded in appointing official censors for religious books from among the doctors, although a double authorisation effectively existed, since the Faculty also retained the right to approve.[16] The chancellor had clearly acted without the Faculty's

13 Martin, *Livre, pouvoirs et société*, I, 441.
14 A. Chevillier, *L'Origine de l'imprimerie de Paris* (Paris, 1694), pp. 402–3.
15 P. Mellottée, *Histoire économique de l'imprimerie*, vol. I, *L'Imprimerie sous l'Ancien Régime 1439–1789* (Paris, 1905), 54.
16 H.-J. Martin and R. Chartier (eds.), *Histoire de l'édition française*, 3 vols. (Paris, 1982–5), II, 78.

knowledge, because the Faculty later complained about three named persons having accepted the royal invitation to the detriment of their colleagues.[17] The University had in any case weakened its own position by seeking assistance from the king and the *parlement* in 1605, when it recognised its own powerlessness before the production of 'mauvais livres'.[18] The chancellor acted openly in the appointments from 1653 when the Faculty's rights of privileged access to texts, except for class text-books, officially ceased. The Faculty no longer had any independent control of the space of orthodoxy and could only make retrospective complaints once a work had been printed, a right it shared with the *parlement* and factions from among the clergy or the religious orders. But it is obvious that the system did not always work in the way it was intended. From 1625 to 1636, during the troublesome *querelle des réguliers*, over a hundred publications appeared, many of which were published not after the approval of a royal censor but after approval of one or two doctors contacted by the author or the bookseller.[19]

The transfer of powers of censorship to the secular power did not lessen the concern of royal authority for the protection of the Church. It simply reduced the authority of the Church to act on its own behalf. Article 52 of the Code Michaux stated that the law was being strengthened because of the 'introduction des mauvaises et pernicieuses doctrines', while the *arrêt du conseil* of 1662 makes reference to 'libertinage et . . . impiété'.[20] From 1678 more than half the works seized by the authorities were of a religious nature. Within the tightening up of censorship laws in France, certain aspects of religious production were given greater prominence, images meriting a specific mention. In article 23 of the statutes regulating the newly founded Communauté, the syndic and *adjoints* were especially enjoined to ensure through visits that those trades concerned with the production of images did not print or sell 'peintures dissolues'.[21] Of course the Church itself could not afford to publish works in which images did not conform to the stipulations of Trent. Even so, two breviaries published in 1654 for the diocese of Clermont contained illustrations which were not in accordance with the specifications of the Council.[22]

The Faculty of Theology nominally had other rights in the organisation

---

[17] Martin, *Livre, pouvoirs et société*, I, 442–3.
[18] M. Ventre, *L'Imprimerie et la librairie en Languedoc au dernier siècle de l'Ancien Régime, 1700–1789* (The Hague, 1958), p. 79.
[19] Martin, *Livre, pouvoirs et société*, I, 185.
[20] E. Hatin, *Manuel théorique et pratique de la liberté de la presse, 1500–1868*, 2 vols. (Paris, 1868), I, 12–13, and G. Lepreux, 'Contribution à l'histoire de l'imprimerie parisienne', *Revue des bibliothèques*, 1–2 (1910), 316–19 (pp. 317–18).
[21] Duportal, *Etudes*, p. 8.
[22] Ibid., pp. 239–40.

of the book trade, such as providing certificates of reception to the various trades, thus effectively regulating numbers, and the right to order residence within the precincts of the University. All that ceased definitively in 1686. Royal power took other steps to regulate the industry: the doubling up of trades was strictly limited (booksellers could not present themselves for vacant places of printers); the right to receive apprentice printers and the right to visit premises were accorded exclusively to the syndic and *adjoints* of the Communauté. The University had not even been consulted. In 1689 the University enumerated its grievances against the edict and demanded that its rights be restored. These included the right to visit premises, and the authority to demand of printers and binders a knowledge of Greek and Latin to be subsequently verified by the University. Another demand of the Faculty was the presence of two doctors at the opening of packages of books.[23] The University failed in its appeal. The Faculty of Theology in Paris was still sensitive to the real loss of its powers at the beginning of the eighteenth century, as is demonstrated by the title of the Jansenist Dupin's *Défense de la censure de la Faculté de Theologie de Paris du 18 octobre 1701*. But after lengthy argument and lamentation, he is forced to admit that 'les facultés n'ont point de jurisdiction'.[24] From the second half of the seventeenth century the whole process of censorship was quite simply laicised.

This process had partially begun in the sixteenth century, first when the Faculty of Theology was reduced to the control of religious books only (works of history and law were submitted to the *maîtres des requêtes*), and second through royal grant to a printer of a *privilège* which in principle represented a monopoly of production for a fixed period, but eventually acted as both a grant of monopoly and the official and superior seal of approval for publication. Increasing intervention on the part of royal power in censorship did not necessarily lead to the introduction of greater consistency in the system. The *privilège* was not in itself a guarantee that a book would not be prosecuted at some future stage. In 1641 the Faculty of Theology found itself examining Bauny's *Somme des péchés* which was already in its sixth edition. Later in the century the printing of Fénelon's *Télémaque* was interrupted despite the book having obtained a *privilège*. It was then printed clandestinely and went into twenty editions in the second half of 1699. Even the translation of the *Augustinus* appeared with a *privilège* accompanied by the approval of three Sorbonne and two Carmelite doctors. Arnauld's *Fréquente communion* received the approval

---

[23] Ch. Jourdain, *Histoire de l'Université de Paris au XVIIe et au XVIIIe siècle*, 2 vols. (Paris, 1862–6), I, 264–5.

[24] L. E. Dupin, *Défense de la censure de la Faculté de Theologie de Paris du 18 octobre 1701* (Paris, 1701), p. 561.

of twenty doctors and sixteen prelates. This inconsistency derived in itself from a more deep-seated problem in the wider space. If the institution of a tighter régime of censorship was supposed to protect the space of orthodoxy, there was a problem if the censors did not always have a clear idea of what that orthodoxy was. The space of the word reflected the confusion that reigned in so many of the other spaces I have considered. What these particular examples demonstrate yet again – and they are two of many – is that the boundaries of the space of orthodoxy could never be fixed in advance. The repressive aspects of censorship thus played their role in the definition of orthodoxy by negative – and inevitably – retrospective means.

The Faculty's relations with government did not always cause friction, and the doctors could be circumspect, even compliant, in their deliberations. One incident of note, recounted in the memoirs of the Jansenist sympathiser Hermant, was the discussion in 1638 focusing on Séguenot's *Sainte virginité*, a work in favour of contrition which reflected the Jansenist position on moral teaching, which conflicted with Richelieu's preference for attrition and which apparently disturbed the king's sleep. The Faculty decided therefore to examine the work. Bishops were sent from the Court in order to ensure that the final decision conformed to the official view of the Church. What is important here is the invasion of royal power, through the agency of the Church itself, of the space of the Church as represented by the Faculty of Theology. The Faculty on this occasion was not in fact beneath currying favour with Richelieu and sought approval of its decision by sending a letter to the cardinal conveying, in Hermant's words, 'des marques honteuses de sa servitude'.[25] Hermant, admittedly biased, regarded the Faculty as in the pocket of the cardinal, which perhaps demonstrates the atmosphere in which royal censors might be appointed from among its ranks. The Faculty was not an homogeneous space in itself. Its independence could also sometimes be called into question.

Heterogeneity in the space of the Church is reflected in the various examples of censorship surrounding bishops who, given their particular status, could within certain limits avail themselves of a good deal of independence. Matters of censorship in seventeenth-century France were to reveal the nature of those limits. Another incident recounted by Hermant turned out retrospectively to be of rather special significance. Jean-Pierre Camus produced a translation of St Augustine's work on monastic life which had to be withdrawn after a ruling of the *conseil du Roi*.[26] Camus was bishop of Belley, and it became increasingly clear over

[25] G. Hermant (ed. A. Gazier), *Mémoires de Godefroi Hermant sur l'histoire ecclésiastique du XVIIe siècle, 1630–1663*, 6 vols. (Paris, 1905–10), I, 157–9.   [26] Ibid., p. 60.

the following years that the status of bishop was no protection in the space of the word. Certainly, a number of cases were allied to circumstance, like that of Fénelon whose flirtation with quietism and with an oppositional circle to the king earned him a special place in the demonology of the régime. In 1698 Pontchartrain, on learning that Fénelon's *Nouvelles lettres* had been published in Brussels, ordered that all booksellers should be searched for copies and indeed 1,000 were discovered. The king however ordered that the seizures should cease 'n'estimant pas qu'on doive empêcher l'archevêque de Cambrai d'écrire pendant que les autres prélats le font'. This indulgence did not last for long because a few months later Fénelon's correspondence was seized. In 1704 the *lieutenant de police*, d'Argenson, prevented the circulation of one of Fénelon's pastoral letters. Pontchartrain congratulated d'Argenson, not on the grounds of recognising defective doctrine, but because the letter had been circulated outside the diocese without permission.[27] Fénelon had exceeded the limits of his own space.

In the beginning of the century bishops had complete freedom in the publication of missals, breviaries and catechisms for use in their own dioceses, something also true of religious orders and congregations. Bishops also had the power to censure books in their pastoral letters, but such condemnations could give rise to 'appels comme d'abus' in which the civil power could intervene in ecclesiastical affairs.[28] In 1686 the publications of bishops were brought into the general régime of censorship by the order that all books or printed productions should bear the name and provenance of the printer, a practice which had seemed unnecessary in the dioceses.[29] Another call to order had occurred earlier in the century when, in his letters published without a *privilège*, the Cardinal d'Ossat revealed delicate negotiations of the time of Henri IV. He was reminded that all authors had to submit to ordinary legislation.[30]

The most spectacular incident of prelates having to submit to the ordinary régime of censorship was that involving Bossuet and the Cardinal de Noailles in their dispute over the rights of prelates in the condemnation of books. This incident brought to a head the tensions that had existed between the secular and religious powers in the censorship of books, and to a certain extent redefined the position.[31] The subject of dispute was the publication of Richard Simon's *Nouveau Testament de*

[27] J. Saint-Germain, *La Vie quotidienne à la fin du Grand Siècle* (Paris, 1965), pp. 132–3.
[28] Mellottée, *Histoire économique*, p. 48.
[29] L. Morin, *Histoire corporative des artisans du livre à Troyes* (Troyes, 1900), pp. 158–9.
[30] Martin, *Livre, pouvoirs et société*, I, 464–5.
[31] The details of this episode can be found in John D. Woodbridge, 'Censure royale et censure épiscopale: le conflit de 1702', *XVIIIe siècle*, 8 (1976), 333–55, Auvray, *Richard Simon*, pp. 127 ff. and Steinmann, *Richard Simon*, pp. 334 ff.

Notre-Seigneur Jésus-Christ in 1702. Two essential points were at issue: the bishop's right to grant permission to works of a religious nature, and the right of a bishop to grant permission for a work with religious content before the *privilège* granted by the king could be considered of legal status.[32] The award of a *privilège* and the publication of the text were thus, in Bossuet's view, conditional upon episcopal permission.

Simon's work was granted a *privilège* in France, subject to certain corrections being made, after its initial publication in the independent principality of Trévoux. In order to give the *privilège* more respectability it had been arranged that a favourable article, written by Simon himself with Bignon's permission, appear in the *Journal des savants*. This enraged Noailles who published an *ordonnance* condemning the *Nouveau Testament* and forbidding people to read it on pain of excommunication. Bossuet's strenuous intervention (based on a reading of the table of contents) then led Pontchartrain to believe that he was the victim of a plot,[33] although the situation was almost certainly the reverse. A letter upholding episcopal rights had also been sent by Noailles's secretary to the bishop of Châlons, Noailles's brother. This letter invoked a right based implicitly on the concept of the apostolic succession whereby bishops had a duty to watch over everything to do with the Scriptures and mentioned that such a right was enshrined in the Council of Sens of 1528. Another precedent was the action taken over the *Nouveau Testament de Mons* on the express grounds that the text had been published without the approval of any bishop. Furthermore Noailles's *ordonnance* implied that a bishop had the right to place limits on the extent of royal authority in matters of publication.

Pontchartrain's response was to reiterate the subordination of the Church in the space of the word: he forbade bishops to publish without first obtaining a *privilège*, which meant in practice that their ordinances and pastoral letters all had to be submitted to the chancellor's office for scrutiny. He also sought legal advice on the primacy of the authority of the king over the precedents of tradition. Simon, who had been given another *privilège* provocatively four days after Noailles's ordinance, argued in this version of his work the case for gallican liberties over decisions of the councils. To make matters worse, Simon, under the protection of Pontchartrain, published a reply to Noailles's pronouncement which appeared without permission or *privilège*. Bossuet submitted his *Instructions* on Simon's *Nouveau Testament* for scrutiny but then withdrew them because of the humiliation this would represent for other bishops who were rallying to Noailles's course of action.[34]

---

[32] Woodbridge, 'Censure royale', 354.   [33] Ibid., 338–9.   [34] Ibid., 342–4.

It is impossible to underestimate the shock felt by Bossuet at being treated like just another author since, implicitly, bishops became suspect of purveying false doctrine. The depth of his reaction is contained in a letter sent to Noailles at the height of the dispute, in which he raises the wider question of the domains of temporal and spiritual power, thus revealing a very real tension within the domain of gallicanism itself, especially in the area of episcopal gallicanism. Bossuet felt able to pass over the first insult, that of the requirement of prior scrutiny, something not requested by five previous chancellors, but was unable to stomach the second, that is to say the appearance in the published work of the examiner's attestation, a condition not previously applied to bishops.[35] Attaching the name of the censor in this way was not only new, tailored to the specific occasion and redolent of blatant partiality, but it interfered with the rights of bishops 'dans l'essentiel de leur ministère, qui est la foi'.[36] Bossuet clearly perceived that the action of Pontchartrain not only submitted the Church to secular authority but it submitted bishops to examination on matters of faith by subordinates. When Pontchartrain replied in defence that the crown must ensure that bishops write nothing against the state, Bossuet's indignation was barely contained. The final blow came when the public notice containing the ordinance against the offending book of Simon was made subject to the new rules. Bossuet was not consulted over its printed form which he did not see.[37]

At this stage all parties made submissions to the king. Pontchartrain repeated that bishops possessed a right of approval but not of permission. Their rights could not supersede those of the king. Pontchartrain subsequently conceded some ground when he reiterated that bishops had no right to grant permission but could give approval to a printed book in their dioceses (it is difficult in fact to see how royal authority could remove this right), but that this would not dispense them from the need to seek authorisation from the chancellor's office. Another apparent concession (only because Pontchartrain had introduced a new ruling anyway) came with the statement that a bishop could publish his ordinances and pastoral letters for diocesan use (a clever move because Bossuet had no jurisdiction in Paris) without examination or *privilège*. Finally, Pontchartrain conceded to Bossuet (but not to others) the right not to submit to examination, invoking the case of Fénelon as a precedent. This was a slur in itself because of Bossuet's hostility to Fénelon over quietism. Subsequently, despite the chancellor's efforts, bishops won back some control of their own space when they were dispensed from the need to submit their works to a cleric, only to a lay person who would not comment on doctrine. The

---

[35] Bossuet, *Œuvres*, XIII, 427.   [36] Ibid., p. 423.   [37] Ibid., p. 433.

agreement reached in 1702 ordered the suppression of Bossuet's first ordinance on the grounds that, among other things, it mentioned the Council of Trent. After all that, Richard Simon's *privilège* for the *Nouveau Testament* was revoked at the beginning of 1703. It had served its purpose.[38]

What the Simon incident reveals most of all is that royal intervention in censorship was so often linked to the policy of the moment, one more reason why consistency was so difficult to achieve. Direct intervention in the religious space of the word by the king or his representatives was in this way not uncommon from the very beginning of the century. Henri IV, known for having a somewhat relaxed attitude to censorship, was none the less keen to prevent a return to the religious and political passions of the wars of religion, and, for example, interfered in *parlement* proceedings directed against the Jesuits.[39] Richelieu too imposed silence on the gallican question when it suited him, and few works of this sort were published between 1630 and 1635. In 1636, however, pro-gallican publications became useful again: two were published probably on his orders despite being subsequently banned.[40]

Political intervention of this sort, according to Hermant at least, continued during the period of Mazarin, and focused particularly on the Cardinal de Retz. In 1654 St Augustine's polemic against the Pelagian heresy was published with a dedicatory epistle to Retz, certain passages of which, Mazarin allowed himself to be persuaded, were damaging to the king. He ordered publication of the whole work to cease. But the work had its protectors, including Senault, the conservative superior of the Oratory, who could in no way be identified as subversive. Mazarin relented but prohibited the publication of the praise of Retz.[41] Another case of manipulation was Voisin's translation of the liturgy, published amidst great expectation and with approval emanating from the entourage of the archbishop of Paris. The archbishop of Rouen, however, called a meeting of the Assembly of the Clergy of France whose judgement was that the translation should be suppressed. Although Mazarin, or so it was believed, did not disapprove of the translation, the outcome of delicate negotiations with Rome over Retz – Rome would not have been displeased with the decision of the French Church – took first place. Mazarin reported his agreement with the Assembly's decision to the nuncio and to Rome which, sufficiently encouraged, eventually withdrew its protection of the exiled French cardinal.[42] Hermant's account points to a certain irony in the conclusion to this affair. Mazarin's niece, the princesse de Conti, set

---

[38] Woodbridge, 'Censure royale', 351.   [39] Martin, *Livre, pouvoirs et société*, I, 461.
[40] Ibid., pp. 184–5.   [41] Hermant, *Mémoires*, II, 368–71.
[42] Ibid., IV, 504–7.

much store by the translation, and, when the chancellor withdrew its *privilège*, she managed to save all the copies of it which she spirited away in two cartloads.[43]

The mention of relations with Rome introduces another factor in achieving a consistency of policy but also in respect of dissension in the space of religion as reflected in the space of the word. Any promotion of gallicanism after Trent was enough to cause friction, and Pontchartrain's complaint about Bossuet's public mention of the Council has a special significance here. In specific terms the Index of Forbidden Books possessed no legal status in France. This meant that books placed on the Index (like many but not all gallican works) could be published in France, and that books not objected to by Rome could be banned in the kingdom. Being placed on the Index was on some occasions almost an incitement to success. Pierre Charron's *La Sagesse* (1601–4), which had been placed on the Index in 1605, had been printed in thirty-nine editions by 1672.[44]

Rome was no less a presence for all that in the space of the word in France, and on a number of occasions this presence gave rise to anxious discussion, not least in a Faculty of Theology highly sensitive about its rights in the domain of censorship. On one occasion some doctors tried to prevent discussion of a particular issue on the grounds that the matter was already under discussion in Rome. The firm reply was that the Faculty was well within its rights, especially as the Holy See had itself consulted faculties in the past. More importantly, it was put to the complainant that the independence of the Faculty would be severely curtailed if his position were to be accepted.[45] Royal power had its own reasons to insist on the Faculty's independence during the controversy surrounding Pascal's *Provinciales* in 1658. Some doctors had stated that the Faculty had abstained from considering them as a result of Rome's prior condemnation. The representatives of the king demanded that this opinion, considered 'prejudiciable aux droits du Roïaume, aux libertez de l'Eglise gallicane & à l'honneur de la Faculté', be eliminated from the Faculty's records.[46]

Sometimes, however, the remonstrances of Rome were successful. In January 1665 the *Journal des savants* published a defence of a work by Pierre de Marca, archbishop of Toulouse, on gallican liberties after it had been placed on the Index, and followed it with other attacks on the ultramontanes in subsequent editions. Royal authority had on this occasion to yield to Rome's complaints and the journal was suspended. Colbert was all too aware of the journal's usefulness and decided to

[43] Ibid., p. 507.
[44] A. Soman, 'Pierre Charron: a Revaluation', *Bibliothèque d'Humanisme et de Renaissance*, 32 (1970), 57–79 (p. 76).
[45] Dupin, *Défense*, pp. 524–5.   [46] Ibid., p. 526.

replace the editors with the abbé Gallois who promised, probably on Colbert's orders, to adopt a more moderate tone.[47] Generally, however, the *parlement* and the Faculty were constantly on their guard against any outside interference.

One particular reason for vigilance was the physical presence of the nuncio in Paris. The status of the nuncio in France was strictly that of an ambassador who had no powers of enactment, although he was an important channel of communication of Rome's views. He for example conveyed to the superiors of the orders and the universities the pope's renewal of a previous decree forbidding any publication on the matter of grace. A new decree forbidding the publication and reading of the *Augustinus* in 1641 was addressed by Cardinal Grimaldi, the nuncio at the time, to the archbishop of Reims, who was enjoined to ensure its observation in his province.[48] The nuncio's jurisdiction was thus limited, and one suspects that he was listened to only when it suited royal policy. To have any influence at all, he had to rely on friendly prelates, influential laymen and ultramontane theologians in the Faculty.[49]

But he trod on gallican toes at his peril. On the initiative of the Jesuits the Inquisition condemned two French works of theology in 1647. The pleasure some may have derived from this incident was, according to Hermant, short-lived because it was pointed out that: 'sous prétexte de favoriser la passion des Jésuites, on travaillait, sans y penser, à introduire en France le tribunal de l'Inquisition'. The nuncio had conveyed the decision in a doctrinal decree, a clear breach of gallican liberties in the eyes of the ever watchful *parlement* which itself made representations to the Court. The position of the *parlement* was eventually accepted. All copies of the decree, possession of which was regarded as an offence, were seized and any further publication of it was banned.[50] In 1659 a printer was imprisoned for publishing a papal bull at the request of the nuncio.[51]

The nuncio had the authority to protest at the actions of the French authorities, as in the case of Sanchez's treatise on matrimony which contained a chapter on sexual perversion. Because it was considered obscene, it was banned. The nuncio complained that a work of canon law for confessors could not possibly be proscribed when an obscene publication like Aretino's *Ragionamenti* circulated freely in a French translation (much toned down in fact).[52] The nuncio's objections to Charron's *De la Sagesse* had more success, but only because Charron

[47] Bellanger (ed.), *Histoire générale*, II, 129–31.   [48] Hermant, *Mémoires*, I, 140.
[49] Soman, 'Pierre Charron', 71–2.   [50] Hermant, *Mémoires*, I, 406–9.
[51] Martin, *Livre, pouvoirs et société*, II, 664.
[52] A. Soman, 'Press, Pulpit and Censorship before Richelieu', *Proceedings of the American Philosophical Society*, 120 (1976), 439–63 (pp. 444–6).

had no important protectors, and Henri IV wanted to try to influence the conclave that would take place at the death of Clement VIII.[53] The nuncio also managed to persuade the *conseil du Roi* to ban publication of Dupuy's *Traité des droits et libertés de l'Eglise gallicane* which had none the less obtained a *privilège* (later revoked).[54] This was a very different situation from that which obtained during the Venetian Interdict of 1606–7 when the king made it clear that no papal or Venetian propaganda could be published in Paris. On this occasion the nuncio found a willing ally in the garde des Sceaux who gave verbal permission to some printers to publish papal tracts supplied by the nuncio, the latter offering them immunity from any action taken by the *parlement*.[55] But such collusion between the space of gallicanism and the 'intruder' from Rome was rare, and in the space of the word the Roman Inquisition had no lasting effect.

Jansenism and censorship

Religious controversy of any sort was a sure way of attracting the attention of the authorities to the press. Jansenism represented simply a very acute form of this phenomenon, and a correlation can be established between the volume of printing production and the controversies surrounding the *Augustinus* and Arnauld's *La Fréquente communion*.[56] The impact of Jansenism was such that severe limits, officially at least, were placed on Jansenist publication from the 1640s onwards, although the same level of severity was not applied in all periods. From 1647 obtaining a *privilège* for a Jansenist work of polemic proved difficult, but for a time works produced clandestinely were rarely prosecuted. Arnauld, despite a certain suspicion, seems to have put some faith in seeking official approval, as his part stewardship of the first edition of Pascal's *Pensées* showed.[57] The key date for a harsher attitude towards Jansenist publications was certainly Arnauld's final condemnation by the Faculty of Theology in January 1656 when Chancellor Séguier, who clearly favoured the Jesuit side, thought the real moment for action had come.[58]

The success of royal authority depended on a complex network of interests. At the same time it could not depend on the homogeneity of the space of the word, for Jansenism certainly had supporters within the ranks of the officers of the Communauté, which meant that surveillance of the circulation in general of Jansenist works in Paris or their entry into the

[53] Soman, 'Pierre Charron', 74.
[54] Mandrou, *Des Humanistes*, p. 167.   [55] Soman, 'Press', 456.
[56] Martin, *Livre, pouvoirs et société*, II, 564.
[57] Ibid., I, 215–16.   [58] Ibid., II, 587.

capital from elsewhere in the kingdom was half-hearted. The religious affiliation of printers also played a part, as did the composition, for example, of the Paris *parlement*. The convergence of all these factors provided Jansenism with something of a breathing space. Desprez's career as a bookseller (he made a fortune from selling Jansenist books and pamphlets) tells us much about the protection that people like him in the trade could expect from certain quarters. In 1657 he was arrested but avoided a whipping on the intervention of the curé of Saint-Eustache. Instead he was banished from the kingdom for five years. On his release, after apparently having promised not to appeal, he appealed to the *parlement* who annulled the sentence of the Châtelet. It so happened that Bellièvre, a friend of Port-Royal, was *premier président* of the *parlement* at the time.[59] In fact the support offered to Jansenists was such that printers and booksellers were able to return to their shops and workshops to resume their activities only months or even weeks after the intervention of the police.[60] Desprez was something of a recidivist because five years later, in 1662, he was back in the Bastille during the controversy over the formulary. He was later given the responsibility of the publication of the *Pensées*.[61]

The most instructive period in the history of printing and Jansenism comes after the condemnation of Arnauld at the Sorbonne when the Jansenist party went on the offensive with Pascal's *Provinciales*. To do justice to the story of the publication of these letters would require thriller-writing of a high order: at times the situation approached high farce, with printers and their wives hiding on the roofs of houses or smuggling out manuscripts while the police weren't looking. Pascal was constantly on the run from his own domicile, living in hiding, sometimes staying with his friend, the duc de Roannez, sometimes making journeys outside Paris to Port-Royal.[62] Desprez, who became involved when the going got a little too rough for some of his colleagues, was eventually forced into hiding.[63]

Printers began to feel the heat around the ninth letter but the situation held owing to sympathy within the Communauté. Protection was forthcoming from Ballard, the syndic of the Communauté and the printer of the king's music, who intervened with Fouquet and Séguier. The printer Langlois, increasingly fretful, had promised to show Ballard everything given him to print. Ballard calmed him down, turned a blind eye and let

[59] H.-J. Martin, 'Guillaume Desprez, Libraire de Pascal et de Port-Royal', *Fédération des sociétés historiques et archéologiques de Paris et de l'Ile de France, Mémoires* II (1950), 205–28 (pp. 214–15).
[60] Martin, *Livre, pouvoirs et société*, II, 591.
[61] Martin, 'Guillaume Desprez', 216–17.
[62] Ibid., 207 8.   [63] Hermant, *Mémoires*, III, 6–7.

pass packages from abroad.[64] Baudry, the *solitaire* in charge of the practical details of publication, noted in his journal that there was no need to hide since the magistrates themselves enjoyed reading Pascal's presentation of Jesuit moral teaching. Baudry also profited from this respite to have other Jansenist works printed. The situation changed in December 1656 when it was ruled that nothing could be printed or sold without permission or a *privilège*. Even Ballard requested that Baudry suspend the printing of Jansenist pamphlets. But Baudry went ahead with the seventeenth and eighteenth letters.[65] After that the Court became more and more determined to pursue defaulting members of the trade who, in some cases, found themselves on the end of some harsh treatment.[66]

It happened however that few members of the trade were excluded from the space of the word on account of their record in either clandestine printing or selling. Indeed exclusion or inclusion followed no particular logic. Desprez's involvement with the publication of the *Provinciales* was not held permanently against him and he became 'imprimeur du Roi' in 1686, despite his exclusion from the thirty-six officially accredited printers. Although he was not received into the Communauté as a printer until 1706, he was permitted by La Reynie to purchase presses, characters and tools from the widow of another printer.[67] In view of the fact that such sales were subject to very strict legislation, Desprez must have become useful in some way. Pralard was another bookseller with a Jansenist track record who later served royal power.[68] Indeed allegiances could operate in reverse. Arnauld's *Fréquente communion* was printed by Vitré, one of the most important figures of the trade in his time. He had been favoured in his commissions by the Assembly of the Clergy of France.[69]

In the course of the century the Paris book trade was not the only source of problems for the authorities. Outside the capital several cities were active in the publication and circulation of Jansenist texts, with Rouen being increasingly identified by the representatives of royal power at the beginning of the eighteenth century as particularly irksome. Pontchartrain complained in 1703 that works on grace were emanating from Rouen presses. Penalties could be severe. One printer accused of producing a pro-Jansenist text saw his mastership annulled.[70] For reasons already suggested, success in monitoring the trade was uneven and eventually it

---

[64] Ibid., p. 72.
[65] Martin, 'Guillaume Desprez', 210–12.
[66] See Hermant, *Mémoires*, IV, 385, 168, 347 and 381.
[67] Martin, 'Guillaume Desprez', 207 and 220.
[68] H.-J. Martin, 'Un Libraire de Port-Royal, André Pralard', *Bulletin du bibliophile et du bibliothécaire*, 45 (1961), 18–38.
[69] Martin, *Livre, pouvoirs et société*, II, 566.
[70] J. Quéniart, *L'Imprimerie et la librairie à Rouen au XVIIIe siècle* (Paris, 1969), p. 208.

had to be policed by inspectors sent directly from Paris rather than by officers of the trade itself.

The other source of books inspired by Jansenism was Holland, almost a universal refuge for all sorts of French dissidents. Prominent among the printers of Jansenist texts were the Elzeviers whose products found their way into France, usually through Rouen. Daniel Elzevier published the *Provinciales* in 1657 along with the texts of Wendrock, otherwise known as Pierre Nicole. Le Maistre de Sacy's translation of the New Testament was also printed on Dutch presses.[71]

The existence of Jansenist books in circulation in France and abroad did not achieve the total disappearance of the hostile space of Jansenism from the kingdom that royal power might have liked. The space of Jansenism survived in the space of the word in a quite different way. In the first place the memory of the leading lights of Port-Royal was enshrined in the memoirs of Lancelot, Fontaine and du Fossé: secondly, the patient transcription of manuscripts by a number of dedicated nuns meant that the most important works of Jansenist figures were all published by the middle of the eighteenth century. In fact the archives of Port-Royal had been confiscated by d'Argenson but returned by what Catherine Maire calls 'un mystérieux scrupule de conscience'. From before the end of the seventeenth century moves had begun to preserve the Port-Royal archives, and were confirmed especially by Louis-Adrien le Paige (1712–1803), a Jansenist lawyer. The archives have survived into our own day in the form of the Société de Port-Royal.[72] It is an acute irony that, whereas the space of Port-Royal was all but completely destroyed in the declining years of Louis XIV's reign, the Jansenist space of the word should have transcended the boundaries of time in the form of a library.

Protestantism and censorship

The space of the word in respect of Protestantism was of particular importance given the reliance of Huguenots on personal possession of texts, including the Bible and the Psalms. A Protestant presence in the book trade, not always determined by religious affiliation, was essential to a level of survival of the community. It was a presence which came gradually under attack over the years of our period with a view to eliminating it altogether. This, supposedly, was to be finally achieved by the Revocation of the Edict of Nantes. But then the reduced number of people printing books in some areas of the kingdom was not enough to

---

[71] Martin, *Livre, pouvoirs et société*, II, 593.
[72] Catherine Maire, 'Port-Royal', in *Les Lieux de mémoire: les Frances*, Part III, vol. I (Paris, 1992), 471–529, especially pp. 498–504.

produce the works of polemic necessary for raising or maintaining the consciousness of the Protestant faithful in the increasingly hostile environment to which they were subject.

The Edict of Nantes in fact addressed aspects of Protestant participation in the production of the printed word, not always to its long-term advantage. Article XXI restricted the printing of Protestant works to those towns and places which constituted 'lieux d'exercices', that is to say where the Reformed Religion could be exercised freely. Here the authorities had no right to control or to seize books on grounds of religion without a further clearly defined reason.[73] Books of doctrine, edification and controversy could not in theory be printed in Paris: production of these texts was relegated to a place outside the capital, Charenton, where no fixed presses were installed and where books were sold at stalls in the open air at the door of the temple.[74] Two Protestant printers did install a press there in 1620 on which they turned out what was regarded as an inflammatory pamphlet. They were ordered to remove it within twenty-four hours and all copies of the offending text were burned.[75] Other sorts of book could be produced elsewhere but they were subject to inspection by royal officials and Faculty theologians.

The tight régime of surveillance in respect of Protestant printing led to a good deal of clandestine activity, as when Duplessy-Mornay kept the whole print-run of the *Mystère d'iniquité*, condemned in 1611, in his country residence, releasing copies from time to time for sale at foreign fairs. On his departure from Saumur in 1621 all the remaining copies were burned by soldiers in the courtyard.[76] Some cities were keener than others on the surveillance of Protestant books, Toulouse prominent among them.[77] As the century progressed, the publication of Protestant works came under ever closer scrutiny. Two rulings of 1663 stated that, prior to publication, Protestant works of religion had to be submitted to a pastor for approval and then to a royal magistrate for permission to publish. This ruling was renewed in 1670. But just in case any confusion about Protestant approval for publication might have crept into anybody's mind, a ruling of 1671 made it clear that pastors had no absolute right to inspect books in this way.[78]

The space of Catholicism protected itself against the full strength of

---

[73] Van Deursen, *Professions et métiers*, pp. 85–6.
[74] J. Pannier, *L'Eglise réformée de Paris sous Henri IV* (Paris, 1911), p. 534.
[75] J. Pannier, *L'Eglise réformée sous Louis XIII de 1621 à 1629 environ*, 2 vols. (Paris, 1931–2), II, 387.
[76] Ibid., p. 374.
[77] See M. Desbarreaux-Bernard, *L'Inquisition des livres à Toulouse au XVIIe siècle* (Toulouse, 1874), pp. 4–6.
[78] Van Deursen, *Professions et métiers*, pp. 88–9.

Protestant attack by the restrictions placed on the number of presses on which Protestant works of polemic could be produced. In any case Huguenot communities wished to attract as little attention to themselves as possible: consequently, works of this kind emanated largely from presses outside the kingdom, Sedan or Geneva among them.[79] This could only have compounded the perception of Protestantism as hostile. There were some who wished to restrict the Protestant space of the word even more and prohibit Protestant participation in the trade in all other places except the 'lieux d'exercice'. It is significant perhaps that in one town a group of fanatics burnt down the bookshops even before they destroyed the temple.[80]

Protestant attempts to control their own space were based on a number of considerations. Chapter XIV, article 5 of the *Discipline* forbade Protestant members of the trade in particular along with the faithful in general to have any commerce 'qui dépende directement des superstitions de l'Eglise romaine'. In 1610 a Protestant bookseller was denied communion for a time on the orders of the Paris consistory for having printed a Catholic pamphlet, and he was forbidden to sell his books at Charenton. He complained that if ministers had the same power as Jesuits they would be a good deal worse.[81] Commercial pressures however thwarted attempts at regulation on the part of Protestant authorities. The Paris consistory had forbidden the publication of a letter written by the pastor Pierre du Moulin. The problem was that Catholic *colporteurs*, not under Protestant jurisdiction and on the lookout for a good sale, hawked it about Charenton themselves.[82]

Pure commercial interests were not alien even to the Protestant space. No lack of evidence exists for Protestants working for Catholics, even engravers, a good example of a professional task involving a confessional difficulty. The Reformed Religion rejected and abhorred the use of images by Catholics. However, the work of Protestant engravers was included in the Bible of Frizon which was supposed to refuse all compromise with the 'heretics'. Van Lochom seems to have had the monopoly of a certain type of pious work such as the *Catéchisme royal* of le Père Bonnefous. Duportal explains this phenomenon as an activity involving a purely mechanical fabrication of certain images which therefore deprived it of any emotional involvement. At the most it was a question of pride in craftsmanship.[83] One might add money, of course, or even tolerance. When the demands of

[79] Martin, *Livre, pouvoirs et société*, I, 170–1.
[80] Van Deursen, *Professions et métiers*, p. 89.
[81] Pannier, *L'Eglise réformée de Paris sous Henri IV*, p. 541.
[82] Pannier, *L'Eglise réformée sous Louis XIII de 1621 à 1629 environ*, II, 372.
[83] Duportal, *Etudes*, pp. 222–3.

the Revocation produced an upsurge of printing from the Parisian and provincial presses in terms of books of special use to *Nouveaux Catholiques*, it is inconceivable from a practical point of view that former Protestants themselves were not involved in this operation. Between October 1685 and January 1687 a million books of this sort were published.[84]

In any case, in some places, a Protestant printer might be the only one for miles. From 1634 an ardent Huguenot, Pierre Coderc, worked for the bishop of Montauban, and in Montpellier, even more curiously, Gillet produced *L'Idolatrie huguenote* for the Jesuit Richeôme,[85] although Andrieu recounts the same story for Agen and denies the existence of such a printer there of that name.[86] Jacques Roger of Pau published works by both le Père Audebert and the pastor Abbadie who had confronted each other in a public polemic. This can only have resulted surely from Protestants having the monopoly of the trade. This was not so in Paris where Vendôme, another Protestant, was involved in the production of the *Provinciales*. As Van Deursen comments, looking at the production of an individual printer would not necessarily indicate his religious affiliation.[87] The cross-sect trade of the Protestants seems to prove the point made by Elisabeth Labrousse that, religion apart, Protestants could quite easily integrate into Catholic space, which, in terms of business, represented quite simply a social and economic space.

Equality within that space was not however a foregone conclusion. Although the Edict of Nantes made no mention of restriction of trades, the concept of free exercise did not sit easily with the Catholic orientation of corporation statutes which could theoretically exclude Protestants. Clearly they had not always been read in this way, for they did not rigorously prevent Protestant membership.[88] Pannier identifies fifteen Protestant families who had been continuously involved from the sixteenth to the seventeenth centuries in the Parisian bookselling trade.[89] In any case Protestant representation had not always been free in an absolute sense because, according to legislation of 1535, their number had been fixed at twenty-four.[90]

Certainly the statutes of corporations have led to differing interpretations, as in the case of Poitiers. Chauvet argues that from 1634 reception into the mastership was closed to Huguenots, whereas Van Deursen

[84] Martin, *Livre, pouvoirs et société*, II, 676.
[85] Van Deursen, *Professions et métiers*, p. 86.
[86] J. Andrieu, *Histoire de l'imprimerie en Agenais depuis l'origine jusqu'à nos jours* (Paris, 1886), p. 55.
[87] Van Deursen, *Professions et métiers*, p. 87.
[88] Ibid., pp. 85–8.
[89] Pannier, *L'Eglise réformée sous Louis XIII de 1621 à 1629 environ*, II, 391.
[90] Pannier, *L'Eglise réformée de Paris sous Henri IV*, p. 535.

interprets the statutes to read that an apostate Catholic could not become a member (in 1648 a printer who had converted was threatened with expulsion).[91] That the free exercise of the trades was regarded as important, even as overriding confessional considerations, is exemplified by those cases where the exclusion or expulsion of Protestants was unsuccessful. In principle, members of the book trade in Rouen had to be of the Catholic faith from 1666. In that year its officials were unable to block the reception of a Protestant into their number.[92] Nor were Huguenot printers and booksellers necessarily concerned by the ruling of 1649 that apprentices should be French, of good morals and of the Catholic faith (no such conditions attached to the 'alloués' who performed the tasks of apprentices when the latter were in short supply).[93]

Official intervention was sometimes necessary in order to enforce the reception of Protestant booksellers, as in the case of Antoine Cellier's son in 1666. This did not however prevent the omission of his name from the register.[94] In the same year Jacques Lebourgeois of Caen won his case against the corporation of Rouen. It is possible that the status of printer was more difficult to achieve than other printing-trade practices. Charles, another son of Antoine Cellier, was received as a bookseller-binder in 1661 but opted to remain a binder in 1686 when legislation prevented binders from acting also as booksellers. As Van Deursen comments, the fact of being a printer and at the same time a Protestant may just have been an aggravating factor in a context where established members of the trade wanted no more rivals.[95] This is not to say that pressures were not put on Protestant members of the trade, as indeed the need for official intervention demonstrated. As early as 1624 an individual named Royal, who had been caught selling seized copies of Marot's version of the Psalms, was forbidden to set up shop in Agen on the grounds that he was 'factionnaire et seditieux'.[96] Clearly Renaudot, whose *Gazette* was soon to become the official organ of government, found it expedient to abjure his Protestant faith in 1626, at a time when Louis XIII was departing on a crusade against those who had been until then Renaudot's co-religionaries.

The vice-like grip on Protestants in the book trade tightened in terms of legislation in May 1685. An *arrêt du conseil* forbade the further reception of Protestant printers and booksellers, and Protestant booksellers had to

[91] P. Chauvet, *Les Ouvriers du livre en France des origines à la révolution de 1789*, 2 vols. (Paris, 1959), I, 255, and Van Deursen, *Professions et métiers*, pp. 87–8.
[92] Chauvet, *Les Ouvriers du livre*, I, 239.
[93] Mellottée, *Histoire économique*, p. 211.
[94] Pannier, *L'Eglise réformée sous Louis XIII de 1621 à 1629 environ*, II, 385.
[95] Van Deursen, *Professions et métiers*, p. 87.
[96] Ibid. and Andrieu, *Histoire de l'imprimerie en Agenais*, p. 81.

close their shops. In July Huguenots exercising these professions before May (those who had already abjured were excluded) were obliged to cease their activities, because it had been decided that the publication and dissemination of 'livres et autres écrits mêlez de discours scandaleux et diffamatoires, et même contre le respect dû à la Religion Catholique, Apostolique et Romaine' would be forbidden.[97] The term 'diffamatoire' could in effect be interpreted to include any statement whatever relating to Protestant doctrine, which was by its very nature anyway considered heretical. This interpretation was in fact anticipated in the Edict of Nantes where it appears in Article XXI. This whole article was never destined to be in the interests of Protestants themselves.

In the period immediately before the Revocation all excuses served to harass Protestant booksellers. An edict of August 1685 ordered a search for all anti-Catholic books: the *parlement* of Toulouse followed suit and books were impounded at Niort. In Toulouse the *parlement* had decreed that booksellers would only be tolerated in the 'lieux d'exercice' and, on the orders of the archbishop, three Montauban booksellers had to close, ostensibly for the possession of heretical works, although none was found in two of the three. Two of them abjured in order to be able to continue with their livelihood.[98] The fate of all Protestants in the trade was sealed by the Act of Revocation enshrined in the Edict of Fontainebleau on 17 October 1685 and registered by the *parlement* five days later. But in the eyes of many the Revocation simply made official restrictions in the Protestant space of the word which had already operated *de facto* if not *de jure*.

Was this the end of Protestant representation in the greater space of the word? Clearly not, and officialdom was sometimes involved in persuading Huguenots to stay in France. The Lyon bookseller Huguetant, even while suspected of wishing to flee abroad (a criminal offence), was not pursued by the *intendant* who instead was obliged to try and keep him, in the end unsuccessfully.[99] In Niort, *la veuve* Bureau was allowed to take her stock of 'heretical' works to Holland in 1686. At the same time she was more or less invited to stay by being given a Catholic psalter to print. The closing down or enforced exile of Huguenot printing specialists was rapidly seen to have implications for Catholic activities. Many abjured (like Charles, son of Antoine Cellier) but often only in appearance, as with the Moulins of Montauban and the Rigauds of Montpellier. Others continued, along with some Catholics, to satisfy a continuing demand for Protestant books

---

[97] Van Deursen, *Professions et métiers*, pp. 89–90.
[98] Ibid., pp. 90–1.
[99] M.-E. Vingtrinier, *Histoire de l'imprimerie à Lyon, de l'origine jusqu'à nos jours* (Lyons, 1894), pp. 355–7.

particularly in Rouen.[100] The printing and even possession of Protestant books remained a criminal offence for which anyone could be sent to the galleys.[101]

But harsh treatment was not always the rule, and a Protestant background was not always a disadvantage. Rigaud of Montpellier became director of the Bibliothèque royale and Jacob Desbordes became the only printer of Niort when the three others, by an *arrêt* of 1704, had to be content with the humbler title of bookseller.[102] As I have suggested, commercial reasons dictated a less rigorous attitude to Protestant representation in the French book trade after 1685. Significantly, while the *arrêt* of July 1685 was not abrogated in 1698, the exclusion of Protestants from the book trade did not figure in the second act of revocation in that year. The government in effect gave up hope of stemming the traffic of Protestant books, partly because their distribution by *colporteurs* in rural areas, especially the Cévennes, Vivarais and Dauphiné, undermined what the legislation set out to achieve. The bishop of Châlons received the following reply to his complaint concerning the circulation of Protestant books: 'Il n'y a point de remède.' In the end the religious convictions of printers and booksellers seem to have been disregarded, and they were left in peace.[103]

One of the consequences of the Revocation of the Edict of Nantes, as in the case of Jansenism, was that the space of Protestantism widened to include the United Provinces, since that was a place of refuge chosen by a large number of Huguenots. Holland was particularly important in the context of the space of the word because of its proximity – the importation of books into France was easier than from other countries – and in the tradition of commerce in the book trade, especially in the illegal trade where the port of Rouen had its own traditions from the very early years of the Reformation. Huguenots in Holland were far from cut off from their co-religionaries in France and indeed from their Catholic friends. A sort of cultural space managed to establish and maintain itself beyond the national frontiers of hostility, in part due to the enormous energy of Pierre Bayle in particular, whose *Nouvelles de la République des lettres* was a much sought after publication in France. Although Bayle expressed his intention to eschew politics, the *Nouvelles* became a way of defending French Protestantism by publicising books concerned with the faith, which had the effect of provoking the indignation of Arnauld, another refugee in Holland.[104]

---

[100] Van Deursen, *Professions et métiers*, pp. 91–5, and Chauvet, *Les Ouvriers du livre*, I, 239.
[101] See Van Deursen, *Professions et métiers*, p. 97.
[102] Ibid., pp. 96–7.   [103] Ibid., p. 96.
[104] Bellanger (ed.), *Histoire générale*, II, 152 and 154.

The space of refuge itself was not always as tolerant as one might expect, for policy matters dictated that an openly aggressive opposition to Louis XIV could not be allowed to get out of hand. The Dutch authorities were aware of the dangers as early as 1653 when it was forbidden to print French gazettes, the most common form of oppositional publication. Dutch gazettes were forbidden to print anything against political and religious institutions.[105] French gazettes were again proscribed in 1686. However, such legislation may well have been largely cosmetic because of the real indignation aroused by the Revocation outside France, particularly in Protestant countries. The edict of 1686 was never rigorously implemented and was renewed just for the form in 1687 and 1691. Even the representative of the French authorities, the comte d'Avaux, knew that much.[106]

The indignation of the French authorities at the attacks on the régime emanating from abroad did not prevent them from having dealings with the Dutch book trade. The Dutch effected regular exchanges with their French counterparts and often had good relations with French authors. More curiously perhaps, especially in view of complaints about the Dutch press towards the end of the century and Holland's status as a refuge for Jansenists and Protestants, royal power preferred to negotiate with its representatives, especially during the recession suffered by the French book trade in the 1690s, a matter of great concern to the literary world inside the kingdom.

One of the major figures in all this was the Dutch publisher Rayner Leers, who even at the time of the Revocation of the Edict of Nantes was visiting Paris. He was particularly interested in maintaining good relations with the office of the chancellor to avoid obstacles to the entry of his books into France. No less a figure than Bossuet wrote to Pontchartrain asking that, given the difficulties of the French presses, books which did no harm to the state or religion should be allowed to be freely imported. Leers became such a friend of the chancellery that Bignon made him the official supplier of works required by the Bibliothèque royale, especially after the theft and translation to Holland of a number of important manuscripts, among them texts on the subject of grace. Even more curiously, Bignon prevented French publishers from pirating texts published by Leers when he himself did not scruple to pirate texts of French publishers.[107] The space of the word was above all the space of pragmatism. In 1707 a Dutch boat delivered four cases of Protestant books to two booksellers in

---

[105] E. Hatin, *Les Gazettes de Hollande et la presse clandestine aux XVIIe et XVIIIe siècles* (Paris, 1865), pp. 90–1.
[106] Ibid., pp. 96–7.
[107] Martin, *Livre, pouvoirs et société*, II, 740 and 751–3.

Bordeaux. Boat and books were impounded. Because the authorities were reluctant to put obstacles in the way of trade with Holland, the merchandise and the captain were rapidly released.[108] Yet again, the authorities had to accommodate intentions and reality.

Ideas and control

The interrelation of the space of the word with other spaces is illustrated perhaps most completely by the space of ideas. Not only was the Church itself anxious to contain the adoption of new directions by its own members, but the civil authorities became involved at moments when disputes over ideas threatened to disrupt the order of the state. Inevitably, the assault on authority in science and the contribution that such an assault might make on other types of authority demanded some sort of control. Rapin summarises the general attitude to what was regarded as 'novelty' when he asserts that the law suffers no innovation 'dans l'usage des choses universellement établies'. No alternative can be envisaged to the philosophical method current in the University. The passion for new opinions has dangerous consequences for a well-ordered state, especially in view of the fact that 'la Philosophie est un des organes dont se sert la Religion, pour s'expliquer dans ses décisions'.[109] While Poullain de la Barre considers the problem from a rather different angle (he was a Cartesian), he suggests none the less that 'savants' can be dangerous men and that the control of disorder in ideas is the proper domain of royal power and authority.[110]

One of the major controversies surrounding novelty in ideas was that of Galileo's confirmation of the heliocentric explanation of the universe. Galileo had after all been condemned at the seat of the Roman Church which had in this way sent out a warning at the very least to all forward-looking men of science. A dilemma arose here. Clearly, scientists who accepted the new system could not think themselves into the past. As Arthur Koestler brilliantly put it: 'We can add to our knowledge, but we cannot subtract from it.'[111] Men of science had to discover some way of negotiating possible censure in respect of what they held to be a central scientific truth. The condemnation of Galileo threatened no less than the future of all science. In that sense, as Descartes understood, Galileo's contribution and the reaction to it could not be considered as an isolated issue. The major difficulty following from Galileo's condemnation was

---

[108] Van Deursen, *Professions et métiers*, p. 97.
[109] Rapin, *Réflexions sur la philosophie*, p. 392.
[110] Poullain de la Barre, *De l'Education des dames*, pp. 96–7.
[111] A. Koestler, *The Sleepwalkers* (London, 1964), p. 20.

less the fact of the heliocentric system itself than the method by which it, and all other scientific discoveries, could be substantiated. Individual discoveries were neither here nor there. The important thing lay in the philosophical structure which included all of them. Rome's condemnation of Galileo attacked the very heart of the Cartesian method, whereupon it became necessary to safeguard the system of deduction allowing one to move from principles to proof: 'le mouvement de la terre, ce n'est pas une solution particulière qu'il s'agit de sauver, c'est l'ensemble de la physique, c'est l'armature de la philosophie'.[112] The urgency of this matter was compounded by the abandonment of one philosophical system for another. The fact was, of course, that Descartes knew that the decision on the heliocentric system did not constitute an article of faith and for that reason was not absolute. The infallibility of the Church was not at stake. The decision for the philosopher was what Gouhier nicely calls a 'gaffe'.[113] In any case Descartes was not bent hell for leather on publication and was quite content to let the matter blow over.[114] Lenoble's view is that, since Galileo's condemnation had had a limited effect on important members of the Church, the risk of writing on the subject in France had been exaggerated by Descartes and overemphasised by his modern editor, Charles Adam.[115]

Mersenne was an active publicist for Galileo in the first half of the seventeenth century. His initial adoption of a cautious approach meant that it was some time before he came to espouse the Galilean system, but he certainly never believed in designating heliocentrism as a heresy. Indeed, Mersenne's support for Galileo preceded Rome's condemnation, that is to say around 1630–1. After 1634 he came more openly to Galileo's defence. Even in 1634 he had some doubts but, mitigated sceptic that he was, he regarded the new idea as the most probable solution.[116] For Mersenne it was a matter of interpretation and approach. The censors had never intended to exclude the use of the Copernican hypothesis in the calculation of eclipses and the movement of the heavenly bodies, an activity which did no harm to the status of Scripture (presumably especially if the calculations were correct). Mersenne was none the less adamant that if scholars proceeded with more caution and prudence in the sciences, 'they would not be subject to censorship, and would have no occasion to complain or to retract'.[117]

The position Mersenne adopted on censorship seems to be finely balanced between the need for a certain freedom of thought and the

---

[112] Gouhier, La Pensée religieuse de Descartes, pp. 84–5.
[113] Ibid., pp. 171–2.   [114] Ibid., pp. 86–7.
[115] Lenoble, Mersenne, p. 405.   [116] Ibid., pp. 392–8.
[117] See Brown, Scientific Organizations, p. 37.

protection of the space of orthodoxy. On the one hand, he opposes a facile form of censorship which fails to proceed in a careful, disinterested and dispassionate way. On the other hand, ecclesiastical authority has a right to forbid the reading of books which can be used by heretics and the enemies of the Church to overturn belief, even though the books may themselves contain nothing contrary to the truth.[118] Mersenne's wording is interesting because he does not seem to forbid the writing of such books, the implication being that their circulation should be limited. Overall, censorship should be concerned with the progress and advancement of truth, of the Catholic faith and the glory of God. The way in which Mersenne sought to attempt this conciliation of the space of science and religion within the space of the word derives in part from the time at which he was writing. After the wars of religion, any philosophy casting doubt on the moral order was to be mistrusted. The task of religion and morality was to stabilise social order, so that scientific activity could be undertaken without danger. So critical thought had its limits.[119] The control of the space of orthodoxy depended on the advancement of science undertaken prudently.

In the light of this, the more crucial aspect of Mersenne's behaviour is the way he protected himself in his own writings. The first edition of the *Questions théologiques*, while it included the substance of Galileo's dialogues condemned in 1633, also included the decision of the cardinals, as he admitted to Peiresc, 'pour médecine'. He admitted further that he had prepared expurgated versions of this work in which he had not refuted the controversial propositions.[120] Despite the different situation in France that Lenoble evoked in the case of Descartes, it still didn't do to be imprudent. For his own self-protection, Mersenne's works are full of deliberate obscurity and 'protective verbiage'.[121]

Mersenne was not alone in such attempts at 'self-control'. According to Pintard, Gassendi's style was such that it would be difficult to find 'ni une proposition condamnable ni une page rassurante': in typically ungenerous fashion he regards this as the fruits of forty years of hypocrisy.[122] Naudé's procedures were no different. In his distinctions between Christian truth and the folly of unbelievers, his real opinions are concealed beneath a mass of erudition.[123] In 1658, Gui Patin explained that, in his meetings with Charpentier and Miron, if they discussed religion or the state, 'ce n'est qu'historiquement, sans songer à réformation ou a sédition'.[124] Bayle however warns against an excess of self-policing and against the sup-

---

[118] Lenoble, *Mersenne*, pp. 223–35.
[119] Ibid., p. 532.   [120] Ibid., pp. 392–401.
[121] Brown, *Scientific Organizations*, p. 38.
[122] Pintard, *Le Libertinage érudit*, p. 303.
[123] Ibid., p. 465.   [124] Quoted in Mandrou, *Des Humanistes*, p. 208.

pression of certain types of fact, however unpalatable they may be. After all they can probably be read in a thousand other authors.[125]

The Church attempted on many occasions formally to stem the tide of new opinion and to exclude it from its immediate space, that is to say the institutions it controlled, a need made especially apparent by the spread of Cartesianism in society at large. Moreover ecclesiastical authority often sought the help of civil authority in its endeavours. The *parlement* and the University had combined in 1624 when anti-Aristotelian theses favouring alchemy and chemistry had been advertised in Paris. On this occasion the Faculty alerted the civil authorities who then condemned the theses and had printed versions of them torn up in the presence of one of the culprits. It was this incident that led to the ruling that the holding of any doctrine contrary to old and approved authors would be a capital offence.[126] Under the impact of Cartesianism the Sorbonne attempted to renew the ruling in 1671 and provoked the famous *Arrêt burlesque* of Boileau. By that date, hostility towards Cartesianism had considerably hardened. Descartes's works had been placed on the Index of Forbidden Books in Rome on 20 November 1663. The Index may not have had force of law in France, but there were many in France who would no doubt have agreed with the decision. Initially the decision was not final in the sense that it was accompanied by the words 'donec corrigantur', that is to say that republication would be conditional on certain corrections being made. On the other hand no precise indications were given as to what exactly had to be corrected. In 1722 the Roman censors closed the issue by placing the 1709 Amsterdam edition of the *Méditations* on the Index without the qualification of 1663, although some claimed that this was because observations by others than Descartes had been added.

It is from around 1662 that the first wave of anti-Cartesian censorship was imposed. Indeed Descartes's appearance on the Index may have been the result of Clerselier's over-vigorous campaign to gain acceptance for Descartes's interpretation of the Eucharist. During Clerselier's campaign, convergent with that of the Benedictine Desgabets, one of the former's texts had been printed without his permission and shown to Louis XIV as an example of a pernicious book, whereupon the king requested that the archbishop of Paris have it examined and censured. Eventually, Clerselier and Rohault were ordered to cease their active propaganda on behalf of the Cartesian cause.[127] What is noteworthy in this incident is the chain of

---

[125]   P. Bayle, *Dictionnaire historique et critique* (Rotterdam, 1702), II, 1565.

[126]   L. Thorndike, 'Censorship by the Sorbonne of Science and Superstition in the First Half of the Seventeenth Century', *Journal of the History of Ideas*, 16 (1955), 119–25 (pp. 120–3).

[127]   McLoughlin, 'Censorship', 571–2.

command from king to archbishop and not the other way round. The king could be considered to have acted in precisely the way that Mersenne had recommended in the preservation of public order. The pressure was such at one stage that Rohault moved towards a reconciliation of Aristotle and Descartes. In any case he adopted a more cautious attitude in his writings, avoiding matters which touched on articles of faith and concentrating less and less on metaphysics.[128] In 1669 candidates could apply for the chair of philosophy at the Collège de France only by advancing anti-Cartesian theses.[129]

The coalescence of secular and religious space in the control of Cartesianism went a spectacular step forward in 1667 when Descartes's remains were transferred to Sainte-Geneviève-du-Mont. The Court forbade Lallemant to give the funeral oration and indeed forbade any funeral oration at all to be delivered. The University authorities had already made clear to him that it was inappropriate for the chancellor of the University abbey to afford such public approval to Cartesian doctrine. In 1671 Harlay called together all the highest dignitaries of the faculties and colleges to announce the king's wish that Cartesianism should be rejected. The faculties rushed to obey the declaration led by the Faculty of Theology.[130] In 1685 the Paris *parlement* requested that the archbishop of Paris draw up a list of books which he thought should be suppressed, a list which included some 500 titles. The *parlement* subsequently ordered their suppression.

But it was ultimately impossible for the Sorbonne to halt the advance of Cartesianism. The repetition of prohibitions serves only to prove this fact. The condemnation of eleven propositions in 1691 clearly attracted little notice with the result that, in 1704 and 1705, in order to bring peace to the disputes between theologians and philosophers, especially with regard to the Eucharist, the rector assembled all the professors of philosophy and enjoined them to obey the will of the king in the matter of the condemned propositions of 1691.[131] To avoid further condemnation some teachers resorted to subterfuge. Jean Courtillier, at the Collège de Montaigu in 1679–80, publicised Cartesian theses by refuting them.[132] Pourchot published in 1695 a course in which Descartes was obviously preferred to Aristotle but used arguments of the latter to prove propositions of the former. In his preface he even declared his adherence to the University's condemnation of Aristotle's critics: but instead of aligning himself with

[128] Ibid., 580.
[129] A. Adam, *Histoire de la littérature française*, 5 vols. (Paris, 1948–56), III, 20.
[130] McLoughlin, 'Censorship', 565–6.
[131] F. Bouillier, *Histoire de la philosophie cartésienne*, 2 vols. (Paris, 1854), I, 468.
[132] Spink, *French Free Thought*, pp. 190–1.

the contemporary position of the University, he preferred to quote the much more generally worded statute of 1598 which could not have made any reference to Cartesianism.[133]

A rather curious part of this story is the ease with which Cartesian works could be published in France right into the 1670s. While the *Discours de la méthode* was published in Leiden in 1637, the *Meditationes* were published in Paris in 1641 with a royal *privilège* but without the approval of the Faculty of Theology. After Descartes's death, no problems were experienced with the publication of his writings, and an edition of his correspondence appeared between 1657 and 1667. The French version of the *Meditationes* was republished in 1673, the *Passions de l'âme* in 1679, and the *Principia* in 1681. This seems to suggest that some were perhaps more sensitive to the fact that Descartes's followers were causing more problems than Descartes himself would have countenanced. It was the highly public nature of the dispute which was frowned upon. Descartes stood aside from the polemic in death as in life.

The attack on Cartesianism was, however, pursued with the utmost vigour in the religious space where the Church was able in theory to control its own personnel. Prohibitions were imposed on the members of the Maurist Congregation at Saint-Germain-des-Prés in 1675, the Faculty of Theology of Caen in 1677, and in 1678 the Génofévains in all of France (in this case the prohibition was accompanied by one concerning the theology of Jansenius). After a period when the fathers of the Christian Doctrine were, it seems, totally hostile to new ideas, a mass conversion took place at the beginning of the eighteenth century which led to a ban on Cartesian theses in 1711.[134] In Protestant academies novelty in philosophy and theology was banned as early as 1637 when professors had every six months to send to official examiners extracts of theses taught in public.[135]

The most important regulation of individual spaces within the overall space of orthodoxy concerned the Jesuits and the Oratorians. The Society was never uniformly hostile to the new ideas and did not therefore present itself as a homogeneous space. Fournier praised Descartes in his *Hydrographie* of 1643. Le Valois's evaluation was initially mixed but he certainly never regarded Descartes as an atheist, although this did not prevent him from participating later in moves to designate Cartesianism a heresy even outside the world of teaching, and from denouncing Descartes and his followers as 'fauteurs de Calvin'.[136] Later in the century, once

[133] Kors, *Atheism in France*, pp. 276–7.
[134] Viguerie, *Une Œuvre d'éducation*, pp. 545–50.
[135] Prost, *La Philosophie à l'Académie protestante de Saumur*, p. 52.
[136] Bouillier, *Histoire de la philosophie cartésienne*, I, 469.

Malebranche provided in his work a more attractive integration of Cartesianism with Christian thought, the minority position of Descartes's supporters changed radically.[137] This attractiveness on the other hand was precisely what worried the authorities. The General Congregation of the Society in Rome met in 1682 and forbade the teaching of new opinions: it needed to eet again however in 1696 to bring renewed order to the situation. Even then the superior of the Parisian province complained that several of his charges 'donnent hautement dans la nouveauté'. At the fifteenth General Congregation of the Society in 1706 thirty propositions were drawn up which it was forbidden to teach in the colleges. Some individuals paid heavily for their adherence to this novelty.[138]

Perhaps the most agonising debate over Cartesianism among the ranks of the religious orders was conducted within the Oratory whose Augustinianism in some ways predisposed them towards it. Precisely because of Jesuit opposition to the order on these grounds the hierarchy of the Oratory was determined to be particularly severe with those who publicly espoused the new system. Prominent among the proponents of this conservative policy were Bourgoing and Senault. The history of the Oratory in the second half of the century was, in the domain of thought, largely one of warnings and prohibitions. In 1652 André Martin was suspended from his teaching function in Marseille for adopting Cartesian theses in a book on St Augustine. In 1654 refutation of Aristotle in a thesis earned another Oratorian refusal to publish. Other examples followed, one banishment being the result of an examination of lecture notes by the Faculty of Theology. An additional problem was the infusion of a degree of political radicalism into the writings of Peland and especially Bernard Lamy who taught that social inequalities did not exist in the state of innocence.[139] Sanctions against those who promoted Plato at the expense of Aristotle were adopted in 1656, and in 1658 the General Assembly approved a policy decidedly hostile to new opinions. As a result, Nicolas Poisson had to abandon a plan to write a biography of Descartes.

In 1674 Lamy was at the centre of a particularly complex affair in Angers which involved almost everybody, including the king. The incident proved once again that civil as well as ecclesiastical authority had an interest in regulating the space of orthodoxy. The Jesuits certainly wanted Lamy branded as a heretic and saw to it that his works were examined after the discovery in his physics course of an 'impious' proposition. The University of Angers called together all the college principals, the Oratorian professors of philosophy and the priors of

---

[137] Sortais, *Le Cartésianisme chez les Jésuites français*, p. 20.
[138] Ibid., pp. 20–36.
[139] Spink, *French Free Thought*, pp. 194–5.

monasteries and ordered their submission. One who resisted that decision was Coquery, principal of the Collège d'Anjou, who appealed successfully to the Paris *parlement*. Meanwhile more Cartesian theses had been printed, this time with the permission of the *lieutenant général* of Anjou. Lamy took advantage of the situation and, at the end of a physics course, intended to preside over the presentation of a nakedly Cartesian thesis. The rector forbade it but Lamy was ordered to proceed by Coquery. Finally the rector managed to obtain a ruling from the *conseil d'Etat* which overruled the Paris *parlement*. Lamy's resistance was thus broken. One secretary of state tried to persuade Louis XIV to imprison Lamy, but the king was content to order that Lamy discontinue his teaching and preaching, and he was exiled to Saint-Martin-de-Misère in Dauphiné.[140] The Oratory unquestionably came off worst in this affair. After pressure from the archbishop of Paris and the Jesuits, the General Assembly of the Oratory was forced in 1678 to adopt a concordat with the Society in which the Oratory had to eliminate from its statutes its preference for St Augustine and St Thomas, and to declare its respect for the followers of the theology of Molina.[141]

Control of the space therefore proved difficult, especially because the control exercised by royal and ecclesiastical authority could only ever really be retrospective. Moreover, the immediate space of the Church could not be isolated from the world outside where Cartesian theses had advanced considerably. Quite simply an audience existed which required to be satisfied, an audience clearly divorced from the old ideas and an audience divorced in some ways from the structures that had produced those ideas. The immediate space of the Church was thus an island within the larger space, constantly trying to arrest the erosion of its shores. Not even the intervention of the king could prevent individual minds from thinking differently. The spaces of novelty were beginning to link up in an alarming way. The refusal of the Church to embrace the new system and to deal with it from within was unquestionably a contributory factor to its declining influence in the space of ideas. The space of orthodoxy was threatened by the very processes intended to protect it.

---

[140] Bouillier, *Histoire de la philosophie cartésienne*, I, 460–3, and F. Girbal, *Bernard Lamy, 1640–1715: étude biographique et bibliographique* (Paris, 1964), pp. 33–7.
[141] Bouillier, *Histoire de la philosophie cartésienne*, II, 465.

Conclusion

In the course of the seventeenth century the French Church attempted to reconstruct culture in a way consonant with the requirements of the Council of Trent. The precondition for the transformations in existing culture to take place, among both the rural and urban masses and the social élites, and for the invention of new forms of religious cultural promotion, was the establishment of a space of orthodoxy according to whose norms, under the guidance of authority, everything within that space could be measured. The space of orthodoxy was therefore all-inclusive and could not in theory be separated either from the space of temporal power or, more generally, from the space of the world. The boundaries of one were at the same time those of the other.

The French Church was certainly a different institution at the end of the century from what it had been at the start. Its activities were spread over a remarkably wide area. Much attention was paid to the improvement of the clergy and to the reform of the orders. Churches were built or restored, and greater contact of the clergy with believers existed through schooling and charitable activities. A crusading spirit was encouraged throughout the kingdom with the regeneration of spiritual life in parishes and dioceses, and missionary activity took the Church into the countryside to the extent that its presence had never been previously so keenly felt. A large number of truly great figures emerged in the course of the century and the development of the printing industry contributed to the personal possession, and to the writing, of pious works and works of theology. The space of the Church in terms of its accessibility to the faithful, and the faithful's accessibility to the Church, was undoubtedly impressive.

In a way the success of the Church has to be measured by the degree of authority it could exercise, since the spirit behind the promotion of the new spirituality brooked no compromise. Orthodoxy could concede no ground to its opponents nor could there be any margin for doubt. The concept of an autonomous space outside the authority of the Church was inconceivable. Protection of the Church from forces outside its immediate boundaries very much depended on the rule of authority over its own members if the institution was to function effectively as an example of the spiritual government of souls. A number of factors, however, combined to weaken the position of the Church in the course of the seventeenth century. Despite its obvious renewal, the history of the Church turns out to be a history of the limits of its influence.

In the first place, the public face of the Church presented difficulties in giving the impression of a united force in the establishment of the space of orthodoxy. Virtually no period in the seventeenth century was untouched by doctrinal problems of some sort, from the *querelle des réguliers* to the quietist controversy and the reaction to Louis XIV's acceptance of *Unigenitus*. The increasingly uncompromising stand of some members of Port-Royal over the confusion of the theological tradition of St Augustine with the tradition of the Church as a whole must also have contributed to the image of the Church as composed of a body of warring factions. Moreover, as Pascal's *Provinciales* unquestionably showed to an avid pamphlet-reading public, disputes over doctrine were all too often in reality political disputes, providing the opportunity for one party to score points off another. Indeed, in the case of the quarrels over grace, the root of the problem can be traced back to the failure of Trent itself to give any adequate guidance.

Another element to be set against the successes of the Church was its too frequent ability to produce situations which achieved consequences that were the opposite of its intentions. The Tridentine emphasis on the special nature of the sacerdotal aspect of the priesthood, where in many respects the priest separated himself from the day-to-day concerns of his flock, led eventually to a cultural divide, if not among the social élites at least in rural areas. Allied to this distancing of the priest from believers, the onslaught in the countryside, especially on what was seen as too great a familiarity with the sacred, may not have turned people away from the Church but may not at the same time have strengthened their adherence to reform. Time and again historians point to the resistance of believers to attempts to eliminate traditional practices or representations of the sacred. The Church perhaps managed to instil a new docility among its members, but that docility did not necessarily betoken acceptance of change.

The ability of the Church to fill its own ranks with reformed and reforming priests was limited in an organisation where the power structure was still rather diffuse. The space of the Church was not in this sense coherent. Bishops did not have total control of the priesthood in their own diocese and parish priests found themselves in constant competition with the regulars. The education of the priesthood in general and the establishment of seminaries in particular depended on the initiative of individuals and the uneven availability of financial resources. The Church had no central budget for such a venture. Moreover, a Church which, through its various agencies and from the bottom to the top of its hierarchy, provided an important means of social advancement was bound to demonstrate widely differing levels of vocational commitment. Changes in the spiritual culture of the faithful could only be truly effective once the Church itself had been reformed throughout its structure. By the time this may have been true, other factors had intervened in sending the faithful in different directions.

Where the Church could exercise institutional influence, at least within its own immediate boundaries, it did not necessarily meet with unqualified success and affords another example of the Church being responsible for producing its own opposition. The issue of Cartesianism is crucial in this respect. The Church's refusal to contemplate giving the new science or philosophy any sort of official status within the space under its control more or less consigned it to a space over which it had little or no control. The Church itself thus contributed to the idea of a purely secular space for scientific thought, despite the intentions of its originators. The secular space was allowed to set the agenda. The crowning blow was the royal creation of a space for science from which the Church was formally excluded. Interventions of the temporal authority in matters of thought and theology, except perhaps under Richelieu, were more often than not made essentially for reasons of preserving order rather than on grounds of intellectual partisanship. The fight against atheism too led in no small way to its intellectual legitimacy. Bossuet's treatment of Richard Simon could only have given the impression of an intellectually closed Church. And the disreputable attempts to to bring Protestants back into the fold enhanced even further the Church's reputation as a repressive institution.

The Church's control over the spaces outside the immediate space of the Church turned out to fall far short of the totalising ambitions I wrote about in my introduction. It is worth repeating that the failure of the state to integrate fully Tridentine decrees in law meant that the Church started from a weak position since the Church's influence in the secular space was thereby institutionally much reduced. The issue of censorship offers a good example of the limits of influence, especially after Pontchartrain's positively disrespectful challenge to Bossuet and Noailles. An even more telling example was the organisation and definition of charity which changed significantly under the influence of the temporal authority.[1] Despite the refusal of many in the gallican Church to adopt Roman

---

[1] See J.-P. Gutton, *La Société et les pauvres: l'exemple de la généralité de Lyon, 1534–1789* (Paris, 1971).

leniency in the domain of theatre, religious moralists could only urge the faithful not to attend public performances of plays. The Church never seriously came near to closing theatres and could do no more than exercise a purely moral influence on individual consciences. While many diocesan rituals included the actor among those refused the sacraments if they did not first renounce their profession (the diocese of Metz included spectators), many more did not. Bossuet, the scourge of Molière, never altered the ritual of his own diocese of Meaux.

The difficulty experienced by the Church in respect of the secular space was very much related to frontiers. The Church and the world largely shared the same culture. In some respects the secular space could be regarded as setting the cultural agenda, especially as regards literary or artistic forms which were then appropriated for religious purposes. Many members of the clergy participated directly in the culture of the secular space and provided it with some of its most effective theorists. What had to be faced was that this shared culture originated in a pagan world. At times the dividing line could be found not so much between secular and religious culture, but between those within the immediate space of religion who accepted and assimilated the culture of antiquity and those who rejected it. Epic poetry became one area of debate in literary terms but, much more crucially, stoicism and other elements of ancient philosophy became another. What qualities could be positively accorded to humanity, qualities identified and exalted by those who had not benefited from God's grace, without fundamentally harming teaching on original sin and grace itself? The moral and theological issue was very much a cultural one. Christian humanism for many seemed to be a contradiction in terms, and this was a tension running through the whole of the century which, while it was rich in cultural invention, could not at the same time forsake its cultural heritage. The two antiquities, Christian and pagan, were either qualified friends or unconditional enemies.

The movement of certain agencies of the Church into the secular space met sometimes with spectacular success, as in the case of schools. Often the presence of the Church in a space which it wished to reconquer was much more controversial, and the secular space was considered to have absorbed the Church rather than the reverse. Again, the *Provinciales* of Pascal act, rightly or wrongly, as a stinging rebuke to an opportunism which ended with results contrary to those which may have been intended. Even the possibility of maintaining the purity of the religious space was a divisive issue, particularly among Jansenists. The limits relating to the participation of the laity in the religious space were in themselves a source of frustration for some, especially in the controversial area of translations of the liturgy. The reaction to the papal bull *Unigenitus*, destined to put an end to the Jansenist controversy, demonstrated the divide between Rome and some sections of the French Church. Louis XIV could not fully have realised the implications of his alliance with the pope at this time.

It is here that Catholicism contrasts most strongly with Protestantism in questions of ownership of the space. Participation of the laity could only go so far. No wonder then that many felt that the secular world, in itself a creation of the Church with its emphasis on the distinct nature of the priesthood, was one over which they could exercise some measure of control on their own terms, at least in the cultural domain. Translation there was not an issue of exclusion. Many were clearly happy to be part of a lay culture which did not contradict religion but which did not actively promote it either. The secular space was far from a space of conversion, and Bossuet's *Oraisons funèbres* provide, in their very magnificence, illustrations of the exception rather than the rule.

The structural difficulties of the Church, and the limits that could be set to its action and authority in seventeenth-century society, find their ultimate source in the relation of the Church to another agency with totalising ambitions. Royal power seems to have had its own agenda which did not altogether correspond with that of the Church. How did Church and state combine? Together did they constitute an alliance or a conflict? Did the spaces of religion and political power share exactly the same boundaries or did one space 'contain' the other? Could one space exist independently of the imperatives of the other? What were the principles which underpinned these imperatives? It might be useful in the first instance to explore a number of approaches to this relationship which illustrate different models of influence of Church on state or state on Church. In this way we will then be able to consider the degree to which these models reflect the practice of reform in seventeenth-century France. We will also be able to return to some of the issues I have just raised and to focus more closely on them in terms of the frontier between the sacred and the profane, so much an issue in the course of this study.

Although the period of Richelieu is associated with the elaboration of a theory which made a case for the extension of the power of the state, that theory also had to take into account the accommodation of royal policy to the religious foundations of the state. What makes this particularly interesting is that Richelieu was a cleric and a prince of the Church. A common perception of the period of Richelieu is that the interests of religion and politics, as articulated through the concept of the *raison d'état*, became confused to the extent that there occurred nothing less than the secularisation of politics, a view which has been forcefully challenged by William F. Church. While Church admits that 'some of his tactics opened the way for the growth of the modern state which eventually became a lawless and thoroughly secular affair' (something of an overreaction, perhaps), this position was not one espoused by Richelieu himself. Church argues further that Richelieu's own religious convictions could not reasonably be doubted despite the pressures of political decisions whose rationale, on the surface at least, resembled the theories of Machiavelli.[2] Richelieu none the less found it necessary to defend points at which a religious position appeared to deviate from, if not contradict, the policies he was pursuing, particularly with regard to his foreign alliances. This defence rested largely on the principle of the divine right of kings which placed the ruler directly within the space of religion. This then became the ultimate space within which politics operated. Whatever the merits of this position, it was, as Church notes, not a secular one and did not deny the dictates of morality.[3]

On the other hand royal policy had to accommodate itself to a context which had lost its religious unity, but this in itself did not alter the concept of monarchy based on traditional religious assumptions. Since the nature and purposes of the French state were founded on religion, acts in French interests could only enhance the cause of religion.[4] For this reason contemporary political theorists had recourse to the notion of the Catholic of state which involved a sort of political fideism: 'the true Catholic of State or believing subject should submit to the will of God and the king's policies as a matter of faith. All persons regardless of their vocations should remain in their stations and refrain from criticizing royal actions which were beyond their comprehension.'[5] Church admits that there was at least a partial autonomy of the space of politics which rested necessarily on 'a relatively loose application of religious morality to temporal affairs'. But this, along with an adherence to religious liberalism, remained one essential element of a single ideological pattern.[6] It is difficult to imagine it in any other way, given the absence in France of an alternative framework within which to operate. Life within politics was still a life within the Church: 'Richelieu and the great majority of Frenchmen continued to regard the Roman Church and the French monarchical state as the two great, coordinate, interlocking, divinely instituted agencies for the government and guidance of the people in their respective but closely allied spheres.'[7]

The principal architect of the theory of the state as belonging to the religious domain was Bossuet, who outlined his position in the *Discours sur l'histoire universelle* (1681) and the *Politique tirée des propres paroles de l'Ecriture sainte* (begun in 1677 but left unfinished). A central historical

[2] William F. Church, *Richelieu and Reason of State* (Princeton, 1972), pp. 8–11.
[3] Ibid., p. 53.   [4] Ibid., p. 288.   [5] Ibid., p. 134.   [6] Ibid., pp. 91–2.
[7] Ibid., p. 89.

principle of his was that kings play an essential role in a universe which is directed according to the laws of divine providence on which kings themselves are dependent. This knowledge should make them 'attentifs aux ordres de Dieu, afin de prêter la main à ce qu'il médite pour sa gloire dans toutes les occasions qu'il leur en présente'.[8] God governs history and not men. Kings are more governed than governing, and should heed the lessons of mortality.[9] Does the Church then have supremacy over the temporal domain, as this position might imply, since the Church is the direct representative and interpreter of the will of God? As one might expect of a servant of the king, the situation is rather one of mutual support. God is not only the source of 'sacerdoce' in the spiritual domain, but of 'empire' in the temporal. Just as the ecclesiastical order recognises the power of kings, so they must recognise themselves as 'humbles enfants de l'Eglise'. In this way: 'Tout l'état du monde roule sur ces deux puissances. C'est pourquoi elles se doivent l'une à l'autre un secours mutuel.'[10] Since God is the source of power for Church and state, both occupy the same space. But matters of jurisdiction remain. One of the privileges accorded the sovereign by the Concordat of Bologna was the right of kings to nominate to certain ecclesiastical offices. Bossuet asserts quite forcefully that, while kings have the right to choose 'pasteurs', they should not think that they can choose just anybody, but must choose according to the advice of the Church.[11] The king is thus the guardian of reform which is directed, however, by the Church itself.

This position is reinforced by the status of the king within the domain of the spiritual in that he is the lieutenant and minister of God on earth, and it is at this point again that the spiritual and the temporal form a single space ruled by the same imperatives: 'Le service de Dieu et le respect pour les rois sont choses unies.'[12] In these circumstances, political rebellion is sacrilege, as Bossuet himself states.[13] This coincidence of the space of the secular and religious powers works to protect the position of even a bad king who can under no circumstances be deposed. The Christian, who recognises the order of God in the king's legitimate possession of power can but suffer and obey.[14] The model of behaviour in the political space is the early Christian who, while persecuted, never attempted to challenge the legitimacy of the temporal power.[15]

This is not however the subordination of religion to politics, whatever the emphasis on obedience, the actions of the king continuing to be measured according to the yardstick of Christian morality. Thérèse Goyet

[8] Bossuet, *Oeuvres*, xv, 7. Bossuet's *Discours* are in vol. xv, his *Politique* in vol. xvi.
[9] Ibid., xvi, 374 and xv, 61–2.   [10] Ibid., xvi, 349.   [11] Ibid., p. 352.
[12] Ibid., p. 86.   [13] Ibid., p. 76.   [14] Ibid., xiv, 280.
[15] Ibid., xvi, 268 and xiv, 101 and 299–300.

goes as far as to say that 'Bossuet subordonne *absolument* la politique à la morale chrétienne'.[16] This relationship is even more reinforced by the very context of the discussion since by relating contemporary political action to history as recounted in and interpreted through Scripture in both the *Discours* and the *Politique* Bossuet anchors the actions of kings in the space of God which by its very nature includes all other spaces and allows not even for partial autonomy.

The most systematic account of the combination of Church and state by a modern historian is that of Robert Muchembled for whom the imposition of a unified belief according to the dictates of orthodoxy matched perfectly the ideal of unification and harmonisation at the centre of absolutist politics. In their increasing hierarchisation and authoritarianism, Church and state were mirror images of each other.[17] The Church is regarded as having attempted to destroy the relative autonomy of certain units of social organisation by mounting a systematic attack on the structure of belief on which these units rested. By destroying previous structures of belief the consequent effects could only contribute to and reinforce the attempt to establish new political structures.[18] The role of education was to provide a teaching not only centred on obedience to the Church but on obedience to the king as an integral accompaniment. In addition the social élites aimed at the impossible in offering the mass of the population cultural models which they could not hope to aspire to, all this in the name of a cultural unification along the lines of the political model.[19] Essentially, the whole system was therefore recruited in the elimination of diversity and in the establishment of norms.[20] Absolutism in that sense was truly a totalising space which accompanied the totalising ambitions of Trent.

A model of the relation of Church to state which reverses the trend of Bossuet's arguments is offered by Michel de Certeau, who regards the Church of the seventeenth and eighteenth centuries as facing the fragmentation of a space where the unicity of reference constituted by God as the source of both morality and religion was challenged, after the Reformation, by the growth of science and the discovery of new worlds difficult to integrate into the former system of reference. With the advent of different forms of religion and discourse, what was previously presented as a totalising force became one particularism among others and the resulting relativisation of religion(s) led to the search for a new legality.[21]

[16] Th. Goyet, *L'Humanisme de Bossuet*, 2 vols. (Paris, 1965), II, 466 (Goyet's emphasis).
[17] Muchembled, *Culture populaire*, p. 256.   [18] See ibid., p. 270.
[19] Ibid., p. 266.   [20] Ibid., pp. 228 and 209.
[21] M. de Certeau, 'Du Système religieux à l'éthique des Lumières (XVIIe–XVIIIe siècles): la formalité des pratiques', in *La società religiosa nel età moderna* (Naples, 1973), 447–509 (pp. 447–52).

De Certeau identifies three important elements which were symptomatic of this religious disaggregation and which therefore fail to provide either theory or practice with general laws. Atheism, associated with the city, is a mark of detachment on the part of the *libertins* from the unitary thought supported by faith. Witchcraft, associated with the countryside, is equally a mark of detachment from religion to the extent of forming 'le lexique imaginaire d'une anti-société'. Mysticism represents a space for living a certain type of religious life separate from previously dominant institutional and theological discourses. This disarticulation of religious thought and practice could not be tolerated by a temporal authority whose concern was an ordered society, and the *raison d'état* of the time of Richelieu filled the void by regulating ways of behaving. The state thus opted for 'une raison *de la pratique*' (de Certeau's emphasis) and appropriated belief for its own purposes: 'Gouverner, c'est faire croire.'[22]

He argues further that the content of religious belief, what he calls 'formalité', is provided with another function, and Christian organisations and institutions are re-employed in an order which they no longer determine. At this level of practice the Church plays an important part in promoting the cult of monarchy in the period of Louis XIV. And it is all Churches which follow this route, Protestant as well as Catholic, even during the Church of the Refuge.[23] Within the Catholic Church this emphasis on practice is reflected in the creation of new religious orders which are organised according to social functions in the way that had hitherto not been the case. In this sense, the social order provided the spiritual domain with the principles of its organisation and hierarchy.[24]

De Certeau is far from asserting that such a position commanded universal assent, since at the same time within the Church there developed a movement which privileged the 'interiorisation' of Christian life, where belief was lived in private, and which reflected an incompatibility with the new socio-political demands of the Church. Thus 'avant d'être une doctrine, la rupture est une situation'. This situation derives in the first instance from the dissociation of 'dire' and 'faire': 'L'affirmation d'un sens chrétien s'isole dans un dire et semble de moins en moins compatible avec l'axiomatique des pratiques.'[25] But Jansenism seems not to have remained in the realm of 'dire'. De Certeau reduces the emphasis on theological and ideological differences between the Jansenists and others, and insists that they argued over practices, and that Jansenist isolationism constituted above all else 'un mode *pratique* de *résistance* au milieu ambiant'.[26] But there is a greater complexity to the argument. In the beginning Jansenism could be distinguished by its sacramental practice.

[22] Ibid., 455–8.   [23] Ibid., 460–2.   [24] Ibid., 472.   [25] Ibid., 466.
[26] Ibid., 474 (de Certeau's emphasis).

But the socialisation of religious practices meant in effect that religious difference was no longer perceived in these terms but in social terms. Jansenism thus became a social difference for those outside its immediate circle.[27] Given the enrolment of the Church at large in the political programme of the state, the Jansenists, in their culture of separation, could only be considered a threat to order because they could not accommodate themselves to its imperatives.

How can we match these different models to the realities of the time? As Church himself observed, Richelieu's personal commitment to certain aspects of religious reform cannot seriously be doubted. His support for the reform of the regular clergy entrusted to an ultramontane, the Cardinal de La Rochefoucauld, his position on the heretical nature of the Reformed Religion and his efforts to reduce its influence, his own stated and published positions on spiritual matters such as the relative merits of contrition and attrition, and his concern for the role and discipline of the clergy in the kingdom, including the promotion of theologically trained bishops, all attest to the close interest he took in ecclesiastical and religious affairs. On the other hand, it was on Richelieu's initiative that the powers of censorship came ultimately to rest with the state. At the same time, the space of orthodoxy was strengthened in some way by the commitment of a centralised political authority to the control and prevention of heterodox ideas.

It is obvious however that the relationship between the two powers was an uneasy one. During the period of Richelieu, the claims made for the religious foundations of the state did not prevent contradictory positions from emerging. Opposition to the pragmatic nature of Richelieu's policy came from the *parti dévot* which did not contest the principles of absolutism but contested the nature of the general good with which Richelieu sought to underpin them.[28] A pamphlet by Mathieu de Morgues urged the king to rid himself of Richelieu in order to restore to political imperatives an ethical direction.[29] Bérulle, whom we associate with the *parti dévot*, believed in the primacy of the space of religion and in particular in the larger space of Catholic Christendom to whose unity political and temporal doctrine should be subordinated.[30] Bérulle wrote a pamphlet to the queen emphasising the superiority of Jesus to kings of this world.[31] But the possibility of even a figure like Bérulle holding absolute and uncompromising positions was limited. According to Church, although they hoped that their role as servants of the crown would act as a source of influence, Bérulle (who acted as a negotiator for the cardinal) and others supported Richelieu's policies which they considered to be in

[27] Ibid., 476.   [28] Church, *Richelieu*, p. 95.   [29] Ibid., p. 212.
[30] Ibid., p. 233.   [31] Ibid., p. 379.

the interests of France.[32] The *parti dévot* was not therefore in itself homogeneous, since it was during this time that the more intransigent stance of Saint-Cyran inaugurated the reputation of the Jansenist grouping for a more uncompromising form of political opposition.

Muchembled's suggestion that the state was a direct beneficiary of post-Tridentine reform of culture and structures of belief is supported by other historians. King asserts that in his *Politique* Bossuet legitimated some of the notions we would readily associate with mercantilist thought which constituted the economic foundation of the kingdom. Gold and silver as major contributors to a flourishing state, trade and navigation as the first source of wealth, then the importance of natural resources and production, and judicious taxation, all found a place in his political theory drawn from Scripture.[33] This position was not unchallenged. Fénelon was opposed to the mercantilist policies of Louis XIV which were regarded as impoverishing the kingdom and placing an unfair fiscal burden on those who could least support it.[34] The position of Fénelon did not contest the basic assumptions of Bossuet but placed them on a different foundation. Indeed Fénelon subordinated perhaps even more than Bossuet the political to the religious dimension.

François Lebrun too regards the strict 'encadrement' of the faithful as contributing greatly to the absolutist ideal of Louis XIV, particularly in the teaching of obedience to God and king, and of resignation before a divinely ordered society. The power of this message was such that centralisation and absolutism were perhaps the work of bishops and priests issued from the seminaries rather than of the *intendants* and their entourage: 'L'Etat et l'Eglise ne se sont jamais autant identifiés l'un à l'autre, unis dans un même projet réducteur, la soumission des corps et des âmes de vingt millions de Français.'[35] Delumeau notes conversely the support that the state gave to some of the initiatives of the bishops. Royal authority regulated in the name of appropriate religious observance a large number of aspects of public behaviour such as prohibition of games and the closure of taverns during holy office. The net was cast even wider in the regulation of numbers at wedding feasts and other popular pastimes, so that the faithful were constrained in ways that had hitherto been unknown.[36]

These are perhaps perfect examples of the points at which political and religious initiatives combined to the mutual benefit of each, and they raise

---

[32] Ibid., pp. 108–9.

[33] King, *Science and Rationalism*, p. 47.

[34] See L. Rothkrug, *Opposition to Louis XIV: the Political and Social Origins of the French Enlightenment* (Princeton, 1965).

[35] Lebrun (ed.), *Histoire des Catholiques*, pp. 147–8.

[36] Delumeau, *La Peur en Occident*, p. 407.

a number of questions concerning the premises on which some historians have based their analysis of the relation between Church and state. The problem with Muchembled's position, and in a sense with that of de Certeau, is that absolutism and the imposition of orthodoxy are presented as having been realised. The approaches of Muchembled and others seem to rest on the assumption of two well-run and perfectly organised spaces with clearly defined and successful programmes. In one sense that may be true, for certainly royal authority wished to see the extension of its power and the Church responded to a reforming spirit. But the ability of each to deliver was uncertain. The state never managed completely to defeat the vested interest of some sections of the population and the success of its economic policies, under great pressure from the need to finance wars, was limited. In terms of its interest in ecclesiastical affairs, while under Louis XIV it more or less controlled the ecclesiastical hierarchy, temporal authority made no real impression on the circulation of heterodoxy. Louis XIV may have bent the Church to his will in his conflicts with the pope, but for many in the Church he did incalculable and lasting damage to gallican liberties by accepting *Unigenitus*. Even the Revocation of the Edict of Nantes did not universally enhance his reputation among Catholics in the kingdom. Louis's own piety had no durable effect and things went back under the Regency to where they had been, more so than even before.

This lack of absolute control of the temporal authority over its own space is reflected in the space of the Church itself. The Catholic Reform in France was by no means a unified phenomenon. In organisational terms, Muchembled certainly, along with others perhaps, underestimates the slowness with which the new priest was (and could be) produced in the seventeenth century. It was some time, and not many years preceding the end of the century, before the distance between the priest and his flock required by Trent was achieved. But even this was not necessarily to the Church's advantage. How could the Church claim any sort of lasting control when the boundaries of the space of orthodoxy had constantly to be reassessed? In this context there seems to be a disjunction between doctrinal conflicts among theologians which must have been a source of great anxiety for many, and the certainty with which all sections of the Church's hierarchy and its cadres approached popular culture. It would also be a mistake to believe, as Muchembled seems to, that the intellectual élites were united in the cultural models on offer or even interested in their circulation.

De Certeau's approach is too one-sided in his assertion that temporal power determined the direction of spiritual reform by providing the focus for a unity shattered during the Reformation and by factional disruption.

It must surely be argued that many of the great reforming figures were educated and received their pastoral vocation before the absolutist pattern, as we have often thought of it, emerged in France. The concept of social action in the Church was evident in sixteenth-century Italy which provided the iconic Borromeo as a model of pastoral action. The ministry of St François de Sales, an equally influential figure, originated in a see far from the political centre of France.

Unquestionably it can be demonstrated that the policies of Church and state coincided at various points and that in their totalising ambitions they resembled each other. The centralising tendency within the space of orthodoxy and the attempts at homogenising the space of religion matched perfectly the same tendencies in the space of politics. For this reason, perhaps, the temporal authority happily afforded autonomy to the ecclesiastical authority where it identified no obvious points of conflict. Bishops had within their own jurisdiction a good deal of freedom and were able to undertake quite radical initiatives in the dioceses. The most remarkable sphere in which the Church operated more or less independently was education. Resistances to the schools came from vested corporate interests or from local authorities but only in very limited areas. Occasionally, in the domain of education, royal authority expressed the negative view that the number of schools was excessive but this did not address the issue of the place of education within reform as such. Royal authority did intervene when it was made aware of the circulation of heterodox ideas which, as at Angers, might be a threat to order. The political space had effective power and made clear its expectations of the Church to put its own house in order. In this the Church needed no encouragement.

Indeed notions of order worked in two mutually helpful directions. No doubt, with the help of the educators and the bishops, royal authority took the opportunity to promote a more rigorous concept of public order. Equally, the interest of the state in public order contributed surely to the progress of the reform movement. France became a potential space of conversion because of the developing climate of order that was established through the extension of royal power and the decrease in civil disruption, still active and significant where it occurred but sporadic already by Richelieu's death. After the Fronde, the increased power of the *intendants* brought a new dimension to the influence of royal power in the provinces, however unevenly it may have been ultimately implanted. The Church certainly needed the power of the state, both political and military, to destroy heresy in the form of Protestantism within the kingdom. That is still a long way from advancing the thesis of a close and deliberate alliance. The degree to which the two spaces came together on a number of issues can be explained in another way, for it would be entirely wrong and anachronistic to think of the state and the Church as separate in any absolute sense since both spaces recruited from the same educated sectors of the population. Education was in any case provided, even by the end of the century, to only a few, and by the religious orders at that.

Implicit in the discussion so far has been the extent to which there may have existed a secular space which excluded the religious. This is of course a large issue whose constituent elements can only be sketched here. The word 'secular' is problematic because it can represent exclusion of the religious but is not necessarily to be defined outside a religious framework. Moreover, the clergy was divided into its regular and secular components. But even the secular clergy was, according to the Tridentine reform, supposed to maintain its distance from the laity and forbidden to engage in activities inappropriate to a religious calling but which possessed their own legitimacy in the social space as a whole. On the other hand this did not mean that those activities could not themselves be regulated by religious imperatives, such as economic relations between individuals and the nature of recreation. In literature and art this could mean that writers and painters were not obliged to include an explicit religious element in their works but that their works should not espouse values which could not be accommodated to Christian morality and doctrine.

But it was possible to charge those in a religious calling of some kind with compromising too much with the secular to the detriment of their vocation. Accusations of compromise with secularism were of course frequently directed at the Jesuits whose activities were often regarded as ruled by other than purely religious imperatives. In particular they were held to have constructed a form of moral teaching which, in order to bring individuals or peoples into the fold of the Church, allowed for a margin of interpretation determined from without rather than from within Christian morality and doctrine. In stark terms the Jesuits stood in contrast to those, most notably the Jansenists, who preached a purer version of life within religion and who emphasised life in the world as an obstacle to a state of prayer and spiritual recollection.

The Jesuits, while constituting perfect examples of the Church militant, in fact illustrate the tensions and risks emanating from a position which privileges action in the world. Trent itself contained these tensions by its very existence, since its task was one of reconquest in a fractured world. Catholicism was suddenly engaged in a struggle within Christendom and had to invent the modalities of reconquest and reconversion. There is no doubt that the Jesuits believed in the space of religion and the space of society as having the same boundaries, since the object of their mission was the same as that articulated at Trent, that is to say that no realm of social and political life could be excluded from religious imperatives. Certainly, in the course of the century, this entailed some accommodation, in terms of their allegiance to the pope, and to the distance the French Church and crown maintained with Rome. In time, therefore, the Jesuits had come to temper their natural ultramontane reflexes and had espoused the interests of royal power. But this transformation was not necessarily all it seemed. It constituted rather a stance within the movement of reform against the representatives of radical Augustinian theology. Politics in this sense served their version of the space of orthodoxy.

Social action was not of course the preserve of the Jesuits. There is no other way to describe Pavillon's initiatives in the diocese of Alet. But the degree to which that could be sustained in the religious space as a whole is questionable, especially given the wide range of interpretation by bishops from extremely diverse backgrounds of the notion of pastoral action. Jansenist purity of that sort could only ever be localised. The model of Port-Royal represented a contraction of the space of religion towards which its converts moved, as is symbolised by those aristocratic women who had apartments close to or in the convents. Jansenism is marked by a sort of stasis, as befits its emphasis on introspection. By contrast the mobility of the Jesuits in the world was crucial, both in France and in the world at large. The Jesuits aimed at inclusiveness. No space was uninhabitable. Indeed the space of orthodoxy as they conceived it was not a single unit but a sort of confederation of spaces whose own existence they did not challenge and through which they moved with ease. Their ambition was to establish a system of alliances rather than to integrate the different spaces into one monolithic space. Hence the negotiation required of these alliances led, rightly or wrongly, to the perception that they had compromised the space of orthodoxy rather than strengthened it.

Was there then a space without religion or where religious imperatives were irrelevant? Was the seventeenth century in France a period which moved towards a greater secularisation of society? The question needs to be answered on two levels, the institutional and the personal, one of which is easier to negotiate than the other. Institutionally, the Church had to yield some of its ground to temporal power. In the domain of family legislation more and more was handed to temporal jurisdiction which sorted out wrangles over dowries and separations. It was recognised that in marriage the sacramental was accompanied by a civil contract.[37] Emphasis on public order dictated new attitudes to the poor where the act of alms-giving, an essential element of the believer's efforts to gain

---

[37]   Latreille (ed.), *Histoire du catholicisme*, II, 378.

salvation, no longer constituted a charitable act in itself irrespective of the bona fides of the recipient. Charity had to be organised and the poor provided with a space of confinement in workhouses. By a royal ordinance of 1662 an *hôpital général* was set up in every town. In this sense de Certeau is right to emphasise the Church's action in society as determined by secular demands. The Faculty of Theology also lost its rights in the world of censorship, but this cannot be defined as an attack upon the Church because the *parlement*'s rights in this respect were much reduced at the same time.

The docility of the Church in the face of royal policy, especially in the various conflicts with Rome, illustrates the degree of its enrolment in the space of politics during the period of Louis XIV. This does not however demonstrate the autonomy of the two domains. The very fact that Louis felt it necessary to take the Church along with him shows that the temporal authority did not believe it could act alone. Against that the affair of the *régale* was an indication of the risks the Church ran in such a close association with royal power, however unavoidable that was, for the state of the Church and its pastoral activity in the provinces was seriously weakened during that time.

It is impossible to provide an adequate account of the absence or presence of personal belief in seventeenth-century France, since the evidence is either lacking or difficult to interpret. *Libertinage* and atheism certainly represented presences in the space of culture, but the first is notoriously difficult to define and the second notoriously difficult to prove. An added complexity is that for many contemporaries in the Church they were one and the same thing. I do not believe that atheism, despite current theories on its existence in reality, was in any way a real force in our period: it existed only in the margins. *Libertinage* does not necessarily exclude some form of belief although its critical stance may not fit easily into the space of orthodoxy. One must also take into account Peter Burke's warning that anti-clericalism is not the equivalent of the secular.[38]

Certainly there were those *libertins* who espoused a political position which upheld the absolute independence of temporal power but, as Pintard points out, largely as a result of the horrors of the religious wars.[39] The state is again regarded as the only agency which can restore order in a society riven with factions. But religion is not absent from the *libertins'* conception of social organisation and in itself promotes order. On a doctrinal level the content of religion may be evacuated in the process, but

---

[38] P. Burke, 'Religion and Secularisation', in P. Burke (ed.), *The New Cambridge Modern History*, vol. XIII (Cambridge, 1980), 293–317 (p. 302).

[39] Pintard, *Le Libertinage érudit*, p. 12.

many *libertins* cannot think of the social space without its religious component. The position of the *libertins* resembles in a curious way the stasis of the Jansenists, although Port-Royal represented a space with a much higher profile than the libraries of Naudé and others. The political conservatism of the *libertins*, with its unquestioning acceptance of monarchy as a system of government, was the guarantor of their ability to believe and think in the way they did. Their individualism was in no way a revolutionary fervour. Religion too helped preserve the order they required for the continuation of their intellectual activities.

It would also be difficult to assess the religious state of France at the end of our period which is none the less associated by some historians with the notion of 'dechristianisation'. The term is not without its difficulties in that, as Peter Burke remarks, 'Christianity has meant something different at different times.'[40] Contemporary evidence in particular cannot be taken at face value. Madame de Maintenon for example found little fervour for religion in the provinces. This does not indicate unbelief and in any case may be a function of the standards of piety of 'la veuve Scarron'.[41] Clair asserts that in the second half of the seventeenth century little enthusiasm for religion was evinced by the cultured élites and *libertinage* was an attitude connected with 'une vie facile'. But forgetting God is not the same as unbelief.[42] Religion may well have acted as a 'publicly available background'.[43] Jansenist practices and the onslaught on popular structures of belief may well have led, however, to an abandonment of belief. In this regard it is interesting that Madame de Sévigné should remark that what struck her in Provence were the exterior manifestations of belief rather than adherence to its substance.[44] It may be likely therefore that traditional forms of belief were much more tenacious than they have been given credit for. The conformism of large numbers of the faithful should not be taken at face value. Silence was not always assent. But nor was it absence of belief of any sort at all.

Peter Burke helps focus the discussion of secularisation by defining it as 'the process of change from the interpretation of reality in essentially supernatural, other-worldly terms to its interpretation in terms which are essentially natural and focused on this world'.[45] In the course of the period the map of knowledge changed considerably, particularly but not exclusively through the influence of Cartesianism. The importance of Cartesianism is that it finally obliged serious scientific thinkers to abandon

[40] Burke, 'Religion and Secularisation', 294.
[41] P. Clair, *Libertinage et incrédules, 1665–1715?* (Paris, 1983), p. 71.
[42] Ibid., pp. 84–5.
[43] Taylor, *Sources of the Self*, p. 491.
[44] See Busson, *La Religion des Classiques*, p. 17.
[45] Burke, 'Religion and Secularisation', 302.

Aristotelian categories on which key aspects of Christian belief were none the less founded. Moreover, scientific explanations could be formulated in ways which dispensed with the need that they should form an integral and logical part of an overall philosophical and theological system. Mathematics could in one perspective be regarded as essential to the secularisation of the 'mysteries' of the universe.

Contemporaries did not see it this way. Mersenne, Malebranche and other Oratorians did not hesitate to combine their belief in mathematics as an indispensable scientific tool with their Christian belief. For Mersenne science itself is a space of conversion since scientific activity is the best way of serving God. The revelation to be found in heaven will be a scientific revelation.[46] Descartes himself would not have recognised that science constituted a threat to religion. Arnauld experienced no difficulty in accepting that the old philosophical system was an obstacle not only to scientific progress but to the reputation of religion and belief. What could be said on the other hand is that the importance of science in the seventeenth century lay not in its challenge to religion as such but to inadequate standards of Christian explanation. Both Arnauld and Pascal attempted to answer the difficulties that arose from belief being subject to imperatives which did not derive from belief itself. That an adequate answer may not be forthcoming was the anxiety of those who held to 'pre-Cartesian' explanations. In this context it is also true that an assault on authority in one field could lead to the transfer of that assault to others. Again that need not represent a secular view but the desire for a greater independence of belief on the part of individuals. Not all critical stances stood outside the space of orthodoxy, as Descartes and Richard Simon demonstrate. The damage to the Church derived not so much from systems of unbelief as from its intransigence in rejecting or mistrusting any challenge to its own official conception of orthodoxy, as in the case of Cartesianism.

In the end one has to say that tensions were at work within the system which challenged the concept of a unified space of orthodoxy ruled by a seemingly unyielding authority. Inevitably, the state, perceived as the political guardian of that space, also ended up as the target of that challenge. But the forces which would build on and 'decontextualise' the critical stances adopted within the space of belief or which held views formulated outside the space of belief were still marginal in the seventeenth century itself. Atheism, *libertinage* and deism, along with the political challenge issuing from disaffected Protestants, were either self-contained or in exile. For the most part, there may indeed have been

[46] Lenoble, *Mersenne*, pp. 75–6.

spaces without religion but there were no important spaces outside religion. In France, an alternative mind-set was not yet available which could arrive at a militant secularism which would in its turn reject religion outright. The state and the Church may sometimes have had imperatives which one found incompatible with the other, but for the moment they were the last representatives of the concept of substantial forms: like body and soul they were incomplete realities in themselves.

Bibliography

Adam, A., *Histoire de la littérature française*, 5 vols. (Paris, 1948–56)
  Du Mysticisme à la révolte: les Jansénistes du XVIIe siècle (Paris, 1968)
Alpatov, M., 'Poussin peintre d'histoire', in A. Chastel (ed.), *Nicolas Poussin*, 2
  vols. (Paris, 1960), I, 189–99
Andrieu, J., *Histoire de l'imprimerie en Agenais depuis l'origine jusqu'à nos jours* (Paris,
  1886)
Arnauld, A., *Examen du Traité de l'essence du corps* in *Oeuvres*, vol. XXXVIII (Paris,
  1780)
Arnauld, A. (ed. A. Gazier), *Mémoire sur le règlement des études* (Paris, 1886)
Arnauld, A. and Nicole, P. (ed. L. Marin), *La Logique ou l'art de penser* (Paris,
  1970)
Auvray, P., *Richard Simon, 1638–1712: étude bio-bibliographique* (Paris, 1974)
Banier, A., *Explication historique des fables* (Paris, 1715)
Barbeyrac, J., *Discours sur l'utilité des lettres & des sciences par rapport à l'état*
  (Geneva, 1714)
Barbier d'Aucourt, J., *Sentiments de Cléante sur les Entretiens d'Ariste et d'Eugène*
  (Paris, 1738)
Barnard, H. C., *The Little Schools of Port-Royal* (Cambridge, 1913)
Barnard, H. C. (ed.), *The Port-Royalists on Education* (Cambridge, 1918)
Bayle, P., *Dictionnaire historique et critique*, 3 vols. (Rotterdam, 1702)
Bayle, P. (ed. A. Niderst), *Bayle: Oeuvres diverses* (Paris, 1971)
Bayle, P. (ed. A. Prat), *Pensées diverses sur la comète*, 2 vols. (Paris, 1984)
Bellanger, C., Godechot, J., Guiral, P. and Terrou, F. (eds.), *Histoire générale de la
  presse française*, 5 vols. (Paris, 1969–76)
Bergin, J., *Cardinal de la Rochefoucauld: Leadership and Reform in the French Church*
  (New Haven, 1987)
  'Richelieu and his Bishops? Ministerial Power and Episcopal Patronage under
    Louis XIII', in J. Bergin and L. Brockliss (eds.), *Richelieu and his Age*,
    175–202
Bergin, J. and Brockliss, L. (eds.), *Richelieu and his Age* (Oxford, 1992)
Betts, C. J., *Early Deism in France from the So-called 'déistes' of Lyon (1564) to
  Voltaire's Lettres Philosophiques (1734)* (The Hague, 1984)
Bezard, Y., 'Autour d'un éloge de Pascal: une affaire de censure tranchée par
  Louis XIV en 1696', *Revue d'histoire littéraire de la France*, 32 (1926), 215–24
Birn, R., 'La Contrebande et la saisie de livres à l'aube du Siècle des Lumières',
  Revue d'histoire moderne et contemporaine, 28 (1981), 158–73

'Book Production and Censorship in France, 1700–1715', in K. E. Carpenter (ed.), *Books and Society in History* (New York, 1983), 145–71

Bloch, O., *La Philosophie de Gassendi: nominalisme, matérialisme et métaphysique* (The Hague, 1971)

Blunt, A., *The Paintings of Nicolas Poussin* (London, 1958)

Boileau-Despréaux, N. (ed. F. Escal), *Oeuvres complètes* (Paris, 1966)

Bollème, G., *Les Almanachs populaires aux XVIIe et XVIIIe siècles: essai d'histoire sociale* (Paris, 1969)

La Bibliothèque bleue: littérature populaire en France du XVIIe au XIXe siècle (Paris, 1971)

La Bible bleue: anthologie d'une littérature 'populaire' (Paris, 1975)

Bossuet, J.-B., *Oeuvres*, 48 vols. (Paris, 1828)

Bossy, J., *Christianity in the West, 1400–1700* (Oxford, 1985)

'The Counter-Reformation and the People of Catholic Europe', *Past and Present*, 47 (1970), 51–70

Bouillier, F., *Histoire de la philosophie cartésienne*, 2 vols. (Paris, 1854)

Bourchenin, P.-D., *Etude sur les académies protestantes en France aux XVIe et XVIIe siècles* (Paris, 1882)

Briggs, R., *Communities of Belief: Cultural and Social Tensions in Early Modern France* (Oxford, 1989)

'The Académie Royale des Sciences and the Pursuit of Utility', *Past and Present*, 131 (1991), 38–88

Brochon, P., *Le Livre de colportage en France depuis le XVIe siècle: sa littérature, ses lecteurs* (Paris, 1954)

Brockliss, L. W. B., *French Higher Education in the Seventeenth and Eighteenth Centuries; a Cultural History* (Oxford, 1987)

'Aristotle, Descartes and the New Science: Natural Philosophy at the University of Paris, 1600–1740', *Annals of Science*, 38 (1981), 33–69

'Copernicus in the University: the French Experience', in J. Henry and S. Hutton (eds.), *New Perspectives on Renaissance Thought: Essays in the History of Science, Education and Philosophy* (London, 1990), 190–213

'Richelieu, Education and the State', in J. Bergin and L. Brockliss (eds.), *Richelieu and his Age* (Oxford, 1992), 237–72

Broutin, P., *La Réforme pastorale en France: recherches sur la tradition pastorale après le Concile de Trente*, 2 vols. (Tournai, 1956)

Brown, Harcourt, *Scientific Organizations in Seventeenth-Century France, 1629–1680* (Baltimore, 1934)

Burke, P., *Popular Culture in Early Modern Europe* (Aldershot, 1978)

'Religion and Secularisation', in P. Burke (ed.), *The New Cambridge Modern History*, vol. XIII (Cambridge, 1980), 293–317

'The "Bibliothèque bleue" in Comparative Perspective', in *La 'Bibliothèque bleue' nel seicento o della letteratura per il popolo* (Bari-Paris, 1981), 59–66

Busson, H., *La Pensée religieuse française de Charron à Pascal* (Paris, 1933)

La Religion des Classiques, 1660–1685 (Paris, 1948)

Catherinot, N., *Traité de peinture (18 octobre, 1687)* (no place, no date)

Certeau, M. de, 'Du Système religieux à l'éthique des Lumières (XVIIe–XVIIIe siècles): la formalité des pratiques', in *La società religiosa nell'età moderna*

(Naples, 1973), 447–509

Chadwick, O., *From Bossuet to Newman: the Idea of Doctrinal Development* (Cambridge, 1957)

Charles-Daubert, F., 'Le Libertinage érudit', in H. Méchoulan (ed.), *L'Etat baroque: regards sur la pensée de la France du premier XVIIe siècle* (Paris, 1985)

Charmot, F., *La Pédagogie des Jésuites: ses principes – son actualité* (Paris, 1943)

Charpentier, F., *De l'Excellence de la langue française*, 2 vols. (Paris, 1683)
  Carpentariana, ou Remarques d'histoire, de morale, de critique, d'érudition et de bons mots de M. Charpentier de l'Académie françoise (Paris, 1724)

Chartier, R., *Lectures et lecteurs dans la France d'Ancien Régime* (Paris, 1987)

Chartier R. (ed.), *A History of Private Life*, vol. III, *Passions of the Renaissance*, trans. A. Goldhammer (Cambridge, Mass. and London, 1989)

Chartier, R., Compère, M.-M. and Julia, D. (eds.), *L'Education en France du XVIe au XVIIIe siècle* (Paris, 1976)

Châtelet, A. and Thuillier, J. (eds.), *La Peinture française de Fouquet à Poussin*, 2 vols. (Paris, 1964)

Châtellier, L., *The Europe of the Devout: the Catholic Reformation and the Formation of a New Society* (Cambridge, 1989)

Chaunu, P., 'Jansénisme et frontière de catholicité, XVIIe et XVIIIe siècles: à propos du Jansénisme lorrain', *Revue historique*, 227 (1962), 115–38

Chauvet, P., *Les Ouvriers du livre en France des origines à la révolution de 1789*, 2 vols. (Paris, 1959)

Chevillier, A., *L'Origine de l'imprimerie de Paris* (Paris, 1694)

Church, William F., *Richelieu and Reason of State* (Princeton, 1972)

Clair, P., *Libertinage et incrédules, 1665–1715?* (Paris, 1983)

Clarke, Desmond M., *Occult Powers and Hypotheses: Cartesian Natural Philosophy under Louis XIV* (Oxford, 1989)

Colletet, G., *L'Art poëtique* (Paris, 1658)

Copleston, F., *A History of Philosophy*, 7 vols. (London, 1958–64)

Coras, J. de, *Jonas, ou la Ninive pénitente* (Paris, 1663)
  Josué, ou la Conqueste de Canaan (Paris, 1665)

Cotin, L'Abbé Ch., *Poésies chrestiennes* (Paris, 1668)

Coustel, P., *Traité d'éducation chrétienne et littéraire*, 2 vols. (Paris, 1749)

Crousaz, J.-P. de, *Traité de l'éducation des enfans*, 2 vols. (The Hague, 1722)

Dainville, F. de, *La Naissance de l'humanisme moderne* (Paris, 1940)
  L'Education des Jésuites XVIe–XVIIIe siècles (Paris, 1978)
  'Collèges et fréquentation scolaire au XVIIe siècle', *Population*, 12 (1957), 467–94
  'Allégorie et actualité sur les trétaux des Jésuites', in J. Jacquot (ed.), *Dramaturgie et société*, vol. II (Paris, 1968), 433–43

Davidson, N., 'Atheism in Italy, 1500–1700', in M. Hunter and D. Wootton (eds.), *Atheism from the Reformation to the Enlightenment* (Oxford, 1992), 55–85

Dear, P., *Mersenne and the Learning of the Schools* (Ithaca and London, 1988)

Debus, Allen G., *The Chemical Philosophy: Paracelsian Science and Medicine in the Sixteenth and Seventeenth Centuries* (New York, 1977)

Delassault, G. (ed.), *La Pensée janséniste en dehors de Pascal* (Paris, 1963)

Delumeau, J., *Le Catholicisme entre Luther et Voltaire* (Paris, 1971)
  La Peur en Occident, XIVe–XVIIIe siècles: une cité assiégée (Paris, 1978)
  Le Péché et la peur: la culpabilisation en occident, XIIIe–XVIIIe siècles (Paris 1983)
Desbarreaux-Bernard, M., *L'Inquisition des livres à Toulouse au XVIIe siècle* (Toulouse, 1874)
Descartes, R. (ed. Ch. Adam and P. Tannery), *Œuvres de Descartes*, 11 vols. (Paris, 1964–71)
Desmarets de Saint-Sorlin, J., *La Verité des fables* (Paris, 1648)
  Clovis, ou la France chrestienne (Paris, 1661)
  Marie-Madeleine, ou le Triomphe de la grâce (Paris, 1669)
  L'Excellence et les plaintes de la poësie, in *Esther* (Paris, 1670)
  Discours pour prouver que les sujets chrestiens sont les seuls propres à la poësie heroïque (1673), in F. R. Freudmann (ed.), *Clovis* (Paris, 1972)
  Traité pour juger des poëtes grecs, latins et françois (1673), in F. R. Freudmann (ed.), *Clovis* (Paris, 1972)
  La Défense du poëme héroïque (Paris, 1675)
Deyon, P., *Amiens, capitale provinciale: étude sur la société urbaine au XVIIe siècle* (Paris, 1967)
Dorival, B., *Philippe de Champaigne, 1602–1674* (Paris, 1976)
Dubu, J., 'L'Eglise catholique et la condamnation du théâtre en France', *Quaderni francesi*, 1 (1970), 319–49
Du Fresnoy, C. A., *L'Art de peinture* (Paris, 1668)
  L'Art de peinture (Paris, 1673)
Dupin, L. E., *Défense de la censure de la Faculté de Theologie de Paris du 18 octobre 1701* (Paris, 1701)
Duportal, J., *Etudes sur les livres à figures édités en France de 1601 à 1660* (Paris, 1914)
Dupront, A., *Du Sacré: croisade et pèlerinages; images et langages* (Paris, 1987)
Dupuy du Grez, B., *Traité sur la peinture pour en apprendre la teorie & se perfectionner dans la pratique* (Toulouse, 1699)
Febvre, L., *Le Problème de l'incroyance au XVIe siècle: la religion de Rabelais* (Paris, 1947)
Félibien des Avaux, A., *Entretiens sur les vies et sur les ouvrages des plus excellens peintres anciens et modernes*, 4 vols. (London, 1705)
Ferté, J., *La Vie religieuse dans les campagnes parisiennes, 1622–1695* (Paris, 1962)
Fleury, C., *Traité du choix et de la méthode des études* (Paris, 1686)
Foigny, G. de (ed. P. Ronzeaud), *La Terre australe connue (1676)* (Paris, 1990)
Fontaine, A. (ed.), *Conférences inédites de l'Académie royale de peinture et de sculpture* (Paris, 1903)
Fontenelle, B. Le Bovier de (ed. R. Shackleton), *Entretiens sur la pluralité des mondes: digression sur les Anciens et Modernes* (Oxford, 1955)
Fontenelle, B. Le Bovier de (ed. L. Maigron), *Histoire des oracles* (Paris, 1971)
Foucault, M. (trans. A. M. Sheridan), *Discipline and Punish: the Birth of the Prison* (New York, 1977)
Foucault, M. (trans. A. M. Sheridan), *The Birth of the Clinic: an Archaeology of Medical Perception* (London, 1989)

Histoire de la folie à l'âge classique (Paris, 1989)

Frain du Tremblay, J., *Discours sur l'origine de la poësie, sur son usage et sur le bon goût* (Paris, 1713), (reprinted Geneva, 1970)

François de Sales, St (ed. Ch. Florisoone), *Introduction à la vie dévote*, 2 vols. (Paris, 1961)

Fréart de Chambrai, R. (ed. A. Blunt), *Idée de la perfection de la peinture démonstrée par les principes de l'art* (Farnborough, 1968)

Frijhoff, W., 'L'Etat et l'éducation, XVIe–XVIIe siècles: une perspective globale', in *Culture et idéologie dans la genèse de l'état moderne* (Rome, 1985), 99–116

Fumaroli, M., *L'Age de l'éloquence: rhétorique et 'res literaria' de la Renaissance au seuil de l'époque classique* (Geneva, 1980)

Héros et orateurs: rhétorique et dramaturgie cornéliennes (Geneva, 1990)

' "Temps de croissance et temps de corruption": les deux antiquités dans l'érudition jésuite française du XVIIe siècle', *XVIIe siècle*, 131 (1981), 149–68

Funkenstein, A., *Theology and the Scientific Imagination* (Princeton, 1986)

Furet, F. and Ozouf, J., *Reading and Writing: Literacy in France from Calvin to Jules Ferry* (Cambridge, 1982)

Garrisson, J., *L'Edit de Nantes et sa révocation: histoire d'une intolérance* (Paris, 1985)

Gibson, W., *Women in Seventeenth-Century France* (Basingstoke, 1989)

Gilbert, C. (ed. M.-S. Rivière), *Histoire de Calejava: ou De l'Isle des hommes raisonnables* (Exeter, 1990)

Gilson, E., *The Christian Philosophy of Saint Thomas Aquinas* (London, 1957)

The Christian Philosophy of Saint Augustine (London, 1961)

Girbal, F., *Bernard Lamy, 1640–1715: étude biographique et bibliographique* (Paris, 1964)

Gobinet, Ch., *Instruction sur la manière de bien étudier* (Paris, 1690)

Godard de Donville, L., *Le Libertin des origines à 1665: un produit des apologètes* (Paris–Seattle–Tübingen, 1989)

Godeau, A., *De la Poësie chrestienne*, in *Oeuvres chrestiennes* (Paris, 1633)

Poësies chrestiennes (Paris, 1654)

Saint Paul (Paris, 1654)

Goldmann, L., *Le Dieu caché: étude sur la vision tragique dans les Pensées de Pascal et dans le théâtre de Racine* (Paris, 1955)

Gouhier, H., *La Philosophie de Malebranche et son expérience religieuse* (Paris, 1926)

La Vocation de Malebranche (Paris, 1926)

La Pensée religieuse de Descartes (Paris, 1972)

Cartésianisme et augustinisme au XVIIe siècle (Paris, 1978)

Goyet, Th., *L'Humanisme de Bossuet*, 2 vols. (Paris, 1965)

Gutton, J.-P., *La Société et les pauvres: l'exemple de la généralité de Lyon, 1534–1789* (Paris, 1971)

Gwynn, R., *Huguenot Heritage: the History and Contribution of the Huguenots in Britain* (London, 1985)

Hahn, R., *The Anatomy of a Scientific Institution: the Paris Academy of Sciences, 1666–1803* (Berkeley, 1971)

Hall, H. Gaston, *Richelieu's Desmarets and the Century of Louis XIV* (Oxford, 1990)

Hatin, E., *Les Gazettes de Hollande et la presse clandestine aux XVIIe et XVIIIe siècles* (Paris, 1865)

Manuel théorique et pratique de la liberté de la presse, 1500–1868, 2 vols. (Paris, 1868)

Henry, J. and Hutton, S. (eds.), *New Perspectives on Renaissance Thought: Essays in the History of Science, Education and Philosophy* (London, 1990)

Hermant, G. (ed. A. Gazier), *Mémoires de Godefroi Hermant sur l'histoire ecclésiastique du XVIIe siècle, 1630–1663*, 6 vols. (Paris, 1905–10)

Hirschfield, J. M., *The Académie Royale des Sciences* (New York, 1981)

Huet, P.-D. (ed. F. Gégou), *Lettre-traité de Pierre-Daniel Huet sur l'origine des romans* (Paris, 1971)

Hunter, M. and Wootton, D. (eds.), *Atheism from the Reformation to the Enlightenment* (Oxford, 1992)

Jean-Baptiste de la Salle, St, *Conduite des écoles chrétiennes* (Lyons, 1811)

Jouin, H., *Conférences de l'Académie royale de peinture et de sculpture* (Paris, 1883)

Jourdain, Ch., *Histoire de l'Université de Paris au XVIIe et au XVIIIe siècle* (Paris, 1862–6)

Jouvancy, Le Père J. de (trans. H. Ferté), *De la Manière d'apprendre et d'enseigner* (Paris, 1892)

Julia, D., 'La Réforme post-tridentine en France d'après les procès-verbaux de visites pastorales: ordre et résistances', in *La Società religiosa*, 311–415

King, James E., *Science and Rationalism in the Government of Louis XIV, 1661–1683* (Baltimore, 1949)

Koestler, A. *The Sleepwalkers* (London, 1964)

Kolakowski, L. (trans. A. Posner), *Chrétiens sans église: la conscience religieuse et le lien confessionnel au XVIIe siècle* (Paris, 1969)

Kors, A. C., *Atheism in France, 1650–1729*, vol. I, *The Orthodox Sources of Disbelief* (Princeton, 1990)

Labrousse, E., *Pierre Bayle*, 2 vols. (The Hague, 1963–4)

'Une Foi, une loi, un roi?': la Révocation de l'Edit de Nantes (Paris, 1985)

'La Doctrine politique des Huguenots: 1630–1685', *Etudes théologiques et religieuses*, 47 (1972), 421–9

Lachèvre, F., *Le Procès du poète Théophile de Viau*, 2 vols. (Paris, 1909)

Latreille, A., Delaruelle, E. and Palanque, J.-R. (eds.), *Histoire du catholicisme en France*, 3 vols. (Paris, 1957–62)

Le Bossu, Le Père R., *Traité du poème épique* (Paris, 1675)

Lebrun, F. (ed.), *Histoire des Catholiques en France* (Paris, 1980)

Lebrun, F. (ed.), *Histoire de la France religieuse*, vol. II, *Du Christianisme flamboyant à l'aube des Lumières* (Paris, 1988)

Le Comte, F., *Cabinet des singularitez d'architecture, peinture, sculpture et graveure*, 3 vols. (Brussels, 1702)

Leibacher-Ouvrard, L., *Libertinage et utopies sous le règne de Louis XIV* (Geneva, 1989)

Le Laboureur, Le Père L., *Sentiments de l'autheur sur la poësie chrestienne & prophane*, in *La Magdelaine pénitente* (Paris, 1643)

Charlemagne (Paris, 1666)

Lelevel, H., *Entretiens sur ce qui forme l'honneste homme et le vray sçavant* (Paris, 1690)

Lettres sur les sciences et sur les arts (Paris, 1704)

Le Moyne, Le Père P., *Discours de la poësie*, in *Hymnes de la sagesse divine et de l'amour divin* (Paris, 1641)

Peintures morales, 2 vols. (Paris, 1643–5)

Dissertation du poëme héroïque, in *Œuvres poétiques* (Paris, 1672)

Lenoble, R., *Mersenne, ou la naissance du mécanisme* (Paris, 1943)

Lepreux, G., 'Contribution à l'histoire de l'imprimerie parisienne', *Revue des bibliothèques*, 1–2 (1910), 316–19

Ligou, D., *Le Protestantisme en France de 1598 à 1715* (Paris, 1968)

Lux, David S., *Patronage and Royal Science in Seventeenth-Century France: the Académie de Physique in Caen* (Ithaca and London, 1989)

Mabillon, Dom J., *Traité des études monastiques*, 2 vols. (Paris, 1691)

Réflexions sur la réponse de Monsieur l'abbé de la Trappe au Traité des études monastiques (Paris, 1692)

McKenna, A., 'Madeleine de Scudéry et Port-Royal', in A. Niderst (ed.), *Les Trois Scudéry: actes du colloque du Havre (1–5 octobre 1991)* (Paris, 1993), 633–43

McLoughlin, T., 'Censorship and Defenders of the Cartesian Faith in Mid-Seventeenth-Century France', *Journal of the History of Ideas*, 40 (1979), 563–81

Maire, Catherine, 'Port-Royal', in *Les Lieux de mémoire: les Frances*, part III, vol. I (Paris, 1992), 471–529

Mâle, E., *L'Art religieux après le Concile de Trente: étude iconographique de la fin du XVIe siècle, du XVIIe, du XVIIIe; Italie, France, Espagne, Flandres* (Paris, 1932)

Malebranche, N. (ed. G. Rodis-Lewis), *De la Recherche de la vérité*, 3 vols. (Paris, 1945–62)

Mandrou, R., *De la Culture populaire aux XVIIe et XVIIIe siècles: la Bibliothèque bleue de Troyes* (Paris, 1964)

Des Humanistes aux hommes de science, XVIe et XVIIe siècles (Paris, 1973)

Marolles, M. de, *Traité du poëme épique* (Paris, 1662)

Martin, H.-J., *Livre, pouvoirs et société à Paris au XVIIe siècle, 1598–1701*, 2 vols. (Paris, 1969)

'Guillaume Desprez, Libraire de Pascal et de Port-Royal', *Fédération des sociétés historiques et archéologiques de Paris et de l'Ile de France, Mémoires*, II (1950), 205–28

'Un Libraire de Port-Royal, André Pralard', *Bulletin du bibliophile et du bibliothécaire*, 45 (1961), 18–38

Martin, H.-J. and Chartier, R. (eds.), *Histoire de l'édition française*, 3 vols. (Paris, 1982–5)

Mellottée, P., *Histoire économique de l'Imprimerie*, vol. I, *L'Imprimerie sous l'Ancien Régime 1439–1789* (Paris, 1905)

Ménestrier, Le Père C.-F., *Des Représentations en musique anciennes et modernes* (Paris, 1681)

Des Ballets anciens et modernes selon les regles du théâtre (Paris, 1682)

Bibliothèque curieuse et instructive (Trévoux, 1704)

Moisy, P., *Les Eglises des Jésuites de l'ancienne assistance de France* (Rome, 1958)

Morin, L., *Histoire corporative des artisans du livre à Troyes* (Troyes, 1900)

Mouy, P., *Le Développement de la philosophie cartésienne, 1646–1712* (Paris, 1934)

Muchembled, R., *Culture populaire et culture des élites dans la France moderne, XVe–XVIIIe siècles: essai* (Paris, 1978)

L'Invention de l'homme moderne: sensibilité, moeurs et comportements collectifs sous l'Ancien Régime (Paris, 1988)

La Violence au village, XVe–XVIIe siècles: sociabilité et comportements populaires en Artois du XVe au XVIIIe siècle (Paris, 1989)

Nadler, S., *Arnauld and the Cartesian Philosophy of Ideas* (Manchester, 1989)

Niderst, A., *Fontenelle à la recherche de lui-même, 1657–1702* (Paris, 1972)

Nourrisson, J.-F., *La Philosophie de Saint Augustin*, 2 vols. (Paris, 1865)

Nussbaum, F. L., *The Triumph of Science and Reason, 1660–1685* (New York, 1953)

Orcibal, J., 'Le Patriarcat de Richelieu devant l'opinion', in *Les Origines du Jansénisme*, vol. III (Paris, 1948), 108–46

Ornstein, M., *The Role of Scientific Societies in the Seventeenth Century* (Hamden, Conn., 1963)

Pannier, J., *L'Eglise réformée de Paris sous Henri IV* (Paris, 1911)

L'Eglise réformée sous Louis XIII, 1610–1621 (Strasbourg, 1922)

L'Eglise réformée sous Louis XIII de 1621 à 1629 environ, 2 vols. (Paris, 1931–2)

Parker, D., *The Making of French Absolutism* (London, 1983)

Pascal, B. (ed. L. Lafuma), *Œuvres complètes* (Paris, 1963)

Perouas, L., *Le Diocèse de La Rochelle de 1648 à 1724: sociologie et pastorale* (Paris, 1964)

Perrault, Ch., *Le Siècle de Louis le Grand* (Paris, 1687)

Parallèle des Anciens et des Modernes en ce qui regarde les arts et les sciences, 4 vols. (Paris, 1692–7)

Phérotée de La Croix, A., *L'Art de la poësie françoise* (Lyons, 1675)

Phillips, H., *The Theatre and its Critics in Seventeenth-Century France* (Oxford, 1980)

'Les Chrétiens et la danse: une controverse publique à La Rochelle en 1639', *Bulletin de la Société d'histoire du protestantisme français* (1977), 362–80

Picard, R., *La Carrière de Jean Racine* (Paris, 1956)

Piles, Roger de, *Conversations sur la connoissance de la peinture* (Paris, 1677)

Dissertation sur les ouvrages des plus fameux peintres (Paris, 1681)

L'Idée du peintre parfait (Paris, 1707)

Cours de peinture par principes (Paris, 1708)

Pintard, R., *Le Libertinage érudit dans la première moitié du XVIIe siècle* (Paris, 1943), (new edition Geneva, 1983)

Popkin, R., *The History of Scepticism from Erasmus to Spinoza* (Berkeley, 1979)

Portalié, E. (trans. R. J. Bastran), *A Guide to the Thought of St Augustine* (London, 1960)

Pottinger, D. T., *Censorship in France during the Ancien Régime* (Boston, 1954)

Poullain de la Barre, F., *De l'Education des dames pour la conduite de l'esprit dans les sciences et dans les moeurs* (Paris, 1674)

Poutet, Y., *Le XVIIe siècle et les origines lasalliennes*, 2 vols. (Rennes, 1970)

Prost, J., *La Philosophie à l'Académie protestante de Saumur, 1606–1685* (Paris, 1907)

Pumphrey, S., 'Non-Aristotelianism and the Magnetic Philosophy', in J. Henry and S. Hutton (eds.), *New Perspectives on Renaissance Thought: Essays in the History of Science, Education and Philosophy* (London, 1990), 177–89

Quéniart, J., *L'Imprimerie et la librairie à Rouen au XVIIIe siècle* (Paris, 1969)

Rabb, Theodore K., *The Struggle for Stability in Early Modern Europe* (New York, 1975)

Rancé, A. Le Bouthillier de, *De la Sainteté et des devoirs de la vie monastique*, 2 vols. (Paris, 1683)

Réponse au Traité des études monastiques (Paris, 1692)

Randall, J. H., *The Career of Philosophy*, vol. I, *From the Middle Ages to the Enlightenment* (New York, 1964)

Ranum, O., *Paris in the Age of Absolutism: an Essay* (New York, 1968)

Rapin, Le Père R., *Réflexions sur la poétique* (Paris, 1674)

Réflexions sur la philosophie ancienne et moderne (Paris, 1676)

Rapley, E., *The Dévotes: Women and the Church in Seventeenth-Century France* (Montreal, 1990)

Remsberg, Robert G., *Wisdom and Science at Port-Royal and the Oratory: a Study of Contrasting Augustinianisms* (Yellow Springs, Ohio, 1940)

Roche, D., *Le Siècle des Lumières en province: académies et académiciens provinciaux, 1680–1789*, 2 vols. (Paris, 1978)

Rodis-Lewis, G., *Descartes et le cartésianisme hollandais: études et documents* (Paris, 1950)

Rothkrug, L., *Opposition to Louis XIV: the Political and Social Origins of the French Enlightenment* (Princeton, 1965)

Roumeliote, A., 'Bossuet gendarme de l'augustinisme face à Richard Simon et Jean de Launoy', in P. Ranson (ed.), *Saint Augustin* (Giromagny, 1988), 398–405

Saint-Amant, M.-A. (ed. J. Lagny), *Moïse sauvé* in vol. V, *Œuvres*, 5 vols. (Paris, 1967–79)

Sainte-Marie, Le Père H., *Réflexions sur les regles et l'usage de la critique touchant l'histoire de l'Eglise*, 2 vols. (Paris, 1713)

Saint-Germain, J., *La Reynie et la police au Grand Siècle* (Paris, 1962)

La Vie quotidienne à la fin du Grand Siècle (Paris, 1965)

Salomon-Bayet, C., *L'Institution de la science, et l'expérience du vivant* (Paris, 1978)

Sauvy, A., *Livres saisis à Paris entre 1678 et 1701* (The Hague, 1972)

Scudéry, G. de, *Alaric* (Paris, 1654)

Sedgwick, A., *Jansenism in Seventeenth-Century France: Voices from the Wilderness* (Charlottesville, 1977)

Simon, R., *Histoire critique du Vieux Testament* (Amsterdam, 1685)

Histoire critique du texte du Nouveau Testament (Rotterdam, 1689)

Snyders, G., *La Pédagogie en France aux XVIIe et XVIIIe siècles* (Paris, 1965)

Solomon, Howard M., *Public Welfare, Science and Propaganda in Seventeenth-Century France: the Innovations of Théophraste Renaudot* (Princeton, 1972)

Soman, A., 'Pierre Charron: a Revaluation', *Bibliothèque d'Humanisme et de Renaissance*, 32 (1970), 57–79

'Press, Pulpit and Censorship before Richelieu', *Proceedings of the American Philosophical Society*, 120 (1976), 439–63

Sortais, G., *Le Cartésianisme chez les Jésuites français au XVIIe et au XVIIIe siècle* (Paris, 1929)

Spink, J. S., *French Free Thought from Gassendi to Voltaire* (London, 1960)

Steinmann, J., *Richard Simon et les origines de l'exégèse biblique* (Bruges, 1960)

Stroup, A., 'Royal Funding of the Parisian Académie Royale des Sciences during the 1690s', *Transactions of the American Philosophical Society*, 77, part 4 (1987), 1–167

Tallon, A., *La Compagnie du Saint-Sacrement, 1629–1667: spiritualité et société* (Paris, 1990)

Taton, R., *Les Origines de l'Académie royale des sciences* (Paris, 1965)

Tavard, G., *La Tradition au XVIIe siècle en France et en Angleterre* (Paris, 1969)

Taveneaux, R., *Le Jansénisme en Lorraine, 1640–1789* (Paris, 1960)

Le Catholicisme dans la France classique, 1610–1715, 2 vols. (Paris, 1980)

Taylor, Ch., *Sources of the Self: the Making of the Modern Identity* (Cambridge, 1989)

Testelin, H., *Sentimens des plus habiles peintres sur la pratique de la peinture et sculpture* (Paris, 1696)

Thomassin, Le Père L., *La Méthode d'étudier et d'enseigner chrétiennement et solidement les lettres humaines par rapport aux lettres divines et aux écritures*, 3 vols. (Paris, 1681–2)

Thorndike, L., 'Censorship by the Sorbonne of Science and Superstition in the First Half of the Seventeenth Century', *Journal of the History of Ideas*, 16 (1955), 119–25

Tocanne, B., *L'Idée de nature en France dans la seconde moitié du XVIIe siècle*, 2 vols. (Lille, 1978)

Tromp, E., *Etude sur l'organisation et l'histoire de la Communauté des libraires et imprimeurs de Paris, 1618–1797* (Nîmes, 1922)

Van Deursen, A. Th., *Professions et métiers interdits: un aspect de l'histoire de la Révocation de l'Edit de Nantes* (Groningen, 1960)

Ventre, M., *L'Imprimerie et la librairie en Languedoc au dernier siècle de l'Ancien Régime, 1700–1789* (The Hague, 1958)

Viguerie, J. de, *Une Œuvre d'éducation sous l'Ancien Régime: les pères de la doctrine chrétienne en France et en Italie, 1592–1792* (Paris, 1976)

Vingtrinier, M.-E., *Histoire de l'imprimerie à Lyon, de l'origine jusqu'à nos jours* (Lyons, 1894)

Wade, Ira O., *The Clandestine Organization and Diffusion of Philosophic Ideas in France from 1700 to 1750* (Princeton, 1938)

The Intellectual Origins of the French Enlightenment (Princeton, 1971)

Walker, D. P., *The Ancient Theology* (London, 1972)

Waterworth, J. W. (trans.), *The Canons and Decrees of the Council of Trent* (London, 1888)

Williams, C., *The French Oratorians and Absolutism, 1611–1641* (New York, 1989)

Wittkower, R. and Jaffe, I. B. (eds.), *Baroque Art: the Jesuit Contribution* (New York, 1972)

Woodbridge, John D., 'Censure royale et censure épiscopale: le conflit de 1702', *XVIIIe siècle*, 8 (1976), 333–55

Wright, A. D., *The Counter-Reformation: Catholic Europe and the Non-Christian World* (London, 1982)

Index